ADULT LEARNING,
CRITICAL INTELLIGENCE AND
SOCIAL CHANGE

P

We would like to dedicate this book to all our students past and present; to the spirit of collective resistance and to the possibility of transformation. We would also like to acknowledge and thank Marion Junor for keeping collective track of all our contributions.

Adult Learning, Critical Intelligence and Social Change

Edited by
Marjorie Mayo & Jane Thompson

NIACE
THE NATIONAL ORGANISATION
FOR ADULT LEARNING

Published by the National Institute of Adult Continuing Education
(England and Wales)
21 De Montfort Street, Leicester LE1 7GE
Company registration no. 2603322
Charity registration no. 1002775

First published 1995

Reprinted 1997, 1998

Cataloguing in Publication Data
A CIP record for this title is available from the British Library

ISBN 1 872941 61 3

Printed in England by Antony Rowe Ltd, Chippenham
Printed on acid-free paper

Contents

Preface

Jane Thompson

In 1980 some of us who are included here contributed to a collection of essays entitled *Adult Education for a Change* (Thompson, 1980), which made a small but significant contribution to the recent history, theory and practice of radical adult education. The book was welcomed by many teachers and organisers working on the left, providing inspiration to some and validation to others. Recognised as something of a 'seminal text' during the early 80s, it acted as an irritant to many of those who viewed adult education from a liberal perspective, but who were also sliding away from the liberal tradition towards new vocationalism under the jurisdiction and direction of successive conservative governments.

Even before *Adult Education for a Change* made it to the bookshelves, however, the seeds of radical right-wing reaction were already sown. Some attribute the original articulation of education's alleged failure to 'properly meet the needs of industry' to the speech delivered by Jim Callaghan at Ruskin College, Oxford in 1976, when he was opening a new hall of residence in memory of Steve Biko. Such are the many contradictions of labour history!

But it was the policies of Thatcherism and the New Right which helped to make the apparent need for change into a reality and arranged to turn the education system into one more outpost of the enterprise culture, operating according to business principles and driven by the so-called logic of the market. The consequences were considerable reorganisation, relocation, cuts and closure. As Rebecca O'Rourke (see 'All Equal Now?' in this volume) comments:

> *Every adult education institution I have worked in – and I dare say most of those I haven't – displays a copy of Caius Petronius' comment on reorganisation – 'a wonderful method for creating the illusion of progress while producing confusion, inefficiency and demoralisation'.*

But the changes were more than a method designed to save money and alienate and de-skill teachers at great expense, they also acted as a way of re-inventing education as a means of people-processing and control, rather than as a potential tool for their liberation. It is not coincidental that the language of 'total quality management', 'quality control', accreditation, modularisation, vocationalism and 'progression' has largely served to disguise (although only thinly) a fairly determined departure from left-radical, progressive and even liberal definitions of education as a way of assisting in the democratic creation of knowledge and the development of practical and critical intelligence, in favour of various kinds of training and measurements of competency.

I shall not anticipate the arguments of those who have criticised these developments, because they are elaborated in this volume, and because our contributors speak eloquently and variously for themselves, except to say that it has been the overwhelming domination of the education debate, in adult and continuing education anyway, by those who have more readily acclimatised themselves to the 'new realism' of New Right orthodoxy, that has helped to provoke this long overdue collected response from those of us who have not been so easily persuaded by either its logic or its objectives.

In 1993 I wrote a brief but heartfelt polemic in *Adults Learning* (Thompson, 1993) after a period of absence from adult and continuing education circles. I was commenting on how comprehensively the focus of debate in the popular journals and everyday conferences had shifted to matters of institutional re-organisation and CATs administration, rather than those of politics and purpose, teaching and learning and curriculum development. Organisers and academics alike seemed pre-occupied with questions of funding, marketing, accrediting and monitoring. Few people mentioned students or adult learners. Equal opportunities seemed as out of date as Wills Whiffs or Ford Cortinas. Tokenism in high places had ensured that there were sufficient women dressed in management suits to stand beside the men to pretend that women's liberation was no longer needed. No one very much appeared to notice the absence of other minority groups. The nature of knowledge, teaching and learning methodologies and curriculum development were glaring omissions from local conferences on Access and APEL.

At a NIACE conference to mark International Women's Day 1993 [1] only the occasional lone voice paid any attention to equal opportunities, feminism or politics. At another in November about quality assurance [2] the talk with senior education managers and institutional principals was all about performance indicators, customer throughput and the statistical analysis of quality. Since few of the audience either questioned the speakers or contributed from the floor, and whilst most of the energy exerted to try to produce a semblance of debate was exercised by the Director of NIACE, in the guise of 'devil's advocate', it was difficult not to conclude that both reflection and discussion had suffered terminal exhaustion. Until afterwards, in the bar, when it became clear that another feature of so many years of Tory rule was that the price paid for holding on to jobs, and even achieving promotion, had been widespread demoralisation and incorporation – in the original, political sense of the term. People felt silenced, some were scared, most believed there was nothing else that could be done except to go along with the new order and live in the cracks. The creation of new jobs in quality and marketing seemed to provide their own logic.

Hence the *cri de coeur* in *Adults Learning* to 'whoever was left', which helped to set the record straight. Not everyone responded like Malcolm Barry (Barry, 1993), one-time music critic of the *Morning Star* and now

Head of Continuing Education at Goldsmiths College, London University, who praised others like himself for their capacity to recognise reality and their powers of adaptation. Those who kept their heads down and worked quietly 'on the inside' for decent educational opportunities for adults within the boundaries of what was possible.

Compared to Barry, others who responded to my piece in *Adults Learning*, and who helped to provide the impetus for the publication of this book, were dismissed by him as somehow responsible for their own exclusion and marginalisation in contemporary debate and practice. His caricature was of erstwhile feminists 'in dungarees' and radicals whose political commitment to the dispossessed had convinced no one but themselves about the significance of the class struggle. His response expressed the fashionable concern of 'modernisers' and 'new realists' to distance themselves from old style 'loonies', now increasingly re-afflicted by 'political correctness'.

This collection of essays offers our response – not to Barry particularly – but to all of those who have imagined, during the last 15 years or so, that 'the way the world is' is how it inevitably 'has to be'.

The contributions come from workers in different branches of adult, community and continuing education with differing pre-occupations – from universities to centres for the unemployed; in formal systems and in community projects; with varying degrees of influence and responsibility. For the most part we have also been around a long time, not simply like dinosaurs, but as cultural workers engaged in political struggles. Most of us have continued to argue for alternative practices and to pursue different goals from those identified as 'necessary to industry'; to recognise the continuing importance of traditional understandings of what counts as 'Really Useful Knowledge' (see Katherine Hughes in this volume) and 'critical intelligence' (see Allman and Wallis in this volume) but in a contemporary context and in which ordinary people's grip on the possibilities of democratic participation, and any semblance of control over their own lives, has been massively eroded. The influence of the New Right in all areas of social policy and public services, not simply education, has been the attempt to transform citizens and voters with influence in the democratic process at a variety of levels, into clients and consumers who make individualised complaints through quangos, which are unaccountable to anyone except those in government who provide their funding and organise their appointment.

But although the sea change in dominant values and perceptions has been enormous, it has not been total. The contributions made to this collection reflect not simply the continuing engagement with radical adult education ideas and practice rooted in an important tradition, but also an alternative and contemporary reason for promoting the acquisition of critical intelligence as a defence against the dangerous totalitarian mentality of governments, and dominant ideologies, which have been in power too long and think they are inviolate.

The arguments collected here come from teachers and organisers working not, as Barry assumes, from up-turned soap boxes at Speaker's Corner but from *within* education institutions (so long as we still have full-time jobs), and from part-time and temporary employment (when we have little other choice). All of us remain engaged in the process of contesting the purpose and significance of learning, as distinct from 'measuring everything that moves on a five-point scale'[3] or accrediting everything that breathes in the name of spurious progression routes. As John McIlroy has commented (personal communication), it is important to remember that the debates that exert influence and lead to change are not simply conducted by those who 'keep their heads down' and 'work quietly on the inside'. It is also possible, and characteristic of the purpose of many of those whose words are included here, to 'stand up for principle, and argue for principle, and to develop work on the basis of principle – without being excluded.'

This collection is a testimony to some of that work and to some of the initiatives which have endured, despite successive conservative governments, and despite a pretty cold climate for the left in recent years. The arguments point to ways of moving forward, not simply to recapture lost ground, but to shift the possibilities of what might be done in the future.

Notes

1. 'Keeping women on the agenda in education and training', Birmingham, 8 March 1993.
2. 'Quality matters: how can adult learners get consistent quality across sectors?', London, 24 November 1993.
3. Terry Melia, Chief Inspector of the FEFC, speaking at the NIACE conference, November 1993 referred to above.

References

Barry, Malcolm (1993) 'Learning, humility and honesty' *Adults Learning*, vol. 5, no. 2, October 1993.

Thompson, Jane (ed.) (1980) *Adult Education for a Change*, Hutchinson.

Thompson, Jane (1993) 'Learning, liberation and maturity: an open letter to whoever's left', *Adults Learning*, vol. 4, no. 9, May 1993.

One

Adult Education for Change in the Nineties and Beyond: Towards a Critical Review of the Changing Context

Marjorie Mayo

Writing in 1979, in her introduction to *Adult Education for a Change*, Jane Thompson argued that 'The notion that any kind of education, however pure its motives or esoteric its subject matter, can ever be considered neutral is now a difficult position to maintain'. She quoted from Freire to endorse her view that:

> *there is no such thing as a neutral education process. Education either functions as an instrument which is used to facilitate the integration of generations into the logic of the present system and bring about conformity to it, or it becomes the 'practice of freedom', the means by which men and women deal critically and creatively with reality and discover how to participate in the transformation of their world (Thompson, 1979: 26).*

Thompson went on to argue that adult education could provide relatively more space for education for social transformation, because it had been less concerned with control through measuring and labelling people, and because the students, as adults, had political rights as citizens and brought their own life experiences which could lead them to question and challenge rather than legitimise inequality.

Fifteen years on, from the vantage point of the mid-nineties, there has been both continuity and change, including changes in adult education which have re-emphasised the continuing and increasing significance of key aspects of the earlier analyses. Since 1979, adult education has been profoundly affected by wider processes of economic, social and political restructuring, processes which have to be analysed within the global context, although they have certainly been particularly marked in Britain during the Thatcher years and beyond. One consequence of these changes has been that adult education has become more directly subjected to precisely that concern to measure and label which had been previously more characteristic of schooling. This issue of measurement and labelling has been an important theme, and one which is explored in a number of chapters (including the chapters by Fraser, Martin and Alexander, O'Rourke and Shaw and Crowther). Whilst important in its own right, however, this is symptomatic, rather than the cause of wider processes of restructuring.

The combined effect of these wider processes has been that it has become increasingly difficult to argue that 'knowledge is neutral'. Adult education, like education more generally, has been demonstrably less neutral, and more overtly controversial; more visibly a mechanism for either social integration or social transformation. The significance of these differing and potentially contradictory outcomes is crucial to analyse, and digest, if adult educators are to develop clear perspectives and effective strategies for change.

In the following sections, reviewing the context for adult and continuing education, I argue that over the past decade it has become even clearer that strategies to reform education in general, and adult education more specifically, have to be analysed in the context of the state's wider economic, social, political and ideological strategies, in capitalist societies, during a decade or more of global recession. As a starting point, I note some of the ways in which theoretical debates about the interconnections between education and the state in capitalist society have moved on since 1979. This, in turn, relates to the discussion of some of the key features of underlying economic, social and political changes, which have been particularly crucial in understanding the changing context for adult education in the nineties and beyond. And finally, I point to some of the varying ways in which adult educators and the individuals and groups they work with have identified creative strategies for adult education for transformation, creative strategies and practices which are considered in more detail in the chapters which follow. My conclusion is that adult education is demonstrably more vital than ever, both in providing essential knowledge and skills *and* in developing alternative visions for democratic social change. This is the starting point for the chapters which follow.

Before tackling these questions, however, I should like to emphasise that my particular focus is upon these specific aspects of the changing context for adult education. This is in no way intended as a comprehensive reflection on the focus and themes which were developed in *Adult Education for a Change* 15 years ago. Whilst *Adult Education for a Change* did engage with theoretical debates around the relationships between education, the state and ideology in capitalist societies, the collection also engaged with a number of other vital areas of debate both in terms of theory and in terms of practice. The collection represented a process of questioning the concepts and practice of adult education, as these had developed historically and were being applied in Britain and beyond.

Adult Education for a Change set out to question underlying ideologies and their implications for the practices and outcomes of adult education. For example, the chapter by Keddie explored the implications of ideologies of individualism and choice, and examined the ways in which the ideology of individualism related to the curriculum and teaching methods, as well as to policies for providing education for 'disadvantaged' adults, focusing upon them and their needs and supposed deficits without relating these back to wider structural causes of disadvantage and social inequality (Keddie, 1980). This critical debate about adult education and the disadvantaged was developed in a number of chapters, including contributions by Jackson, Lovett and Thompson, contributions which included questions about community education and community action (Jackson; Lovett; Thompson, 1980). Chapters in this collection take up some of these threads and develop them in the contemporary context, exploring strategies for positive, progressive practice.

Adult Education for a Change also posed questions around gender as well as questions around class. Over the past 15 years the significance of both gender and race has become even clearer, both in their own right and in terms of their relationships with other forms of exploitation and oppression. The chapter by Thompson in this collection develops this discussion, along with a number of others, including Fraser, O'Rourke, Reynolds and Swindells. These themes are key to the present collection.

In *Adult Education for a Change* debates were also located within their historical context, including the history of workers' education and the labour movement (the chapter on the Labour College movement and the Workers' Educational Association before the Second World War by Brown, 1980). The importance of understanding the historical context of working-class culture and education for social change, and long-standing debates about 'Really Useful Knowledge', in contrast with technicist approaches to 'Useful Knowledge', are taken up and developed in a number of chapters in the present collection, including those by Hughes, Kean, Ross and Swindells. And the chapter by Yarnit is amongst those which include critical reviews of recent history in relation to adult education and the working class.

Before moving into these debates, past and present, in the subsequent chapters in this collection, however, I want to explore some of the particular features of the changing economic, political, social and ideological context, with a view to questioning the impact for adult education. How and why is it being argued that adult education is potentially more vital than ever, in this changing context? And what might be the theoretical basis for making such a claim?

So what were the key features of the theoretical debates on the relationships between education and the state in capitalist society, which informed the arguments in *Adult Education for a Change* at the end of the seventies? In his foreword, Keith Jackson reflected upon the critical assessment and development of the liberal adult education tradition, both in theory and practice, as academics like himself and his colleagues in the Liverpool Community Development Project engaged with the theoretical implications of progressive practice, working with political and social movements in the inner city. His references to the relevance of Marxist analyses, drawing upon the contributions of Gramsci in particular, were developed in the chapter by Sallie Westwood (Westwood, 1980).

Westwood summarised Marxist contributions to the sociology of education in the seventies, focusing upon the functions of education for social reproduction, that is for the reproduction of the social relations and the ideological climate within which capitalism can thrive. Capitalist society, she argued, like any other society, must reproduce itself, and that process of reproduction requires the reproduction of social relations and ideologies, as well as material goods. Alongside the media and other institutions of modern capitalist societies, education had what she described as 'a vital role to play in the reproduction of capitalism' (Westwood, 1980: 35).

Similar insights had, of course, been explored by mainstream functionalist sociologists (e.g. Parsons, Davis and Moore), who had argued that the educational system had unique significance in modern industrial societies, both for transmitting relevant knowledge and specific skills, and for wider processes of socialisation into the values and culture of modern advanced capitalism. In this sense, the education system was seen to have replaced the church, in preindustrial societies in the West, as the key mechanism for transmitting values and culture from one generation to the next. The modern education system, then, socialises the young into the basic values of society. Only the functionalists viewed this state of affairs, and this emphasis upon the promotion of social integration and continuity, as representing a desirable goal (given that they saw modern, industrial capitalist society as the objective of social development). Whereas Marxists such as Althusser, Bowles and Gintis, and Bourdieu drew fundamentally different conclusions about capitalist society, and thus about the role of the education system in reproducing it. Although capitalism, from this perspective, is inherently dynamic, Marxists have argued that the dynamism of capitalist society rests upon social inequalities which can only be ultimately resolved under socialism.

Westwood quoted Bowles and Gintis' view that the education system's ties with the requirements of capitalist production inevitably led it 'to reproduce economic inequality and to distort personal development'. 'The education system', she argued, 'reproduces workers for capitalism by its emphasis upon control, discipline and by teaching children the authority relations of the capitalist division of labour' (1980: 36–37). By extension, adult education was also affected by the social class bias of the education system more generally, disproportionately used as it has been by the middle class, whilst the working class tends to view adult education provision as equally alienating as school. Even trade union education, according to this perspective, is infected by pressures for incorporation, rather than challenging the framework of capitalist economic and social relations of class subordination which underpin the workplace. The chapter by John McIlroy in this volume explores some of the contemporary implications of these dilemmas for trade union education and training in Britain, over the past period of restructuring. And in parallel, the education system has been criticised for reproducing capitalist social inequalities in terms of gender and of 'race'. As has already been suggested, concerns to do with gender in education, and specifically in adult education, are explored in the chapter by Jane Thompson in this volume and developed in both theory and practice in her chapter and in the chapters by Fraser and O'Rourke.

In *Adult Education for a Change*, Westwood went on to argue, as Jackson had done, and as McIlroy and Allman and Wallis do in this collection, for the importance of Gramsci's contributions to these theoretical debates. In particular Gramsci's concept of hegemony provided the tool for analysing the ways in which ruling classes strive to dominate the framework of ideas; so that the hegemonic culture, in capitalist society, is a culture in which capitalist economic and social relations, in the market economy, are seen as normal, and indeed natural; the only 'common sense' way in which society could be organised. (Gramsci's critical examination of this notion of 'common sense' is further explored, too, in the chapter by Alexander and Martin, together with alternative, progressive ways of understanding the notion of 'common sense'.)

Education in general, according to Gramsci, including adult education specifically, may serve to further legitimise this 'common sense'. Or alternatively it may serve to challenge this hegemony, to promote fundamental questioning and the discussion of alternatives. This was precisely the way in which Gramsci himself contributed to adult education in terms of political education, questioning existing social class relations and posing issues around workers' control in the Factory Councils in Italy, after the First World War.

This emphasis upon education, and specifically adult education, as a site of struggle in the battle of ideas is particularly relevant, both in terms of subsequent theoretical debates and in terms of analysing more recent policies and practice. Education in general and adult education and training specifically need to be so contested precisely because of the potential economic, social, ideological and cultural implications. There are potential connections with the requirements of economic restructuring (which involve tailoring education and training more precisely to employers' estimated skills requirements). And adult education and training has relevance for processes of social, ideological and cultural restructuring; for promoting the pre-eminence of market values as uncontestable – the common sense view that there neither is nor realistically can be an alternative. In recent debates this view that there is no alternative has taken a number of forms, including the 'TINA' formulation of the Thatcher years (There Is No Alternative) and the 'death of socialism' and the 'end of history/ideology' debates which accompanied the collapse of former socialist governments in Eastern and Central Europe in 1989.

Meanwhile, the Marxist analyses of the seventies have been contested in contrasting ways. The debate moved on. As several of the chapters, including Thompson's, argue, the New Right challenges of the eighties can be traced back not only to the Black Papers, but also to Callaghan, the then Labour Prime Minister, speaking at Ruskin in 1976 and launching the 'Great Debate' about how the education system should be geared more specifically to the requirements of industry. The New Right project for the restructuring of education and training, including adult education and training, is explored in a number of chapters, including those by Fraser, Grayson, Hughes, Martin and Alexander, O'Rourke and Shaw and Crowther.

As they argue, the New Right project was particularly marked in Britain and in USA in the Thatcher/Reagan years of the eighties, although the restructuring of social spending has been exported to Third World countries, with devastating effects, as part of World Bank and IMF

Structural Adjustment programmes to promote market-driven development globally. The chapter by Payne, for instance, illustrates these processes in the case of Nicaragua.

Alternatively, the development of postmodernist theories has provided another critical perspective on Marxist approaches. Whilst postmodernism itself has been slippery to define, being more readily characterised in terms of what it questions, postmodernists have broadly shared a profound scepticism about the grand theories of the past. This profound scepticism applies particularly to Marxism, with its structured analysis of the economic basis of class-divided societies under capitalism and its belief in the possibility, indeed the inevitability in traditional Marxist accounts, of the ultimate triumph of socialism. Postmodernism rejects both the categories and the projected conclusions of the Marxist analysis. The chapters by Allman and Wallis, Steele and Thompson include more developed discussions of postmodernism, and specifically discussions of the implications in relation to debates on adult education.

Steele comments on the ways in which postmodernism's stance of scepticism leads to a distanced and increasingly ironical standpoint, a type of nihilism, in its extreme forms, which 'refuses to distinguish between social life and its simulations'. As Steele demonstrates, postmodernism can be seen in terms of cultural/ideological configurations of late capitalism, with postmodernist intellectuals as a 'class' of taste creators hooked on fashion. And Thompson argues that the postmodern pre-occupation, in some academic feminism, has acted to deradicalise the subversive potential of academic women's studies through undermining the links with the social movement for women's liberation.

Whatever the criticisms of the ultimate logic of the more relativist and nihilistic versions of postmodernism, however, the postmodernist critique of the rigidities and potential reductionism of structuralist Marxism and essentialist feminism (as these were developing by the late seventies), *has* had to be taken seriously and has been taken seriously by Marxists and feminists. Indeed, there has been a longer-term critical review of the potential reductionism of structuralist Marxism and the limitations of essentialist feminism from within Marxism and feminism, themselves, critical trends which anticipated many of the criticisms of postmodernism.

Brian Simon, for instance, has been profoundly critical of the type of structural Marxism which has led to fatalistic and mechanistic conclusions about the possibilities for educational reform, let alone for seeing the education system as an important site of ideological struggle. Simon has included Bowles and Gintis, for instance, in this characterisation of an approach to Marxism which sees capitalism as fixed and inevitable, with the education system as inexorably meeting the requirements of capital. In contrast, Simon has argued for the importance of a more dialectical approach, which allows for the relative autonomy of education, with space for contradictions and unintended outcomes which do not fit so neatly with the supposed logic of capital; and most importantly with space for struggles, including struggles around working-class adult education. 'The future', according to Simon, 'is open and undecided', and it is, he suggests, 'of supreme importance that those closely involved in education recognise and struggle consistently to realise its potential' (Simon, 1985: 30). In many ways, this reflection summarises the key message of this collection.

Similarly, Andy Green, for instance, has demonstrated, through his comparative historical analysis, the continuing relevance of Gramsci's approach and the importance of understanding both structural factors and constraints, *and*, as Simon has argued, the importance of human agency in relation to struggles for educational reform. Through analysing the changing patterns of state intervention in education in England, France, Prussia and the USA he has shown both the increasing centrality of education (the secular church, in terms of ideology and socialisation) and the ways in which state intervention is ideological, rather than simply repressive. In other words, there can be relative spaces for educational reform as part of wider strategies for transformation. And following Gramsci, he concludes that popular education can be transformative of popular consciousness, rather than simply or mechanistically reproducing capitalist ideology (Green, 1990).

Following Gramsci, too, and combining the insights of Gramsci with those of Freire, Peter Mayo has similarly argued for the possibilities as well as for the significance of adult educators' contributions to progressive practice (Mayo, 1993). The logic of this position, as it is argued in this collection, is that given the wider processes of change and restructuring over the past 15 years or so, adult education has potentially more significance than ever, in terms of education for social transformation.

Whilst these theoretical debates have had a life and importance of their own, however, they have certainly not been taking place in a vacuum. On the contrary, the logic of the Marxist perspective is that although theoretical/ideological debates have key importance in their own right, theories and ideas are not free-floating, or totally removed from their economic, social and political contexts. And the context for these debates has been one of economic recession and restructuring on a global scale, a context in which New Right ideas were promoted and exported, and New Right remedies were applied in Britain and the USA and beyond.

Without going into detail here, the scale of these changes since the seventies does need to be emphasised. The impact of worldwide economic recession has been compounded by New Right responses, attempting to free up market mechanisms and reduce employers' costs, to revive profitability for capital. The consequences for labour have included increased unemployment and increased casualisation, low pay and reduced employment rights. And free market economics have been accompanied by free market social policies, to reduce public spending and divert resources towards the requirements of profitability, in both First and Third Worlds (typically via Structural Adjustment Programmes).

The results of these combined factors have been literally catastrophic for the world's most vulnerable, with dramatic increases in poverty for many millions in the Third World. Between 20% and 30% of the world's population was, by the end of the eighties, living in households which were too poor to obtain the food necessary to maintain energy levels. Every day, it has been calculated, some 40,000 children die of poverty, an economic holocaust the equivalent of an Auschwitz every three months (Latouche, 1993). The impact has been less fatal in the West, although even in Britain and the USA there have been persistent differentials in infant mortality according to families' economic and social circumstances; and in Britain, for instance, the proportion of children living in poverty tripled during the eighties.

In terms of the debates in this book, however, the key aspects of New Right policies which have been criticised are those concerned with education and training. And these have been contradictory. On the one hand, there has been increasing emphasis upon the contribution which education and more specifically training could make to economic growth and development, and this has been a powerful trend, both in the West and in developing countries of the Third World (e.g. Rogers, 1992). A number of chapters explore the implications, including the implications for the focus upon competence, defining educational outcomes increasingly narrowly, in terms of measured effects on productivity (Alexander and Martin, Crowther and Shaw, Yarnit, this volume).

This emphasis upon the potential links between education and training and economic growth and development has also been particularly marked in relation to adult education and community education (Jolly, 1987; Rogers, 1992) in both First and Third Worlds. Once again, however, it is important to emphasise the contradictory aspects of these connections. From the Marxist perspective, employers' interests cannot be equated with the interests of their workers. But that is not at all to imply that workers do not share an interest in economic growth and development. The point to stress, here, then, is absolutely not to argue against development *per se*, but to challenge the New Right's assumptions that economic growth and development will 'trickle down' to benefit all sections of society, eventually, if the market is only left to itself. The experiences of the past decade or so, both in Britain and in Third World contexts, demonstrate only too clearly that the result may be quite the reverse – that unrestrained growth for the benefit of some is accompanied by increasing poverty and polarisation for others. The key issue then becomes what type of education and training is used to promote what types of economic growth and development, for whose benefit? In the current climate of recession and restructuring, these questions have particular significance. But they form part of a longer series of debates about adult education in relation to the workplace and workers' education, debates which were explored in a number of chapters in *Adult Education for a Change*, and which are taken up and developed in this collection (Forrester, Hughes, McIlroy, Ross).

Whilst there has been increasing emphasis upon the economic implications of education in general, and adult education and training in particular, however, this has not precluded the importance of more ideological factors. On the contrary, and as the earlier discussion about the relationships between education, the state and ideology suggested,

education and training systems have also been geared towards the reproduction of social relations and the ideologies which render these acceptable becoming the 'common senses' of everyday life. During a period of
profound economic, social and political change, such as the period since
the seventies has represented, however, this 'common sense' view of nor-
mality has also needed profound renegotiation. The abnormal has
needed to become 'normal'. Previously accepted patterns of social relations have had to be reviewed, and previously uncontested norms have
been challenged. The unthinkable has become not simply thinkable but
apparently inevitable; the view that there is no alternative, whether this
is to previously unthinkable rates of unemployment, poverty or homelessness or to erosions of what used to be seen as essential civil liberties,
including the right to strike – or even, more specifically, to fundamental
erosions of access to education for critical understanding, rather than
simply to training in marketable skills.

This collection follows and explores different aspects of these underlying ideological changes, in relation to the restructuring of adult education. The key point to emphasise here, then, is that adult education, like
education in general, has become more sharply defined as an arena of
struggle. And this has been in terms of ideological and cultural struggles,
not simply in terms of strategies to match adult education and training
more precisely to the changing requirements of the market economy. (Although working-class communities, especially women in those communities, have, of course, also been deeply and absolutely understandably
concerned to acquire the knowledge and skills for economic survival,
and this concern continues to be expressed. The chapter by Sonia
Reynolds on the links between adult education and training and community economic development in South Wales provides a contemporary illustration.)

This emphasis upon the contested nature of education and training is
crucial. As has already been argued, and as a number of the chapters, including Steele's, for instance, demonstrate, ideological changes have not
been unproblematic; ideological restructuring has been the site of struggle. Different chapters explore a range of strategies for carrying out these
ideological and cultural struggles and identifying spaces for critical practice. Steele has also suggested that the marginal, non-mainstream position of adult education has historically been important, in enabling
intellectuals to open up dialogues with working-class people and in its
more radical forms has enabled social movements to temper intellectuals
to their needs. It is this marginal space which, he argues, it is particularly
important to re-occupy. But it is important to emphasise too that occupy-
ing marginal space does not have to involve *being marginal*. On the contrary, this marginal space can be the site for the development of
alternative analyses and alternative practices, as a number of the chapters, including those by Duke, Hughes, Grayson, Lovett, McIlroy,
O'Rouke, Thompson and Yarnit, show.

Spaces have been potentially opened up by the very processes of restructuring. This has applied even in the context of adult education and
training in relation to economic restructuring and the changing require-

ments of the market economy. Ironically, British governments since the seventies have stressed the importance of targeting education and training far more precisely, in relation to specific areas of knowledge and skills in short supply in the labour market. This has been key to the entire project of restructuring education and training, including the emphasis upon narrow definitions of competence. But this has also been problematic, in practice. So the state has been grappling with the contradictions of how to impose these changes whilst retreating from direct state provision and leaving the processes of restructuring open to greater influence from the market and directly from employers (via the Training and Enterprise Councils). And in the meantime, a number of employers have become increasingly concerned with an alternative perspective, the need for a more broadly educated workforce, with a sounder basis of transferable knowledge. The example of Ford's EDAP scheme is one of the better known and documented case studies (although Ford had a range of objectives in addition, besides providing workers' education, including objectives related to the goal of restructuring industrial relations along more consensual, Japanese-style lines). The chapter by Keith Forrester explores some of the issues and tensions involved in such employer initiatives to promote a wider view of education for their workforces. Similar issues and tensions have also emerged in the US context (Mayo, Meyer and Rosenblum, 1992). But these have been potentially creative contexts, both for adult educationists and for the trade union organisations concerned. For example, the Chicago Consortium For Worker Education (CCWE) has provided a range of examples of workers and their unions shaping employer sponsored education programmes for the benefit of the workers concerned.

Whilst workplace-based education and training has been an increasingly important theme, the relationships between community-based education and community action have also been increasingly vital since the publication of *Adult Education for a Change*. Once again, there are aspects of continuity and aspects of change, both in the issues which are explored and in the authors and their contexts (including contributions from Lovett, in both volumes). *Adult Education for a Change* included chapters which critically analysed the contemporary focus on adult education and community education in relation to strategies to tackle poverty and social deprivation. Poverty had been 'rediscovered' in the sixties, and adult education in the seventies was linked to meeting the needs of the 'deprived/disadvantaged adult', through the debates following the Russell Committee Report in 1973. This critical analysis in the 1980 collection provides the backdrop for the discussion of 'Russell revisited' in the chapter by Jackson in this collection.

Since the late seventies, community-based strategies have been reinvented once again. The new 'communitarianism' has emerged on the agenda, across party political divides, and in different national contexts. So why has the (broken) wheel of community-based strategies to tackle wider structural problems been applied, yet again? There may be a number of reasons, some of which relate directly to previous discussions of global restructuring processes, more generally.

In particular, the contemporary focus upon community participation in the Mixed Economy of Welfare has provided justifications for the retreat of public provision, promoting self-help for a mixture of reasons, including reasons associated with public sector cuts. But whilst community participation has been promoted as part of free market strategies to reduce public expenditure and enhance cost effectiveness, both in the First World and in the Third World, community participation has also had a more progressive edge, with genuine potential for more transformatory strategies (Craig and Mayo, forthcoming). Community participation as part of strategies for people-centred development has been put forward as representing potential hope in addressing the global development crisis (e.g. Korten, 1989; UNDP, 1993). And linked to this, voluntary and community-based organisations, non-governmental organisations (NGOs) and people's movements have been identified as having potentially vital and radical contributions (Clarke, 1991). John Payne's chapter considers the implications of these contradictions in the context of Nicaragua, where, ironically, the extraordinary Sandinista government programme of adult education for social transformation was halted, following the defeat of that government in 1990, only to be at least partially revived through the NGO sector, creatively working to begin to fill the spaces which had been left.

Community participation in and through adult education may be and has been promoted for differing reasons, in varying circumstances. These have related to regressive goals and objectives. And, conversely, they have included both government and voluntary/NGO sector initiatives with a transformatory agenda (see, for example, Srinivasan, 1992; Poster and Zimmer, 1992).

Adult and community education geared towards the promotion of participatory action research (PAR) have similarly been promoted in a range of contexts, both in the First World in the North and in the Third World in the South. The collection of case studies edited by Orlando Fals-Borda and Muhammad Anisur Rahman (1991) provides such examples from different Third World contexts as well as from North America. In these cases, participatory action research is conceptualised as part of a process of adult education for social change and transformation, geared to the acquisition of 'serious and reliable knowledge upon which to construct power, or countervailing power, for the poor, oppressed and exploited groups and social classes – the grassroots – and for their authentic organisations and movements' (*ibid.:* 3). The ultimate aims of this liberating knowledge and power, it is argued, are 'to enable the oppressed groups and classes to acquire sufficient creative and formative leverage as expressed in specific projects acts and struggles; and (2) to produce and develop sociopolitical thought processes with which popular bases can identify' (*ibid.:* 4). Such an approach has vital relevance both to Third World contexts and to the more local contexts in Britain, as these feature in a number of the chapters in the present volume, including, for example, that by Reynolds. This is also relevant to the chapters by Grayson, Hughes and Ross, in particular.

Community participation and the role of participatory action research have particular significance, too, in relation to earlier theoretical debates. In addition to the criticisms and debates within Marxist approaches, which have already been explored in relation to structuralism, more recent criticisms have also renewed debates about socialism and democracy. Miliband, for instance, was amongst those Marxists who argued that by far the most important lesson to be learnt from the collapse of socialist governments in 1989 was to do with the subject of democracy and the importance of developing more genuinely democratic forms of socialism (Miliband, 1991: 11). Clearly this is part of a larger debate, which there is not the space to develop here. But the point to emphasise is that community participation in general, and participatory action research, can also be considered in terms of their potential for contributing to wider and more thorough-going strategies for democracy.

This brings the argument back to the starting point for this collection, that despite the problematic nature of the period since the publication of *Adult Education for a Change*, and without in any sense underestimating the significance and extent of the challenges and dilemmas which the past decade has posed for those concerned, nevertheless, despite all of this, adult educators *have* managed to identify creative spaces, both in Britain and beyond. This collection illustrates these achievements, in working with individuals and in working with groups and organisations providing opportunities for critical educational experiences in the workplace and in the community. And in addition, it is being argued, the significance of adult education for change is greater than ever. Over recent years, education and training in general, and adult education more specifically, have been the focus of attention, precisely because education can be seen as the means for promoting integration and conformity in a rapidly changing world. And education and training, including adult education, should also be the focus of attention precisely because, as Freire argued, education can also be the means by which men and women deal critically and creatively with reality and discover how to participate in the transformation of their world.

References

Althusser, L. (1971) 'Ideology and ideological state apparatuses', in Althusser, L. *Lenin and Philosophy and other Essays*, New Left Books.

Bowles, S. and Gintis, H. (1970) *Schooling in Capitalist America*, Routledge.

Brown, G. (1980 'Independence and incorporation: the Labour College movement and the Workers' Educational Association before the Second World War', in Thompson, J. (ed.) (1980).

Clarke, J. (1991) *Democratising Development*, Earthscan.

Craig, G. and Mayo, M. (forthcoming) 'Community participation and empowerment', in Craig, G. and Mayo, M. (eds) *Community Empowerment*, Zed Books.

Fals-Borda, O. and Rahman, M. (eds) (1991) *Action and Knowledge*, Intermediate Technology Publications.

Green, A. (1990) *Education and State Formation*, St Martin's Press.

Jackson, K. (1980) 'Foreword', in Thompson, J. (ed.) (1980).

Jolly, R. (1987) 'Education', in Cornia, G., Jolly, R. and Stewart, F. (eds) *Adjustment with a Human Face*, vol. 1, Clarendon Press.

Keddie, N. (1980) 'Adult education: an ideology of individualism', in Thompson, J. (ed.) (1980).

Korten, D. (1990) *Getting to the 21st Century*, Kumarian Press.

Latouche, S. (1993) *In the Wake of the Affluent Society*, Zed Books.

Lovett, T. (1980) 'Adult education and community action', in Thompson, J. (ed.) (1980).

Mayo, M., Meyer, P. and Rosenblum, S. (1992) 'Workplace-based education and economic development', *Economic Development Quarterly*, vol. 6, no. 4, pp 444–453.

Mayo, P. (1994) 'Synthesizing Gramsci and Freire: possibilities for a theory of radical adult education', *International Journal of Lifelong Education*, vol. 11, no. 2, pp125–148.

Miliband, R. (1991) 'Reflections on the crisis of Communist regimes', in Blackburn, R. (ed.) *After the Fall*, Verso.

Poster, C. and Zimmer, J. (eds) (1992) *Community Education in the Third World*, Routledge.

Rogers, A. (1992) *Adults Learning for Development*, Cassell.

Simon, B. (1985) *Does Education Matter?*, Lawrence and Wishart.

Srinivasan, L. (1992) *Options for Educators*, PACT/CDS.

Thompson, J. (1980) 'Adult education and the disadvantaged', in Thompson, J. (ed.) (1980).

Thompson, J. (ed.) (1980) *Adult Education for a Change*, Hutchinson.

UNDP (1993) *Human Development Report*, Oxford University Press.

Westwood, S. (1980) 'Adult education and the sociology of education: an exploration', in Thompson, J. (ed.) (1980).

Yarnit, M. (1980) 'Second Chance to Learn, Liverpool: class and adult education', in Thompson, J. (ed.) (1980).

Two

Challenging the Postmodern Condition: Radical Adult Education for Critical Intelligence

Paula Allman and John Wallis

> *An historic act can only be performed by 'collective man', and this pre-supposes the attainment of a 'cultural-social' unity through which a multiplicity of dispersed wills ... are welded together with a single aim, on the basis of an equal and common conception of the world ... where the intellectual base is so well-rooted, assimilated and experienced that it becomes passion ... (Gramsci, 1971: 349–50).*

> *[A critical/dialectical] perception is necessary, but not a sufficient condition by itself for liberation; it must become the motivating force for liberation (Freire, 1972: 26).*

The Basic Ingredients of Radical Education

Critical thinking is the most basic ingredient of radical education. A critical and continually developing intelligence is its most fundamental aim. Without these means and objectives radical educators have little hope of enabling others to develop the motivation, the passion, to challenge present social/economic conditions and to engage in creating a social form more conducive to the fulfilment of human potential in harmony with the natural world. But to achieve the 'unity' to which Gramsci refers depends on how we conceptualise critical thought/intelligence.

In many academic communities there seems to be a fair amount of agreement that critical thinking entails the systematic questioning of extant knowledge. Often this means, or includes, the systematic questioning of both received academic knowledge and the prevailing common sense. For the radical educator this approach to thinking and learning should never be undertaken as an academic posture or routinised mode of establishing one's identity as an 'educated' person. The radical educator engages in critical thinking, and encourages others to do so, in order to 'unveil' the oppressive nature of our current circumstances, to understand what is happening and why it is happening, as well as the history of these conditions. Radical education can only be initiated by someone whose critical thought is dialectically, reciprocally, related to a subjective desire to create a more just world, a person with a vision and therefore a strategy which might enable a 'critical mass' of humanity to engage in the achievement of social justice.

However, the radical educator also must be realistic. It is crucial that we do not misunderstand the relation between vision/strategy and the, more short term, tactical processes we need to employ within the prevailing social relations of oppression. Far too frequently, radical educators have disappointed themselves and invited the ridicule of others because we have lacked, or at least not stressed, a degree of realism. We should never have assumed, or permitted others to assume, a direct or automatic, sequential relation between radical education and macro-level social change. Realistic radical education aims to prepare people, who will go on to prepare others, to transform their social relations at all levels. Ultimately this involves transformations of the national, and now almost global existence of an oppressive social form. However, if transformations at these levels are to be effective, people will need to have developed a critical understanding of what needs to be changed. This will include their involvement in a collective struggle to transform themselves so that they are prepared to initiate the creation of a humanised, i.e. non-oppressive, social order. In other words, we are talking about a long and arduous process, and our acceptance of the educative value and necessity of this struggle, rather than pinning our hopes on a sudden leap from 'enlightenment' to revolutionary change (Marx, 1853, in Vol. 11, 1979).

This advocacy of realism bears no resemblance to the one now current in education and many social movements. The latter is based on defeat and resignation, whether or not this is recognised by its proponents. It is a realism that retreats from the quest to identify universal goals and values which are applicable to all of humanity. This is a realism content with focalised resistance to oppression within the finite, fragmented experiences of social groups or 'communities of interest' whose only affinity with other such collectivities is expressed in recognition and celebration of how different we all are. It is a realism produced by a long overdue flash of insight – the realisation of the plurality of human interests. Unfortunately it is an insight lacking in a critical awareness of how the social relations of capitalism compound or unnecessarily accentuate human differences. This is the realism of the postmodern condition, a realism which spells the abandonment of the search for common and, therefore, potentially shared human goals.

Our plea for realism is based on a materialistically derived vision of what could be achieved for all humanity through, for starters, the development of critical intelligence. This realism does not require us to abandon either plurality and diversity or 'universality'; it requires us to dialectically grasp them as reciprocally related and to experientially treat them as such in the present and future. We will return to these points later when we discuss why and how radical educators must challenge the experience and consciousness, the praxis, which are characteristic of the postmodern condition.

So far we have suggested some basic ingredients of radical adult education, viz. critical thinking/intelligence; realism and vision. The relation among these three implies that we need to dig a bit deeper, think a bit more critically/radically, to identify an ontology and an epistemology appropriate for radical education. Whether acknowledged or not, all forms of education rest on some theory, or at least assumptions, of what it means to be a human being, an ontology. They also rest on a theory of the origin and nature of knowledge, an epistemology, which produces in its adherents the acceptance of a particular relation to knowledge. We propose that a radical educational ontology must begin with a critical assessment of the human condition, what it means to be a human being within the limiting social relations of capitalist societies. Then it must go on to argue that even within these limitations, a potential to become more human can be witnessed – a potential which could be realised and developed by all humanity if we were to transform the given social relations, creating new ones. Therefore a radical ontology is both critical and hopeful because it requires us to analyse 'being' with criteria derived from a concretely-based vision of 'becoming.' Concretely-based visions are not utopian. They are derived from evidence of what some people, through struggle, manage to achieve even in oppressive circumstances.

A radical epistemology is impossible to achieve or even 'think' in the absence of a radical ontology. However, to formulate a radical epistemology we need to employ additional theoretical 'tools'. As with developing a radical ontology, we must critique present theories of knowledge and the consequent ways in which teachers and learners relate to knowledge and, of course, propose the necessary radical transformations. However, to engage in that process effectively, we must employ a critical/dialectical theory of consciousness which enables us to utilise a negative or critical concept of ideology (Larrain, 1983).

In a nutshell, this means a theory which postulates that consciousness arises from our social being, our human activity within the given social relations of our experience, together with the conscious thought produced, in the same way, by people in the past (Marx on Engels, 1846). This historical consciousness will continue to be accepted so long as it continues to address some real aspect of an individual's present circumstances. Therefore, as a baseline, consciousness is conceived of dialectically as a unity of thought and action (praxis). If this unity is created solely within the given social relations, without question or challenge, we only can think and act, have praxis, within the existing framework of our social relations. In other words, we can only reproduce the framework or resist within its overall parameters. If we think that human beings can become critically conscious agents in creating their own history, the origin or source of consciousness becomes extremely problematic, especially when the given framework is comprised of oppressive social relations. We can change our approach, resist in accord with conjunctural variations in our social formation but to no long-term effect. To prepare ourselves to authentically challenge, and eventually change, this social formation, we have to propose and then engage with others in alternative social relations which allow us to develop, or begin to develop, a critical/radicalised consciousness. This is a consciousness which arises from a unity of knowing and being in completely different, humanised ways.

Ideological thought and practices emerge within present social relations. This form of thinking and behaviour produces explanations that
conceal or naturalise the contradictory/dialectical relations that constitute our lived experiences, e.g. the class relations of capitalist societies. It
is not a false way of thinking. The explanations of our reality which are
produced could never appear coherent and convince us if they bore no
relation to our real experience (Hall, 1982). Nevertheless they distort the
quest for critical intelligence because these explanations, and their behav-
ioural counterparts, draw on partial or fragmented aspects of our reality.
This is how they distort or thwart the development of criticality. The relation between these fragmented aspects must be mentally grasped, even
when our immediate experience militates against this opportunity. This
means that we must learn to understand our reality dialectically. Therein
lies our only possibility for the development of critical intelligence and,
in the longer term, an authentic transformation of our social formation.

Several implications follow from these theoretical elements which we
are suggesting are integral to a radical epistemology and its relationship
to education. First, teachers and learners must exist in changed relations
which enable them to become the co-investigators of all forms of existing
knowledge, and they will need to use the theoretical tool of dialectical
analysis, and ideology critique, in order to develop an understanding of
our real or material circumstances, and the ways in which people currently understand these. Dialectical analysis implies, even demands, historical analysis but the necessity of such still needs to be stressed. We will
say more, later, about dialectical analysis. Our main point here is that
radical education involves the simultaneous transformation of our experience of being, struggle on the ontological front, and our experience of
knowing/thinking, struggle on the epistemological front.

Together with our educational experience, and as inspiration for it
over the last decade and more, are two people who would, no doubt, acknowledge their intellectual foundations in Marx, viz. Freire and Gramsci. Both have been interpreted in various, often antagonistic ways. Since
Freire discusses education in more detail than Gramsci, and to set the record straight on how he conceives the dynamic and reciprocal relation
between ontology and epistemology, we will close this section by para-
phrasing what he says, particularly about the latter (Freire, 1974).

After talking extensively about the teacher-student relation, a certain
aspect of the ontological transformation, he goes on to discuss the relation to knowledge in terms of the didactic or 'banking' educator he is famous for castigating. His example is unfortunate as it leads many
progressive, experiential, student-centred educators to think they are not
culpable vis-à-vis this critique. However, it is clear that this is not a critique of method but a critique of a relation to knowledge. The teachers he
challenges go to their studies, or wherever, and work very seriously to
research and prepare the way in which the results of their researches will
be presented to the 'class', but when they complete this endeavour their
own 'act of knowing/learning' is complete; it is finished in the knowledge they now will offer, in whatever way, for the learners to 'consume'.
Freire says he is convinced of the opposite. For him or for any radical

educator/learner to know more, we need another 'subject of knowing', an individual or preferably a group, with whom we can engage in a dialogical 'act of knowing', i.e. the critical co-investigation of knowledge presented as the beginning of the learning experience rather than as the only desired end. Out of this relationship to knowledge, 'new knowledge', or a deeper and more critical understanding, can emerge.

In combination, these basic ingredients of radical education can provide what we have called, elsewhere, an 'abbreviated experience' of what it means, and feels like, to 'be' and to learn in alternative and more humane social relations, an experience aligned to the vision, the strategy, we discussed earlier (Allman and Wallis, 1990). Also, it should provide, at the very least, an introduction to, or the beginning of, the life-long and continuous process of developing critical intelligence. We have not offered a methodological 'blue-print' for this process; nor did we intend to do so. The principles, ingredients, of radical education we have identified, and perhaps others, must be worked out in specific contexts; however, they can serve as common criteria for continuously evaluating whether the radical educator is achieving a coherence between short-term tactics and longer-term strategy.

Radical education necessarily rubs against and should challenge the grain of tradition, the *raison d'être* or the interests served by the current forms of education which have developed within or been given further shape within capitalist social relations. It must confront the current context in which the lived experience of being educated – being the 'object' of either the didactic or progressive educator – provides the material for the ideological understandings of what it means to be educated or to know. We 'know' when we can return to teachers what they already know or when we can question that knowledge in ways which are considered to be academically sound. The ideology inherent in this context is extremely pervasive and therefore difficult to challenge. As a consequence, radical education is not easy to achieve, but as Freire argues, for those who are committed to a radical transformation of the social/economic order, there is no other choice than to try.

Radical Education in our Context

Our own most sustained effort to engage in radical education has been in the highly conventional setting of university education. This involves courses for adult and community educators, from a wide variety of contexts, who express a commitment to working collaboratively to develop critical intelligence. The learning groups are cross-cut by different experiences of class, gender, ethnic, etc., social relations and therefore different initial perspectives on the importance individuals attribute to any form of oppression. Successful completion of the course is signified, according to the institution, by the award of a qualification. As a consequence of all these factors, we cannot assume that the individuals who form these 'groups' share any semblance in the way in which they understand our careful pre-course explanations of what we mean by critical intelligence, or the necessity of a commitment to 'read' or critically understand the world. In an extensive interview we say that we cannot guarantee the achievement of the radical objectives of the course, it is not 'in our gift'. We explain that we will initiate the process and continue to challenge our learning colleagues to join us in the necessary transformations but that we can only achieve these objectives 'with' them, in collaboration. We cannot do it 'for' them or 'to' them. Sometimes it takes a long time, on the course itself, for these explanations to be understood. We would be naïve to expect otherwise. Again we must be realistic but also hopeful – the latter means clinging on to a realistic appraisal of human potential. Experience has confirmed our belief that the majority of participants will become committed to the necessity for radical transformations, will become more radicalised, the more they are enabled to engage in a radical 'reading' of their world.

However, to have any prospects of success, we, and any other radical educator, must portray our own commitment and transformed relations to knowledge. This entails a great deal of hard work, especially in the form of constant, critical self-scrutiny. We have to think deeply about our own assumptions, objectives and rationales. Then we need to explain our thinking about these clearly and explicitly and to introduce learners, from the beginning, to some level of understanding of the intellectual 'tools' like dialectical analysis and ideology critique which we will need in order to co-investigate the world critically. And we must be willing to repeat any explanation, as often as necessary. If we truly know that we cannot deposit knowledge, that human minds are not blank but already full, we must accept that people will only 'hear' a particular explanation when they are ready to do so; in other words, when their consciousness has undergone some degree of qualitative transformation which enables them to be able to integrate radical or counter-hegemonic ways of understanding. Our experience has demonstrated that such transformations of consciousness are possible only within the alternative social relations of the type of radical education approach we have described.

This approach involves listening carefully so that participants' current ways of thinking as expressed within our sessions can be understood, analysed and then problematised, i.e. questioned in a manner that helps people, when expressing their thinking, to reconsider or explore the origins of their thoughts. Effective problematising develops gradually and only to the degree that trust evolves from the shared commitment of the learning group. And this can develop only through the joint and explicit agreement to engage in the struggle to transform teacher-student relations and the relation to knowledge wherein any source of authority is open to critical scrutiny.

All of the above is only possible if we explicitly introduce our learning colleagues to a new concept and experience of group communication, viz. dialogue. Dialogue is not a method but, as Freire says, 'the seal of the transformed relations'. Therefore it involves all the principles we have been discussing and must be evaluated on each occasion that a group meets according to criteria derived from these principles. The ability to dialogue is not a 'competency' which can be filed away or accomplished in a finite sense. The achievement of dialogue must be faced afresh on each occasion that a group meets.

In our context, and many others which we have examined, it seems difficult to envision that the transformations we have advocated could be realised without adopting a thematic curriculum. The current professional rendition of this type of curriculum has been called 'Issue-Based' work, but often this means short-term educational encounters which focus solely on a single issue or problem which is not connected or seen to be related to many others. As a consequence, participants are engaged in yet another experience of fragmentation. In contrast, we would argue that a thematic curriculum must be coherent, developmental and integrated. In preparation, we begin with a continually updated dialectical analysis of our material reality and therefore a fair notion of the way in which the dialectical contradictions of capitalism are currently being experienced in daily life. Then we listen carefully to hear how our learning colleagues either express these or sometimes ignore them. Silence with reference to a crucial theme is an important indicator of how people may be adapting to their real circumstances. When talking about their work or broader social existence, people might express a theme in different jargon or from different angles of perception. Again we must listen carefully and then suggest themes which might unite participants' curiosities and concerns. Freire calls these 'generative themes' because they arise from the dialectical movements in our real world; because they have both local and global significance and because such themes can 'fan out' or be related to other crucial themes which share the same characteristics (Freire, 1972).

For us this type of curriculum can be truly developmental when the qualitative changes of consciousness which are achieved in the co-investigation of one theme lead to a collective decision regarding the next theme we want to study. This can sound like the popular notion of a negotiated curriculum, but it is really something quite different. Let us offer an example. In one group we had two people from 'developing' countries who were engaged in development work primarily financed by 'aid'. This group came together at the time when the British media had focused attention on the issue of aid, but not in a critical manner. Many people had participated in mass jamborees or spectacles, one-off events, like 'Live Aid'. Besides the two development workers, our group was comprised of British adult and community educators who had begun to think that aid was an important issue that could be used, in some way, to encourage people to participate in adult/community education. Therefore we began with the group's collective expression of an interest in a common issue. However, because we studied aid, within the radical education approach we have described, the curriculum 'fanned out', developed into further explorations of other related themes, viz. poverty, development and underdevelopment, racism and sexism. And then the course was over. Nonetheless people knew, in a very critical way, the connection between all of these themes, and therefore it was unlikely that their learning, their critical thinking, had come to an end.

For some participants the learning we did together was painful, for others it was energising. To deal with the pain and sometimes feelings of helplessness, we always make sure, within our dialogues and by the resource readings we supply, that each theme is investigated in terms of its local as well as more global manifestations. As a result, people usually realise that something can be done, a start can be made.

Needless to say, there have been problems in implementing radical education in our context. In terms of the institution, we have survived because of the quality of written/assessed work that many learning colleagues have produced. But in terms of the problems we have encountered, and increasingly encounter, with the students themselves, it is hard to believe that our experience is so very different from those of you who target your educational work within contexts that seem to promise more radical outcomes. Whether the site of work is within a mining community, a centre for unemployed people, a trade union, a tenants' group, an access course or our context, all of us face participants whose consciousness is being increasingly shaped within the postmodern condition.

Marx's theory of consciousness, which informs our work, postulates that our social being determines our consciousness in all its objective and subjective dimensions. Radical education must afford an alternative experience of social being if critical thinking is to flourish. Nevertheless, given Marx's theory, it should be no surprise that we currently face certain tendencies within ourselves and learning colleagues that create additional challenges.

The Postmodern Condition

This is the term used by many people to signify the condition of social being during this conjuncture of human history (Jameson, 1984; Harvey, 1989). Critical analysis provides a strong case for the argument that the condition derives from the current phase in the development of capitalism, some commentators claim its most fully developed or mature stage (Mandel, 1975), together with the related collapse of alternative forms on which many radicals had pegged their hopes for a socialist future. Before discussing the lived experience and consciousness of the postmodern conjuncture, it must be stressed that the linking of cultural forms to a historically specific material reality does not imply a reductionism in analysis based on a crude reading of Marx's base–superstructure analogy. The relation between seemingly separate realms of existence is dialectical, therefore reciprocal. The results, as a consequence, are not mechanically uni-directional.

The experience of the postmodern condition encourages people to focus on pluralistic aspirations derived from difference and to deny the legitimacy or possibility of universal values and goals which used to be the constituent elements of a radical vision. In our discussion of contemporary realism we focused on some of these postmodern aspirations or elements of 'conventional wisdom'. The quest for individualism, individual fulfilment, and an authentic identity, in isolation from a quest for common or shared social objectives, seems to lie at the heart of so many of these postmodern tendencies. Our argument, derived from our concept of a radical ontology, is that within humanised social relations entirely different experiences and ideas about authenticity and individuality would emerge.

Increasingly it seems that the only element of the social, or broad scale communality, that remains is the social world of commodities. This is a social world in which our relation to 'things' increasingly becomes more important than human social relations for the continuous reconstitution of 'the self', the paraphernalia of the 'commodified self'. Those who embrace a life-style based on the acquisition of commodities, on consumption, seem to ignore the fact that such a life-style is not exactly a universal, or even wide-spread, option in the contemporary world. Personal desires, wants and the rights of individuals or sub-groups, constituted around some assumed shared aspects of life-style, seem to have become, for many people, the only worthwhile arena for political and social engagement. Such engagements, and the individuals who move in and out of them, tend to lack coherence. The celebration of diversity and even fragmentation has become the order of the day.

The idea that values, experience and knowledge have a potential resonance for most of humanity seems to have evaporated. Therefore concepts such as 'truth' and 'humanity' have lost all but very localised or particularistic significance. Relativism is the primary characteristic of many types of contemporary thought – that there is no truth, no universal values, is the 'new truth' promulgated in celebration of human diversity. In other words, the celebration of diversity has meant simple recognition of difference, not a coming together to work through our diverse experiences. As a consequence, any person or group's 'truth', i.e. explanation of the real world, is just as legitimate as any other. This is what is meant by relativism. However, it is only the scope and degree of this relativism that is 'new' in this historical experience of capitalism.

Relativism in thought is a tendency which seems to arise during periods of capitalist crisis; therefore it is a periodic tendency with a history that spans at least the last 150 years (Hughes, 1959). Nevertheless some new features are emerging from the experience of the postmodern condition which are extremely problematic for radical educators and political activists, features which if not challenged could mean the end of any possibility of radicalism, critical intelligence and vision of a better future for the whole of humanity. These features run counter to objectives which have guided human striving for centuries. For example, they are completely contrary to the human quest to create a coherent self (Lovibond, 1989; Gramsci, 1971). The coherent self was a self or identity which individuals had to struggle to create. It was based on developing values and beliefs that were logically consistent and which could help us make sense of our diverse experiences. But these values and beliefs were not derived from individual whims or trivial aims. They were social values and beliefs that developed within and became valued within human social relations (Taylor, 1991). Radical social values developed within and informed historical struggles for freedom and a realisation of a fuller humanity. For example, striving for the belief in 'freedom of choice' only became a value, in its own right, because individuals could choose from and then embrace values that were significant in terms of both the social good and the individual's fulfilment.

The contemporary experience of relativism and fragmentation has been accentuated by the loss of a concept of social significance or its relocation in particularised experience. As a result, individuals may still value 'freedom of choice' in the creation of their identities, but the choice is made from a collage of fragments, and other than the value of diversity, there is nothing left of broad social significance to provide a coherence to the self which is created. The proponents of this 'kaleidoscopic self' express no sense of loss, but surely there is a loss. On one hand, what possible reason can there be for radical education or the pursuit of a radical vision if we accept the 'death of the coherent self', the 'death of the subject'. Indeed, what reason could we give for promoting critical intelligence? One does not need to be critical or even intelligent to live in and to adapt to a fragmented world, within a fragmented identity, where the only task is to satisfy individual wants and desires and establish the 'rights' to do so. All one needs to do is to succumb to the intoxication of the market place, the world of capitalist commodities, and to create lifestyles and 'cultures' from these previously commodified or processed raw materials. Clearly there is more at stake here than just radical values and objectives. The very meaning of being human or of realising our human potential is also at stake. Of course, it always was. Throughout human history there has been the possibility that we might uncritically choose to become less human rather than as choosing, critically, to become more fully human. Radical education, politics and critical intelligence were intended to be the means by which we struggled for the latter.

To work out a radical challenge to the tendencies of the postmodern condition, requires a critical analysis of the material relations which are shaping the features we have described. A complex and collaborative analysis will be necessary in the near future; in fact it's long overdue. Here we are able to offer only a brief sketch but one which, nevertheless, allows us to explore some ideas about how we might begin to create an effective challenge to postmodern consciousness.

Prelude to the Sketch based on Marx's Economic Analysis of Capitalism

We must begin with some basic 'truths', historically specific truths, about capitalist social formations. First, crisis is an inherent and recurrent feature of this form of social/economic organisation. These are not necessarily crises that signal collapse. More often they involve a necessary process of destruction so that the system can be cleansed, i.e. the results of the movements and developments of capitalism's dialectical contradictions can be temporarily corrected. Most people know that the production of goods and most services can only take place if a profit is produced. However, they may not fully understand that competition, which also is an inherent and related feature of the system, demands that certain rules must be followed by all competitors. One of the basic rules is that as many commodities as possible, impregnated with as much unpaid or surplus labour as possible (i.e. labour in excess of that which repays the wage), must be produced in the shortest possible time. And they must be circulated and sold as quickly as possible so that the profit realised in sale (although created within production) can be re-invested in the next production run or some area of investment that expands or augments the total sum of capital in the possession of each competitive unit or enterprise.

Although there is no other choice but to play by these rules, following them produces crises of 'over-production' in terms of existing markets of effective demand – demand backed by purchasing power. The competitive agenda underpins the drive to increase or intensify the productivity of workers through the application of technological innovations and/or new ways of organising the work process. Sometimes these drives for increased productivity involve an expansion of the workforce, but at present in the 'developed' economies of the West it has meant a contraction of the number of people in paid employment. But this also means a contraction in the base of capitalist profit, viz. the ratio between paid and unpaid/surplus labour, or at least the number of workers creating the surplus. Therefore, over time, there will be a fall in the rate of profit, firstly for individual firms. Eventually this will affect the overall, global rate of profit. The interplay of all of these processes heightens the competitive struggle which is relieved only by periodic crises or a 'cleansing of the system' until the contradictions re-emerge later, usually on an augmented scale. Interestingly, contemporary capitalist discourses seem more willing to acknowledge these tendencies, referring frequently as they do to the 'business cycle'. In the past, when nation states seemed more in control of their economies, slumps in the cycle were blamed on individuals, trade unions and national governments. Now that capitalism is more extensively and totally, than ever before, a global system and extra-national culprits can be identified, even the proponents of capitalism are more willing to admit, albeit unwittingly, to some of the system's internal flaws and to admit that government policy can no longer alleviate the worse effects, but simply encourage us to play by the 'rules of the game' more competitively.

Radical educators must develop a dialectical understanding of how capitalism works. This is not a call for a return to mechanical forms of economic determinism but for a re-engagement in dialectical thinking which, had it been employed previously, would have knocked deterministic interpretation on the head at its inception. Dialectical understanding is the opposite of positivism and empiricism which seek 'truth' or understanding in the immediate datum or phenomenon available to observation, but dialectical analysis does begin with these and traces their historical development. However, it is the essences or causes of the current phenomena which must be traced historically, not just their surface or immediate appearances. The assumption is that these causes or essences are the dialectical contradictions that constitute the capitalist social formation. Radicals must uncover, mentally grasp, the essences of current phenomena because if we are to create authentic transformations we need to focus on the relational/dialectical causes rather than simply the phenomenal symptoms they produce (Marx, 1875).

When we dialectically conceptualise the economic realm of human activity, we understand that it is inter-related to every other aspect of our social existence. As a consequence, the economic realm can shape the other areas and be shaped by them. Sometimes this happens reciprocally or in balance but at others, one realm or area of existence can assume primacy over others. However, because of struggle and resistance, e.g. class struggle, the primacy is never complete or total. Determination is never mechanical, nor can it be conceived of as such within dialectical thinking. Spaces, possibilities, exist for effective radical challenge, and we can identify them when we attempt to understand our current circumstances dialectically. Having applied a dialectical understanding to studies and accounts of the last 30 years of capitalist development, it is possible to offer a succinct overview of global capitalism. We are sure you will see, as we have done, close parallels between certain economic tendencies and many postmodern cultural practices and forms of consciousness. However, when we consider the global economic structures we also can see that postmodern responses mimic only a partial representation of the total process. Therefore postmodernism is a thoroughly ideological response which cannot serve the interests of the poor and oppressed members of humanity.

Capitalist Restructuring

The pattern now referred to as the globalisation of capitalism began to be given shape primarily by the USA in the 1960s. It was a response to a crisis in the economy of the nation which had emerged, for various reasons, after World War Two as the number one economic super-power. The predominant feature of the response was that the resolution had to be sought in the international arena. The USA owed its super-power strength to many factors, but chief amongst these were the facts that it produced for the world's largest domestic market of effective demand, and through aid assistance to war-torn Europe, it had also created a loyal, and often tied, export market. Eventually the export consumption would stimulate renewed production in Europe and heightened competition to supply effective demand. Once again the inherent tendency towards over-production would rule supreme, and this time it would be increasingly experienced within both domestic and international markets (Thrift, 1986; and Harvey, 1989).

By the mid-1960s the USA's domestic rate of profit had begun to decline. It should be noted that politics played a reciprocal role with economics in that process of decline. One of the temporary solutions was the creation or further development of the multi-national firm and the increasing globalisation of capitalist social relations (Thrift, 1986).

For a brief while, the USA had the advantage of being the first nation to employ and learn from these strategies of global profit realisation and capital accumulation. During the 1970s and 1980s many other nations caught up, setting the scene for the intensified round of competition and 'world recession' we have been experiencing ever since.

Surface or partial (ideological) analyses of all of this have lead to some people becoming very enthusiastic about 'new trends'. Dialectical analysis leads to a much more critical perspective. First and foremost, it seems quite clear that capitalists learned during this period that they had to act both globally and locally. They had to employ all the new telecommunications technology to place investment and situate production wherever they could achieve the best returns on investment. And they had to use, in these multiple sites, whichever form of work organisation, control of labour (some of which were not at all new), would best aid the pursuit of profit-making and capital accumulation. Furthermore, with the heightened competition, there is now an endless quest for new markets, whether this means identifying people who are relatively new to commodity consumption or fostering new wants amongst those with an already established addiction to consumption. For the latter, 'niche' products are created, often by slapping an individualised or culturally-specific surface gloss onto a mass-produced product. Globalisation has also meant that 'cleansing' the system can take a new form during periods of crisis. No longer do capitalists have to scrap or destroy technologies and products that have become unviable in existing markets; these can be profitably sold to developing countries or even 'dumped' on unexpecting, technologically starved nations as economically-tied aid or aid linked to creating future effective demand (George, 1986).

With this phase of intensified competition, some people experience the appearance of greater choice, diversity and pluralism and these have become the basis for an idea of progress shared by many on both the left and the right of the political spectrum. However, we also are experiencing a massification or universalising tendency which seems beyond our control. There is a simple but insidious reason for the latter that makes a mockery of contemporary notions of progress. For the economy of any area or nation to grow, survive and satisfy the 'needs' of its population, there is no choice, at present, but to play by the capitalist rules of the game. Therefore there will be a 'sameness' in response to how economies and societies must operate, or at least a tendency towards this, regardless of superficial recognitions of plurality and diversity (Cox, 1987). Disastrously, too many voices on the left have been caught up in celebrating the postmodern concept of progress, whilst seeming to lose any sense of how these 'positive' features could be linked to a radical vision of the future, to the creation of new social relations in which these features could be of benefit to all of humanity and the natural world. Some 'radicals' even think that these features will lead to an evolutionary development of a more humane existence (Gorz, 1985). All human subjects have to do is sit and wait and, if they can, enjoy the present.

Challenging Postmodernism

This brief overview enables us to suggest a few ideas about how we could begin to challenge the impasse in radicalism created by the postmodern condition.

First we need to reclaim the original theoretical sources that can inform a radical praxis of education and politics. This will involve confronting the type of 'theoretical amnesia' that results from relying solely on secondary and tertiary sources. We are thinking primarily about the original writings of Karl Marx, Antonio Gramsci and Paulo Freire, as well as primary source historical studies of radical education. We need to reclaim our history and critical theory.

The first suggestion would help us fully develop a dialectical theory of consciousness and a critical concept of ideology as well as the ability to analyse the world dialectically. Then we would have the critical tools which would enable us to challenge ideological thought and practice as expressed by people on the right or the left, or anywhere in between.

We need to preserve the belated recognition by postmodernists that difference and diversity are important components of human experience, whilst also strongly promoting the common needs and goals of humanity and the natural world. We will have to argue that there is a human ontological vocation which not only recognises but appreciates diversity and our dialectically reciprocal relation with the natural world. This would mean a radical challenge to abstract notions of equality. We need to develop a new and concrete idea of equality that celebrates our individuality, our diversity, and considers these as qualitative riches which could benefit both individuals and the 'common good.'

On every front we must challenge the relativisation of truth. And to engage in this challenge we will need to clearly distinguish between dialectical/radical concepts of truth and other, ultimately conservative, enlightenment concepts of truth. The latter focus solely on universal, trans-historical, static or finite truths.

Radicals must search for four types of truth which are valuable only in relation to one another. First there are truths which, thus far, seem to hold across the entirety of human history, e.g. human beings create history. These could be called meta-transhistorical truths; they must always be tested, but it is difficult to think that it could be otherwise. Then there are truths that hold across history to date, but we can envision that it could be otherwise, e.g. yes, human beings make history but so far this is not a history based on the critical choice of the majority of human beings. This need not be the truth for the future. Third, there are truths which pertain to the foundation of a particular social formation; they are historically specific to and necessary for the continued survival of a social form, e.g. exploitation within capitalism rests on the social relation between labour and capital. Finally, within any social form there are conjuncturally specific truths, e.g. currently capitalist enterprises are using multiple or 'flexible' ways of exploiting labour and accumulating capital, often referred to as capitalist restructuring within the regime of flexible accumulation. When taken together, these four types of truth constitute a dialectical concept of truth, a concept we will need if we are to effectively challenge the abandonment of the quest for truth so characteristic of postmodern relativism.

Most concretely we can challenge the postmodern condition and all oppressive experiences within capitalism by initiating educational/political projects in which participants can experience, even if only briefly, the meaning of a socialist/radical vision. We have devoted considerable space to spelling out what we think the ingredients of these radical 'abbreviated' experiences should be so we will not labour them here. But we must stress that radical vision has to include challenges to every form of oppression and the ideological praxes that legitimate them, e.g. patriarchy, racism, ageism.

These are our thoughts to date about how to challenge the postmodern condition of consciousness and educational/political activism. We must always remember that postmodern tendencies are only phenomenal manifestations brought about by the current phase of capitalism, capitalism's restructuring in the face of crisis. However it is a restructuring, like so many others in the past, that will assure the survival of capitalism in the absence of an appropriate radical challenge that aims at the core, dialectical contradictions which make possible and sustain this oppressive social form.

References

Allman, P. and Wallis, J. (1990) 'Praxis: implications for "really" radical education', *Studies in the Education of Adults*, vol. 22, no. 1, April, pp 14–30.

Cox, R. (1987) *Production, Power and World Order*, Columbia University Press.

Freire, P. (1972) *Pedagogy of the Oppressed*, Penguin Books.

Freire, P. (1974) *Authority versus Authoritarianism*, an audio-tape from the series 'Thinking with Paulo Freire', The Australian Council of Churches.

George, S. (1986) *How the Other Half Dies*, 2nd edn, Penguin Books.

Gorz, A. (1985) *Paths to Paradise*, Pluto.

Gramsci, A. (1971) *Selections from The Prison Notebooks*, edited and translated by Hoare, Q. and Smith, G.N., Lawrence and Wishart.

Hall, S. (1982) 'Managing Conflict, Producing Consent', Unit 21 in Block 5 Conformity, Consensus and Conflict of D102 Social Sciences: a foundation course, The Open University.

Harvey, D. (1989) *The Condition of Postmodernity*, Basil Blackwell.

Hughes, H.S. (1959) *Consciousness and Society*, MacGibbon and Kee.

Jameson, F. (1984) 'Postmodernism or the cultural logic of late capitalism, *New Left Review*, no. 146.

Larrain, J. (1983) *Marxism and Ideology*, Macmillan.

Lovibond, S. (1989) 'Feminism and postmodernism', *New Left Review*, no. 178.

Mandel, E. (1975) *Late Capitalism*, New Left Books.

Marx, K. (1853) *Revelations Concerning the Communist Trial in Cologne* in Marx and Engels, *Collected Works*, vol. 11.

Marx, K. (1857–58) *Grundrisse*, translated with a foreword by Martin Nicolaus, Penguin Books, 1973.

Marx, K. (1863) *Theories of Surplus Value*, vols. 1, 2 and 3, Progress Publishers (Moscow), 1963.

Marx, K. (1865–78) *Capital, vol. I, II and III*, Penguin Books, vol. I, 1976; vol. II, 1978; vol. III, 1981.

Marx, K. (1875) 'Critique of the Gotha Programme,' in McLellan, D. (ed.) *Karl Marx: Selected writings*, Oxford University Press, 1977.
Marx, K. and Engels, F. (1846) *The German Ideology*, Progress Publishers (Moscow), 1976.
Taylor, C. (1991) *The Ethics of Authenticity*, Harvard University Press.
Thrift, N. (1986) 'The geography of international economic disorder,' in Johnson, R.J. and Taylor, P.J. (eds) *A World in Crisis*, Basil Blackwell.

Three

Are We Not More Than Half the Nation? Women and 'the Radical Tradition' of Adult Education, 1867–1919

Julia Swindells

Throughout the history of adult education in England over the past 150 years, there has been a tension between the drive towards emancipation and the pressure towards elitism. For the most part, this has been debated in terms of the relationship between independent working men's movements and adult education generated by middle-class men, initially from Oxbridge. This account will redress the balance by arguing that focus on that relationship has tended either to exclude or to distort a recognition of the importance of women's education, both in itself and as a driving force in the radical tradition of adult education.

I date the historical account from 1867, when the Reform Act gave increased democratic powers and rights to working-class men. The struggle entailed in the attempt to extend working-men's rights in the political and industrial fields has been well documented (Jepson, 1973; Williams, 1980). This battle for rights was also being fought, as is frequently the case in relation to a political struggle, in terms of, contested and competing demands vis-à-vis education. The threat of anarchy represented for some by the Hyde Park riots, precipitated in 1867 by the campaign for extended franchise, was experienced primarily as a fear of challenge to the existing culture, particularly to the role of the gentleman, privileged by class and educational background (Williams, 1980). Amongst the range of responses from education, there are a number of significant indicators in that same year, including the establishing in Leeds of the North of England Council for Promoting the Higher Education of Women, and the appointment of James Stuart, one of the central promulgators of the University Extension Movement, to a fellowship at Trinity College, Cambridge.

Before moving to the significance of those events for adult education, though, it is important to register models more recognisable in terms of the radical tradition of adult education, which predate 1867. The Adult School Movement began at the end of the eighteenth century and was for women as well as men. The beginning of the nineteenth century then saw the founding of Mechanics' Institutes, whose aim was to offer workpeo-

ple 'an easily accessible training in the scientific principles of their professions' (Harrop, 1987: 97). In relation to both the Adult School Movement
and Mechanics' Institutes, there are existing histories, some of which
have focused on the issue of gender. In brief, we can see that the ideas of
association, collectivism and equality were in tension with an implicit,
sometimes explicit, exclusion of women, denoted in a celebration of manhood. The manifesto of the Adult School Movement demonstrates this in
its rhetoric, 'associating men together for the free study of the deeper
problem of life', on the basis of 'the ideal of manhood set before them in
the Gospels' (Harrop, 1987: 96). Admission of women to the Mechanics'
Institutes was a 'reluctant' one, and was often based on an assumption
that female and male requirements were quite distinct, education in scientific principles and professional training being the preserve of men, unless this was related to women's family roles (Purvis, 1989: 102–6).

The Working Men's Colleges developed in part as a response to criticisms of the Mechanics' Institutes, which were generally felt to have
failed working men in certain key areas, not least in giving little chance
to discuss politics or determine curriculum design and content. The Colleges were committed to an education that was meant to be characterised
by the pursuit of true, disinterested scholarship, free of constraints imposed by the world of commerce. However, the whole question of 'fellowship' discussed by the founder members, who were largely
academics and clergy, left the position of women at best ambivalent. As
one of the founders put it, 'it did not seem possible to create such a fellowship with the working women' (Purvis, 1989: 168, quoting F.D.
Maurice). The response of one male student indicates that anxiety about
extending the definition of fellowship to embrace women was not peculiar to academics and clergy with historic privileges born of their experience of college life. It is significant that he invokes the phraseology of
'really useful knowledge', associated with the radical tradition, to voice
what he sees as the threat; women's presence is only acceptable to him if
their teaching can take place without disturbing the 'real usefulness' of
his own college education (Purvis, 1989: 168).

Where women did gain access to the colleges, it was often in terms of
a curriculum which was differentiated not only from that of the men, but
also within gender. Middle-class women followed daytime classes in 'la-
dylike' accomplishments, whilst working-class women followed evening
classes in the 'three Rs' and plain sewing. Ironically enough, too, the
Working Women's College, which was set up in part because of women's
suffrage campaigners' recognition that women were being ill-served, if
served at all by the college model, was under pressure to include men as
well as women. This seems to be something of a general pattern which
develops when women attempt to claim for themselves 'the same sort of
educational advantages ... that the men enjoyed' (Purvis, 1989: 171). Of
these colleges, the London version lasted longest. The 1908 Report, *Oxford and Working-Class Education*, records that by that date, the London
Working Men's College is 'the only institution (apart from Ruskin College and the new College at Fircroft, Bournville) which offers workpeo-

ple both a University education and comradeship in learning' (Harrop, 1987: 101).

The Women's Co-operative Guild

It is not until the Co-operative Societies are founded in the later part of the nineteenth century, that we have much sense that women and men are working together to generate their own movement, independently of industrialists on the one hand, or academics and clergy on the other. It is in the Co-operative Movement that we first get a commitment to political education as self-education, carrying with it the naming of women as well as men in relation to citizens' rights. The movement describes itself as including 'the training of men and women to take part in industrial and social reforms and civic life generally. It deals with the rights and duties of men and women in their capacities as co-operators, workers, and citizens' (Harrop, 1987: 99).

Even so, women clearly felt that they needed to create their own groups and movement, which they did so in the form of the Women's Guilds. The Women's Co-operative Guild was formed in 1883 by Alice Acland, who had criticised the Co-operative men's movement for being gender-divisive in encouraging men to agitate for political and social reforms, whilst advocating that women focus primarily on being consumers of Co-operative goods. 'What are men always urged to do when there is a meeting held at any place to encourage or start co-operative institutions? – come! help! vote! criticize! act! What are women urged to do? – come and *buy*! ... Are we not as important as the men? Are we not more than half the nation?' (Liddington and Norris, 1978: 40).

The Guild was committed to a highly politicised model of education, in which 'the true education of women' was an integral part of the movement as a whole (Webb, 1927: 52). Margaret Llewelyn Davies, who was Secretary of the Women's Co-operative Guild from 1889 to 1921, was explicit about the ideological role that education should fulfil.

> *The training given by the Guild starts from the point of view that Guildswomen have common interests as members of a Movement, and that the education needed is in the ideas and facts which will make their movement most effective; while the success in arousing enthusiasm and energy is due to combining appropriate action with education (Webb, 1927: 11).*

Guildswomen soon ensured that meetings broke with the traditional subjects related to domestic economy, to include not only co-operative and labour matters, but also discussions which formed the basis of a wide range of public campaigns. In the 1890s alone, they were at the forefront of agitation for women's suffrage, free education, old-age pensions, sickness benefit, and other rights, not to mention socialism. As one commentator put it, 'cutting-out parties and sewing classes' were replaced with 'the understanding that many of the reforms desired must be secured through *public action*' (Webb, 1927: 123 [original emphasis]).

Working with women in the trades unions, Guildswomen also undertook extensive research and documentation for use in political argument and legislative debate – used, for instance, in discussion of the Factory Acts and 'the minimum wage'. Even to the most sceptical of contemporaries, this must have been evidence of 'a triumph for the progressive power of democratic organisation and a vindication of women's capacity for politics' (Webb, 1927: 120). Margaret Llewelyn Davies solicited, collected and published a number of first-hand accounts of working women's lives, many of which pay tribute to the educative aspect of the Guild (Llewelyn Davies, 1931). Again, the debate about what is an appropriate education for a woman involved in and committed to the Guild is registered in explicitly ideological and political terms. Mrs Layton's account points up the contrast between the type of education she has experienced at Mothers' Meetings, and that which she participates in when she joins the Guild.

> *I had attended Mothers' Meetings, where ladies came and lectured on the domestic affairs in the workers' homes that it was impossible for them to understand. I have boiled over many times at some of the things I have been obliged to listen to, without the chance of asking a question. In the Guild we always had the chance of discussing a subject. The Guild was more to my mind than the Mothers' Meeting, so I gave up the Mothers' Meeting and attended the Guild (Webb, 1927: 40).*

She also comments that, coming to the Guild, she was not used 'to working-women managing their meetings'. Another Guildswoman writes:

> *I used for a short time to attend a Mothers' Meeting, and did so more from a point of duty than anything, but after joining the Guild I did not feel to have patience to listen to the simple childish tales that were read at the former, and did not like to feel we had no voice in its control. There is such a different feeling in speaking of trials and troubles to Guilders (where they are real) than to speak to the ladies of the Mothers' Meeting. You know that they have a fellow-feeling being all on an equality, but there is the feeling in speaking to the ladies that after consulting this one, that one and somebody else, a little charity might be given ... This sort of thing to honest working people hurts their feelings of independence, but when co-operators help them it is done in a different way (Webb, 1927: 40).*

The desire for self-determination, 'control', 'voice' and discussion where the issues are 'real', is in clear opposition to the threat to independence imposed by the reductive and condescending model of education offered by the middleclass. For many Guildswomen, the only liberating model of education they have experienced has been through the Guild. Mrs Wrigley comments, 'I can't say that I have read many books as I have had no time. What I have read has been Guild and Co-operative literature and newspapers, for I have learnt a great deal through newspapers' (Webb, 1927: 66). In Mrs Scott's account, the relationship between education and politics is equally explicit, though of a more visionary and romantic character. She has read widely in George Eliot, Charles Kingsley, George Egerton, H.G. Wells and pacifist literature, as well as 'the old favourites', Dickens, Tennyson and many others. She comments: 'When we think of the great and noble women who have made the path, like the story in Olive Schreiner's *Dreams*, by giving their lives and thoughts to making it easy for those who follow, we cannot feel too much or speak too highly of those who founded our Movement ... which has meant so much to the working-woman, brought new visions and opened the doors and windows' (Webb, 1927: 99–101).

History has not only tended to overlook Guildswomen's search for 'really useful knowledge' and their extensive contributions to political radicalism in the late nineteenth century, it has also, where it has looked, tended to camouflage working-class women's educational aspirations by disparaging as bourgeois a passion for learning, particularly where this is expressed in literary terms such as those which characterise Mrs Scott's account. There has also been a tendency to overplay the antagonisms between 'ladies' and working women. As we see from the Guildswomen's accounts, there was clearly opposition to those ladies of the Mothers' Meetings who could offer only childish tales and charity, but equally there was much solidarity and mutual support between those women of all classes who were campaigning for the suffrage. As the Guild's informal curriculum 'broadened out from domestic and co-operative matters to ... political economy and rational dress', so it began to provide 'one of the most important sources of support' for the Women's Suffrage Movement, which was itself, I shall argue, importantly generative in relation to the University Extension Movement (Liddington and Norris, 1978: 40 and 136).

Even without that connection with university extension, the issue of education was often in the foreground of Guild and Suffrage public campaigns. For instance, when the 1902 Education Bill proposed to abolish school boards and replace them with education committees from which women would be excluded, there was massive protest from Guildswomen. The commitment to education as part of the political struggle was also protracted beyond the effective life of the Women's Co-operative Guild and into the twentieth century. In 1918, the National Union of Women's Suffrage Societies converted itself into the National Union of Societies for Equal Citizenship, which by 1929 had become the Townswomen's Guilds. After the 1919 Sex (Disqualification) Removal Act, which was intended to remove remaining barriers to women entering the professions, and after the extension of the suffrage to women under the age of 30 in the 1920s, the movement's commitment to education became even more explicit.[1]

Once the rights and activities of working-class women have been recognised, it is appropriate to put the history of the Co-operative Women's Guilds into the context of the radical tradition of adult education. However, that recognition has been a long time arriving, and some histories persist in rendering working-class women's participation in the radical

tradition invisible, or marginal, or hopelessly compromised by their relations to middle-class women. The Co-operative Women's Guilds, however, were primarily about working-class women's struggle for their own
educational, social and political agenda and self-determination.

The University Extension Movement – The Traditional Story

What is more problematic is the argument which I want to make next,
which is that women's relationship to other forms of adult education in
the period was also radical or potentially so. However conventionally
mainstream the University Extension Movement was in its male form,
for instance, the relationship of women to it historically is often more politically ambiguous. This raises further questions, to which I shall return,
about what we mean when we talk about the 'independent' tradition of
adult education, and also indeed, what we mean by 'radical' in relation
to adult education movements.

The traditional story of the rise of the University Extension Movement is a story of men. It begins in 1850, when a Royal Commission was
set up to investigate the universities of Oxford and Cambridge, which
had become 'increasingly isolated from the needs of the time and, to a
considerable extent, corrupt and oligarchical' (Jepson, 1973:13). In that
year, the MP for North Lancashire proposed an inquiry 'to assist in the
adaptation of those important institutions [Oxford and Cambridge Universities, and Trinity College, Dublin] to the requirements of modern
times' (Hansard, 1850). One of the figures he quoted related to King's
College – it had an income of £20,000 a year, but only 13 students. In-
censed by the whole issue having been brought before Parliament (and
by an MP from the North), the Member for Oxford University went on to
accuse his not-so-honourable friend of quoting from scurrilous pamphlets which had suggested that 'the interests of religious and useful
learning have not advanced to an extent commensurate with the great resources and high position of those bodies'. The Oxford MP's indignant
speech upholds the rights of Oxbridge to remain independent of accountability to Parliament (particularly to the likes of the MP for North Lancashire), and perhaps even to the Crown.

Nevertheless, the leader of the House, Lord John Russell, apparently
to the surprise of most members, decided that there could be no objection
in principle to setting up a Royal Commission to make an inquiry. Of interest here is that one of the reasons he gives is that the subject is very important to the people of Great Britain.[2] He goes on to suggest, in what
reads as a tone of beguiling calm, that Oxbridge should play its part in a
national education system, and should encourage and foster greater ac-
cessibility to educational resources. Indeed, he appears momentarily to
uphold that commitment to 'useful learning' which we are led to believe
had originated in the scurrilous pamphlet.

In that same year, William Sewell pressed for the extension of university education and a broadening of the Oxbridge curriculum, and also

began to see the deliberations of government in a somewhat satirical light, for, as that 1850 debate stretches over the months, the focus on educational discussion gives way to one about the unassailability of Oxbridge independence. Many of the MPs are, of course, Oxbridge men themselves, and many of their speeches abound with images of 'veneration', of these 'eminent' institutions, for which they harbour 'respectful' and even 'reverential' feelings. The exception is an MP who is an Oxford man, but professes cynicism. Throughout the eighteenth century, he argues, both universities remained in 'a torpid and languid state', and 'the whole system was a perversion of the intentions of the original founders ... to enable poor clerks to educate themselves'. But even Lord Russell had suggested that any inquiry should be conducted in 'a friendly spirit'. After all, these are 'venerable' establishments, well known for their 'literary distinction'.

There is more to be said about the nature of Oxbridge corruption at this time, and about how far Oxbridge being 'isolated from the needs of the time' is a phenomenon which has persisted beyond the nineteenth century as a problem for adult education. And, of course, the 1850 debate had not raised the issues as they related to women at all. It was not until 1922 that Oxbridge was to be discussed in Parliament in ways that would include any analysis of the needs of women students and staff.[3] Even as recently as 1982, we can read that 'Oxford and Cambridge play a determining role in the formation of elites in Britain ... they perpetuate an unjust and divisive class system ... with a disproportionate influence on the rest of higher education' (Labour Party, 1982: 49).

The University Extension Movement – The Less Traditional Story

The debates about working-class men's involvement in adult education have often rehearsed openly the tension between dependence on existing educational resources and institutions on the one hand, and self-generated, politicised conceptions of education on the other. Even the 1908 Oxford Report, quite radical in its perception that the absence of the working-class from the universities meant not only that working-class people were being 'wronged', but also that the universities had 'sterilized' themselves, played out its fears around such stereotypes as the one that working-class people who entered Oxford might be 'carried off their feet by the social life ... and forget their own people'. The debate about whether the working class should be 'given' access to dominant culture rather than the political means to generate and develop a distinct curriculum persists into our own time, highlighting the political reality that elite groups remain in a position of patronage.[4]

In relation to working-class women, these tensions are exacerbated by a history which has placed women in a position of social, economic and educational dependence on men, which has rendered political struggle for women problematic in any clearly 'independent' form. What we have seen in relation to the Adult School Movement, the Mechanics' Institutes, the Working Men's Colleges, and even the Guilds, are some of the difficulties for women in attempting to educate themselves either alongside or independently of men. And what we frequently see in the history of the Women's Suffrage Movement, even again in the history of the Guilds, is the seemingly necessary intervention of middle-class women in order to secure any kind of 'independent' activity for working-class women, precisely because of working-class women's greater economic and ideological dependence on men (so notions of independence must always be qualified by the question of independence from whom).

As well as 'independence', the question of 'radicalism' has been a fraught one vis-à-vis women. The Women's Suffrage Movement, in itself, has often been dismissed as a middle-class movement, in relation to which the term 'radical' is inappropriate. And mention of the history of the University Extension Movement sets up flashing lights, signalling that this is the liberal tradition, outside the jurisdiction of questions of radicalism. The usual story of university extension *does* focus on liberal men, showing the movement emerging from within Oxbridge, after those debates in 1850, to meet the challenge of the criticisms that had been made of the two universities. As a sole explanation, however, this does not account for that delay of 17 years, between 1850 and 1867, after which the movement got under way.

My argument is that the pressure on Oxbridge came from political developments and independent groups outside of Oxbridge, at least as much from the consciences of the educationally over-privileged at Oxford and Cambridge or from government intervention. By 1871, four years after James Stuart was appointed to his fellowship at Trinity College, the Cambridge University Extension programme was being seen as a potential educational provider to what would have previously seemed the most unlikely groups of people to be corresponding with Oxbridge colleges. In that year, at least four known bodies approached Cambridge about the possibilities of help with their educational provision – the Crewe Mechanics' Institute, the Rochdale Equitable Pioneers' Society, the North of England Council for Promoting the Higher Education of Women and the Mayor of Leeds. Indeed, it is possible to argue that at least some of these groups, far from wanting to eschew their own independence in determining education, were deliberately seeking to redistribute and increase educational resources only available until that time to a small elite. The women included in these independent groups were often also involved in the Women's Suffrage Movement, making demands for educational resources as part of their commitment to the political struggle on behalf of women, and we therefore also need to raise the question of whether their activity represents a form of radicalism which often passes unrecognised.

The case for a less traditional, more radical story of university extension is perhaps made easier by the fact that, historically, women's relationship to the University Extension Movement is vastly and therefore patently different from that of men's. The men were the providers. The women were not. We could say, somewhat perversely, that women were independent in this late Victorian history in one clear sense – that they were independent of access to the key institutional providers of post-school education for most of the Victorian period – Oxbridge, London and Dublin. Women were not alone in thinking that an approach to these institutions, particularly once the signal of these liberal men involved in university extension had been given, did not come from a position of hopeless political compromise, uselessly sullied by what Oxbridge represented in terms of dominant culture and elitist education. In other words, the Rochdale Pioneers too believed that their position of exclusion gave them every right to believe that it was high time to attempt to grasp some 'privileged' resources. (There are many instances, though, of liberal Oxbridge men believing and continuing to believe that the dominance of women in their extension classes was a distraction from the real purpose.)

Even women's struggles vis-à-vis Oxbridge itself tell an illuminating story, as 'the women's degree campaigns at Oxford and Cambridge can be seen as microcosms of the national struggle for female enfranchisement' (McWilliams-Tullberg, 1977: 118). It is not within the scope of this account to review those battles, but it is important to register that 'the story of the admission of women to degrees at Cambridge is a telling illustration of masculine ambivalence toward women's struggle for emancipation' (McWilliams-Tullberg, 1977: 117). In other words, whilst some Cambridge men were attempting to open up aspects of university education to women, a persuasive body of others was actively resisting women's attempts to define education on their own terms.

Prominent figures such as Emily Davies and Josephine Butler clearly felt under pressure to drop certain political commitments in relation to the liberation of women, in the act of prioritising the struggle for educational reforms. Emily Davies, who played such a forceful part in the history of women's entry to Cambridge, felt she had to resign from the Women's Suffrage Committee when she took up that cause. The association of Cambridge with the Women's Suffrage Movement is often given as part of the reason why it took so long for the university to facilitate access to degrees for women. There is ambivalent commentary on this, ranging from the rather depressing but familiar idea that women were somehow to blame for being too outspoken, to the more convincing explanation that it was men's resistance, not to education for women *per se*, but to women's organisation of the campaign, which was the problem. Certainly, in Oxford, male dons objected explicitly to women's attempt to control their own education, voicing the lingering prejudices about the possible ill-effects of study on women's minds and bodies (Brittain, 1960: 69). In Cambridge, 'anti-feminist sentiments' persisted (Brittain, 1960: 70). When women agitated for degrees, they were scorned and outvoted. When men did so on their behalf, the battle was won.

We see these tensions reflected in debates between women within Oxbridge. The running argument between Emily Davies and Anne Clough about whether women should follow the same curriculum as men or a different one, is well documented (McWilliams-Tullberg, 1977; Bryant, 1979). And we could here move the argument back outwards again, to suggest that that controversy had bearing on adult education as a whole in the period, revealing 'the dilemmas involved when trying to equalize educational opportunities for women and men without changing the power structure of "male" colleges', and indeed of male education as a whole (Purvis, 1989: 174). It is not until the 1920s and 1930s that the attack on those structures is articulated, but it is forceful when it comes (most notably in Woolf, 1938). However, that is another story.

The important story here is one that goes beyond women's battles, symbolic or literal, to gain access to Oxbridge or even higher education as a whole. Groups like the Leeds Ladies' Educational Association were campaigning, primarily, on behalf of women in the under-privileged 'regions', particularly the big Northern cities, whose access to educational resources were minimal. Crucially, too, their campaigns were often linked to debates, not only about their own education, but to the national education system as a whole, where the expansion of public education was increasingly to demand women as teachers, particularly those of young children, and where the inadequacies of girls' experience of secondary schooling had come to light (Miller, 1992).

Against this background, we could re-write some of the story of the University Extension Movement to show additional characters to those of William Sewell, James Stuart, Edward Carpenter, and other enlightened male reformers in Oxbridge. The Leeds Ladies' Educational Association, created in the same year as James Stuart's Trinity appointment, appears to have been instrumental both in establishing the North of England Council for Promoting the Higher Education of Women, and in campaigning for educational resources for the women of Leeds. It figured its own, lesser-known protagonists, including Lucy Wilson, Miss Heaton and Theodosia Marshall.

Star-Gazing versus Suffrage

Perhaps more importantly, though, we can examine the illuminating discrepancies between the intentions of these bodies in approaching Cambridge University and the actuality of the type of provision that the University's incipient extension programme could offer. In his autobiography, Edward Carpenter, one of the early extension lecturers transmitted to the provinces by James Stuart, is persuasively genial about his meeting with the Leeds Ladies, and his lecture programme in Leeds (Carrpenter, 1916). What the Leeds Ladies had wanted from Cambridge was resources to support a teacher training programme, a course in pedagogic theory and method, a means of developing women's teaching skills in themselves and as part of the way of addressing the inadequacies of the teaching of girls. They had stipulated this requirement in their letter to James Stuart. What the latter has to offer, though, is Edward Carpenter, along with his particular subject specialism, astronomy. Edward Carpenter knows nothing whatever, he readily admits, of teacher training. Having secured a contact, having managed to tap into what one Oxbridge man described as the golden stream of Cambridge resources, the Leeds Ladies keep Carpenter on for astronomy, the final irony being that, however fine the Rosse telescope, and however committed Edward Carpenter is to a somewhat progressive pedagogic method, wishing to support theory with practice, seeking to encourage his students to use telescopes as well as be informed of their findings, it is difficult to see the stars through the smoke of industrial Leeds.

Edward Carpenter has urbane and charming things to say, too, about the Leeds Ladies themselves. He sees himself as a gentleman mediator between women of competing passions, drawing him into 'deadly plots'. There is perhaps another perspective that could be adopted here to tell a different story, including a whole story about Lucy Wilson herself, who is described in the following terms: 'Like many "advanced" women she was very *doctrinaire*; and having swallowed a principle (like a poker) would remain absolutely unbending and unyielding, and, in the second place, she hated men. On one occasion she got up a "Women's Rights" Meeting in Leeds' (Carpenter, 1916: 82). Edward Carpenter is not slow to recognise the predicament of many Victorian women: 'Certainly the disparity of the sexes and the absolute non-recognition of sexual needs – non-recognition either in life or in thought – weighed terribly hard upon the women of that period' (Carpenter, 1916: 95). But his attitudes to the Leeds Ladies reflects some of the tensions in male attitudes at the time; that telling witticism about the poker and the slightly jocular, disparaging use of 'got up' to describe Lucy Wilson's organisation of a meeting about women's rights.

The important argument, though, is about what this glimpse at the supposed character of Lucy Wilson can show about women's involvement in the struggle for adult education, for women's self-determination through education, and for access to educational resources on their own terms. The history of the Guilds, the Extension Movement and of late nineteenth-century Oxbridge, is a story of highly-charged connections with the Women's Suffrage Campaign. It is, to that extent at the very least, about a coherent strategy on behalf of women's self-determination in relation to education for political and social change, a strategy under considerable and sometimes coercive pressure to fragment.

As 1867 has carried real and symbolic force in this account, so we can see some significant events in 1919. The Sex Disqualification (Removal) Act removed existing legal barriers to women entering the professions, a sub-group of Lloyd George's Reconstruction Committee recommended that universities should generate extension programmes as 'a normal and necessary part of their functions', and, symbolically enough, though perhaps somewhat surprising in its belated aspect, Ruskin College agreed to accept women students (Kelly, 1970: 267–81). As I mention earlier, the National Union of Women's Suffrage Societies, with the vote for at least some women newly won, was metamorphosing from a political campaign to one for 'citizenship education'. In many ways, though, 1919 was only the beginning of the struggle. The issues raised, implicitly and explicitly, by Guildswomen and by women's intervention in the University Extension Movement, were too dramatic in their social and political configurations to be solved by legislation alone, and without a continuation of the struggle for independent movement, which women abandoned at their peril.

A handful of Oxbridge dons may have seen the issue as being about channelling the golden stream of Oxbridge resources to what they no doubt saw as particularly worthy representatives of the deserving masses, but the stark fact remains that they could not supply what the Leeds Ladies' Educational Association required from them. Women's attempts to gain the tools by which to further their own education for social and political change were met by Oxbridge men with either resistance, incomprehension or plain lack of skill. Whether we see groups like the Leeds Ladies attempting to seize or appropriate resources, or simply asking, perhaps misguidedly, for help, we remain confronted with that inadequate response; that, however inappropriately, Oxbridge dons could at best supply their own expertise – the authority of the specialist subject discipline, whatever it might presume to be. They were approached for teacher training, badly needed by women striving to educate themselves, their sisters, their daughters, to enter the public sphere on better terms, in the struggle for political rights and liberation. That the best the men had to offer to that struggle was a particularly opaque form of star-gazing, is a story which continues.

Notes

1. For another occasion, though, there is a whole twentieth-century history to be written about the extent to which the Townswomen's Guilds lost, or at least the accounts of it have lost, a sense of how to maintain a politicised commitment to education. Readers can see the tension in Mary Stott, *Organization Woman. The story of the National Union of Townswomen's Guilds*, Heinemann, 1978.
2. The connection John Russell makes between Oxbridge and a national education system is one which, as we see later in this account, is also made by women campaigners for the suffrage and educational change.
3. Royal Commission on the Universities of Oxford and Cambridge, Hansard, volume 153, 1922, recommended that there was a need to discuss the position of women students and teachers.
4. The construction of this polarity, with dominant culture on the one hand and self-determination on the other, has dogged the discussion of working-class children and schooling. Here, the issue of class has often been confused with the issue of compulsory state schooling, as if to argue that if working-class children have rights of access to dominant culture, then we (? professional educators? whoever?) have the right to force it upon them. Surely, we have to dispense with the polarity, if working-class people are to generate education on their own terms?

References

Brittain, Vera (1960) *The Women at Oxford*, Harrap.

Bryant, Margaret (1979) *The Unexpected Revolution: A study of the education of women and girls in the nineteenth century*, University of London Institute of Education.

Carpenter, Edward (1916) *My Days and Dreams*, Allen & Unwin.

Hansard (1850) *Inquiry into Oxford, Cambridge and Dublin Universities*, Hansard, volume CX, April, 1850, p 691.

Harrop, Sylvia (ed.) (1987) *Oxford and Working-Class Education* [1908], Department of Adult Education, University of Nottingham.

Jepson, N.A. (1973) *The Beginnings of English University Adult Education: Policy and problems*, Michael Joseph.

Kelly, Thomas (1970) *A History of Adult Education in Great Britain*, 2nd edn, Liverpool University Press.

Labour Party (1982) *Education after 18: Expansion with change*, A Labour Party Discussion Document.

Liddington, Jill and Norris, Jill (1978) *One Hand Tied Behind Us. The rise of the women's suffrage movement*, Virago.

Llewelyn Davies, Margaret (ed.) (1931) *Co-operative Working Women, Life As We Have Known It*, Hogarth Press [reprinted by Virago, 1977].

McWilliams-Tullberg, Rita (1977) 'Women and degrees at Cambridge University, 1862–1897', in *A Widening Sphere: Changing roles of Victorian women*, Indiana University Press.

Miller, Jane (1992) *More Has Meant Women: The feminisation of schooling*, University of London Institute of Education/Tufnell Press, London.

Purvis, June (1989) *Hard Lessons: The lives and education of working-class women in nineteenth-century England*, Polity Press.

Webb, Catherine (1927) *The Woman with the Basket: The story of the Women's Co-operative Guild, 1883–1927*, Co-operative Press, Manchester.

Williams, Raymond (1980) 'A hundred years of culture and anarchy', in *Problems in Materialism and Culture*, Verso.

Woolf, Virginia (1938) *Three Guineas*, Hogarth Press [reprinted by Penguin Books, 1979].

Four

Cultural Struggle or Identity Politics: Can There Still be a 'Popular' Education?

Tom Steele

This chapter argues that the seed of a cultural struggle in Britain after World War Two found fertile soil among the ranks of the new generation of adult educators. Many of them saw it as key element in the creation of a New Left which would be liberated from both Stalinised Marxism and Fabian philistinism and believed that the members of the adult education movement could be prime actors in the new politics. What came to be installed in universities as a new academic discipline of Cultural Studies owes its development to the work of this generation of adult educators, who saw it as programme of popular education. The chapter concludes, however, that the popular project has run into the sand of academic specialisation, leaving a political vacuum at its heart. It asks if a 'popular' educational movement is still possible, given the particularisation implicit in the rise of the identity politics of the past decade and whether a renewed sense of the vocation of adult education can connect the academy with the new social movements.

Opening up the cultural struggle was the reason many radicals went into adult education in the post-war period. Many felt that a decisive shift from the politics of the point of production to the politics of representation, ideology and hegemony was strategically necessary if a new political common sense was to be constructed. If art and literature were to serve the people, the argument ran, a critical popular consciousness had to be developed. Meanings had to be wrested from their bourgeois contexts, democratic controls had to be created over communications, popular forms had to be nurtured and hegemonic culture to be revealed for what it was – a means of organising the consent of the subordinate classes. In the immediate post-war period the attempt to reconstruct a common culture within an alternative inscription of 'Britishness' which emphasised popular resistance and democratic production was one, if not the dominant, motivation of liberal studies adult education tutors. From this ethos of experimentation and interdisciplinary work emerged what in the late 1960s came to be called Cultural Studies.

In the intervening 20 years an extraordinary body of cultural analysis has been produced, little of which came directly from adult education. The centre of gravity shifted away from adult education to departments of English Studies and Left political journals. Richard Hoggart coined the term 'cultural studies' at Birmingham University, where he founded the Birmingham Centre for Contemporary Cultural Studies. Stuart Hall was recruited from the editorship of *New Left Review* to promote sociological and theoretical developments, which developed Hoggart's 'rituals of resistance' orientation into pioneering studies of popular and sub-cultures. Hoggart subsequently moved to UNESCO in Paris, while Hall developed the Centre and then himself moved into the Open University, then a dramatically new form of adult higher education. In the 1970s and 1980s much of the cutting edge was developed in the polytechnics, whose less hidebound approach to academic compartmentalisation allowed for much freer interdisciplinary work in a more radical atmosphere.

But, ironically, the study of popular culture increasingly departed from the project of popular education envisaged by its founders. Instead it developed into a new mainstream academic discipline with a quite fierce body of methodologies and increasingly arcane internal debates over 'Theory'. Curiously, while theoretical debates became almost stratospheric, a cultural populism emerged which enthusiastically embraced manifestations of popular culture which would earlier have been declared anathema. Fears that Cultural Studies may have lost its way were being voiced in the late 1980s and early 90s by many of those who pioneered it. Stuart Hall, Angela McRobbie and especially Raymond Williams became anxious about the specialisation, narrowness and lack of engagement with social life of an area of studies which owed its lifeblood to it (Hall, 1990; McRobbie, 1991; Williams, 1989). I want to outline here some of the beginnings of cultural studies in Britain and, skipping lightly over the innovative and unrepeatable years of their full-flowering, suggest how their crisis might enable us to rethink the project of popular education.

In one of his last papers Raymond Williams was particularly exercised by accounts of the history of British cultural studies which embedded it in texts such as *Culture and Society, The Uses of Literacy,* and *The Making of the English Working Class.* Valuable as some of these accounts have been they omitted what for Williams is the key difference of Cultural Studies as an intellectual activity, which was the study of the relationship between *project* and *formation* (Williams, 1989). To account for the development of cultural studies simply through an examination of the books produced by a number of its luminaries, which of course included Williams himself, he argued, failed to locate the source of the texts in actual social process. He noted how his own book *Communications* had been commissioned as the result of a National Union of Teachers Conference on Popular Culture and Personal Responsibility in the early 1950s. He had been able to write it quickly precisely because it was based on his own notes used in adult education classes over the previous 15 years. It had belonged therefore to a very specific extra-mural practice.

By the 1980s the by now conventional text-based story was that cultural studies had emerged from a form of left-Leavisism as a convergence of intellectual disciplines. It seemed to have forgotten the baggy and loose collection of practices worked out in negotiations with adult students. Elsewhere John McIlroy, Ioan Davies and I have attempted to articulate alternative genealogies (McIlroy and Westwood, 1993; Davies, 1993; Steele 1987, 1994). Williams suggests obliquely that this parapraxis may no doubt have been because of the shift of cultural studies into mainstream academic departments and the marginalisation of its own innovators, because this is indeed what had happened, in a previous era, with the development of English studies in the late nineteenth century. At that time, Williams argues, following the lead given by some provincial universities, Cambridge University's first modern English courses were little more than the formalised syllabuses of Oxford Extension lecturers. Here too adult education had responded to the needs of neglected and repressed areas of society and negotiated an area of studies without the benefit of academic departments. From the demands of especially women and men from the lower-middle and working classes for the study of literature came the development of English studies.

> But then look what happened: having got into the university, English studies had within twenty years converted itself into a fairly normal academic course, marginalizing those members of itself who were sustaining the original project. Because by this time what it was doing within the institution was largely reproducing itself, which all institutions tend to do: it was reproducing the instructors and the examiners who were reproducing people like themselves (Williams, 1989: 153).

Subsequently, in the 1930s, F.R. Leavis was also marginalised by Cambridge English studies and was forced outside the university in search of the more general original project. However, says Williams, because of his insistence on seeking a critical *minority*, he only partially succeeded in renewing the spirit of the original project.

Williams implies that this same process of incorporation and forgetting has been repeated in the Cultural Studies project – an example perhaps of 'eternal recurrence'. While the subsequent project of cultural studies had been to some extent analysed, its formation, which included those doing the analysis, had not and as a consequence the original project had been lost. The point was, as far as Williams was concerned, that although the Richards, Leavis, *Scrutiny* project of close textual criticism and attention to popular forms had indeed been the point of departure of many of those who worked in adult education in the 1930s and 40s, they had *not* chosen simply to remain with it. For the Leavis project had been a consciously elitist one of reproducing that cultural minority which itself would work in minority institutions such as grammar schools and universities. Many, like Williams, had then chosen to work in adult education precisely as an alternative to Leavis's project of minority culture in what Williams calls 'an attempt at a mass democratic education' (Williams, 1989: 154). This was truly vocational work, a continuation of the tradition that Williams himself analysed in *Culture and Society* of the work of the 'public intellectual', such as Ruskin, Morris and Tawney.

They had been engaged in a vocation of popular education which, after World War Two, Williams, Hoggart, Thompson and hundreds of others now joined.

To a greater or lesser extent, the new generation broke with elements of this tradition, which despite its engagement with social life and popular culture was emphatically high cultural. Many of the new post-Leavisites were prepared to give popular culture a hearing and not, like Leavis, to treat it as a menace. They studied popular culture as much to detect its signs of strength and resistance as to expose its corrupting elements. This was not altogether unproblematic. As Williams notes, for all his attention to the strengths of working-class culture Richard Hoggart sees nothing to celebrate in 'commercial' popular culture. Similarly, Edward Thompson's celebration of working-class culture is of its high 'moral realism' rather than its leisured and recreational aspects. Williams's own advocacy of a 'common' culture, too, is little interested in aspects of working-class culture other than those of the collective institutions it created and was frankly dismissive of its literary content. But then socialism too, as Göran Therborn says, has to be considered as a high cultural product (Therborn 1992: 19).

Outside the university, the nineteenth century project of a democratic popular education had continued into the twentieth century through a variety of educational forms including the WEA, the Plebs League, the Labour Colleges, the settlements and host of religious and political groupings. In the early 1920s a government report on *The Teaching of English in England*, otherwise know after its chairman, Sir Henry Newbolt, as the Newbolt Report, radically raised the profile of English Studies. It wanted to make English Studies the pivot of a renewed project of humanity, 'Englishness' and citizenship, and it assigned adult education the role of knight errantry: 'University Extension lectures and classes were almost the first attempt to fill a gap in our higher education and they did a service in promoting the study of our national literature which should never be forgotten' (*The Teaching of English*, 1921: 267).

But this interpellation of the 'nation' had been greeted sceptically by the more politicised educational groups who saw the promotion of English Studies as little more than an intensification of bourgeois ideology. Indeed there was fine line, and many like George Thompson, the district secretary of the North Yorkshire WEA district, held literature and the arts generally at a distance and, instead, concentrated on developing social studies, political philosophy and history. The arts were for him 'women's subjects' (Steele, 1987). During the 1930s the teaching of literature and the arts in adult education inspired furious debate between the 'traditionalists' like Thompson and the 'modernisers' like W.E. Williams, the editor of the *Highway* and subsequently first general secretary of the Arts Council, who wanted less politics and more culture. In the tension between these arguments a many-sided, cross-disciplinary approach developed. Its signs were obvious initially in the teaching of economics and international relations as Williams points out, but also in music, the visual arts, town planning, film studies and in approaches to sociology which, inspired by Karl Mannheim, stressed its holistic social studies aspect. In this atmosphere some tutors seized on Leavis's *Culture and Environment* with alacrity, as evidenced by Storm Jameson's review of it in *The Highway*. Many Leavisites and even the founder of *Scrutiny*, L.C. Knights, commitedly taught classes for the WEA using Leavis's work in analysing advertisements and newspapers. The arguments were continuing when the war broke out and almost settled the matter, for with the absence of so many men in the forces, in the WEA 'women's subjects' became dominant, even in Yorkshire.

But it was the end of the war, the election of the Labour government with a programme of reconstruction and ultimately after 1947 the intensification of the Cold War that forced the issue. It was in this highly politicised context that the need for 'the *cultural* struggle' seems to have been first articulated – although the formation of popular front politics in the late 1930s was certainly a forerunner. As Raymond Williams makes plain, the teaching of cultural subjects in adult education was intimately bound up with the emergence of a New Left politics. Cultural Studies may even have been an anti-Cold War strategy of teaching politics by other means. Williams and many others of the post-war generation of tutors in adult education saw adult education as the natural constituency for a new politics which was both critical of a Fabian-inspired Labourism but not content with the dogmas of Soviet-constructed Marxism.

One major, and mostly unwitting, source for the emergence of this new politics was the Communist Party itself. For long, as Andy Croft makes clear, one of its most vibrant aspects was its cultural activity (Croft, forthcoming). The party was indeed a source of patronage and education for young writers during the 1930s, for whom it could offer publication in literary journals and introduction to left publishing houses like Lawrence and Wishart. At the same time its active historians' group under Dona Torr and Christopher Hill was setting a new agenda for British social history. It was also a profoundly cosmopolitan group into which refugees from Nazism could introduce non-Soviet European Marxism like that of the Lukacs group and the first translations of Antonio Gramsci. The party acted both as a club for mutual support and education and as a mentor group. Dissident intellectuals and writers were attracted to it in part because it provided various arenas for serious cultural debate not commanded by Bloomsbury or the aesthetic elite so hated by Leavis, but also offered a partisanship with working people to which Leavis was unsympathetic. Initially, the party affected a relatively *laissez-faire* approach to its cultural groups and allowed them considerable rein, but later cultural disputes grew bitter. During the 1930s the Central Committee was relatively uninterested in culture or intellectuals, which it regarded as largely ornamental, so long as there was no attempt to interfere with party policy. With the onset of the Cold War, however, it took a renewed interest in culture and in 1947 established a National Cultural Committee to 'co-ordinate' the work of the 10 specialist cultural groups, including the Writers' Group, under the chairmanship of Emile Burns. As Andy Croft again notes, the Cold War was shaping up on the literary high ground as exemplified by Crossman's *The God that Failed*.

Although the party now wanted greater control of its intellectuals, as the orthodox Marxist models of economic determination became less defensible, it had also become more sensitised to the power of ideologies and representations in forming class consciousness. The Twenty Second Party Congress called for a cultural struggle alongside the political struggle, inspired in part by the writing of Mao Tse Tung. 'The British Road to Socialism', the party's new political programme, had to be supported by some more developed understanding of what Britishness actually was. Under the auspices of *Arena*, another of the party's cultural journals, a series of important conferences on aspects of culture were called, to which many of the party's intellectuals contributed, including the young Edward Thompson. British culture was represented as under threat from the corrupting forces of American commercialism – a perception with which Leavis himself would not have disagreed.

These conferences were important for establishing the ground on which the cultural struggle should be fought. In one important sense it was to construct alternative senses of national identity to those associated with imperialism and oppression. This was the Britain of patriotism without jingoism, of 'dear old England', and the *British* Road to Socialism. In the key conference, which was given over to an examination of Britain's cultural heritage, George Thomson, the classicist and one of the party's most respected intellectuals, argued that it was wrong to think of 'culture' as bourgeois only, since in Britain this so-called bourgeois culture was also the heritage of socialism. It was, as the proletarian philosopher Tommy Jackson had argued, in some senses a revolutionary culture and English literary realism, as Gorky had said, was pioneering (Thomson, 1952: 13). Thomson saw the cultural struggle as having two main thrusts. The first was to encourage 'worker-writers', so that writing was seen not simply as a class-bound activity, which would have the effect of uniting intellectuals with the workers and, most importantly, being *tempered* by them. The second was to interpret this cultural heritage in the light of Marxism-Leninism. He gave the fairly uncontroversial example of Gay's *Beggar's Opera* but also he quoted Caudwell's dictum that the struggle should 'drag the past into the present and force the realisation of the future'.

But, since Caudwell's unorthodox approach was regarded by the leadership as heretical if not schismatic, this was more controversial. A fierce debate over Caudwell raged in the pages of another party journal, *The Modern Quarterly*, during 1950–51 in which most of the party's big guns were lined up to sink him. But his staunch defence by George Thomson, in particular, inspired Edward Thompson into re-thinking the terms of the cultural struggle. In particular he was persuaded by Caudwell's refusal of the reduction of consciousness to passive reflection and mechanical materialism in orthodox Marxist theory (Thompson, 1977: 244). This broke with the base/superstructure analogy and allowed a much more flexible interpretation of cultural determinants to be developed, a kind of 'relative autonomy' of the spheres and theory of ideology which paralleled Gramsci and pre-dated Althusser.

In his own contribution to the conference, called 'The American Threat to British Culture', Thompson's position was that 'we' had to win people for life and not wait for a new kind of person to appear until after Socialism has been won: 'We must change people *now* for that is the essence of all our cultural work' (Thompson, 1952: 30). Morris's 'moral realism' was clearly in his sights at this time but he converted the *political* project of the party into an *educational* aim. In the pages of the journal of the tutors in adult education, the *Tutors' Bulletin*, Thompson had already urged the WEA to adopt a cultural policy, in effect to argue for the same energy to be given to campaigning for the extension of *cultural* facilities to the people as they had for educational facilities (Thompson, 1950: 11). He urged that the WEA should change its attitude on cultural matters from high-minded and distanced study to actual engagement with living cultural activities. The Shakespeare class, for example, should not turn up its nose at the local amateur dramatic production but get stuck in and dirty its hands with what he saw as *popular* culture.

Thompson's intervention evinced the serious change in direction younger intellectuals were taking, away from 'pure' politics classes towards the cultural. In what must have appeared a serious deviation, he argued that workers' education had to take into account the 'cultivation of the individual' which was necessary for the education of the 'citizen'. The point of cultural education was to ensure more active participation of 'the movement's' students in the social activity represented by the art under study.

> There is no case for attacking a class in music or literature because it does not produce a crop of Labour councillors, but there may might well be a case against a class in which no member became actively engaged in local dramatic or musical societies, gave services on a library committee, promoted the activities of the Arts Council, entered controversies in the local press upon municipal theatre or music, or kept abreast in an alert and communicative way with contemporary developments in the arts (Thompson, 1950: 8).

Here then was a definite shift of focus, the opening up of a cultural struggle alongside the political struggle. Essentially it was about a struggle over resources for fostering the emergence of regional and local cultures rather than the mainstream Arts Council approach of imposing a 'national' culture upon a supine provinciality, but: 'the scales today are weighted so heavily by commercial forces interested in the degeneration of standards, by forces of mass suggestion, by the environment and routine of industrial life against any healthy cultural activity that every sign of health must be carefully fostered' (Thompson, 1950: 9). This marks both the continuity with the language of Leavisism in anathematising commercial trivialisation but also the rupture with it in its emphasis on local self-determination and democratic vitality. In effect this was the original version of the cultural struggle. It was not intended as the formation of a new academic discipline but an active politics conducted on the margins of the academy – rough, moralistic, unrefined but responsive to popular movements and for the tutors concerned, vocational. What happened to it?

In a sense what happened to it is also the story of the social and cultural transformation which later came to be called postmodernism. While the cultural struggle re-energised the left and made possible the construction of a New Left politics, it ironically accelerated the demise of the class formations upon which the old politics was built. The politics of the point of production gave way to those of reproduction. As Fred Inglis remarked in his study of British socialism, Edward Thompson's *Making of the English Working Class* provides 'a new past to live from; it changes the social memory so that differently understanding how the present came about, the agent thinks forward to a new set of possibilities' (Inglis, 1984: 199). That text which Thompson called his West Riding book, the outcome of his engagement with his adult education classes and political work in Yorkshire, effectively created a new history from which a younger generation of militants could break with the established political institutions and imagine alternative futures.

However, if the past could be so fickle as to transform itself under the pen of a gifted historian, what other wonders lay in store? In a sense the trap had been sprung. The 'culturalism' which Thompson had encouraged was tempered in his case and that of the 'old' New Left by the materialist discipline of submission to historical evidence and empiricism. But the young Turks it encouraged had fewer reservations. Under the newly discovered sign of 'Theory' the 'new' New Left of the early 1960s unlocked the gates for a more fully fledged idealism. As he famously recorded after the palace coup which ditched himself and the other adult educationists who had been involved in the formation of *New Left Review*, Thompson wrote:

> we found we had appointed a veritable Dr Beeching of the socialist
> intelligentsia ... Old Left steam engines were swept off the tracks: way
> side halts ('Commitment', 'What Next for CND?', 'Women in Love')
> were boarded up; and the lines were electrified for the speedy traffic
> from the marxistentialist Left bank ... Finding ourselves redundant we
> submitted to dissolution (Thompson, 1978: 35).

There was more to it than this, of course, not the least of which was the re-emergence of the feminist movement in part inspired by Althusser's use of the concept of ideology, which although it debunked Thompson's use of the term 'experience', nevertheless worked in ways he had encouraged, to recreate new subjects of knowledge. But the metaphor holds. Arguably through the rediscovery of the continent and the subsequent programme of translations by *New Left Review* of European Marxism and post-Marxism, the *trans-manche* theory express dumped an extremely ripe mound of manure on the seedlings of British cultural studies. After a long period of isolation it seemed that once again British intellectual life had been opened to the European ideas centres.

Other significant developments followed, led by the formation of the Birmingham Centre for Contemporary Cultural Studies by Richard Hoggart, which, under Stuart Hall, used a synthesis of Althusserian and Gramscian theory to launch extraordinarily fruitful analyses of popular culture. Raymond Williams left the Oxford Delegacy to confront Cambridge English head on, Thompson went to Warwick 'Business' University and John Rex went to Durham, so that by the mid-sixties adult education had lost many of its most energetic iconoclasts to internal university departments (though in Thompson's case not for long). The same expansion of the higher education system that allowed them in, also included many children from lower-middle-class and working-class families, who previously might have looked to the WEA in mature life. Harold Wilson's Open University, later in the decade, for the first time offered systematic structured degree programmes to adults which made the old extra-mural provision look distinctly jaded.

The effect of this epochal change in adult education was that the yoking together of the political struggle and the cultural struggle urged in the immediate post-war period was only fitfully possible. Cultural Studies moved into the academic mainstream and despite its interest in popular culture became increasingly mandarin in its discourses. It was discussed in ways that even the intelligent lay members of adult education classes found hard to grasp, often leaving the field free for the return of a more conservative liberal studies 'art appreciation' mode to operate instead. Thus the mainstreaming of cultural studies left the initial project of a popular critical education in a New Left politics stranded in a time-warp, which eternally celebrated the moment of the *Making* but seemed not to be able to move on – the exceptions being, perhaps, in the development of local studies and creative writing.

By the late 1980s mainstream Cultural Studies appeared to be in crisis. Jim McGuigan has suggested why this was the case in a recent typically incisive polemic (McGuigan, 1992). Despite the undoubted successes of its mapping of the terrain of popular culture, for McGuigan one of the more damaging features of the mainstream approach to cultural studies has been the dogmatic insistence on separating contemporary cultural studies from the political economy of culture. Because mainstream cultural studies regards attempts to map cultural phenomena onto accounts of capitalist development as economic reductionism, (ironically, exactly the demon Thompson was trying to exorcise), it has lost the possibility of political engagement with social life. Instead, it comments upon social life from a distanced and increasingly ironic standpoint. In some of its more recent manifestations, mainstream cultural studies adopts an aristocratic nihilism which utterly refuses to distinguish between social life and its simulations – with ludicrous results, such as in Baudrillard's analysis of the Gulf War.

Another effect has been a kind of uncritical populism which in a simple inversion of Leavisite concerns has celebrated virtually every manifestation of popular culture as politically progressive. While there is an understandable wish to understand and value everyday meanings in the manner of Williams's insistence that 'culture is ordinary', McGuigan insists that such a stance 'produces inadequate explanation of the material life situations and power relations that shape the mediated experiences of ordinary people' (McGuigan, 1992: 244). It's also not much help, he believes, for falsely modest intellectuals merely to record how well people are doing in the face of overwhelming odds.

However, there has been a growing *sociological* commentary on postmodernism which, stemming from the work of Habermas, Bourdieu, Giddens and others has been sceptical of the claims of theory. With the work of Frederic Jameson and David Harvey, McGuigan suggests that it has been possible to return to sophisticated analyses of the political economy of cultural studies without falling into the trap of crude reductionism. Through this work it is possible to see postmodernism as a cultural/ideological configuration of late capitalism, which has produced both an authoritarian populism and its antagonists in new social movements. Another effect is that intellectuals themselves have become part of a new postmodern 'class' of taste-creators, hooked on fashion (McGuigan: 218).

Is there are renewed role for adult education here before the millennium? If there is, then it could be found in what Thompson, following William Morris, has called 'the education of desire'. Although utopias are currently out of fashion as collective projects, Ruth Levitas has argued that utopian thinking is still possible as a critical tool (McGuigan: 247). Without being necessarily prescriptive, it can stimulate a desire for a different way of being from which standpoint it can interrogate the present. One of adult education's traditional functions has been to address that mode of thinking and help people work with it – whether it was constructing the Labourist commonwealth in the earlier part of the century, or enabling working-class women to work through their needs in the New Opportunities and Access movements of the 1980s. The marginal, non-mainstream position of adult education has historically enabled intellectuals to open up dialogues with working people and in its more radical forms has enabled social movements to temper intellectuals to their needs. This marginal space has to be re-occupied and used once more by educators to leave for a moment the hermetically sealed rituals of the academy, where the internal debates reach scholastic dimensions of dizziness, to join the dialogues of intelligent lay persons who seek out 'liberal adult education'.

The benefits are obvious to both sides. The mere process of trying to communicate the more extreme flights of cultural theory to adult students often renders its absurdity patent. Adult education also engages with the *experience* of mature students, which is so different from that of those fresh out of school. It should also be a space in which communities and new social movements can secure the services of academics for their own projects. The undoubted excellence of many studies of popular culture could be of even greater value if it were put at the disposal of groups and agencies such as ethnic minorities, gay rights, women's movement, disabled and aged groups. On a broader scale, cultural studies can enable the project of 'citizenship' to be reconsidered with much more flexible narratives of subjectivity, identity and cultural needs and with less aesthetic impoverishment than the old Labourist cause. If Cultural Studies then began reflexively, to understand *itself* as a formation, as Williams asked, then it might renew its project of a popular education.

References

Croft, A. (forthcoming) 'Authors take sides: writers in the Communist Party, 1920–1956', in Morgan, K. Fishman, N. and Andrews, G. (eds) *Opening the Books: New perspectives in the history of British Communism*, Pluto.

Davies, I. (1993) 'Cultural theory in Britain: narrative and episteme', *Theory, Culture and Society*, vol. 10, no. 3, pp 115–154.

Hall, S. (1990) 'The emergence of Cultural Studies and the crisis of the humanities', *October*, 53, pp 11–23.

Inglis, F. (1984) *Radical Earnestness*, Oxford University Press.

McGuigan, J. (1992) *Cultural Populism*, Routledge.

McIlroy, J. and Westwood, S. (eds) (1993) *Border Country: Raymond Williams in adult education*, NIACE.

McRobbie, A. (1991) 'New times in cultural studies', *New Formations*, 13, Spring.

Steele, T. (1987) 'Class consciousness to Cultural Studies: the WEA in West Yorkshire, 1914–1950', *Studies in the Education of Adults*, vol. 19, no. 2, pp 109–126.

Steele, T. (1994) 'Representing the people', *Studies in the Education of Adults*, vol. 26, no. 2, pp 180–200.

The Teaching of English in England, Being the Report of the Departmental Committee appointed by the President of the Board of Education to Enquire into the Position of English in the Educational System of England (1921), HMSO.

Therborn, G. (1992) 'The life and times of Socialism', *New Left Review*, 194, July/August.

Thomson, G. (1952) *Britain's Cultural Heritage*, Arena Publications.

Thompson, E.P. (1950) 'A cultural policy', *Tutors' Bulletin*, Summer, pp 7–12.

Thompson, E.P. (1952) 'William Morris and the moral issues today', in *The American Threat to British Culture*, Arena Publications.

Thompson, E.P. (1977) 'Caudwell', in Saville, J. and Miliband, R. (eds) *Socialist Register*, Merlin Press, pp 228–276.

Thompson, E.P. (1978) 'The peculiarities of the English', in *The Poverty of Theory*, Merlin Press.

Williams, R. (1989) 'The future of cultural studies', in *The Politics of Modernism*, Verso.

Five

Radical Adult Education: The Reader and the Self

Hilda Kean

The recent FEFC circular on measuring achievement gives a clear resumé of the current context for state priorities for adult education. The emphasis is on the construction of performance indicators to assess students' commitment to their learning 'programmes', not defined through enthusiasm or enjoyment but as 'reflected in continuation rates'. Achievements of individual students are to be categorised by the extent to which they contribute to the 'national targets for education and training'. These are evocatively described as 'the number of adults achieving lifetime target 3' (FEFC, 1994: 4,5,6).

This emphasis on regulation, quantification and definition – and denial of pleasure – threatens to erode further the radical practices in adult education which still exist, albeit in isolated forms (Edwards and Usher, 1994). As Duke and Taylor have noted in their critique of the CAT system 'the voice of institutional rationalisation deafened out those protests of students who feared, or were not interested in, having their study assessed for credit' (Duke and Taylor, 1994: 94).

The focus on rationalisation and standardisation continues to undermine the distinctive experiential nature of adult education, as Tom Steele has analysed in his chapter in this volume. In looking at alternatives to the current ethos I believe we need to explore anew what we mean by such experience and see how this can be used oppositionally. In particular we should explore and validate the intellectual, political and emotional experiences of adult students and the way in which this has already been incorporated into the students' personal growth (Wainwright, 1994: 76–78). I believe that more importance needs to be attached to the reading experiences of students prior to their entry into adult education, since this performs a variety of functions. Reading not only helps define the individual's relationships to society but provides a mechanism for understanding and developing the self and constructing an identity. As one Ruskin student recently described his past and present reading habits:

> *Reading on a functional level just for (academic) work has led me into a much more voracious appetite for reading, not just for my subject, but also outside of it, which possibly I wouldn't have had before. Certainly I've always had an appetite for it but never the same as it is now ... I see*

the importance of it more now, not just in terms of my work but important in terms of my own personality, my own personal development, and my personal enjoyment as well (interview with 'Michael Blades' by Hilda Kean, June 1994; part of research in progress on reading and identity).

This emphasis on self is not, I would argue, a nineties phenomenon but one which is integral historically to the ways in which reading, especially fiction, has been seen by socialists and feminists and which has been acknowledged within radical adult education. Tom Steele has indicated the controversial nature of teaching literature as cultivation of the individual in post-World War Two radical adult education circles. But this emphasis on fiction and its importance to socialist militants was one current much earlier this century. The texts read and the importance attached to reading by early twentieth-century British autodidacts were reflected in the concerns of the Plebs League, Central Labour College and later Left Book Club publications. Reading was seen both as a further development of self and as a means of assisting in engagement in political activity (Torr, quoted Ree, 1984: 8). Reading meant an entry into another group, a 'community of readers'. Reading, too, was a symbol of status, of respectability, which often set the reader apart from their peers. The part it played in the creation of identity was graphically epitomised by the visual, particularly photographic, images of reading which became an important part of socialist iconography (Flint, 1993: 321–330; Dennett, 1991: 72–83).

My intention in exploring the tradition of working-class reading is to look at the way in which socialists and feminists saw education as a mechanism for the development of the self in a community of like-minded individuals. Reading was not simply instrumentalist in its purpose but was a symbol of status and self-enlightment which gave the reader a stronger sense of self and of identity. For reading, especially the reading of fiction and poetry[1] was – and is – an activity undertaken on an individual basis but providing support, pleasure and inspiration to individual socialists and feminists within the community of those who define themselves politically and radically:

I suppose I've always found escape – and I don't mean escapism – through reading. I've found myself able to retreat from what I don't perceive to be particularly happy around me .. or the situation I've found myself in ... I can shut myself off ... If I'm very frank I suppose it's a fulfilment of an unfulfilled side of me (interview with 'Alison Taylor', Ruskin College, June 1994).

Radical Adult Education and Fiction

Historically the syllabuses and classes of radical adult education can be viewed within the context of the experiences which socialist readers were bringing to the courses. The emphasis on the study of literature and poetry was not as an aberration from economic texts but a continuation of the mental growth and increased awareness that socialists had already experienced.The importance of fiction as well to the socialist reader was established within the Marxist education offered by the Plebs League and Central Labour College. The reading of fiction was not portrayed as simply an individual leisure activity but one which merited collective study (Batsleer *et al.*, 1985: 41–69).

The Plebs journal regularly contained articles on literature. In the first three years of publication, for example, the journal contained articles on Burns, Ibsen, and Chaucer; regularly published poetry and serialised Eugene Sue's fictional tale of Druid Gaul, translated by Daniel de Leon, *The Gold Sickle*.[2] In addition the Plebs League welcomed no less prestiguous a tutor than Dennis Hird, the sacked principal of Ruskin College, as an evening class lecturer on literature and biography at the Labour College.[3] While not deprecating the value of scientific, that is Marxist economic, study, the Plebs League saw literature as a valuable distinct genre, which provided a 'step towards sanity' in the midst of capitalist chaos: 'The great literary artists have done not a little to laugh away the hideous carnage of economic conditions, which rages in social, ethical and religious life, where men burn bodies and poison ideas with the solemn gravity of reformed saints.'[4]

Literature was seen by the Plebs as a positive phenomenon. Ibsen, 'a modernist of modernists', was praised for his 'fundamental optimism'; Robert Burns for 'his poetic genius' and 'deep sincerity of feelings'.[5] Poetry, as a genre, was welcomed for making the reader feel 'at home in this world'.[6] That is, the study of literature was not simply situated within a particular socio-economic context but was seen as a way of helping the individual reader exist in difficult situations through providing comfort and reassurance.

The Labour College movement, too, saw the value of reading literature. It could bring to life events from the collective experience of working people. Again, the study of literature was seen as possessing a quality distinct from that of economics in that it gave validation to the self: 'the inner life of man, the thoughts which became, later, interpreted by deeds' (NCLC, 1919). Correspondence and residential courses on literature were run by the Central Labour College. Although the overall object of its syllabus sought to equip 'the organised workers with the knowledge adequate for the accomplishment of their industrial and political tasks' (NCLC, 1922), nevertheless literature courses were broad ranging (NCLC, 1919). Writers studied included Scott and Dickens; Defoe, Fielding, and Goldsmith and from the modern period Wells, Bennett, Conrad, Kipling, Tchekhof (*sic*), Ibsen, Shaw and Galsworthy. For those students studying by correspondence the courses were arranged accordingly to literary schools and social periods including the romantic revival and women writers of the Victorian era, namely 'Mrs Browning', Christina Rossetti, Charlotte Brontë and Mrs Gaskell. Such women, the syllabus claimed, 'finally asserted – and proved – their claim to rank as co-workers with men ... The sordid domesticity to which women had been condemned from early times was at last giving placed to a realistion of women's capabilities' (NCLC, 1919).

Evidently such an approach was popular. During the period in the late 1920s when the Communist Party's membership declined from over 7,000 to under 3,000 (Branson, 1985: 48), the National Council of Labour Colleges was attracting 31,635 students to its courses at its peak in 1926–7, dropping to just less than 20,000 by 1930 (NCLC, 1933: 6). By 1933 it had sold, amongst many other publications, 10,000 copies of its *What To Read: A guide for worker students* (NCLC, 1933: 32).

The Left Book Club of the 1930s, perhaps the most popular twentieth century left adult educators in the nature and extent of its publications and readers' groups, was established initially as 'a movement of education' (Gollancz, 1936c: 167) to build 'a really effective united front of all men and women of good will' (Gollancz, 1936a: 2). In the selection of books chosen for members full credit was intended to be given to books describing 'instances of individual humanity or public enlightmenment' (Gollancz, 1936b: 132). This included poetry, which was described as 'sharpening men's sense of the world about them, its evils and its movement into deeper brotherhood' (Lindsay, 1938: 1007).

The Reading Experiences Students Brought to Radical Adult Education

Much of our written knowledge of the way in which socialists experienced reading and radical study comes from autobiographies, diaries or accounts penned by the readers themselves which tend to take reading as a process as an uncontroversial given. However, an illuminating account by Mark Starr, former south Wales miner and subsequent Central Labour College lecturer – a classic autodidact – explores the practice of reading. For him books were part of 'the other', a step on a journey of adventure, a journey which needed to be related to the self to take on meaning (Starr, 1918: 162). Irrespective of the particular content, books are given meaning through the relationship between the reader and the text: 'For our books are a part of us. They are inseparable from our mental adventures. We roam no longer with discoverers of lands but of new ideas. The reading of a particular book often stands out in our lives like a milestone or a directing post, marking the distance or the taking of a new turn in the long road of mental evolution – a road in which it is impossible to return or forget' (Starr, 1918: 162–3).

Starr incorporates books as entities within his own mental domain.It is not the books *per se* which make them valuable but the relationship created between the reader and the book. As he elaborates, readers 'should never be mere book collectors. They should make earnest endeavour to truly mentally possess their books'. The way books become assimilated is also described. Through discussing with friends, through summary of the reader's opinions, through underlinings: 'Thus you will make the book your own; make it easy for reference, and trace the change of your own opinion in the future' (Starr, 1918: 163). Nor is reading an ascetic pastime but a source of 'solace and pleasure' (Starr, 1918: 163). Starr's article provides insight into the way the personal needs of the individual were both recognised and acknowledged and gives a useful context to a study of autobiographical accounts of reading from autodidacts. The importance autodidacts attached to the needs of the individual socialist is also indicated by the emphasis placed on the study of psychology (Kohn, 1986: 46–48; Ree, 1984: 40–41; Strachey, 1937: 209; Rose, 1931: 392).

Autodidacts' autobiographies include accounts of books read throughout their lives to indicate the ways in which they have developed politically and personally. Here reading as a personal act epitomises interiority. The essence of the genre – the depiction of the self – leads to incorporation of reading within the narrative as both an individual activity and one leading to personal, individual change (Flint, 1993: 330). The concept of the active reader as described by Mark Starr and the part the reader played in the creation of like-minded communities is widespread in the reading accounts within the radical tradition. The experience of reading helped to induct the socialist reader into a new way of life. As one later explained to Robert Blatchford, the author of *Merrie England*, 'You taught us to read; you taught us to see; you gave us crowds of delightful friends in books; we can never repay the debt' (*Labour Book Service Bulletin*, 1940: 8).

Even prior to organised study the reading of books could mark out radicals from their peers: it was a personally rewarding experience but one which could distance readers from their workmates. As Sheffield shop steward J.T. Murphy explained in his autobiography, *New Horizons*, the reading of books was an activity which characterised his workmates as socialists. 'The men who read books were usually Socialists and the men who read nothing but the Early Bird (the local racing paper) were Tories' (Murphy, 1941: 32). Yet the potential isolation of this activity was counteracted by a move into a different socialist, reading, environment. Reading provided an entree into a community of like-minded socialist readers and thinkers. As Tom Bell explained it: 'With (Socialist Labour) Party work, with three or four companions, and my books, my life at this time was rounded. In our spare time we visited each other to talk and discourse on all manner of subjects and the books we were reading' (Bell, 1941; Griggs, 1983: 227ff).

Nor was it simply that autodidacts read, but that they read widely. Margaret McCarthy, herself a 'voracious reader', nevertheless saw the Young Communist League readers she encountered in the 1920s as different types of reader: 'They studied deeply and were very glib in everything from economics to political theory to the latest novels. They even quoted poetry – the first young workers I had ever met who did so ... The conversations with the young communists left me always in a state of awestruck admiration' (McCarthy, 1953: 78). The effect of these encounters was to make her read more widely and expand both her intellect and, she explained, her whole existance: 'Life had become suddenly full, suddenly rich; the world and my own place and purpose in it had suddenly expanded' (McCarthy, 1953: 101). The act of studying, whether in political organisations or adult education classes, brought together previously individual experiences within a collective framework.

Reading as a Mechanism for 'Conversion'

Even when socialist autobiographical writing does not follow the strict norm of Puritan autobiographical writing, reading is often used as a metaphor of the reader's 'conversion', from the darkness of ignorance to the light of socialist knowledge (Samuel, 1993: 209; Vincent, 1977: 3*ff*). In some cases the transition to socialism was conversion in the sense of converting away from religion. J.T. Murphy for example had been a primitive Methodist. For him reading provided an answer for his doubts about religion: 'after I had read (Spencer's) *First Principles* I felt that he had completed the process of stripping me of my long-held religious conceptions' (Murphy, 1941: 28; see also Englander, 1977 for an account of transition from Congregationalist preacher to SDF Marxist). For Winifred Griffiths the effect of reading a short article on the economic organisation of work caused 'a profound change in my thinking about life ... the impact on me of this article was somthing akin to a religious conversion. It changed my thinking about life so completely that I no longer felt the urge of personal ambition' (Burnett, 1974: 116). As I have indicated elsewhere, the concept of 'conversion' is also found in suffrage feminist autobiographers' attempts to explain their politicisation. However, for the suffrage feminists this was invariably through their own public action or witnessing the harsh treatment women suffragists suffered, not through reading (Kean, 1994; see also Vincent, 1977 for a discussion of Puritan autobiographies).

But for those involved in adult education reading prior to this collective experience was very important.

Sometimes 'conversion' occured during an enforced break from work through injury: reading passed the time.[7] Even the absence of reading is seen as significant when this was then followed by entry into the community of readers. As Tom Mann recalled: 'I knew nothing of Shelley; Ruskin only very superficially; and nothing whatever of Malthus or Marx. Still, I was groping my way, if not directly, towards the light. At least I was becoming conscious of mental darkness'. However, this activist soon became a 'reader' after he was introduced to Shakespeare 'and from that time I was never lonely so long as a volume of Shakespeare was available' (Coates, 1967). Interestingly, despite his extensive political reading it was again fiction which provided the significant step into 'another world'.

The Growth and Experience of Self

It is not just the languge of the transition from the darkness of ignorance to the light of knowledge which has religious connotations. In describing the change brought about by books socialist readers use the language both of spiritual and physical consumption. On the one hand readers are 'filling themselves up', books are 'devoured': their content provides nourishment to enable the intellect to grow. But the exercise of reading is also an act of spiritual consumption; books acting metaphorically as the bread of heaven. Religious discourse is used even by Marxists and atheists to describe a significant change to the self. As Tom Bell put it 'love of literature ... I regard as being as important for a man's soul as meat and drink are for his body' (Bell, 1941: 15–16).[8] For SLP member James Stewart (Kean, 1990: 68), reading was an essential factor in the development of the human mind: books were the food the mind needed in order for it to grow (*Young Rebel*, 1917: 44).

This process of growth and re-creation of self is well documented in the fascinating discussions of Ruth Slate and Eva Slawson, two working-class socialist women from East London attempting to educate themselves in the first decades of this century (Thompson, 1987). The language used shares phrases with that of Mark Starr and Tom Bell. One book provides 'so much food for thought' (Thompson, 1987: 48), another opens 'new worlds to me' (Thompson, 1987: 89), while overall reading has helped construct Ruth Slate as 'a traveller on a voyage of discovery' (Thompson, 1987: 96). The process of reading is seen as an induction into another world of different ideas and life experiences through which the reader herself is incorporated into another life and fellowship. It was this discussion of literature which led them into further systematic study.

Reading and Pleasure

A particular insight into socialist working-class women's reading for pleasure can be found in the material collated by the Women's Co-operative Guild. What is noticeable is the differentiation made in the accounts between reading for duty (to the socialist cause) and reading for (personal) pleasure. The language of consumption of food, we noted earlier, is present. But here it is consumption as a form of indulgence: a guilty and surreptious activity taking the reader away from her household tasks – or political reading: 'I steal a few moments'; 'When I get too old for public work (I hope) I will be able to indulge'; 'My reading ... is done in time stolen from my sleeping hours'; 'to read a book is one of the luxuries I am looking forward to with great longing' (Llewellyn Davies, 1931: 114–115, 120, 128–129).

This process of reading by stealth is seen too in accounts of women working-class readers engaged in paid work. Wheareas men described reading on the way to work on workers' trams or at lunchtime in the workshop these options were not open to women engaged in domestic service (Tillett, 1931: 94; Murphy, 1941: 32–34; Bell, 1941: 65). In this paid employment reading was perforce a surreptitious and forbidden activity, sometimes resulting in harsh consequences. Winifred Foley, for example, describes being hit by her employer for reading *Uncle Tom's Cabin* (Burnett, 1974: 231). Another servant describes snatching time to read while making the beds and thus never having the opportunity to read a book openly – or at leisure (Swindells, 1985: 134).

Julia Swindells sees this process of reading by women domestic servants as potentially subversive and clandestine. Reading, in early Victorian working women's autobiographies, is not seen as self-improving but rarely as 'anything other than dangerous' (Swindells, 1985: 134). However, similar methods of expression are seen in the later Women's Co-op-

erative Guild accounts of women not engaged in paid work. The guilt expressed by the correspondents in the Women's Co-operative Guild survey would seem here to relate not to the process of reading as such but to
the type of reading undertaken. The novels cited, for example, are not
predominantly those of the typical autodidact but are by popular contemporary 'pulp' writers such as Rafael Sabatini and Florence Barclay.[9]
Perhaps the attitudes of working women to reading might also be placed
within the context of the sometimes hostile views of their husbands towards this. In his autobiography, Jack Jones, a former south Wales miner,
describes his illiterate father castigating his mother for encouraging her
children to read: 'Women (have) got enough to do about the house without reading. Ay, if it's only fighting these bugs' (Jones, 1987: 35).

Continuity of Experience

In terms of experience, reading as a process is able to provide continuity.
Books read at certain times in the reader's life can help recall emotions
and experiences of that time as well as providing a stability in a changing
world. For Mrs Hood, a correspondent of the Women's Co-operative
Guild survey, reading preceded activity in the Guild. It was a source of
regret that reading historical novels, of which she was fond, was not possible because of the pressures of meetings – and housework. Reading
then became a surreptitious activity: 'I steal a few moments when dust-
ing' (Llewellyn Davies, 1931: 114). For other Women's Co-op Guilders
too, reading was a thing of the past. Indeed extensive reading is seen as a
feature common to youth: 'one can call up ideas and knowledge gained
when one was young and was reading a great deal' (Llewellyn Davies,
1931: 123).

Although reading was seen by past autodidacts as bringing change
to their lives the activity of reading itself provided a stability, a continuity between the past and the present. This is so of the content of the
books: the names of texts read as a new reader are often remembered as
significant in leading to other books and areas of discovery (Thompson,
1987: 89; Englander, 1977: 85). However, the process of becoming a
reader is seen as integral to the autodidact's changing and developing
self. It is not just the case that names of books are remembered as significant intellectual or political influences but that they are seen as part of
the reader's own personal past and through this have become incorporated into their life in the same way,say, as their childhood. However, the
references are not contemporary: reading is a past influence which had
helped make the person who they were.[10]

Conclusion

The forms of adult education we have referred to did acknowledge the
intellectual experiences of their students as readers; it was not just their
work or political experiences which were seen as relevant. Such experiences still exist and although the particular form of autodidactism has in-

deed changed from earlier this century we should be wary of dismissing it as merely of historical interest. The practice of entering as an engaged indiviudal into a radical communtiy of readers is not tied to a specific historical setting, although the particular books which fire the imagination may well be. Adult students who enter institutions such as Ruskin College have intellectual experiences in common with their comrades of earlier times. It is this continuity of experience which needs to be acknowledged and built upon. Certainly Raymond Williams's description of miners coming to WEA classes not just to study the coal industry but to engage in discussions on politics and literature still has its resonances today (McIlroy and Westwood, 1993: 311).

John McIlroy may be accurate when he states that 'Within adult education itself radical work with the working class constitutes small islands, scarcely a minor archipelago, far from a movement' (McIlroy and Westwood, 1993: 315). But to let such a perspective be the framework for current action would, I think, be misguided.

Contemporary adult students still know what it is to read and to feel part of a wider – historical – experience. In our attempts to step through the minefield of validation and performance indicators it is tempting to ignore the living experience of those students we teach: the present is all.

It is the knowledge and the identity as readers which surely we must both encourage and draw inspiration from in maintaining and reininvigorating radical traditions in the 1990s. As Alan Cook, a Ruskin student in 1994, put it:

> *Without reading the only way you can actually build up any wisdom, if you like, is (through) experience. So you might be 50 or 60 before you've built up any sort of wisdom from your own experience of life. If you read a book you can accumulate someone's whole lifetime of wisdom in a couple of days. Perhaps that's a bit simplistic but I think it's important to read ... and go back to things.*

Notes

1. The political, rather than the fiction, reading of such auodidacts has already been well covered in publications such as MacIntyre, 1986; Ree, 1984; Phillips and Putnam, 1980.
2. See *Plebs*, vol. 1, no. 4, May 1909, p 74; vol. 2, no. 2, March 1910, p 30; vol. 2, no. 3, April 1910, p 61; vol. 2, no. 4, May 1910, p 92; vol. 2, no. 6, July 1910, p 141; vol. 3, no. 1, Feb. 1911, p 19; vol. 3, no. 6, July 1911, p 125, etc.
3. 'Evening classes at the College', *Plebs*, vol. 4, no. 10, November 1912, p 227.
4. *ibid.*
5. Perkins, Frances 'Henrik Ibsen the iconoclast', *Plebs*, vol. 2, no. 1, Feb. 1910, p 6, continued in vol. 2, no. 2, March 1910, p 30; Ballantyne, Jas. 'Scotland's poet – Burns', *Plebs*, vol. 1, no. 4, May 1909, p 74.
6. 'What's the use of poetry?', *Plebs*, vol. 4, no. 6, July 1912, p 133.

7. Philip Snowden, future Labour Chancellor of the Exchequer, attributed his 'socialism' to the books he read whilst recovering from an accident, as did William Watson Bracher; see *Herald Book of Labour Members*, 1923, pp 172, 198.
8. See also Alfred Russell, secretary of the Socialist Sunday School Union in Glasgow: 'From early years I have had a taste for reading, and general enquiry into the why and wherefore of things', *Young Socialist*, August 1903.
9. Florence Barclay was a popular writer of historical romances such as *The Rosary*. Sabatini was a prolific writer of swash-buckling tales (see Richard Boston, 'Ripping yarns', Guardian, 12 February 1994, p 29).
10. Bracher, *Herald Book of Labour Members*, 1923, pp 34, 63, 134.

References

Batsleer, Janet *et al.* (1985) *Rewriting English: Cultural politics of gender and class*, Methuen.

Bell, Thomas (1941) *Pioneering Days*, Lawrence and Wishart.

Branson, Maureen (1985) *History of the Communist Party of Great Britain 1927–1941*, Lawrence and Wishart.

Burnett, John (ed.) (1974) *Useful Toil: Autobiographies of working people from the 1820s to the 1920s*, Allen Lane.

Coates, Ken (ed.) (1967) *Tom Mann's Memoirs*, MacGibbon and Kee [originally published 1923].

Dennett, Terry (1991) 'Popular photography and Labour albums', in Jo Spence and Patricia Holland (eds) *Family Snaps: The meaning of domestic photography*, Virago.

Duke, Chris and Taylor, Richard (1994) 'The HEFCE review and the funding of continuing education', *Studies in the Education of Adults*, vol. 26, no. 1.

Edwards, Richard and Usher, Robin (1994) 'Disciplining the subject: the power of competence', *Studies in the Education of Adults*, vol. 26, no. 1, pp 1–14.

Englander, David (ed.) (1977) *The Diary of Fred Knee*, Society for the Study of Labour History.

Flint, Kate (1993) *The Woman Reader 1837–1914*, Oxford University Press.

Further Education Funding Council (1994) *Measuring Achievement: Circular 94/12*.

Gollancz, Victor (1936a) 'Editorial', *Left Book News*, May.

Gollancz, Victor (1936b) 'Editorial', *Left Book News*, November.

Gollancz, Victor (1936c) 'Editorial', *Left Book News*, December.

Griggs, Clive (1983) *The TUC and the Struggle for Education 1868–1925*, Falmer Press.

Jones, Jack (1987) *Unfinished Journey*, Hamish Hamilton.

Kean, Hilda (1990) *Challenging the State? The socialist amd feminist educational experience*, Falmer Press.

Kean, Hilda (1994) 'Searching for the past in present defeat: the construction of historical and political identity in mid-war British feminism', *Women's History Review*, Spring.

Kohn, Grigorio (1986) 'Notes on the history of the psychoanalytic movement in Great Britain', in Kohn, Grigorio (ed.) *The British School of Psychoanalysis: The independent tradition*, Free Association Books.

Labour Book Service Bulletin (1940), no. 6, January.

Lindsay, Jack (1938) 'Poems of freedom, ed. John Mulgan', *Left Book News*, October.

Llewellyn Davies, Margaret (ed.) (1931) *Life As We Have Known It*, Hogarth Press [reprinted by Virago, 1977].

MacIntyre, Stuart (1986) *Proletarian Science: Marxism in Britain 1917–1933*, Lawrence and Wishart.

McCarthy, Margaret (1953) *Generation in Revolt*, William Heinemann.

McIlroy, John and Westwood, Sallie (eds) (1993) *Border Country: Raymond Williams in adult education*, NIACE.

Murphy, J.T. (1941) *New Horizons*, John Lane, the Bodley Head.

National Council of Labour Colleges (1919) *Subjects Taught in the Correspondence Department*.

National Council of Labour Colleges (1922) *Prospectus of the Labour College*.

National Council of Labour Colleges (1933) *Education for Emancipation*.

Phillips, Anne and Putnman, Tim (1980) 'Education for emancipation: the movement for independent working class education 1908–1928', *Capital and Class*, Spring.

Ree, Jonathan (1984) *Proletarian Philosophers: Problems in socialist culture in Britain 1900–1940*, Clarendon Press.

Rose, William (ed.) (1931) *Outline of Modern Knowledge*, Gollancz.

Samuel, Raphael (1993) 'The discovery of puritanism 1820–1914: a preliminary sketch', in Garnett, J. and Matthew, C. (eds) *Revival and Religion since 1700: Essays for John Walsh*, Hambledon Press.

Starr, Mark (1918) 'Books and the young socialist', *The Revolution*, vol. 1, April.

Strachey, John (1937) 'Introduction to R. Osborn's *Freud and Marx*', *Left News*, January.

Swindells, Julia (1985) *Victorian Writing and Working Women*, Polity Press.

Thompson, Tierl (ed.) (1987) *Dear Girl: The diaries and letters of two working women 1897–1917*, Women's Press.

Tillett, Ben (1931) *Memories and Reflections*, John Long.

Torr, Don *Tom Mann and His Times*, Lawrence and Wishart.

Vincent, David (ed.) (1977) *Testaments of Radicalism. Memoirs of working-class politicians 1790–1885*, Europa Publications.

Wainwright, Hilary (1994) *Arguments for a New Left*, Basil Blackwell.

Young Rebel (1917) 'Editorial', October.

Six

Piecing Together the Fragments: Thoughts on Adult Education in a Vanished Era

Martin Yarnit

Flicking through the pages of *Adult Education for a Change*, it is tempting to wallow in nostalgia for the radical era of post-war adult education, that period of 15 years from the late 1960s to the early 1980s, which was marked by some notable triumphs, but also some lost opportunities. After an assessment of the strengths and weaknesses of the radical era, I want to outline the key issues now confronting us and to make some proposals which build on past insights and achievements.

In what follows, I want to focus on the education of adults, not as a thing in isolation, but as a vital part of the whole national apparatus of education and training. The terms 'adult education' and 'adult learning' are here used interchangeably for the sake of simplicity, although I do recognise that adult learning implies both a broader field of activity, including informal and self-directed activity, and a more active role for the learner. I do not propose to spend much time in defining what I mean by radical adult education – that is best drawn out from what follows – except to say that it is about developing an accessible and democratically accountable system of lifelong education which would:

- enable the development of a critical analysis so as to improve our capacity to intervene singly and collectively for a more just and equal society
- provide the capacity and ideas for individual and collective social and economic development, including skills for work.

Part 1: An Overview of the Period

The late 60s and early 70s marked the emergence of radical forces which were to disturb the settled and consensual world of adult education in the universities, the WEA and LEAs. In retrospect, it is clear that the upsurge of the left, feminism, the shop stewards' movement and a more challenging spirit in working-class communities had largely passed their high point by 1976, when the Labour Government of James Callaghan rediscovered the political uses of unemployment after 40 years of disuse. But by then, some important discoveries had been made, among them the writers' workshop, second chance to learn, access courses, women's groups and community education. These are the developments recorded in *Adult Education for a Change*, the volume we published in 1980.

Second Chance: A Unifying Practice

Second Chance to Learn, the Liverpool project about which I wrote in *Adult Education for a Change*, set itself the task of overcoming the fragmentation of working-class politics and experience through a unifying educational practice (Yarnit, 1980). There were two key underlying themes to the project:

- the abstract definitions of the economic and the social had to be challenged and re-written through people's experience
- education is a resource to be claimed for the working class.

Let me, briefly, explore some of the developments in the relationship between education and society through these themes in the period from the late 60s through to Thatcher's early years.

Economics and Society

Our study of the causes of Merseyside's decline enabled us to confront the boundaries between work and the home, between paid employment, unemployment and domestic labour, and between the roles of men and women and the relations between trade unions and community organisations. When Second Chance moved from the University to become the responsibility of the WEA, which at that time also mounted the bulk of trade union education on Merseyside, the next step should have been obvious. But it was late in the day, in 1979, before we first brought together trade unionists and community organisers at the Northern College to discuss ways of regenerating the local economy in an initiative which was to lead directly to the creation of Merseyside Trade Union, Community and Unemployed Centre, still a significant force in local politics.

Local community and economic regeneration was first put on the agenda as a result of the work of the Home Office-funded Community Development Projects but with the winding up of the scheme in the early 70s, the issues were kept alive, not without some difficulty, by organisations such as Coventry Workshop and the trade union studies centres in Newcastle and Leeds. The economy slipped off the agenda of adult education. What remained was a fragmented interest in unemployment, in trade union studies and in vocational education. I know of no institution or initiative which considered the three together even though they spoke, potentially, to the interests of millions of workers, employed and unemployed. Vocational education, with all its potential for developing a broader view of the labour process and labour relations, was lost almost entirely to the trade unions with the abolition of the industrial training boards early in the 1980s, and trade union studies were forced into the straitjacket of industrial relations narrowly conceived; 'the triumph of technical training', as John McIlroy calls it.

Education

Second Chance began with a piece of collective autobiography. Each student wrote a brief account of their life, with a focus on their school history. From these accounts was drawn out a series of themes, e.g. the foreshortening of education for older students, caused by war and evacuation, the almost complete absence of qualifications in the group as a whole, the very different experiences of school of boys and girls. From the beginning of the course, the intention was to make the experience of learning and education conscious and critical. The study of schooling challenged the students' generalised sense of personal failure and posed instead the reasons for the failure of the education system to serve the needs of the working class. Tutorials built on this understanding to open up a sense of wider educational opportunities, with the result that one in six of Second Chance students have gone on to study for a degree and one in three to study in further education (Edwards, 1986). The challenge to the school system, however, was never directly realised, even though school-based adult education typified our earlier work in inner city Liverpool, including evening taster courses and summer schools (Ashcroft and Jackson, 1974).

Elsewhere in Liverpool, there was a more successful history of linking access to education for adults to tackling the causes of school failure. The Parent Support Programme, which grew out of the Educational Priority Area (EPA) experiment of the late 60s–early 70s, consciously set out to involve adults, especially parents, in schooling, by establishing adult centres in dozens of inner city schools. Evaluations of the project suggest that parents involved in their own education are more likely to support their children's who are more likely, therefore, to succeed at school. What is less certain is the extent to which parental involvement of this kind makes a fundamental impact on the underlying causes of school failure.

Educationally, the 60s and 70s was the era of a breakthrough against the elitist trend which has generally held sway in Britain, before and since. The comprehensive reform of the secondary school system, coupled with ROSLA (raising of the school leaving age to 16), set alongside the opening up of higher education, including the creation of the OU, which gathered pace under Harold Wilson's 1964–70 Labour government, significantly improved the educational life chances of working-class students, as we now know (Glennerster and Low, 1990). This was a large-scale reform which subsequent Conservative governments felt impelled to subvert even though Britain lags far behind its European neighbours: only 30% of 18-year-olds obtain qualifications equivalent to two A-levels, compared with 68% in France (post-ZEP: educational priority zone scheme) and 80% in Japan.

That this pattern of developments in the compulsory and post-school education system was largely lost on those of us working in adult education in the 1970s ought not to be a surprise. It reflects structural and historical differences between the functions of the two sectors, as Sallie Westwood showed in her contribution to *Adult Education for a Change* (Westwood, 1980: 37–8). Schooling has, for very good social and economic reasons, been a matter of abiding concern to the state since at least

1870 (Ashworth, 1960). As the period of compulsory schooling moved from elementary to secondary and then to 15-plus, so the state moved to fund the education, after a fashion, of the entire cohort whilst striving to ensure that schooling was free from any ideological taint of the left. Adult education has always belonged to another world: voluntarist, sometimes critical, and always marginal in its educational impact, its legal position and its funding. Adult educationalists on the left have been freer, than their counterparts in schools, to absorb themselves in radical projects, notwithstanding the sometimes fierce censorship to which we have been subject at crucial turning-points (Fieldhouse, 1991). School teachers, finding their way blocked to a radical expression in the classroom, have perhaps found a means of expression by turning outwards to trade unionism (Barber, 1993).

Some Left Their Mark

Some of the developments I have referred to made their mark and left a permanent trace. Women's groups still meet, so do writers' workshops. Literacy and basic education is an indelible feature of the landscape. Black parents, especially in cities like London, Bradford, Leeds and Manchester, having rid the educational language of the odious term 'educationally sub-normal', are engaged in the battle against the exclusion and criminalisation of their children and for a curriculum which values their achievements. As for community education, for many people it *is* adult education. On MEd courses throughout the land, the recommended reading list would be unthinkable without Tom Lovett, Jane Thompson and Keith Jackson, as well as the longer-established Freire and Williams. Even if the Long March now seems without end, and the radical impulse is weary, there remain some beacons of hope. Ruskin has survived, and the Northern College has helped bring about a partial resuscitation of working-class adult education. The Russell categories have become essential to the work of the WEA, admittedly co-existing uneasily with the traditional strands of the organisation, whilst two or three university departments maintain a lonely but courageous stand, carrying on work with unemployed people, in the inner city and with trade unionists.

It is often from such initiatives that the access movement has arisen which has helped to make mature students the majority in further and higher education. There have been notable advances in access, although far from total success. A MORI poll commissioned by NIACE in May 1994 showed that overall 52% had not studied since leaving school, rising to 70% for those of 65 years and over (NIACE, 1994). Access, some would maintain, has become too successful for its own good, losing any political distinction it once had and becoming effectively a branch of the mainstream. But this is the rub. If we mourn the passing of the radical impulse, how can we find a proper place for the permanent reforms? And access is not alone in this respect. The very pedagogy of adult education, Tawney modified by Freire and the anti-authoritarian spirit of the 60s, that amalgam of student-centred discovery learning and the class secretary tradition of the early WEA has survived, blinking, into the raw, action-planned world of TEC-funded vocationalism, because it works. But student-centred learning has a fatal weakness at its core, as Edwards has shown (Edwards, 1991). It demotes the collective in favour of a largely vapid notion of the education consumer.

A Movement of Disconnected Minorities

If these are some of the successes, what of the weaknesses? Adult education, as an organised phenomenon, has always been a minority interest, regardless of politics. Before the 60s, it was, apart from industrial day release and some WEA classes, a socially exclusive activity, as Russell and other reports showed (Yarnit, 1980: 184). After that, there was a rapid and remarkable expansion and opening up (Doyle, 1980: 134 *ff*). But even so, it reached out only to a small minority, if one excludes the whole area of workplace and vocational education which has, of course, rarely excited the left (Yarnit, 1987: 14). As for the radicals in adult education, despite an ambitious project – education to combat oppression and to awaken resistance – in practice we seemed somehow content to focus almost entirely on a tiny minority of the population. The misfortune of radical adult education was to be trying to find its feet at just the moment when the upsurge of the 60s and 70s was tailing off. For Raymond Williams, one of the towering figures of that current of thought, its heyday was already long since passed. By 1961, it had become clear to him that university adult education was a lost cause and that there had been 'a pretty successful conversion of the WEA into something that could be indifferently called Further Education' (quoted by John McIlroy, 1991). Whilst Williams's version of history does scant justice to the achievements of the 60s and 70s, there was, clearly, in the post-war years no mass movement to compare with Chartism, or the rise of the shop stewards' movement, the Communist Party and the National Council of Labour Colleges after the First World War, or even the ferment in the armed forces and on the home front which contributed to the election of Labour in 1945 (Addison, 1977: 143–154). The result was that without a unifying pressure, radical adult education remained, on the whole, a series of disconnected fields of activity. Explicitly political education has found the going especially hard. The WEA's recent celebration of the ILP's founding or the determination of the miners' wives who created Castleford Women's Centre that learning should serve the needs of their class: these are the rare remnants of the heyday of political education.

A Balance Sheet of the Era

So, if we can attempt a balance sheet of the era, it is clear that it renewed the radicalism of thought and action which has always informed the liveliest adult education. And even though the political tide has ebbed, for the time being, the writing and practice of the 70s has left an imprint which cannot be ignored, even by its detractors. In significant ways, it has changed the methods and structures for good. It provided a world view, however disjointed, when those on the right could offer only empty talk of maintaining standards coupled with a practice which turned out to be fatally vulnerable to the cost-cutting techniques of the

Conservatives and their allies in education. Nonetheless, there were some important lost opportunities. The educational critique of the left fell short of a grasp of the system's underlying rationale. Instead, there were two main types of responses. Some radical adult educationalists found themselves promoting access courses into FE and HE as if these would provide an answer to a fundamentally elitist system. Others, drawn by the attractions of working closely with local communities, centred themselves on the school as a base for community education and development, often discovering in the process just how reluctant headteachers were to involve themselves in such challenging projects. Although both access and community education are an established part of the education mainstream, the system as a whole is still far from providing access to all, throughout life, to forms of learning which would equip us to take control of our lives and to change society for the better.

Part 2. The Current Era: A Different Challenge

Let us try to get the measure of the political and educational era we now find ourselves in. What opportunities does it suggest, what challenges to confront for adult education? I don't intend to review the whole panorama (Bob Fryer, 1992, has had a shot at that in his essay in Brian Simon's collection, *The Search for Enlightenment*), but to focus on several key issues.

The Economy and Education

In their understanding of the relations between production and distribution, the right have traditionally emphasised the importance of wealth creation, especially in recent years. The left, on the contrary, has neglected the economic question in favour of a preoccupation with the division of the spoils between classes. Recent trends render both approaches bankrupt. The UK and Western economic systems generally are characterised by globalisation and specialisation which threaten to push significant sections of the population into a position of permanent exclusion from economic and social entitlement. Such issues cannot be addressed effectively on the narrow terrain of welfarism, as they tended to be in the 1970s; they go right to the heart of the organisation and financing of production, here and elsewhere in the world. At home, in the West generally, the central issue is employment; in the slow to develop world, the question is human sustenance. The fate of the two hemispheres is inseparable.

For a moment, in the aftermath of the Second World War, there seemed to be a way forward which could guarantee incomes for most of the world's population and rising living standards in the West. But the oil price rise which followed the 1973 Arab–Israeli War dealt a severe blow to the post-war settlement, inaugurating a period of growing political turmoil which culminated in the Thatcher–Reagan experiment. The Welfare State, understood in its broadest sense, which had smoothed economic cycles and class relations throughout the 50s and 60s, was anathematised by the Rew Right, which preached deregulation and self-reliance in the market place. The constraints on treating people as commodities – or *de-commodification*, to use the unlovely word of the sociologists – were identified by Thatcher and her allies as both the cause of economic failure and as the stalking horse of communism. In employment, public utilities, education, housing: in every sphere of society, the objective of the New Right was re-commodification. The result has been polarisation, socially, politically and economically, with a growing concentration of power in the hands of a few thousand families.

These developments have thrown the left into confusion. The sweeping away of Soviet power has left the world with no obvious way beyond the market. The implicit assumption by many in radical adult education throughout that earlier period, that there was a socialist road, cannot be made half so easily. If there is a revolutionary strategy, who are its subjects in the 1990s? The most interesting thinking on the left is taking place at the boundary of socialism, feminism and ecologism. Alain Lipietz, for example, proposes a new settlement between labour and capital to guarantee employment and income in return for productivity advances (Lipietz, 1992). Alongside the traded economy, there would be a de-commodified not-for-profit sector to provide welfare services and to mop up unemployment.

The creation and distribution of wealth is a proper subject for critical study as well as an important field in which we must be equipped to intervene effectively as workers, technicians, professionals and planners. That older separation between liberal adult education and vocational education left the industrialist in full control of training whilst failing to provide any clear routes between adult education and employment. Bringing the two together compels both sides to confront the relationship between society and production, at the same time opening up the possibility of the workers' control of production, a theme that Fordism was designed to put an end to in the inter-war period, and did so most effectively. That the post-war nationalisation of the railways, mines and the steel industry is an exception reflects, in part, the significant role of workers' education in tackling the 'commanding heights of the economy'. Paul Hirst explores the forms of economic and social organisation which would enable us to progress beyond the discredited forms of nationalised industries and monolithic welfare provision, whilst James Avis provides a timely warning about the dangers of assimilation to a project for capitalist rejuvenation (Hirst, 1994; Avis, 1993).

Adult education has a role to play in enabling people to earn a living as well as developing common understandings of the new economic events. And this cannot be reduced to the mindless competences which, according to some educationalists, the modern industrial hand requires, even for the least skilled, most peripheral sections of the workforce. The problem, of course, is that the last 15 years have seen the devaluation of education for personal and social development and the rise of a narrow form of vocational education, underpinned by a bureaucracy of learning outcome measurement. What now needs to be done is to re-instate the value of the former and re-invigorate the purposes and content of the latter (see Field, 1991; Ecclestone, 1993, 1994; Parkes, 1993). The realisation elsewhere – France and South Korea to take two contrasting cases – of the importance of raising qualification rates is reflected in the government's support for the National Education and Training Targets, even if the Conservatives contradictorily persist in their belief that the future of the British economy rests on its ability to reduce the labour costs of a barely-educated workforce. This is the driving force which is pushing thousands out of full-time, relatively well-paid employment, and which perpetuates the existence of a reserve army of ill-educated, under-achievers which has been central to Conservative educational philosophy since the 1870 Education Act.

Part 3: Some Ways Forward

1. The Relevance of Political Economy

What should be our response? First, we have to reincorporate the discussion of political economy as the central issue in adult education, as it was in the inter-war period. Wealth creation and the distribution of wealth, full employment, the control of the labour process, the globalisation of production: an understanding of these is indispensable to any attempt to change the world as we find it. Now, more than ever, the debate about how we order the world must take account of race and gender dimensions of economic development, in Britain, in Europe and globally. In a global economy, the relationships between men and women, between white and black, do not develop in isolation.

2. Towards a Unifying Agenda

Secondly, we must find ways of breaking down the barriers between adult education, trade union studies and vocational education. The current regime, of course, is structured to avoid the development of such linkages, but opportunities have to be sought where they can. Students and staff in colleges and universities, operating in the adjacent but separate worlds of EDAP and NVQs, liberal education, trade union studies and mature student access, are not prohibited from sitting down together to discuss the development of new courses or collaborative approaches to the teaching of existing ones. What is required in the first instance is a conception, however schematic, of the possibility of mutual enrichment.

3. Stimulating the Demand for Learning

There has to be a real opening up of education for adults to unleash new pressures for change within the institutions. Perhaps that cannot be achieved without a change of national policy, but in the first instance we need to spell out the type of entitlement we want and press for the local alliances of FE, HE and the WEA, whose development has been stimulated by Adult Learners' Week, to begin to address the needs of the people who are still poorly represented in post-school education. Targeting black people, the low paid, the long-term unemployed (a still growing proportion of the unemployed) and the residents of declining council estates could change the current profile of the adult learner.

There is a growing consensus about the importance of parity of esteem and treatment between different types and modes of learning, lessening the disparity in the funding of courses and support for full-time university students and the part-time mature entrants who increasingly dominate the world of further and higher education, although as a problem this is far from being a recent discovery. (See, for example, the farseeing Labour Party Report on Higher and Further Education, 1973, published just before the Russell Report.) This should not, however, become an argument for switching resources from full-time HE to the priority groups of adult learners referred to above, for that would disadvantage another group of potential working-class university entrants, the 18-year-olds. Rather, it amounts to a call for proper funding and support for continuing education.

One possible framework was advanced in *Time Off to Learn* (Mace and Yarnit, 1987), a collection of essays about paid educational leave and low paid workers. This revolves around a two-tier system of entitlement. The first tier, paid for by the employer – or the state for those unwaged – would provide an entitlement to 30 days per year of paid release, to be taken in a year or saved up and used in blocks, plus the right to longer periods of unpaid leave for higher education but with wider availability of mandatory grants. The basis of the scheme is that students are funded rather than courses, with prioritisation for groups whose educational needs have been neglected.

A second approach to stimulating and framing demand for lifelong education is by creating Learning Development Funds – an idea first proposed by Tom Schuller, albeit in a different context (Schuller, 1986) – against which groups could bid for funds. Criteria would be established to ensure that neglected groups and types of study would be prioritised, but it would be the responsibility of local committees bringing together the main educational interests, including trade unions, to determine the allocation of grants.

Finally, it is worth underlining the significance of the developing notion of the Learning City or Society for this discussion about lifelong learning. The Learning City is a response to the challenges facing big cities all over the world, and the growing sense that the key to the city's future is its people – their imagination, commitment and skills. Donald Hirsch, in a study for the OECD based on the experience of major cities in Europe, North America, Japan and Australia, shows that the city can be a crucial determinant of its own future (Hirsch, 1993). The central ingredient is a conscious attempt to mobilise and focus the resources for education and training to promote urban revival, thus providing a framework for using learning and education to help resolve the city's problems.

Not surprisingly, the idea has been taken up widely, in Britain and abroad. International conferences have taken place in Barcelona, Gothenberg and Bologna. In Liverpool, a wide range of organisations, including the City Council and the two universities, have combined to develop a City of Learning strategy closely tied to economic regeneration. In Edinburgh, local organisations have signed up to a charter which provides a framework for local collaboration to develop the idea of the Learning City and set up a centre. Birmingham has adopted the idea as part of a strategy to improve the quality of its schools. In Sheffield, a series of seminars, involving a wide range of organisations and individuals, has demonstrated the importance of providing the space for a critical overview of the relationship between learning and social and economic development. One important outcome has been to focus attention on the ways in which education could more effectively support and promote local community development.

4. Parental Education

It is vital that we focus on the growing interest in parental involvement in education and schooling. I have recently set out a programme of proposals directed at school governors and parents, including the creation of local learning centres, incorporating childcare, guidance and advice and a base for local campaigns on, for example, jobs and literacy, as well as an interchange point for HE and FE services to communities (Yarnit, 1994). The notion of local learning centres, incidentally, was first advanced in a paper produced by ACACE, the defunct Advisory Council for Adult and Continuing Education, in which it was conceived as a local access point to a 'comprehensive system which is flexible, locally-based and student-centred' (ACACE, 1983). The ACACE concept assumed, I believe, that the staffing would be by professionals. An alternative would be to foster the development of lay adult education workers, drawn from their local communities, much in the same way as the young people recruited as literacy assistants for the Yemeni Literacy Campaign in Sheffield (Shaif, 1992). As well as contributing to local campaigns and education initiatives, they would have the opportunity to enter higher education or gain a significant qualification. Local learning centres, staffed and led in this way, would also enable the development of that network of independent learners' groups which I envisaged as emerging from the creation of a National Adult Learners' Week (Yarnit, 1989).

5. Global Issues

Fifthly, alongside the economic and educational issues to which the previous proposals have been directed, there remains what may become the most significant political issue of the coming decade, the growth of conflicts within nation states between ethnic groups and minority groups such as gays and lesbians. The latest moral panics about juvenile crime, lager louts and single parents – invariably women – are one reflection of the rise of the ghetto of social exclusion. Less publicised is the spread of anti-black violence and harassment. Both are the symptoms of a nation's incapacity to adjust to a post-imperial role and status. The continuing rise in educational standards in our schools is masking a growing polarisation between those bound if not for glory then certainly relatively stable employment and those who will merely survive at the margins, haunting the prosperous with their begging, crack-taking, car-jacking and promiscuity. All this strongly suggests that an understanding of class relations, whilst providing a lynch-pin, constitutes on its own a limited basis for analysis and action. Gender and race must form the other dimensions of a critical analysis of contemporary economic structure, and probably nation and geography, too.

How is this to be approached? In essence, what is required is the invention of new types of study, of a new curriculum, not separate from all the others, but created alongside them. Although the social cohesion measures of the European Union are dwarfed by the social exclusion and polarisation effects of Maastricht and the Single Economic Market, European links – and funding – may offer a way of developing a new curriculum which integrates a study of national and international political economy with its gender and race dimensions. Emphasising the commonalities of oppressed people fighting for power, it would consider the relationship between the environment and economic development and re-interpret the ideas of human rights for the new situations confronting us. It would mean bringing together groups across national and social boundaries to consider joint action as well as to study the common roots of their problems. Mzwanele Mayekiso, a South African civic activist, describing the common ground between her township and the South Side of Chicago, argues for a 'new decommodified form of grassroots development', not to replace the state but because 'we are certain that our own organisations can often deliver services more effectively than an anonymous state bureaucracy'; and also because 'we have positive strategies for establishing the seeds of a new mode of production' (Mayekiso, 1994).

Conclusion: Beyond the Fragments

We are, thus, faced with a daunting agenda, but it is not, in essence, a new one and certainly not a unique one. At other times in British history, movements have arisen which have seized on the entire political, social and economic landscape as a proper subject for analysis and learning. It is the very scale of the obstacles to social development which poses the most fundamental questions about the alternatives. If de-regulation and globalisation make a mockery of traditional notions of national sovereignty, and with them Keynesian social democratic politics, we are compelled to confront the most profound questions about the relationship between democratic politics and economic power, not merely within the UK or even in Europe but at a global level. Certainly, without that broader conceptual framework, it is hard to make sense of the most pressing domestic and local issues. The steep rise in racial harassment, the feminisation of poverty caused by de-regulated labour, the crisis in the NHS: when viewed out of context these appear isolated issues. Effective action to tackle such issues depends on effective understanding of their linked causes. That, in effect, is the landscape which radical adult education needs to address today: causes and solutions.

References

ACACE (1983) *Continuing Education: Local learning centres*, ACACE.

Addison, P. (1977) *The Road to 1945*, Quartet.

Ashcroft, R. and Jackson, K. (1974), in Jones, D. and Mayo, M. (eds) *Community Work One*, Routledge Kegan Paul.

Ashworth,W. (1960) *An Economic History of England: 1870–1939*, University of Liverpool.

Avis, J. (1993) 'Post-Fordism, curriculum modernisers and radical practice: the case of vocational education and training in England', *The Vocational Aspect of Education*, vol. 45, no. 1.

Barber, M. (1993) *Education and the Teacher Unions*, Cassell.

Dispatches (1993) *All Our Futures*, Channel Four.

Doyle, M. (1980) 'Reform and reaction: the WEA post-Russell', in Thompson, J. (ed.) *Adult Education for a Change*, Hutchinson.

Ecclestone, K. (1993) 'Mastering the job', *Education*, 30 July.

Ecclestone, K. (1994) *Understanding Assessment*, NIACE.

Edwards, J. (1986) *Radical Adult Education in Liverpool*, Manchester Monographs.

Edwards, R. (1991) 'The politics of meeting learner needs', *Studies in the Education of Adults*, vol. 23, no. 1.

Field, J. (1991) 'Competency and the pedagogy of labour', *Studies in the Education of Adults*, vol. 23, no. 1.

Fieldhouse, R. (1991) 'Conformity and contradiction in English responsible body adult education, 1925–1950', in Westwood, S. and Thomas, J. (eds) *Radical Agendas?: The politics of adult education*, NIACE.

Fryer, R. (1992) in Simon, Brian (ed.) *The Search for Enlightenment*, NIACE.

Glennerster, H. and Low, W. (1990) 'Education and the welfare state', in Barr, N. and Hills, J. (eds) *The State of Welfare: The welfare state in Britain since 1974*, Oxford University Press.

Hirsch, D. (1993) *City Strategies for Lifelong Learning*, OECD Centre for Educational Research and Innovation (CERI), Paris.

Hirst, P. (1994) *Associative Democracy*, Polity Press.

Labour Party (1973) *Report on Higher and Further Education*.

Lipietz, A. (1992) *New Economic Order*, Polity Press.

Mace, J. and Yarnit, M. (eds) (1987) *Time Off to Learn*, Methuen.

McIlroy, J. (1991) 'Border country: Raymond Williams in adult education', *Studies in the Education of Adults*, vol. 23, no. 1.

Mayekiso, M. (1994) Interview in *Red Pepper*, no. 1, June 1994.

NIACE (1994) *What Price the Learning Society?*

Parkes, D. (1993) 'Is British VET out of step?', *Management in Education*, vol. 7, no.4.

Schuller, T. (1986) *Paid Educational Leave*, Warwick University.

Shaif, A. (1992) 'The community struggle for education', *Adults Learning*, April.

Westwood, S. (1980) 'Adult education and the sociology of education: an exploration', in Thompson, J. (ed.) *Adult Education for a Change*, Hutchinson.

Yarnit, M. (1980) 'Second Chance to Learn, Liverpool: class and adult education', in Thompson, J. (ed.) *op. cit.*

Yarnit, M. (1987) 'Paid educational leave: problems and possibilities, 1976–86', in Mace, J. and Yarnit, M. (eds) *Time Off to Learn*, Methuen.

Yarnit, M. (1989) 'Raising our sights: A better deal for adult learners', *Adults Learning*, November.
Yarnit, M. (1994) 'Rooting learning', *Adults Learning*, December.

Seven

Competence, Curriculum and Democracy

David Alexander and Ian Martin

This account reflects our own experience of the current process of professionalisation within the field of adult and community education in Scotland and, in particular, of the contradictions we have had to confront in
our work between the ideology of competence and the values of critical
enquiry, historical analysis and democratic debate. In this respect, we see
the Scottish case, in which a competence-based/functional analysis approach now dominates professional training for the Community Education Service (see Shaw and Crowther in this volume; also, for example,
CeVe 1990; 1992), as a microcosm of the general trend towards managerialism and impoverished notions of vocationalism and 'quality'. In our
view, a fundamental and urgent purpose of progressive adult and community educators should be to challenge and resist such narrowly conceived and instrumental definitions of competence and to locate them
clearly within the wider New Right project of centralisation, deregulation
and remoralisation. This project is hegemonic in the sense that it aims to
change the way we think about ourselves and each other, essentially
seeking to legitimise self-interest as the basis of moral action. We will argue that the competency movement in education and training is dangerous precisely because its technicising, reductive and individuating nature
lends itself to this process of hegemonic reconstruction.

The task is not to accommodate, manage or even to subvert the facile
equation of professionalism with competence but rather to confront and
deconstruct it in intellectual, historical and ethical terms. Moreover, we
cannot challenge the discourse and discipline of competence if we use the
same language. The focus must, therefore, shift to the fundamentals of
vocation, curriculum and epistemology: what is the role of the educator,
what kind of knowledge counts and how is it selected, constructed and
controlled? To answer these questions demands a vigorous reassertion of
the values of critical autonomy, practical utility and collective commitment that characterised the 'really useful knowledge' of the radical tradition in adult education (Johnson, 1979). In this respect, we find a
significant if neglected 'resource for hope', firstly, in the distinctively
Scottish intellectual and educational philosophy of 'common sense' and
the 'democratic intellect', which is particularly associated with the work
of the philosopher George Davie, and, secondly, in the history of independent working-class education in Scotland. As we struggle to advance

the democratic project in adult and community education, both these Scottish traditions can help us to reconnect with the 'dangerous memory' that is embodied in all progressive social movements, of which radical adult education has been an organic part, and to work with the subjugated knowledges of the majority. In this sense, we argue that the need is to rehistoricise contemporary struggles in order to gain the confidence to challenge and resist the forces of incorporation and control.

Competence: Context and Critique

The spread of the competency movement and, in particular, its current thrust into adult and higher education, sometimes masquerading as 'enterprise', needs to be located in a specific context. This context has structural, institutional and ideological dimensions which are critically considered in other chapters.

In structural terms, the interest in competence-based curriculum development and assessment reflects and effects a concerted attempt at the educational management of economic decline by means of which 'public issues' are transmuted into 'personal troubles', structural contradictions into social pathology. As a particular discursive formation, competence creates a new and reassuring common sense (Edwards and Usher, 1994):

Behind competence stalks the spectre of incompetence; the view is that it is people being unable to do the jobs asked of them to a satisfactory standard, if at all, which leads to uncompetitiveness in the economy as a whole. 'Competence' offers a 'warm' and 'obvious' common sense solution to the problem as constructed. To favour incompetence is surely irrational?

At a time of structural unemployment, the pervasive casualisation of work and a general weakening of the work ethic, a central purpose of the competency movement in social and educational policy is to re-establish labour discipline by means of what John Field (1991) calls a new 'pedagogy of labour'. In education and training, in particular, the emphasis on judging the efficacy of curriculum and pedagogy in terms of the assessment of predetermined outcomes constitutes a contemporary version of 'payment by results'. As such, its basic purpose is to counter professional resistance and institutional inertia. In this respect, the emphasis on competence marks a decisive reallocation of power over education and training in favour of employer and business interests. This is, of course, a fundamentally undemocratic and anti-democratic trend.

The competency movement and technicist reform in education must be located in the global context of the oppressive imperialism of the 'New' World Order.

Our main critique of competence rests upon the claim that in its present manifestation it represents a contextually and ideologically specific discourse about the nature and purpose of education and training. The power of discourse resides in the exclusions, evasions and closures by means of which it constructs reality and demarcates the parameters of debate: 'A discourse defines what can be said, which is based on what cannot be said, on what is marginalised, silenced and repressed' (Edwards and Usher, 1994). The discourse of competence is constructed, in both intention and effect, to impose a particular kind of control and discipline over our work as adult and community educators at several levels: over the education and training system as a whole, the curriculum and the epistemology upon which it is based, the teacher and the student.

Bearing the unmistakeable 'stamp of the industrial-commercial nexus' (Collins, 1987), the competency movement justifies and executes a decisive shift in power and control over education and training in favour of employers, business interests and the central state acting as the agent of international capital. As such, it heralds a 'new Fordism' (Field, 1991) in education and training that effects a simultaneous centralisation of power and deregulation of control. At the same time, it is important to understand how the pseudo-positivism of the competency-based approach ensures that at a pedagogical level issues of power and control are systematically obscured while casualisation and cost-cutting are justified through the de-skilling of students and the limitation of educational objectives (Bowes, 1992).

In terms of curriculum and epistemology, the emphasis moves decisively to prescription and imposition, and away from critical analysis of the social and political construction of knowledge and debate about its control and distribution. The assimilation of approved and authorised pre-selections of knowledge and skill combines with a form of assessment which is frequently justified in crudely behaviouristic and psychologistic terms. For instance, in Scotland the professional capacity of community education workers is now assessed entirely in terms of their ability to 'overtake' a long list of discrete and overwhelmingly technical competences. Significantly perhaps, these do not include the ability to teach or to think.

In this respect, it is important to see the continuities between the current hegemony of competence and the 'ideology of individualism' that has for so long permeated liberal adult education (see, for example, Keddie, 1980; Griffin, 1983). In many ways, the elisions of the latter can now be seen to have prepared the ground for the incursions of the former. And we have to recognise the unwitting collusion of many adult and community educators in the present conjunction of pedagogical individuation with ideological atomisation consequent upon New Right intervention.

Such is the power of this discourse, which integrates liberal humanist methodology with behaviourist outcomes, that the learner is disciplined through a process of 'self-regulation'. The consequences are truly hegemonic because the work competence does is 'to do with disciplining adults through a process whereby adults discipline themselves as learners of a particular type and in a particular way' (Edwards and Usher, 1994). We would argue that the result is fundamentally undemocratic and anti-educational, whatever the rhetorical gloss of 'self-direction' and 'student-centredness' would seem to suggest. The subtlety and the potency of the discourse of competence is that it combines the illusion of autonomy with the reality of a reconstituted behaviourism.

Towards a Democratic Resistance: The Scottish Contribution

In seeking to construct a democratic resistance to the competency movement in adult and community education, we agree with Collins (1991) that this means reasserting its fundamental values and purposes as a progressive and critical vocation. Indeed, we would suggest that the current hegemony of competence within the Scottish Community Education Service is largely attributable to its neglect of precisely the difficult issues and choices this implies. Our view, however, is that Scottish adult and community educators are better served in this respect by their own indigenous histories, democratic traditions and communitarian values than by the alien and alienating discourse of competence. And there are lessons to be learnt from the Scottish case for others who seek to resist the colonisation of competence and the incorporation implicit within it.

It must first, however, be recognised that the predominant response of adult and community educators in Scotland to the New Right project has been to bury their heads in the sands of busy developments. Most of these, particularly in the further education sector (e.g. Scotvec, SVQ, 16-plus programmes, access initiatives and work funded by Scottish Enterprise through Local Enterprise Companies) are based on human investment, human resource development and technicist approaches, which are perceived to be relevant to the needs of industry. The competency movement needs to be seen as an integral part of this wider context. At the same time, responsive, community-based adult education, which has been consistently shown to be effective with people on low incomes and with few or no educational qualifications, exists precariously on minimal, uncertain and short-term funding. In this respect, it is as well to restate the hegemonic thrust of the discourse of competence: 'Cultural hegemony is characterised not only by what it includes but by what it excludes, renders marginal, deems inferior and makes invisible' (Fasheh, 1992).

The retreat into technicism, managerialism and a debased form of professionalism is a betrayal of adult and community education's moral purpose and its historical roots in the democratic movement. In particular, the neglect of curriculum creates a void in which such betrayals and evasions go virtually unnoticed as the contemporary version of merely 'useful knowledge' is pursued with unthinking enthusiasm. Our argument, on the other hand, is that, as adult and community educators, we should be concerned in our work to develop a commitment to a civil society which involves democratic participation, equity and public discussion of fundamental moral and political issues concerning the nature of the curriculum, its selection from cultures, its social distribution and relationships to power. In our view, the debate about curriculum in the education of adults is of major cultural, moral and intellectual significance. It is central to our vocational purpose to seek actively to advance precisely such public discussion in our work. Secret and subversive resistance, sometimes disguised as 'strategic compliance', may comfort individuals but it cannot be a moral or democratic substitute for public debate and collective challenge.

Fundamentally, what we must be concerned with is the critical unity of democracy and intellect. Adult and community educators have a crucial part to play in resisting the dominant hegemony by reconnecting with their historical roots in progressive social movements and reasserting their commitment to building a common critical culture. This, however, involves a self-conscious attempt to problematise and locate the challenges we now confront and to build this process of deconstruction and reconstruction into our curriculum of education and training. And yet such a critical pedagogy is precisely what the exclusions and closures of competence inhibit.

It is deeply ironical that while the cultural politics of contemporary Scotland provides in many ways a peculiarly rich seedbed for such a democratic resistance, the competency-driven professionalisation of the Scottish Community Education Service stands in direct contradiction to this. Some commentators (e.g. Galloway, 1994) use the Gramscian distinction between 'organic' and 'conjunctural' change to examine the current Scottish context. According to this analysis, Scotland's long-term organic development has been characterised by a strong sense of its own distinctive national identity, traditions and values. This includes both material and ideological components, such as a greater investment in collectivist forms of public provision and a deeply felt anti-imperialism. It is true that in recent times the Scots have not been impervious to the blandishments of the New Right: they have bought their council houses, purchased shares in privatised utilities and exercised the 'right to choose' their children's schooling. On the other hand, the general response to the present conjuncture in Scotland has been to view the New Right agenda as embodying an exclusively English and therefore alien vision of the 'good society' (McCrone, 1992), and this has been consistently and overwhelmingly rejected at the polls. Moreover, in seeking to confront the conjunctural crisis in the contemporary politics of the state and the democratic deficit inherent within it, Scots have initiated a range of broadly nationalist and 'spontaneous' counter-politics in civil society. Thus, for example, Galloway (1994) argues that not only has the rejection of the New Right been demonstrated visibly at the polls but also in other areas of cultural life. Campaigns like those of the Anti-Poll Tax Federation, Communities Against the Fuel Tax, the Coalition for Scottish Democracy and the anti-water privatisation lobby were built on strong campaign groups who went on to form cross-community alliances with other groups in a form of civil politics for Scotland unseen since the formation of the Labour movement.

What this demonstrates is the growing dissonance between the cultural politics of Scottish communities and not only the formalised politics of the British state but also, and ironically, with the professional politics of the Community Education Service in Scotland.

We would argue that in the present conjuncture two distinctively Scottish traditions offer us the intellectual and moral resources for a democratic resistance: first, the philosophy of 'common sense' and the 'democratic intellect' expounded in the work the contemporary Scottish philosopher George Davie (see, for example, Davie, 1961, 1986 and 1991); second, the rootedness of radical adult education in Scotland in the independent working-class adult education movement. Our argument is that active resistance (as distinct from subversion) requires a systematic attempt within the adult and community education curriculum to reconnect with both these traditions.

George Davie's work guides us in significant ways and provides the basis for a distinctive vision of a rich and humane civic culture that is worth working for and requires the commitment of all democratic adult educators. Davie (1991) warns of the dangers of ignoring this challenge, of surrendering to the hegemony of 'technical rationality' and thus colluding with the fundamentally divisive and undemocratic logic of the competency movement:

> *For Scottish thinkers, this technicologico-scientific 'rationalisation' of life is not merely repellant from a moral point of view, because of its tolerating or even encouraging the intellectual backwardness of the masses but at the same time it is also inherently an unstable basis for the material progress it seeks to sustain, in that the stultification of the majority, due to their cultural apartheid, is likely to be a species of sympathetic contagion to affect the mental balance of society as a whole, and so undermine the reliability of the science on which it depends.*

He goes on to warn against the delusions of a 'smooth performativeness', or what might be called the technicist and managerial 'quick fix':

> *As for the radical dream of overcoming the cultural leeway by teaching machines and educational technology, the remedy seems to the Scottish thinkers even worse than the disease since the effect would be to substitute a smooth performativeness for the inward Socratic self examination about first principles which, in learned and unlearned alike, gives life a meaning. In so far, therefore, as the strategy of growth requires priorities, it seems reasonable to the Scots to regard their complicated system of spiritual participation as a necessary component of economic advance, in that ... a science-based society can maintain the intellectual standards necessary to material progress only by making it possible for each party to keep the other up to scratch by mutual criticism, in much the same way as, under their religious system, the minister's theological supervision of the congregation was checked and balanced by the congregation's common sense scrutiny of the minister.*

There are two inseparable themes woven into this distinctively Scottish philosophical tradition. The first relates to curriculum and argues the case for a 'common sense', understood in terms of a shared, critical and inter-disciplinary understanding based on the capacity for both inward reflective analysis and public debate. As a result, the blind spots and elisions of any one specialism or area of knowledge may be illuminated by other domains of the intellect and by critical generalist and philosophical understanding (Macdonald, 1993). The principle of common sense, as a public property, is the basis for a democratic and critical culture and it applies as much to the natural sciences as it does to the social sciences and philosophy:

> *Just as in the study of the mind, so in the study of matter, the introverted work of observation and experiment presupposes a self-introverted analysis, which establishes the fundamental concepts by reflection on the appropriate part of common sense (Davie, 1991).*

The second theme concerns the link between democracy and the social conditions conducive to both self-reflection and collective debate:

> *Epistemology is bound up with social practice. The notion of common sense as sensus communis (public or shared sense) both underpins and is constituted by our endeavouring to view our judgements with the eyes of other people, or as other people are likely to view them (Gunn, 1994).*

Specialisation can only be partial and incomplete, and therefore requires comment from educated lay people in a language of commonly understood first principles. This explains the emphasis in traditional Scottish university degree courses on a compulsory grounding in philosophy regardless of subsequent specialisation, if any. The shared understanding of general principles was seen as a precondition for a democratic critical culture in which 'professors and students, specialists and laity can meet on more or less equal terms, and the unlearned no less than the learned have a contribution to make' (Beveridge and Turnbull, 1989). The alternative to such a common intellectual culture is, according to Davie (1991), 'a society split between over-specialised boffins on the one hand and unthinking proles on the other'. It is also important to emphasise that in this Scottish tradition the personal is in a fundamental way the political, because 'one can only think for oneself if one does not think by oneself' (MacIntyre, 1987).

MacIntyre contrasts 'the idea of an educated public', which he bases upon an analysis of the eighteenth century Scottish Enlightenment, with a group of specialists who can only discuss matters among themselves because there is no common language of criticism. He goes on to argue that the vast increase in specialised knowledge in modern times should not be a barrier to its interrogation by common sense and democratic intellectualism unless we are prepared to surrender to 'the kind of professionalisation which excludes the relevance of disciplines to each other'.

It is essential to clarify both the distinctions and, potentially, the connections between the notions of 'common sense' expounded in the work of Davie on the one hand and Gramsci on the other. For Gramsci the key task of the revolutionary educator is to penetrate and problematise the common sense that saturates everyday thinking and popular consciousness precisely because its hegemonic nature effects 'the internalisation of bourgeois ideas, beliefs and values – so much so that they prevent us from thinking about alternatives' (Armstrong, 1988). In this way, common sense masks reality and legitimises oppression – and is, therefore, fundamentally anti-democratic. For Davie, in contrast, 'common' may be read as synonymous with 'democratic' in both intellectual and social terms.

Intellectually, the Scottish philosophy of common sense was intended specifically to counter the undemocratic effects of occupational specialisation and the 'intellectual atomisation' consequent upon it. Common sense, rooted in the philosophical discipline of 'reflective analysis', is ultimately the guarantor of the democratic right to critical autonomy and shared understanding:

> *The Scottish bent for argument about first principles meant that what Davie calls 'the common sense of subjects' was put before questions of detail. It is in this sense that Davie use the idea of 'democratic intellectualism' to characterise the Scottish mind (Beveridge and Turnbull, 1989).*

In our view, 'the common sense of subjects' implies that the ideological and epistemological construction of curriculum is fundamental to the democratic project in education. And yet, it is also precisely what the fragmenting effects of competences disallow.

In social terms, Davie argues for common sense as a counter to the 'social moronisation' that is implicit in the social division of labour, knowledge and expertise in an industrialised society. 'Common' in this respect refers to the social distribution of knowledge and understanding as well as their intellectual quality. Indeed, democracy can only be secured through a particular kind of educational commitment embodied in a common curriculum:

> *While the material growth of a country requires an increasing specialisation in the practical field of production, the spiritual and intellectual growth of the country, if it is to keep pace with the material growth instead of being overwhelmed by it, requires, by contrast, not the promotion but the restriction of specialisation in the theoretic field, by the encouragement, through education, of a general studies mentality ... (Davie, 1991).*

It is necessary therefore to make a clear distinction between Daviean and Gramscian usages of 'common sense' – and, indeed, its colloquial usage as untheorised and a critical gut feeling. For Davie, common sense is as much a precondition of democracy as it is an impediment for Gramsci. Nevertheless, it can also be argued that Davie's notion of common sense, as an intellectual acuity and confidence that is widely shared and deeply rooted in popular consciousness, is an essential prerequisite of the Gramscian counter-hegemonic educational project. In other words, it can be argued that 'good sense' in Gramscian terms is predicated upon common sense in Daviean terms.

This distinctively Scottish commitment to common sense stands against precisely the forces of narrow specialisation and technicist measures of competence which assail adult and community in Scotland today. Our task is to resist these forces because our purpose as democratic educators must be to contribute to the realisation of a common critical culture which MacIntyre (1987) characterises in terms of 'shared standards of justification, with a shared view of what the past of society of which it is a nucleus is, with a shared ability to participate in common public debate'. The challenge for adult and community educators is to ensure that the idea and the ideal of an educated public, which MacIntyre fears has now become no more than a 'ghost haunting our educational systems', is a ghost which is not yet exorcised.

The second vital reconnection that needs to be made is with the robustly independent and counter-hegemonic tradition of working-class self-education in Scotland. In our view, this constitutes a rich yet under-researched 'resource for hope'. It is also a weapon of resistance because it enables us to rehistoricise our sense of ourselves in terms of common values and collective purposes in the face of the ahistorical, technicist and atomistic forces that confront us. In fact, we would argue that one of the reasons for the current hegemony of competence within the Scottish Community Education Service is precisely because the professional training of its workers has lacked historical depth and intellectual substance (see Shaw and Crowther in this volume). In other words, the resources with which to resist the disciplinary power of the discourse of competence have simply not been there.

Scottish traditions of independent working-class education have been particularly strong and closely related to socialist and republican parties and movements. There is not space here to provide a comprehensive analysis of these movements and autonomous educational traditions (see Alexander, 1994), but it is useful to draw attention to the work of John Maclean and the Labour College movement in Scotland, particularly because until recently historians of adult education have given them 'very short shrift' (Simon, 1990). Maclean laid great stress on educational work in order to counteract 'the state educational machine, the churches, the mass media' (Maclean, 1978). In 1902 Maclean, who was an elementary school teacher and gained a national reputation as a radical adult educator, joined the Social Democratic Federation, and 'by 1906 he was conducting classes in economics. Large audiences began to be attracted to the classes held on Sundays. By 1914 he was drawing crowds of over 200 at each meeting' (Roberts, 1970).

Maclean was a man of action, a socialist republican and popular educator who became a legend in his own time, especially in Scotland's industrial heartland in Glasgow and on the Clyde in the early years of the twentieth century. There are significant inter-relationships between developments in the labour movement, the work of the Plebs League, the historical and organic association of adult education with progressive social movements and socialist political parties and Maclean's life and work. (See, for example, Aldred, 1940; Simon, 1965; Milton, 1973; Young, 1992; Ripley and McHugh, 1989; Calder, 1993.) For the purposes of our argument, it is important to emphasise that he was particularly clear and uncompromising about the centrality of independent working-class control of the curriculum because he understood the relationship between knowledge and power – the issue at the heart of the Ruskin Strike, the formation of the Plebs League and subsequently the independent Labour College movement:

Many people are horrified to hear it said that the working-class standpoint in economics is bound to be different from that of capitalists. These tender beings dream of a certain 'impartial' social science bringing about the reconciliation of the hostile classes, as if it were possible to avoid taking sides on economic questions in a society in which the interests of the workers are sharply opposed to those of the employers, the needs of tenants conflict with those of the house-owners, and so on. True, professors of political economy in the universities claim to be impartial men of science. But nobody believes them; their attitude is recognised as a necessary professional pose. Their teaching has become a mere system of apologetics, by means of which they reveal the moral reasons that justify the plundering of the working class. In this respect it is as different as night from day when compared with the work of the economists of the classical school from Smith to Ricardo ... The economists of today write books, abounding in mathematical subtleties, such as have no guidance to give us so far as the control of social productive forces is concerned (Maclean, 1978).

Of course, the two distinctively Scottish traditions outlined here in the work of George Davie and John Maclean are themselves the products of different historical and cultural contexts, and they embody different visions of the good society. While it may be possible to use MacIntyre's 'idea of an educated public' in a comprehensive way to serve both traditions, it is clear that their purposes were not the same. For Davie the social significance of the Scottish school of common sense philosophy as it developed in the nineteenth and twentieth centuries was that 'knowledge serves a social purpose, especially of breaking down the social divisions that the Scottish eighteenth century thinkers saw as a consequence of industrialism' (Paterson, 1993). The inheritors of the Enlightenment traditions were, therefore, concerned to cultivate a wider educated public, and one purpose of popular education was to prevent revolutions on a French or North American model, and later of a radical socialist kind. In defence of this position, it could be argued that a type of humane and civic incorporation may be more conducive to social liberation than the systematic exclusion and oppression evident in other European countries, including England. It can also be argued that Enlightenment traditions as they developed in Scotland ultimately encouraged dissent.

In this respect, it should be noted that John Maclean, as both a school teacher and a radical adult educator, was himself a product of 'democratic intellectualism' and in his own way he was, of course, an exponent of the Scottish philosophy of 'common sense', understood as the sense that must be made common to a class. Addressing a meeting held on 12 February 1916 in the Co-operative Halls in Glasgow at which the foundations of the Scottish Labour College movement were laid, Maclean (1978) urged the case for independence as the only alternative to incorporation:

> It is my hope that you delegates will become just as aware as the masters are of the need for specific forms of education. The state provides an elementary and higher education that certainly needs purging and overhauling: the state may be willing to enforce technical or commercial training on every boy and girl not intending to enter the professions: but the state, because it must be a capitalist state so long as capitalism endures, will not provide a full education to equip workers to carry on the working-class movement or to fight for the ending of capitalism itself.

On the other hand, Maclean would have recognised the contradictions in his own biography. He certainly demonstrated in his vocation as an adult educator an understanding of the Gramscian dictum that 'every relationship of "hegemony" is necessarily a pedagogical relationship' (Gramsci, 1971). Similarly, he would have seen through the meritocratic ideology implicit in the 'lad o'pairts' myth – whereby the village boy (always a boy) makes good – and would also have agreed with Thomas Malthus on the social control rationale of much provided education:

> The knowledge circulating among the common people ... has yet the effect of making them bear with patience the evils which they suffer from, being aware of the folly and inefficacy of turbulence (quoted by Smout, 1986).

Maclean knew only too well that such 'useful knowledge' was insufficient for democracy and social transformation. It has been claimed, for instance, that one of the Enlightenment principles which provides us with a reasonable philosophy of common sense that can be rationally applied to political economy and international law is that duty is a notion independent of interest (MacIntyre, 1987). But, as John Maclean would have asked, in whose interest is this duty? To ask this question and to seek to answer it meant for democratic educators like Maclean, again in the words of Gramsci (1971), 'working to produce elites of intellectuals of a new type which arise directly out of the masses, but remain directly in contact with them to become, as it were, the whalebone in the corset'. Here, in essence, is the historic task with which democratic educators must reconnect.

It is true that Gramsci's use of 'common sense' is radically different from that of Davie. We would, however, argue that adult and community educators today need to study both in order to understand how, if their *praxis* as educators:

affirms the need for contact between intellectuals and the simple, it is not in order to restrict scientific activity and preserve unity at the low level of the masses but precisely in order to construct an intellectual-moral bloc which can make politically possible the intellectual progress of the masses and not only small intellectual groups (Gramsci, 1971).

It may be that these reflections on the nature of democracy and curriculum in adult and workers' education in Scotland appear arcane and irrelevant in view of the changing nature of work and class structures, the excited celebration of postmodern fragments, the politics of consumption and the perceived failures of modernist grand theories. But we would emphasise that John Maclean and his fellow activists did not have closed or determinist minds and saw both education and the state as arenas of struggle. As James Kelman (1992) stresses, what remains most deeply significant about the radical tradition in Scottish adult education is 'not the importance of ideas, but the importance of the *exploration* of ideas'. This is what, in our view, is fundamental to the democratic project in adult and community education today, and it is precisely what the competency movement threatens to marginalise and exclude.

Our claim, therefore, is that an exploration of these Scottish traditions and movements, including the differences between them and the contradictions within them, helps to provide us with a critical basis for a democratic understanding of the social, economic and political forces which underlie curriculum and its relationship to knowledge and power. Such understandings refocus our attention on the possibilities of the counter-hegemonic and democratic decisions educators must make in the selection of a curriculum of resistance. They also enable us in educating educators to locate more clearly the purposes of the competency movement in its historical, epistemological and political contexts. That is, we are concerned with a language of hope and possibility, with subjugated knowledges, with 'dangerous memory', and not a collusion with the language of deceit and moral despair. These critical, difficult understandings form an alternative basis for the education and training of those intending to become democratic adult and community educators. As such, they stand opposed to the 'regime of truth' embodied in the competency movement which seeks only to produce amoral and historically illiterate instructors.

Any truly vocational curriculum with this democratic purpose requires a critical rigour which specifically excludes the separation of conception from practice that is promoted by the competency movement. Such a curriculum is concerned neither to de-skill, to produce ciphers equipped only to deliver a predetermined learning programme and unproblematic content spattered with liberal, experiential and progressive methods, nor to engender a means whereby consenting adults discipline themselves as a 'strategy of governance' (Edwards and Usher, 1994).

Conclusion

> *Solution by the method of partition is always unsatisfactory to minds*
> *with an ambition for comprehensiveness (Collins, 1987).*

If adult and community educators are to be concerned with the cultivation of critical intelligence as a means of social and political engagement, the hegemony of the competency movement in education must be resisted. Both the ideology and the epistemology of competences must be challenged. Moreover, this process must become part of our curriculum in education and training courses. Even when we have to jump through the hoops, we must pause to examine them.

We have argued that competence-based approaches are a form of legitimation in which issues of power and control are masked and evaded. In this sense, they are fundamentally undemocratic and anti-educational, and that is precisely their value to the New Right. The competency movement today is to be seen in the context of the so called 'new world order', and the international division of labour implicit within it, which conflate democracy with the venality of the 'free' market. As such, the competency movement is an ideological instrument for creating hegemonic consent to the globalised de-skilling of not only industrial and agricultural workers but also teachers and adult educators. In the absence of any meaningful forms of industrial and local democracy, capitulation to these forces, which reduce workers to units of human resource management, will inevitably fragment resistance and undermine the possibilities for collective and public challenge. But education is always a key site of hegemonic struggle, and it is in education and by educators that the hegemony of the competency movement must be exposed and resisted. This means making the agencies of state education and all progressive social movements, as well as the education and training of adult and community education workers, both the locus and the focus of such democratic exposure and resistance.

The radical tradition in adult and community education has always been about prefigurative work: capturing in the learning culture we create the vision of more just, democratic and emancipatory social relations and fostering the commitment to struggle for its realisation. In this respect, we could no better than seek to cultivate in our work what George Davie describes as the Scots' 'complicated system of spiritual participation'. Essentially, this means reappropriating the idea of competence and transforming it into what Habermas calls 'communicative competence'. What is required is, in effect, exactly what the current tyranny of competences in education and training prohibits: 'a democratic form of public discussion which allows for an uncoerced flow of ideas and arguments and for participants to be free from any threat of domination, manipulation or control' (Carr and Kemmis, 1986).

Adult and community educators, however beleaguered and marginalised, occupy one of the few educational and cultural spaces that are left for the democratic and emancipatory project in education. We have tried to show how we can rediscover within our own histories, traditions and values the intellectual and moral resources with which to resist, re-engage and reconstruct – and to do so with creativity and confidence.

References

Aldred, G.A. (1940) *John McLean*, 'The Word' Library, no. 3, Glasgow.

Alexander, D. (1994) 'The education of adults in Scotland: democracy and curriculum', *Studies in the Education of Adults*, vol. 26, no. 1, pp 31–49.

Armstrong, P. (1988) 'L'Ordine Nuovo: the legacy of Antonio Gramsci and the education of adults', *International Journal of Lifelong Education*, vol. 7, no. 4.

Beveridge, C. and Turnbull, R. (1989) *The Eclipse of Scottish Culture*, Polygon.

Bowes, S. (1992) 'A critical evaluation of the work of CeVe and its implications for the development of community education in Scotland', Unpublished MEd dissertation, Department of Education, University of Edinburgh.

Calder, A. (1993) 'Heroes, hero worship and the secret state', *Cencrastus*, 45, pp 11–17.

Carr, W. and Kemmis, S. (1986) *Becoming Critical*, Falmer Press.

CeVe (1990) *Pre-Service Training for Community Education Work*, Scottish Community Education Council.

CeVe (1992) *Guidelines for Endorsement of Fieldwork Supervision Courses*, Scottish Community Education Council.

Collins, M. (1987) *Competence in Adult Education*, University Press of America.

Collins, M. (1991) *Adult Education as Vocation: A critical role for the adult educator*, Routledge.

Davie, G. (1961) *The Democratic Intellect*, Edinburgh University Press.

Davie, G. (1986) *The Crisis of the Democratic Intellect*, Polygon.

Davie, G. (1991) 'The social significance of the Scottish philosophy of common sense', in *The Scottish Enlightenment and Other Essays*, Polygon, pp 51–85.

Davies, B. and Durkin, M. (1991) '"Skill", "competence" and "competences" in youth and community work', *Youth and Policy*, no. 34, pp 1–11.

Edwards, R. and Usher, R. (1994) 'Disciplining the subject: the power of competence', *Studies in the Education of Adults*, vol. 26, no. 1, pp 1–14.

Eraut, M. (1989) 'Initial teacher training and the NVQ model', in Burke, J. (ed.) *Competency Based Education and Training* Falmer Press.

Fasheh, M. (1992) 'West Bank: learning to survive', in Poster, C. and Zimmer, J. (eds) *Community Education in the Third World*, Routledge, pp 17–29.

Field, J. (1991) 'Competency and the pedagogy of labour', *Studies in the Education of Adults*, vol. 23, no. 1.

Galloway, V. (1994) 'Community Education: A liberatory cultural approach', Unpublished MEd dissertation, Moray House Institute of Education, Heriot-Watt University.

Gramsci, A. (1971) *Selections from the Prison Notebooks*, Hoare, Q. and Nowell Smith, G. (eds) Lawrence and Wishart.

Griffin, C. (1983) *Curriculum Theory in Adult and Lifelong Education*, Croom Helm.

Gunn, R. (1994) Introduction to Davie, G. (ed. Macdonald, M.) *A Passion for Ideas: Essays on the Scottish Enlightenment, Vol. II*, Polygon, pp xi–xviii.

Hyland, T. (1992) 'Expertise and competence in further and adult education', *British Journal of In-Service Education*, vol. 18, no. 1, pp 23–28.

Hyland, T. (1993a) 'Competence, knowledge and education', *Journal of Philosophy of Education*, vol. 27, no. 1, pp 57–68.

Hyland, T. (1993b) 'Outcome and competence in higher education', *Educational Change and Development*, vol. 13, no. 2, pp 1–3.

Jeffs, T. and Smith, M. (1993) 'A question of competence', *Concept*, vol. 3, no. 1, pp 15–18.

Johnson, R. (1979) '"Really useful knowledge": radical education and working class culture', in Clarke, J., Critcher, C. and Johnson, R. (eds) *Working Class Culture*, Hutchinson.

Keddie, N. (1980) 'Adult education: an ideology of individualism', in Thompson, J. (ed.) *Adult Education for a Change*, Hutchinson, pp 45–64.

Kelman, J. (1992) *Some Recent Attacks: Essays cultural and political*, A.K. Press.

McCrone, D. (1992) *Understanding Scotland: The sociology of a stateless nation*, Routledge.

Macdonald, M. (1993) 'Mutual illumination', *Edinburgh Review*, issue 90, pp 5–8.

MacIntyre, A. (1987) 'The idea of an educated public', in Haydon, G. (ed.) *Education and Values*.

Maclean, J. (1978) *In the Rapids of Revolution*, Milton, N. (ed.) Allison and Busby.

Milton, N. (1973) *John Maclean*, Pluto.

Paterson, L. (1993) 'Democracy and the curriculum in Scotland', *Edinburgh Review*, issue 90, pp 21–28.

Ripley, B.J. and McHugh, J. (1989) *John MacLean*, Manchester University Press.

Roberts, J. (1970) 'The National Council of Labour Colleges: An experiment in workers' education', Unpublished MSc dissertation, Department of Education, University of Edinburgh.

Simon, B. (1965) *Education and the Labour Movement 1870–1920*, Lawrence and Wishart.

Simon, B. (ed.) (1990) *The Search for Enlightenment: The working class and adult education in the twentieth century*, NIACE.

Smout, T. (1986) *A Century of the Scottish People 1830–1950*, Collins.

UDACE (1989) *Understanding Competence*, Unit for the Development of Adult Continuing Education.

Young, J.D. (1992) *John MacLean, Clydeside Socialist*, The Clydeside Press.

Eight

Really Useful Knowledge: Adult Learning and the Ruskin Learning Project

Katherine Hughes

The history and culture of Ruskin College straddles different traditions and purposes, drawing strengths from a liberal educational tradition derived from the extension movement and focused around the university and a more radical tradition related to the trade union and working-class movement, fed more recently by a revival of critical radical adult education and both the women's movement and anti-racist movements. This tradition in summed up in the statement of the College's vocation which reads:

> *Our Mission Statement commits us to work particularly with those individuals and groups who wish to increase their educational abilities and activities or to become more effective in their local, national or international organisations for the betterment of the societies in which they live (Ruskin College, 1992).*

The Ruskin Learning Project, originating in 1988, was established to offer local short course provision to unqualified working-class adults. Courses are free, part-time and open to anyone who wishes to pursue education for whatever purpose. Participants can take several courses at a time over a year and can become involved in other political and cultural events at Ruskin. Courses include History, Social Studies, Women's Studies, Literature, Creative Writing, Economics, and special projects are pursued with the unemployed, older people, women and people in paid work. Approximately 200 people become involved each year.

The Ruskin Learning Project has provided a focus and a forum for many of these debates. The Project operates at the intersection of County Council-supported access provision and a more radical adult educational initiative concerned with education for social change. This history has shaped the project towards the equipping of people for further and higher education but in the context of developing initiatives which seek to understand 'how we are to get out of our present troubles' (*Poor Man's Guardian*, no. 137, 25 September 1834).

Early Connections

Such initiatives have strong historical connections with the radical education of the early 1800s. As today, the early nineteenth century was a period of enormous upheaval for the new industrial proletariat facing the privations of the rapidly growing towns and cities, new forms of working, of timekeeping, low pay and long hours. The spirit of laissez-faire meant a state that challenged combinations (Combination Acts 1799, 1800, 1824–4), pathologised poverty (Poor Law Amendment Act, 1834), sought to suppress political debate (the Newspaper Acts of 1712, 1756 and 1795 taxed newspapers with a view to reducing the circulation of the radical press; they were not reduced until 1836, and the newspaper tax was only abolished in 1855, the paper duty following in 1861) and supported entrepreneurs in their payment of low wages (Corn Laws, 1815). The hardships of the time spawned much political activity, for instance the Chartist and Owenite movements, and a lively radical press.

In the pages of the *Poor Man's Guardian* the hegemonic purpose and utilitarian thrust of contemporary education was challenged:

> *the poorer classes being 'educated' as it was culled by the rich or their undertakings, that is, they were taught just as much as would suit the purposes of the latter. Thus it was in the National Schools and the same spirit prevailed in the Mechanics Institutions where the instruction was strictly confined to science. Men were allowed to have the luxuries but not the necessaries of learning. But what was the use of a man being able to explore all the works of creation if he could get nothing to eat? (Poor Man's Guardian, no. 7, 8 August 1831).*

The work of the Society for the Diffusion of Useful Knowledge, which sought to equip the new workforce with knowledge of use within the economy, was much disparaged.

> *It is safe enough to talk about liberty in the abstract but to attempt to reduce it to practice is to make war on all who profit by our bondage. What we want to be informed about is 'How are we to get out of our present troubles? How are we to break the chains that bind us?' (Poor Man's Guardian, no. 117, 25 September 1834).*

Cobbett too took a swipe at the hypocrisy of those who make supplications to one part of the person while neglecting to consider fundamental material issues. In an impassioned plea he asks: 'But who is to expect morality in a half-starved man who is whipped if he do not work though he has not, for his whole day's food so much as I and my little boy snapped up in six or seven minutes upon Stoke Charity Down? ... Education? Despicable cant and nonsense! What moral precepts can quiet the gnawings and ragings of hunger?' (Cobbett, 1830: 262–3, 265).

In place of 'Useful Knowledge' was posed an alternative idea of really useful knowledge (Johnson, 1979). This meant knowledge that sought to make sense of the causes of hardship and oppression in work-ing-class people's lives:

> to enable men to judge correctly of the real causes of misery and distress
> so prevalent ... to consider what remedies will prove most effectual in
> removing the causes of those evils so that the moral and political
> influence of the people may be united for the purpose of supporting such
> measures as are really calculated to improve their condition (Poor
> Man's Guardian, no. 38, 3 March 1832).

Such knowledge connects the cultural with the scientific, with the practical, makes no crude vocational and non-vocational distinctions and depends for its curriculum of the concerns and interests of those for whom education cannot be the luxury of leisure or progression, but must help to make sense of intolerable circumstances with a view to their chal-lenge.

Fairly Useful Knowledge

The concept of 'really useful knowledge' underpinned many radical adult educational initiatives in the 1970s and 1980s. However, recent pressures have forced much radical education down the safer path of what might be termed 'fairly useful knowledge'. The abolition of the GLC and Metropolitan Counties, the drastic reductions in local authority budgets forcing staffing and grant allocation cuts, the abolition of the Manpower Services Commission, have contributed to the demise of many community and education projects.

The opening up of Access courses against a background of a tempo-rary demographic dip in the numbers of 18-year-olds and the serious skill shortages of an uncompetitive economy, was hailed as a progressive move by many college lecturers, which acknowledged the educability of working-class people and the wastage of talent in an education system designed for failure.

However, both due to its own liberal–individualist logic and the tight control of accrediting bodies and higher education, curriculum ar-eas served progression routes rather than student concerns. They rarely addressed 'our present troubles' (Johnson, 1979).

Other more adventurous and radical adult education initiatives be-came steered into the service of Access with a language of credits, trans-fers and passports. Protesters were meant to be silenced with the jibe that having qualifications of their own, how could they object to other people gaining them? More pressing concerns lie with doubts about the real value of small pieces of credit, and with the accompanying bureaucratic entanglements which limit tutor capacity to negotiate and respond to stu-dent interest. Worse was to come with a major paradigm shift from a dominant liberal education approach to that of the market, affecting the whole Access movement and adult education more widely. The language of production, ironically in an increasingly de-industrialised economy, has become predominant to the extent that a refusal to use it becomes an act of resistance. Unit cost, productivity, turnover, corporations, customers, outcomes, throughput with its concomitant 'bums on seats' becomes what it is all about. The sceptics and heretics are being replaced with the enthusiastic educators who would be as happy running Sainsbury's, and in a sense they are. (It is perhaps a sign of the times that an annual award set up by the National Extension College to mark achievement in innovative programmes in adult education went in 1994 to Sainsbury's plc.)

At the same time problems affecting adult's lives are becoming more pressing. Mass unemployment has left three million people out of work according to the official figures, four million by 1979 accounting, and many more who do not qualify to sign on yet consider themselves 'actively seeking work' (see Unemployment Unit working brief). Between June 1978 and June 1993, 2.9 million full-time jobs disappeared with 1.4 million part-time jobs developing in the same time, an overall loss of 2.2 million Jobs (Hughes, 1994). Poverty too has increased, as is borne out by research by the Institute of Fiscal Studies which claims that: 'The growth in equality in the 1980s dwarfed the fluctuations in inequality seen in the previous two decades ...' (Goodman and Webb, 1994).

The income share of the poorest tenth of the population fell from 4.2% of national income in 1991, while the share of the top 10% climbed from 22% to 25%. The context of this has been the uncompetitiveness of the British economy within an increasingly global environment. Economic responses have encouraged deregulation, casualisation and a low wages economy. Such widening disparities have led commentators of different complexions to talk of a growing underclass of people who are outside the productive process and with the addition of cuts in services are excluded from participation in social, cultural and political activity, made worse in a context of the official sanctioning of individualism and an increasing reliance on the family, or more accurately women, in social policy.

Accounts of the underclass often include single parents and older people who rely on state benefits for their support (Field, 1991). While the value of this idea in sociological terms, rather than in terms of its ability to label and stigmatise, is doubtful, it is the case that important demographic changes are taking place, with more adults in the population in, often enforced, retirement, increasingly a euphemism for unemployment, and changes affecting the family, most notably the growth of one-parent-headed households. Given the way income is acquired, and the relationship between income and a gender division of labour, these changes intertwine with increasing poverty levels and a growing poverty trap, especially for women.

The state in all of this is playing both a 'hands off' economic role, emphasising deregulation and challenging combination, and increasing central control over services while pushing parts of the state beyond democratic accountability. The declining economy is blamed on a failure of morality caused by the laxness of teachers and parents and the creation of a dependency culture, whilst the 'poor law' is tightened most punitively.

It cannot be emphasised too plainly that it is these changes and oc-
currences that are affecting the adults that Russell labels as 'disadvantaged', which Access courses in many regions have been trying to recruit,
and on whom Adult Basic Education targets its work.

Yet at the same time, the language of credits and transfers and progression has eclipsed a content and purpose more relevant to the 'whole
person' which liberal adult education claims to address.

Education and Reaction

The economic upheavals and the lively political responses of the 1970s
and 1980s bear some relation to the early nineteenth century. Both periods experienced a period of reaction which then as now drove adult education into more conventional and safer channels. Political reaction does
not, of course, provide the best environment in which radical education
can flourish. Johnson is right to point out that: 'It may be that radical
education always depends, minimally, on widespread political excitement and especially the expectation of mayor social change and the existence of educational resources including time free from necessary labour'
(Johnson, *op. cit.*)

Free time people may have, but it is called and is usually felt as unemployment or some other form of exclusion. There is little political excitement, rather a sense of powerlessness in the face of inimicable forces.
Education cannot substitute itself for these things, but it may be one
arena in which people can regain a sense of community, of collective interests, of identity and a capacity for personal and collective development and change. It can also tap into what is undoubtedly a groundswell
of political discontent and bring together different views on directions
for social policy and political change. In doing so it can also challenge the
debilitating message that lack of work, poverty, and educational failure
is an individual problem and caused by moral deficiency.

The Ruskin Learning Project is underpinned by these views and operates around several principles. The issue of educability is one that has
never been in doubt at Ruskin, with its history of labour movement and
community involvement. We believe too, in tandem with the wider college, that the notion of 'levels' popular today with Open Colleges is a
misrepresentation of how adults learn. It isn't necessary to be grammati-
cally correct or competent at spelling, or even to be literate, in order to
discuss important issues affecting people's lives. And it is the desire to
have an impact on shaping the debate that encourages the development
of communication skills.

Central to our project is the idea of 'explaining the present troubles
and how to get out of them'. This includes a dialectic between students
grappling with making sense of their own experience and aspirations in a
communal and discussional environment which offers a chance to analyse and also to consider and shape alternatives. In this process barriers
between education and training are broken down. Knowledge is understood as a process of critical engagement with official definitions or academic research measured up against individual and collective experience

and research activity. Equipping people for further study as an important part of our task, but this is entwined with our broader approach. An emphasis on 'culture' is also an important dimension of our work. It is 'ordinary' in both the sense of being about where we come from, who we are, what we want to be. It is also about a direct involvement in shaping and changing meanings, which in the process challenges, demystifies and also shapes a critical appreciation of various forms of cultural productions:

> We use the word culture in these two senses: to mean a whole way of life – the common meanings; to mean arts and learning – the special processes of discovery and creative effort. Some writers reserve the word for one or other of these senses; I insist on both and on the significance of their conjunction. The questions I ask about our culture are questions about our general and common purposes, yet also questions about deep personal meanings. Culture is ordinary; in every society and in every mind (Raymond Williams, in McIlroy and Westwood, 1993: 90).

Above all we aim to make education an exciting and enjoyable individual and community experience, in which no one can fail and which makes people feel that they can continue to develop and contribute for the rest of their lives and which helps to ensure that people feel their own strength.

There is nothing especially unusual about students joining the Ruskin Learning Project, except perhaps the desire for education and the nerve to enter an educational establishment. Most today are unemployed or on other forms of benefit, a few have intermittent or part-time work. Most have few qualifications or little training, and employment has been in semi-skilled and unskilled occupations. A third have no qualifications at all. We attract more women than men, though at around 40%, such levels of male involvement represent a major change. A high proportion of women are lone parents or divorced. We encourage older participants and members of ethnic minorities with both special and integrated provision. We try to remove barriers by charging no fees, offering travel and carer expenses and including people on courses as quickly as possible, often the same day. Around 200 pass through our courses each year and some remain to organise or participate in further activities.

Students joining the Ruskin Learning Project are offered a wide-ranging choice of courses or programmes from which they can join several within a year. We aim to provide a challenging and supported educational environment for as long as is appropriate to each individual. Given the problems that many face, the flexibility to drop out and return is vital.

Students can choose from a number of short part-time courses. These change or are extended in response to demand and where funding permits. They all focus on making sense of the 'present troubles' and approach an understanding from different perspectives whilst offering a diversity of views and experiences. They take an international perspective as well as a local one and seek to make connections between the two.

An emphasis is on informed debate and discussion, with a concern about how situations might be challenged and changed.

Recently we have been offering the following courses: Understanding Economic Issues; British History; Exploring Society; A Social Issues course; Literature and Society; Changing Women's Lives and Issues in Social Work; Literature and Creative Writing; Black Women's History; Maths.

The curriculum in each case involves active negotiation with participants, for instance women attending the 'Changing Women's Lives' course, which runs throughout the year, shape the following term's course content, which remains flexible. This kind of negotiation has so far produced an interdisciplinary course which includes skills such as public speaking, library use and presentational work, an exploration of issues affecting women locally and internationally using various approaches and resources including literature and which draws considerably on students' own very varied experiences. The involvement of women from a range of backgrounds – recently West Indian, Afro-Caribbean, Chinese, Japanese, Iranian – has made for particularly rich experience. In common with the other courses, collective learning, co-operation and the sharing of ideas and experiences is emphasised. Co-operation exists with the full-time Women's Diploma course, with speakers moving in each direction and joint activities such as planning for an International Women's Day event. An emphasis on, participants representing their own topics and undertaking project work helps develop skills of both a political and academic nature. Exploring Society offers another chance for students to explore issues that are of importance to them. Within a curriculum that helps to make sense of some key political theories and concepts, and focuses attention around class, 'race' and gender, topics for study are negotiated and student input encouraged both through participative teaching methods and more substantial involvements. Subjects for discussion include health and welfare, development issues, politics and power and environmental matters.

One student records:

> *Through the various courses which have been immensely enjoyable, I feel I am far more aware of the environment I live in and why it is like it is, how it got to that stage and where it is likely to lead. I am more critical when I read and listen, especially to politicians. I understand the structure of government and indeed society a whole lot more. The courses to me have been enlightening, touching major and smaller issues, eye-opening lessons on what goes on behind the scenes leaving you feeling you've had a small taste and want to learn some more! I am a 28-year-old single parent working recently as a mental nurse, but hoping to study to become a social worker.*

Teachers and Learners

Having the right sort of tutors to work in this way is very important. Qualities required are a commitment to this particular educational approach, a good knowledge of and an excitement about a subject area and a willingness to develop it responsively, a flexible attitude to student needs and a capacity to draw the best out of each person while also working to promote community and a collective culture. What is also required is the capacity for constructive self-criticism and an ability to work in dialogue with student demands and responses.

Recent developments in open learning initiatives, along with the underlying philosophy of learner-centred education, have sought to reduce teaching to box ticking or assignment marking. In tandem with government attacks on professionals, these seemingly progressive ideas of learner autonomy, riding on the back of critical deconstructions of experts and expertise, have in our view done much adult education a great disservice and have led to the more rapid casualisation of an already casualised area of education. It is an irony that students who would gain most value from teaching and tuition are those most often exhorted towards self-help and self-directed learning. It is hard to imagine such an eventuality within the University Colleges of Oxford!

While recognising the value of tutor expertise, the challenging of the special status of 'tutor' is, however, important to the work we do. Part-time and full-time Ruskin students are encouraged, with some training, to run seminars and teaching sessions. One full-time student has recently planned a programme with a group of Afro-Caribbean women to extend her Diploma project exploring Black Women and Racism. The aim is to produce a collective publication with contributions from all members of the group.

This approach is most visible in a second chance course that is taught each year by Ruskin College Diploma students. During a short training course anything from a dozen to 20 full-time Ruskin students prepare an eight-week part-time course for Ruskin Learning Project students. They identify their own aims, course content and means of delivery, divide tasks and work in small teams to prepare sessions. Many of these full-time students have had only two terms' more education than the part-time students and it is this and the strong sense of shared background experiences which makes the course uniquely successful. As one RLP student says:

> *They understand well our problems and are helpful. They understood our feelings and our hesitation. It's a more relaxed atmosphere, less of a teacher–pupil feeling. They all gave us something different and they looked like they were enjoying it (quoted from an evaluation of a course taught by full-time Ruskin students in the summer term 1994).*

As well as rapport, a real exchange is involved in this situation. The Ruskin students gained from the RLP students and there was an atmosphere of collective endeavour:

> *I gained the enjoyment of putting teaching sessions together with fellow students and presenting the session as a team. our own experience as students of Ruskin College would not have been unlike the experience*

encountered by the RLP students – one of oppression, fear of the unknown, taking that all important first step (quoted from an evaluation of a course taught by full-time Ruskin students in the summer term 1994).

The course has the double effect of both breaking teacher–student barriers, while simultaneously raising the profile of teaching adults as being a skilled and complex task. We see no contradiction in this, especially when those skills can be opened up and developed by students within an adult education project.

Changing Directions

In addition to courses we run more substantial programmes of activity. One of these is aimed at unemployed people and is called 'Changing Directions'. This programme was established in response to the Cowley closures and the rapid rise in unemployment in Oxford since 1989. The car factories in Cowley employed 23,000 in the early 1970s and today employ only 5000. The knock-on effects of this, with the drying up of alternative forms of employment have been considerable. The aims of the course are to understand and to collectively challenge unemployment. This involves several aspects. A central task of the course is to make sense of what is going on in the economic and political sphere in Britain and further afield that explains growing unemployment and changing labour markets. This is in part to challenge a sense that many bring with them that being unemployed in a personal failing. It is also to explore the implications of such changes in relation to wider definitions of citizenship (Hughes and Schofield, 1994).

While space is made for individual learning on the course, collective activities are central. In May 1993, the group organised a conference entitled 'Unemployment: Education and training for what?' (Changing Directions Group, 1993). From total silence and a sense of panic when the idea was first mooted, the group moved to booking speakers, organising invitations and publicity, devising workshops, giving presentations and writing a conference report identifying what unemployed people want in terms of education and training. Sixty people attended, including members of the TEC, Social Services, Workers' Educational Association, Community Education, Claimants' Union and many unemployed.

One student describes it:

Somehow I managed to arrive at Ruskin one hour earlier than usual. Today is a very important day as my group are putting on a conference. I have been asked to speak on the stage about my experiences on the Changing Directions course. It is a very difficult thing for me to do, but I feel that I must try and give something back to the course from which I have received so much. So I speak, but not for long as Fiona has so much to say in her presentation. I am very nervous and feel the words come disjointedly out of my mouth. The course has given me the interest and confidence to attend night school and study for some qualifications. After lunch we have some Workshops and I am again in the hot seat, busy being a facilitator. The day has all gone very smoothly and quickly and everyone seems to have enjoyed the experience. I personally have and I feel a great sense of achievement (Changing Directions Group, 1993).

Half of the group are currently learning video-making skills and are making a film about unemployment. In support of this the whole group are producing a publication entitled 'The Experience of Unemployment', to which all are contributing. A conference is also planned on 'The Future of Work'.

In addition to these activities, the group participates in communications classes which culminate in individual presentations and project work. They are also involved in a cultural programme including visits, literature, poetry and drama. The importance of cultural activity is summed up by one student:

We were asked about Dylan Thomas when we applied to the TEC for funding. The chap there though we should be spending each week writing CVs and learning how to fill in application forms! Why? What's the point? There are 19 people chasing every single job in Oxford. We do realise that having a good CV is important, but for our own self-respect and self-help we need drama and discussion, poetry and literature to learn about ourselves, about what we can offer society and about the best way forward (Changing Directions Group, 1993).

Several participants have begun to write poetry, and poetry reading has been incorporated into 'Creative Writing Socials' to which all College members are invited. This has proved a supportive forum for people who have never before read their material and has encouraged wider writing. These activities have generated *Ruskin Writing*, a twice-yearly creative writing magazine aimed at encouraging self-expression across the college community.

The Age Well Initiative

Another programme organised by the Project is the Age Well initiative, which has grown in a context of increasing numbers of people aged 60 or over, joined by increasing numbers forced into early retirement. It grew directly out of the wish of numbers of older people attending RLP courses to establish educational activities which were not necessarily about progression, which could integrate education into a more creative construction of retirement and which could connect with other activities, which challenged ageism, campaigned against poverty in old age and advocated the importance of education for older adults, for whom 'tea and bingo' tended to be the most stimulating offer.

An Age Well Group with minimal tutor support collectively organises weekly discussions for over 20 people each time, around a range of issues and interests, political and cultural, and with presentations from group members. Several participants run an arts group on a different day, and courses in literature and poetry are particularly popular. The Group has also involved itself in running several citywide Age Well Conferences with the Oxford City Council, helped form a Liaison Committee with members of the Pensioners' Action Group, trade union pensioner groups, Social Services, U3A and others to run activities, and members participate in the Pensioners' Forum which advises city councillors.

On the educational front it has launched an educational project based in a community centre in response to members of a pensioners' club complaining about the limits of tea and bingo (Hughes, 1992). A small grant from Charity Projects allowed us to run a course for people in their seventies and eighties whose distinguishing feature was that none has had any educational experiences since leaving school. The results were produced as a study pack (Ruskin College/Oxford City Council, 1992).

With the increasing numbers of people in the 'third age' wanting to remain or become active in the community, however conceived, education can be an important means of opening new doors, creating social spaces and intertwining with political activities and campaigns. A report of a group of 20 older people holding a discussion in Adult Learners' Week 1993 about older learners' needs concluded:

> We specifically need courses that help us to understand changing issues and provisions around pensions, community care, Social Services, Health. This is so we can make sense of what is going on and more readily have a voice in shaping and responding to change. We also need provision in the areas of culture and creativity. Too often, older people as well as younger feel alienated from rich cultural and artistic heritages. We want education that supports and encourage self-help but does not use them as a substitute for provision (Ruskin Age Well Group, 1993).

The Age Well Group has also been holding discussions with the Unemployed Groups in the college revealing interesting similarities in experiences and responses, including a shared sense of marginalisation, of talent and potential being wasted and the importance of education in both understanding and challenging this. Society tends to keep groups separate by age and experiences. Bringing people together can strengthen a sense of diverse but also shared experience and solidarity which is potentially challenging and creative.

Workplace Initiative

The same points about wasted potential and marginalisation can be made about unskilled people in the workplace. Arguments about the need to skill the workforce are today commonplace. In an institute of Public Policy Research pamphlet David Miliband points out:

> In higher paid and higher skilled jobs, education and (re)training are taken more seriously than at lower levels.

The *Training In Britain* survey found that out of the 15% of the working population who have A-level qualifications or better, 52% reported training in the previous three years. Among those without qualifications only 16% said they had received training in the previous three years (Miliband, 1990). Miliband goes on to argue that 'the immediate economic consequence of our failure adequately to train our workforce can be seen in the results of comparative industrial performance'. These arguments are clearly important in terms of equity and in terms of terms of challenging a view from within government that we can compete economically on the basis of a low-paid, low-skilled workforce.

Organisations like Workbase and ALBSU have made inroads into literacy and numeracy deficiencies amongst workers in the workplace and design programmes in conjunction with management, tailored to meet their needs. Like them we also consider that more training, and of high quality, needs to be concentrated on those people who have had least. We consider in addition that an educational content is very important, because it provides the context in which training can be made sense of, and makes training more transferable and therefore useful to the trained. It also increases worker autonomy and this is one of the tensions that managements face. A flexible, skilled, educated workforce has higher expectations of job satisfaction and democracy in the workplace.

However, in terms of 'getting out of our present troubles' we take the view that simply improving literacy levels does little to improve the position of low-paid workers; furthermore, in the way that it is approached, the process is management-centred. Workplace learning must create a better understanding of how the workplace operates so that workers can make a greater impact through unions and other organisations in shaping the way work develops in the future. The Workers' Control movement argues that workers know the workplace in many ways better than management and know what changes to make to improve efficiency (Coates, 1968). Lack of democracy and lack of education in the workplace is inefficient (Glyn and Miliband, 1994).

This approach connects too with issues of equal opportunities. Workplace learning should increase the confidence of workers in their educability and capacity to perform tasks and manage situations. The need for this is particularly strong amongst women and certain ethnic minority groups. The confidence to progress individually can combine with a greater voice in shaping and changing workplace practices and cultures.

Our workplace course was run in conjunction with Oxford City Council and Oxfordshire County Council and was aimed at manual and clerical workers operating on a Paid Educational Leave basis. Its content consisted of discussion of workplace issues such as compulsory competitive tendering, equal opportunities, low pay, quality services. (This course was jointly run with Marjorie Mayo of the Community Education Training and Research Unit of Ruskin College and benefited greatly from her close links with the Take Ten PEL course of Sheffield City Council.) Speakers from the trade unions, personnel department and Council talked about the organisation from different perspectives and how workers could make a greater individual and collective impact on its structures and processes. Skills were developed around individual and group projects and computing and numeracy were included. Guidance was given on applying for promotion and further education and training. The effects of the courses have been to encourage most towards further education and training or promotion.

They have also increased an understanding of the different parts of a large and complex workplace, of important current issues and the possibilities of being effective in making changes.

Conclusions

Ruskin College, along with all other educational sectors, is facing difficult times. The pressures of the Further Educational Funding Council to increase turnover and throughput and reduce unit costs, militates against the more radical and critical aspects of our work.

On the Ruskin Learning Project, the pressures to accredit courses to secure FEFC funding and anxieties about County Council funding withdrawal mean that the environment is one of insecurity and uncertainty. Again, this can operate to encourage uniformity and conformity and to inhibit more radical initiatives.

This, ironically, is occurring at a time when there has rarely been such a need for creative adult education which can help to challenge the serious problems we face, most particularly in terms of poverty, inequality and citizenship, in the context of declining industrial competitiveness, mass unemployment and an increasing number of adults outside the work process.

What working-class adults are being offered may include more opportunity than in the past, though this is questionable. The forms of that opportunity are, however, being strictly controlled and connected to narrow forms of outcome and progression. Fairly useful knowledge in modularised and accredited forms for easy delivery ensures more 'bums on seats' and the survival of providers.

Critical adult education, with its emphasis on the connections between education, democracy and change, with its concern for 'really useful knowledge', has always been a minority tradition. But this is the tradition that does consider the 'whole person' and refuses to split personal growth from changing social arrangements so that all can share in as well as contribute to the common good, that does address 'the real causes of misery and distress' (Cobbett), that challenges those 'who profit by our bondage' (Poor Man's Guardian, 25 September 1834). It is only this tradition that can begin to raise important questions about dealing with unemployment, technological change and new work patterns, that can explore ways of challenging the rise in violence, crime and racism, that can expose the environmental ravages of unaccountable economic systems and the devastation wrought by unequal trading relations and structural adjustment programmes.

In the present climate of reaction, with its attempts to reconstruct a political culture around individualism and self-help, it is perhaps more vital than ever to do our utmost to keep radical adult education alive, to live within the cracks in the system, to challenge the 'new realism' at every opportunity and be part of the process of a regeneration of socialist ideas and practices which will surely come.

References

Changing Directions Group (1993) *Unemployment: Education and retraining for what? Conference report,* Ruskin College.

Coates, Ken (1968) *Can the Workers Run Industry?,* Sphere.

Cobbett, William (1830) *Rural Rides.*

Field, Frank (1991) *Losing Out: The emergence of Britain's underclass,* Basil Blackwell.

Glyn, Andrew and Miliband, David (eds) (1994) *Paying for Inequality: The economic cost of social injustice,* Rivers Oram Press.

Goodman, Alissa and Webb, Steven (1994) *For Richer, For Poorer,* Institute of Fiscal Studies.

Hughes, Katherine (1992) 'Opening doors for older learners', *Adults Learning,* vol. 4, no.4.

Hughes, Katherine and Mayo, Marjorie (1991) 'Opening up personal development: a workplace learning initiative', *Adults Learning,* vol. 3, no. 4.

Hughes, Katherine and Schofield, Ann (1994) 'What has Dylan Thomas got to do with getting people back to work?', *Adults Learning,* vol. 5, no. 5.

Hughes, John (1994) 'How deregulation kills jobs', *European Labour Forum,* no. 12.

Johnson, Richard (1979) '"Really useful knowledge": radical education and working class culture', in Clarke, J., Critcher, C. and Johnson, R. (eds) *Working Class Culture,* Hutchinson.

McIlroy, John and Westwood, Sallie (eds) (1993) *Border Country: Raymond Williams in adult education,* NIACE.

Miliband, David (1990) *Learning By Right. An entitlement to paid education and training,* Institute for Public Policy Research.

Ruskin Age Well Group (1993) *The Educational Needs of Older People. A Report based on discussions held with twenty older people,* Ruskin Learning Project, Ruskin College.

Ruskin College (1992) *CNAA Institutional Self-Evaluation as an Associated Institution.*

Ruskin College/Oxford City Council (1992) *It's Never Too Late To Learn: A study pack for older learners,* Ruskin College.

Nine

All Equal Now?

Rebecca O'Rourke

In this chapter I want to record and reflect upon some of my concerns about the changing context for radical adult education. This won't take the form of a closely-documented account of practice and provision in general, nor am I offering a programme of policy changes. I'm simply inviting you into in my head in an attempt to see if we're having the same conversation and whether and how we can move on from talk to action. My starting point is the contradictory response I've had to the recent changes in the way adult continuing education is organised and funded. Part of me feels vindicated by the moves to draw our work closer into the mainstream work of higher education institutions, but I feel more strongly that these changes will limit an important aspect of adult education work, namely its capacity not only to acknowledge but also to intervene in areas of social and educational inequality.

Although adult continuing education has a significant relationship with mainstream university work, especially through Access and second chance education, they are not co-terminus. Neither the work nor the students will benefit from being restricted to this definition of the relationship. It is particularly worrying that funding follows certain types of work and not others, especially as the squeeze seems to be on work just below formal Access level. This represents a powerful threat to the vital latitude of informality which adult continuing and community education previously had and will undoubtedly affect the numbers and type of students returning to study. Many students who successfully return to formal, accredited education begin their journey back unaware of where they are heading. The danger inherent in the new world of access and opportunity is that it will only work for people who are actively seeking access and opportunity. And, of course, it implies – against the cumulative experience of post-war adult education – that the only valid form of learning to return to is that which models the undergraduate degree.

When educational disadvantage is compounded by other material differences – of gender, ethnicity, poverty, class, disability and sexuality – the effect is often a denial of imagined possibility. Too often education has already written these people off, and they internalise a belief that education is not for the likes of them. This makes it near impossible for them to fulfil the imperative behind the newly constituted 'accessible' institutions of further and higher education. Taking advantage of such opportunities requires students to know their educational goals in advance. Many adults return to education unaware of the full range open to them.

The planned expansion and diversification of higher education will, I believe, result in many adults being lost to education altogether, or having a partial experience of it. I have interviewed many women seeking to become students on Fresh Start or New Opportunities Courses. The commonest ambition which women voice is to do office work. There is nothing wrong with office work, but I know from experience that many of the women who say this do so because it is a respectable ambition. Only by doing the course do they realise what they might be capable of. I don't worry that working-class people, and women especially, will be prevented from returning to learning but rather that the education they return to will offer them a more limited range of options than it has it done during the last decade.

Historically, adult education has been far more engaged with issues of social difference and their consequences for learning and knowledge than higher education. This is partly because the origins of adult education lie in a reaction against a social system that retained educational opportunity for a small elite. Initially a means to provide education for the working man, adult education later became a productive, protected space for the development of women's education – in both its radical and conservative forms – and more recently it has been an important site to develop and sustain work by and for those members of society with special interests and needs, whether they be black and ethnic minority groups, lesbians and gay men, people with learning difficulties or people with physical or sensory disabilities. The common ground between these diverse groups has been, in the context of adult education, an insistence on the social rather than individual nature of experience, and a privileging of experiential over, or at least alongside, other more abstract forms of learning.

The flexibility needed to work in this way, from the needs and interests of the student group rather than to a set of external guidelines, is incompatible with the demands of mainstreaming and accreditation. And it isn't just a question of wanting to preserve a space where, for example, a women's history group or a creative writing group can continue to evolve and direct their own programme of study, important though this is. The totalitarianism of recent changes also has implications for the curriculum, suggesting a narrowing down to instrumental influences through the new partnerships of industry and commerce which makes difficult the kind of curriculum development which adult education has exercised over mainstream academic subjects as diverse as local history, archaeology, cultural studies and women's studies.

Spurious Egalitarianism and Dealing with Diversity

This issue is at the heart of my anxieties. The new definition of higher education as an arena of opportunity risks recasting educational disadvantage as dispossession. If the opportunities are there for all, then we no longer need special provision. The people who aren't there are simply exercising their choice and if they're so churlish as to refuse offers of self-improvement through education and training, why then, they certainly don't deserve any special help. And who needs special help, anyway? We're all equal now, we can all go to college or university if we want to. They say.

The financial and policy implications of the recent changes are disturbing for those sectors of education, such as community or liberal adult education, which are most vulnerable to the charge that they are really social or leisure activities, not proper education at all. They are also likely to be the courses which attract a greater proportion of people who have experienced educational or social disadvantage. In my own institution, important areas of work like New Opportunities for Women and informal, pre-Access courses are starting to look very vulnerable. Within the further education sector, there is a similar pressure on non-vocational and non-accredited work (Kilminster, 1994).

Even if students do get through to higher education, there is no reason to think that higher education will adapt to meet their specific needs and interests. Implicit in mainstreaming is the idea that adult continuing education will adapt to, and conform with, higher education. Of the many issues this raises, I want to focus on the worry that significant achievements in dealing with difference made by adult education will be rolled over as institutions of higher education struggle to homogenise their students. Diversity now plays a significant role in marketing further and higher education: out go images of healthy, fun-loving young people and in come those of older people, some with black faces, some of them women with children. But just how valued are these new constituencies? Perhaps the appeal to diversity is simply a response to demographic change and the falling number of 18-year-olds available for entry into full-time higher education? Certainly the new discourse of diversity currently espoused by higher education is characterised by the assumption that extending diversity threatens academic standards.

A recent staff development response to the change, from a leading centre in this field, illustrates some of the conflicts. It offered a training conference on *Coping with Student Diversity*. Coping with? Immediately a framework is set up of diversity as a problem, a deficiency which must be compensated for. The traditionally elitist nature of British higher education has, they argue, both minimised the problems of diversity and provided a mechanism for coping, through the informality and flexibility of the tutorial system. Increased numbers put pressure on the system at both ends and, they suggest: 'drop-out and failure rates will climb and approach those in countries which already have a diverse student body' (course publicity, Oxford Centre for Staff Development).

Let's unpack that a little. Diversity becomes equated with a tendency to fail and to drop out. And, as our funding is now driven by success in attracting and retaining subsequently successful students, we get jumpy about drop-out and failure rates. But is it true, and what does it mean if it is? Is it really the case that entry in the late teens is the most appropriate and successful means to take advantage of higher education? Are students with diverse experiences innately less able or less motivated than those with homogeneous, normative experiences? It has never been my experience that they are. It has, though, been my experience that the lack of neutrality attached to difference can either fuel ambition and high achievement in, variously, women, working-class and black students or it can destroy them. And sometimes it does both.

As a child from a working-class home I learnt very early how difference makes a difference – to your own expectation of yourself and to others' expectations of you. And these expectations are both psychological and material. We don't have the level playing field of equal opportunity that is cited as an argument against preferential or separate treatment – some of us don't even get onto the playing field. We're in the clubhouse making tea and sandwiches or we are on the other side of the boundary wall, unaware there is a game to be played at all or we're trying to join in with only a partial grasp of the rules.

Mainstreaming university-based adult education could offer an unprecedented opportunity to extend the good practice in equal opportunities developed in adult education into the heart of higher education. If it stands a chance of doing this it needs to retain both its own commitment to this valuable work and its connections with the community and basic skills sectors. Unfortunately, the terms on which the re-organisation is taking places puts both of these imperatives under strain. Training budgets are eaten up with training for accreditation, rather than awareness or curriculum development issues, and our ability to run courses focused around special needs and interests is limited by funding restrictions.

If we lose sight of difference as a site of conflict and social determination we are left with difference as a purely personal or individual concern. This would be entirely in keeping with the individualistic push behind new initiatives in Access identified by Stephen Yeo in the 1991 Mansbridge Lecture (Yeo, 1991).

It would mean that our shiny new Opportunity Universities – and adult education's shiny new pathways into and through them – can continue to fail whole sections of our neighbourhoods and our communities because they didn't make the grade, weren't up to the breaks offered them. The difference between difference and diversity will involve us in conflict over norms and the struggle to shift them, just as radical, socially purposive adult education has always known it would. The old question, Access to what?, is as pertinent now as it ever has been.

Increasingly it feels as if the imperative to deal with difference within educational practice somehow belongs to a privileged, and past, conjuncture. For some, that might be the 70s, when change seemed possible – tangible even – and adult education assumed a powerful, purposeful role in effecting such transitions. For others, it might be the initiatives around unemployment in the mid-80s, and the powerful solidarity – in struggle and defeat – generated by the miners' strike. For myself, it's the Inner London Education Authority, where I worked first as a community education worker in the Centerprise project and then as a return to learning tutor and women's education worker with Hackney and Camden adult education institutes between 1982 and 1992.

The fairy tale feel of this – it was all a long, long time ago and in a different place – is partly a result of ILEA's abolition and my own double move from Hackney to Middlesbrough and adult education institute to university department of adult continuing education. The abolition of ILEA, just like the break-up of the Greater London Council before it, simultaneously demonstrated the importance of the ideas and practices it promoted and their powerlessness. The break-up of ILEA dissolved the infrastructure and networks which play such a key role in sustaining and developing the challenging thinking and practical alliances necessary for radical education to effectively engage with differences of race, gender, disability and sexuality.

It is easy to become sentimental. No one, I think, would argue that ILEA had solved its problems. I certainly can recall many instances of resistance and failure alongside the exhilaration. And class, which ILEA never got to grips with, is deliberately omitted from the above list. But what ILEA did do was to provide space and motivation to begin tackling difference. It established the idea that difference mattered, in the classroom and at a policy level.

I now work in a place which is a long, long way from ILEA's influences on policy and practice. As if I live in a time-warp where none of the issues that were so urgent and engaging for the last decade of my life have ever been raised. The town I live in and the university I work for give a kind of attention to social difference and its implications for social justice that seems cursory to me. Training in equal opportunities for recruitment from the university, for example, but not awareness training which focuses on working practices, values and attitudes. Limited provision, from the local state and the voluntary sector, of, for example, designated activities and spaces for women, lesbians and gay men or ethnic minority communities. It's the same old times, with their heterosexist assumptions, white faces and gendered lines of power. And underpinning this stasis is a process Jean Milloy and I described thus:

> Power operates to subdue difference by ignoring it. We know from our analysis of sexism that ignoring what is 'different' is a highly effective means of silencing it; by pretending, consciously or otherwise, that the different does not exist, we quickly create conditions in which it actually ceases to exist, or is so repressed as to be invisible (Milloy and O'Rourke, 1991: 61).

One effect of this is a sense of I have sometimes, from myself as well as from others, that identity politics, dealing with difference – call it what you will – is something of an indulgence. A luxury we cannot afford in the harsh, real times in which we now live and work. Clearly, in the cultural milieu of inner-city Hackney differences were both more visible and more militantly pursued as issues than they are in Cleveland. But in Cleveland, as elsewhere outside the metropolitan centres, these issues have purchase. Their very absence demands a particular attention, beginning with the asking of simple questions about exclusions which may well have complex answers.

Undoubtedly, the times are hard. But it is naive and ahistorical to think that our differences can be simply set aside or, as the university likes to think, only affect whether we come into the place, not what we do when we get here. It is precisely in periods of retrenchment that structured inequalities gain most purchase. And consequently why a radical response often takes the form of promoting alliances against what are seen as forms of separatism. I have no argument with this, other than to assert the right of minorities to determine their own priorities, which may well embrace acts of exclusion as well as inclusion. I also believe that alliances must be conscious of, and accommodating towards, the full range of experience. It is too easy for one oppressed group to secure its position at the expense of another, as has sometimes been the case, for example in the arguments within women's studies about sexuality, or the complexities of ethnicity and class. Difference is at its most divisive when attempts are made to deny it.

Historically, uneven attention has always been paid to difference in adult education, which reflects the varying emphases – and political analyses – in the history of those institutions. Looking back through reports from adult education classes organised jointly by the University of Leeds and the Workers' Educational Association in West Yorkshire in the 1940s and 1950s, for example, we see that although women make up just over 50% of the student body they do not exert influence commensurate with their numbers. The reports also contain a discourse about worthwhile and legitimate adult education students. Women are here conceived of as undermining adult education's legitimate student body, working-class men engaged in heavy manual work, although these represent just about one-third of all adult education students at that time. Most tutors in the post-war period, it seems, barely tolerate their women students. Women tutors are extremely rare and there are none on the full-time academic staff of either side of the partnership until the late 1960s (Gardiner and O'Rourke, 1995).

A recent study of creative writing provision reveals that although women are even more numerically dominant, at over 80% of the student body, the activity could not be said to be women-centred (O'Rourke, 1994). In fact, it was striking that on several occasions during research visits I observed male members of writing groups talking amongst themselves while women's work was being read out and discussed. Unevenness, then, is not simply a question of history. Equality has not, despite what you hear from some of the more affronted PC watchers, marched in a steady, progressive direction. The university tradition of liberal adult education has always attended to issues of class more readily than it has to those of gender or ethnicity, whereas the voluntary sector, especially where concerned with adult basic education, has tended to be more sensitive to issues of ethnicity and disability. Although gender has been attended to in both contexts, it has often come into conflict with other forms of belonging and these balances have been delicate to hold and to work with. The greater concentration in ABE of students with disabilities or from particular ethnic minority groups, especially travellers and people of Afro-Caribbean descent, reflects both this sector's willingness to accommodate their needs and interests and the systematic failing of these groups by mainstream schooling.

Most ABE tutoring is done by young, white, middle-class women. Often they work as volunteers, sometimes they progress from volunteering to hourly paid, part-time work. Usually they have young children. They are divided from their students by more than their ability to read and write. The students are, on most indices, not only different from, but subordinate to them: significantly older or younger, poorer and often, in the big cities, of Afro-Caribbean descent. Hackney, where I worked in ABE for several years, had an ABE student population that was never less than 80% black. At the time I worked there it employed a number of black tutors and volunteers, but this had only come about because of an earlier initiative to actively recruit and train them. Recruitment, of students and staff, is a cornerstone of equal opportunities work but the further away one travels from ABE, the more likely it is that recruitment accounts for both the beginning and the end of equal opportunities.

Aspects of my work which were taken for granted, integral aspects of being an adult education worker in literacy or return to learning work, have begun to feel almost strange to me in the university context. They are no longer required from me. There is a greater acceptance than I have been used to of provision that reaches some, rather than all, of the community. From about 1987 onwards, every part-time tutoring post I applied for in London required me to address the range of equal opportunities issues across the spectrum of my work and each interview included a micro-teaching element which assessed both teaching skills and how thoroughly I had addressed those issues.

In fact, it is false to make that separation: good teaching was synonymous with understanding and being able to work positively with the full range of social disadvantage and oppression. And it was not an abstract requirement either. In order to work well with my colleagues and my students – who were dazzling in the differences they inhabited – I had to learn about them and their cultures, just as they had to learn about me. The learning took a variety of forms and was motivated by different purposes. Much of it was supported by specialised work, either directly, in the form of awareness training, resource and curriculum development projects, or indirectly, through the circulation of guidelines, policy discussion papers and teaching materials.

I am amazed at how little opportunity there is to pursue this kind of work in the new contexts in which I work. Without such work, it is difficult to guarantee genuine access to people from minority or disadvantaged cultures. It isn't a case of saying: you can come in here – although for many disabled people this apparently simple statement has still to be struggled for – it is a way of ensuring that the place you come to recognises and welcomes you. So, policies about racist behaviour or sexual harassment or the provision of creches or interpreters are all ways to make buildings, courses and institutions genuinely accessible to the full range of potential users.

Also, importantly, attention to equal opportunities addresses the power imbalances that weight difference towards and away from the mainstream. It is an attempt to balance the responsibility for dealing with difference between those who experience it as privilege as well as disad-

vantage. Difference is weighted in ways which make it more or less difficult for certain people to participate or to achieve within education, and
can be extremely isolating. Such differences need acknowledging and,
where possible, valuing positively. It is in this way that equality issues
extend beyond the question of access into questions to do with the nature
and quality of the educational experience on offer.

And how do we do that? It is partly a question of attitude, a self-re-
flexiveness about the assumptions made or condoned in the class-
room/staff room. So, for example, when I taught history and literature to
a return to learning class of 20 women, all of whom were working class,
10 Afro-Caribbean, four Irish, four white, one French and one Bangladeshi, the issue was not just whose history and whose literature I
taught, but how much responsibility I took – and encouraged the class to
take – for the other dynamics and tensions that were always in the room
with us.

Some of the worst fears people have about this kind of attention to
difference might surface in relation to this class (which is a real example)
if I started to talk about the hostility towards the Bangladeshi student.
No one would sit next to her, they said she smelt. Or the impatience with
the white woman whose fear of writing was so extreme that she broke
down in floods of tears whenever she was asked to write anything. Or
the bitter running arguments between the black women, who were divided by different moral and religious values. Or the unease felt towards
the two lesbian mothers, one white and one black, which they experienced as threatening. Or the regular round of dealing with whichever
group felt abandoned or badly done by, convinced that a sub-group of
the class got special treatment because they were: white, Irish, black, lesbians. Dealing with these conflicts, de-personalising them, challenging
them, learning from them all took time and energy.

Isn't this the perfect example of students and tutors avoiding ever
doing any real intellectual, educative work? What's the point of whip-
ping up conflict between students? Meddling with education's clarity
and objectivity, muddying it up with messy emotions and subjectivity.
Isn't this just what you feared would happen with women in charge?
And was it really what they – and I – were there for?

When I first began to teach such culturally and racially mixed
women's return to learning classes, I would have said no, that the students were there to get back into the swing of learning, develop their
skills and explore their choices. I would have said that they needed to
understand what had happened to their first chances in order to make
the best of their second chances, but I would have seen that as introductory, ground-clearing work.

Gradually I came to see that those experiences were not so easily set
aside. They continued to exert an influence, usually a negative and sometimes a destructive one, and they recurred. In order for those women to
progress they needed to understand and deal with the determinants of
their experience. They had to do this in order to be able to set it aside and
get on with learning. And they needed a space clear from the pressures
of racism, sexism or homophobia not just to do that work, but also to al-

low them space for other, more academic learning. The big ism's are personally, as well as socially, destructive and if they thrive unchallenged in the classroom, or the staffroom, they will continue to wreak havoc.

Dealing with difference can never be a one-off, or preliminary affair, as I had thought it could – and as people new to these ideas, and these students, will continue to think. Recently, Jean Gardiner and I presented a paper to a conference of university adult educators which asked the question: What difference does difference make? One member of our audience at least was unshaken in his belief that we were talking about remedial work and if students couldn't set aside their experience of difference then they had no place in the university. But such differences are never entirely set aside by the desire to be simply a student, simply studying maths or history or literature. Femaleness, sexuality, class or racial belonging won't wait patiently outside the door.

And if this was true for a class which met two or three times a week for a year, then did it not also go on being true as those students (as they all did) journeyed on through the education system? Academic freedom guards its privilege jealously, and who isn't bothered by the thought of censorship constraining freedom? But we have to ask whether this freedom is not, like some other freedoms, bought for one set of people at the expense of another? Such a consideration is also not restricted to the intellectual life of the university, it also, perhaps more so than adult education, has implications for the pastoral role in regard to students.

Linked, too, to this question of the need to keep dealing with difference, is the need to guard against the pressure to move on from, or beyond, work with certain interest groups. There is a kind of fashionability about certain sorts of progressive work: where trade unions and the working class gave way to women, who gave way to the unemployed, who gave way to black and ethnic groups, who gave way to the disabled and so on. The point is that we will need to be attending to all these interest groups, sometimes within the same group or individual: that famous disabled black lesbian mother, who may be a joke to some of you, but real enough to the woman herself. We need to continue engaging with difference as long as difference engages with us and our students.

New Opportunities or Fresh Start for Women courses seem at the moment very vulnerable to this trend. You pick up a kind of 'been there, done that' feel about them. This sometimes comes from the tutors, who are inevitably women employed on part-time contracts and are conscious of the ironies of sustaining other women's advancement from their own casualised and limited employment. But it is commoner from organisers and administrators, anxious to move on and do something exciting and innovative, who resent the extra classroom the creche takes up or the noise of 30-odd women and their children. The gloss has worn off, the challenge has gone. Sometimes, too, we get embroiled in destructive hierarchies of oppression: a NOW course is valued solely for its appeal to black women, for example, or developmental money follows new constituencies.

For the women organising the courses, however, the challenges are all too depressingly familiar.

I'm always surprised when the local paper makes an issue of the course being women only. They can't understand that in a mixed group men will control the terms of the discussion ... A lot of women who come to NOW are surprised and apprehensive to find it is a women only course. It's the stereotyped feminist thing they're reacting against. They think they'll have to change who they are (conversation with Gail Heneragan, Course Director, New Opportunities for Women, Middlesbrough, 1993).

Talking to women tutoring a range of adult education subjects – from psychology to archaeology, to literature and history – it becomes clear that the balance of power within the classrooms is still held by men, unless or until a tutor actively creates checks and balances. Men generally have a confidence in their right to time, space and attention that few women in mixed or single sex groups do, but in a single sex group they get a chance to practice and develop that self-possession.

The Changing Value of Education

My generation was probably the last to believe in the great post-war ideal that education made everything and anything possible. I am quite sure that my own commitment to adult education stems in part from realising that the educational opportunities I had could quite easily have been withheld from me had I been born 20 years sooner or later. Education changed my life, and I believed it could do the same for others. I have seen it do the same for others. This makes it hard to stomach the way the quality of the educational experience is being systematically devalued at exactly the point when it comes within the reach of more people than ever before, and furious when they are blamed for declining standards.

This change, or decline, has three components to it. They concern the links between education and employment, the quality of the learning experience and the nature of the curriculum.

Education and training genuinely used to improve job prospects, nowadays it's more likely to be something you do instead of a job. The drive to match education and training to the needs of industry is a double deception: the economy isn't damaged by degrees in the humanities and won't be saved by MBAs but the drive to pretend it will limits many students' choice of study on the spurious grounds that it will help them find employment.

Whether you look in the school classroom, at adult education or in the institutions of higher education themselves you'll find people with the best will in the world losing the fight with an under-resourced, over-bureaucratised system that seems more concerned with speeding up the throughput of students than in giving them an opportunity for growth and development. Collect credits, not experience or knowledge. Ironically, as Stephen Yeo comments, the thinking behind some of the newer, competence-based forms of accreditation seems to be to avoid the educational process altogether (Yeo, 1991).

Even where a commitment to traditional forms of learning exists, the overcrowding and lack of resourcing makes a mockery of them and the enthusiasm with which newer, student-centred forms of teaching and learning are being embraced is too often because they are cheaper and diffuse the problem of crowded tutorials and seminars. The pressures are not confined to students alone, tutors also struggle with large numbers, increased regulation and the pressure to do research. This weakens their ability and willingness to engage pro-actively with difference, whether at the pastoral, policy or curriculum level.

This reflects the extent to which change has been exploited as a form of social control in contemporary British life. Every adult education institution I have worked in – and I dare say most of those that I haven't – displays a copy of Caius Petronius' comment on reorganisation: 'A wonderful method for creating the illusion of progress while producing confusion, inefficiency and demoralisation.' This emphasis on change produces two quite distinct reactions. Some people, as a result of being pushed too hard and too often for no good reason, are unable to see change as at all positive. Others, perhaps embracing the enterprise in higher education philosophy, can only conceptualise change as something they do to others. Each reaction is bad news for those of us committed to working with difference – a process that sets out to encourage change in attitude, behaviour and values. It is also, I believe, bad news for both adult education and the academy.

Adult education has a long tradition of doing valuable curriculum development for the academy and as the two move closer together it is imperative to retain and extend its challenge to the construction of intellectual frameworks and academic knowledge. The universities subscribe to the highly ideological view that knowledge is impartial, that there exists such a thing as academic objectivity which is gender, race and class blind. Blind it may be, but to the ways in which knowledge is constructed, not given, and to the recognition that knowledge construction is and always has been a site of struggle and conflict. The most cursory history of ideas puts to rest the notion of objective truth. Flat earth? Social Darwinism? Zimbabwe built by a lost white tribe? Accepting bias in the selection and theorisation of knowledge gives work on difference an active and constructive role, as well as providing fuel for critiques and challenges to the existing frameworks, whether we see them as Eurocentric, patriarchal, heterosexist or bourgeois. This is partly a question of empirical choices – the including in of women's, black or working-class experience, for example – but it is also conceptual and theoretical: changing the questions we ask of disciplines and their constitutive theories and evidence. The differences have to make a difference.

Socially excluded or disadvantaged groups – women, the working class and black people – have struggled in and over education in a variety of ways. Initially for the right to attend, study and receive awards. Remember, it is less than a hundred years since women could be awarded degrees, less than 50 since it became realistically possible for working-class people to go to university. More latterly, the struggle has been for their substantive academic experience to include and value their personal experience, to generate knowledge which makes sense of and in their lives, rather than demanding they set that experience aside as the price of admission. Radical adult education used to be able to provide the tools, motivation and support for such enquiries, making it possible for some adult returners to take a different set of educational values and frameworks into the academy with them so that the academy itself became aware of an alternative body of research and practice alongside its own.

In promoting and providing wider access to the particular privileges and opportunities that universities can provide it may look as though the radical mission has been achieved. But the critique of education out of which this radical mission came recognised that the absences of inequality are structured absences, speaking about and for the excluded. If wider access involves renouncing the very processes and practices which could interrogate and rearticulate those absences *with the people who experience them*, thereby transforming the nature and culture of the academy, then we will have achieved very little. As adult continuing education meets the mainstream we must try to ensure that we meet on terms which recognise and value our areas of expertise. These include the capacity to work positively with difference, as indicated here, but it may well be another area of adult continuing education's expertise that balances the relationship to the mainstream in such a way as to ensure the continued commitment to that aspect of our work. This is its expertise in the teaching and learning process itself and is reflected in classroom practice, in its long-standing involvement with training issues and in research.

Ironically, the point of intersection of these concerns is the enterprise in higher education initiatives. The struggle to do 'more with less', as the Committee of Vice-Chancellors and Principals styled it (CVCP, 1992), and to do it with and for more students, offers adult education practitioners the possibility of intervention and influence. Higher education, as a consequence of its recruitment and organisational changes, is changing the way it organises teaching, learning and assessment. Placing ourselves in the eye of the storm in this way could offer a degree of stability, but more importantly it guarantees a stake in deciding on and implementing assessment. Assessment will be one of the most powerful determiners of whether or not the student constituency of adult continuing education moves into the mainstream. So far the arguments about assessment in adult continuing education have been stuck at the should we/must we level. We have lost that argument and must now try to win the argument about better and worse forms of assessment. Innovation must come in this area, which poses a challenge to practitioners of adult continuing education to ensure that better forms, rooted in the formative, learning-centred approaches developed through our past practices, prevail.

References

Committee of Vice-Chancellors and Principals (1992) *How to do More with Less*, Circular N92/13, CVCP.

Gardiner, J. and O'Rourke, R. (1995) 'A safe and welcoming place?', *Adults Learning*, vol. 6, no. 5.

Kilminster, S. (1994) 'Changing working-class women's education: shifting ideologies', in *Reflecting on Changing Practices, Contexts and Identities*, papers from the 24th annual SCUTREA conference, SCUTREA.

Milloy, J. and O'Rourke, R. (1991) *The Woman Reader*, Routledge.

O'Rourke, R. (1994) *Written on the Margins: Adult education and creative writing in Cleveland*, Department of Adult Continuing Education, University of Leeds.

Yeo, S. (1991) *Access: What and whither, when and how?*, Department of Adult Continuing Education, University of Leeds.

Ten

Feminism and Women's Education

Jane Thompson

The contribution made by feminism and the women's movement to adult and continuing education has been of tremendous importance in the recognition and creation of what counts as 'really useful knowledge'. Not simply in the recent past, in relation to second wave feminism, but also in relation to the educational imperatives of the Suffragettes and Suffragists, the Co-operative Women's Guilds and the early struggles to establish women's trade unions (Thompson, 1983).

In the late 1960s and early 70s the re-emergence of feminism in Britain was encouraged by the general impetus towards critical consciousness and political resistance associated with the spirit of the new left, civil rights and anti-imperialism. From its beginnings, in the West at least, in consciousness-raising groups and in vociferous political campaigns around equal pay and employment opportunities, contraception and abortion, childcare, sexuality, and in opposition to violence against women, the re-emerging women's movement was always closely associated with self education and re-education.

It soon became clear to those of us involved, as if blinkers had been taken from our eyes, that prevailing orthodoxy and dominant ideas about women were not natural, or inevitable, or objective. They were socially reproduced. Even the political gurus of the left, the creators of 'big ideas' like Marx and Lenin and Trotsky, to whom we initially turned for explanations of our social and economic conditions, had developed their theories in circumstances which were seriously flawed by an intrinsic blindness. Received notions of power, oppression, class, freedom of choice and the significance of experience were largely unexamined in terms of gender or ethnicity. We discovered with astonishment, and then with increasing clarity, that what counted as knowledge, truth and freedom was built upon a mix of ideology and historical selection, in patriarchal circumstances, based on partial information. Women were 'hidden from history' (Rowbotham, 1973), lost within assumptions that either subsumed women's existence within generalisations about the 'human' condition of 'men' in society, or ignored us completely (Spender, 1982).

According to Simone de Beauvoir, women existed as 'the other', locked into Enlightenment notions of men's control over culture and women's constraint by nature. Not only different in kind, because of temperament and constitution , but also, in comparison to the 'stronger' sex, deficient, inferior and less significant. With man as norm, women were frequently found wanting, and expected to fulfil a very different kind of destiny.

The women's movement rapidly outgrew the unreconstructed explanations of the Left, and starting from the basis of personal experience, began to reconstitute new understandings and theories about class, gender, 'race', and sexuality. In the process the very nature of politics and knowledge became transformed. Social and personal relations became identified with political activity, in which the domestic and the personal, as well as the structural, became recognised as significant sites of struggle. Sexual politics, as well as socialist politics, became subject to examination and negotiation, in ways that initiated the collapse of simplistic polarities and unqualified economic determinism.

It was not surprising that those of us who were also students and teachers and writers, as well as women with awakening consciousness about our position, carried the impetus and impatience of feminism into our work and into education.

Throughout the 70s and 80s the growing influence and persistence of feminism was an important irritant and source of agitation. Adult education provided an obvious focus. Although organised and controlled by men, the majority of students were women (Thompson, 1983). The majority of part-time teachers and community education workers, and full-time tutors and organisers in junior positions, were women. The curriculum, although pervasively malestream within the WEA and extramural traditions, relied on received notions of female 'relevance' and 'interest' when it came to local authority and community education classes. Nell Keddie (1980) pointed to the domesticating and conformist nature of the knowledge offered to women in leisure related and liberal education classes provided by the LEAs. In *Learning Liberation* (Thompson, 1983) I drew attention to the concentration on knowledge and assumptions aimed at women which were concerned to adapt us to the logic and requirements of the prevailing system, rather than to assist us in the process of liberation. This recognition, informed by feminism, helped to review the relationship between adult education and 'really useful knowledge'.

The dominant 'liberal tradition' in adult education, associated closely with ideas of 'learning for pleasure' and 'learning for its own sake', was always concerned with 'individual' outcomes and 'personal' growth in the context of predominantly middle-class assumptions and value systems. The voices of working-class, women-centred and black consciousness were largely missing from the record.

The 'radical tradition' (Johnson, 1979), born out of the concern to overcome the oppressions which locked people into ignorance, poverty and powerlessness, provided an alternative analysis and opportunity. Knowledge that was 'really useful', we believed, would raise awareness; provide ways of analysing and understanding how oppressions were structured and sustained; and would lead to educational and social action for change that was informed by theories derived from collective experience. It became imperative to ensure that this tradition did justice to the political and educational concerns of women and minority groups, as well as those men at 'the cutting edge' of the class struggle.

Feminism demanded the same relationship to knowledge. One which would not simply be about 'personal fulfilment' but about validating women's experience and challenging the imposition of ideas and conditions which worked to oppress women as a group.

Demands for a new kind of 'relevance' was related to the process of 'consciousness-raising' and 'changing lives' in a political way, and was also strongly expressed in relation to radical ideas about social class, sexuality, popular activism, adult literacy, black identity and community education.

Out of our criticisms and our reconnections with earlier and more radical roots came a growing dissatisfaction with the prevailing middle-class, gendered and liberal culture of the mainstream.

Feminist commitment helped to establish what became quite widespread alternatives. For example, New Opportunities for Women courses, Second Chance, Fresh Start, Women's Studies Programmes, Training in Non-Traditional Skills, and Women's Science and New Technology initiatives. The WEA, particularly, pioneered a variety of women's political, cultural and trade union courses, as well as assertiveness and self-defence courses and women's studies groups. Women's branches were established, a flourishing women's newsletter was produced and a women's organiser was appointed to a senior position at national office that made the women's studies programme something of a jewel in the WEA crown by the middle 80s.

Encouraged by the radical wing of the Inner London Education Authority (ILEA) and the Greater London Council (GLC), local authority provision in the capital made equal opportunities a seminal priority. Pioneering work in adult literacy and community education highlighted the need to recognise and respond to class, cultural, ethnic and gender diversity when providing education aimed at the least powerful and most discounted groups within society (O'Rourke, 1995). Both curriculum development and teaching-learning methods underwent a sustained process of transformation, based on the commitment to student-centred learning, conscientisation (Illich, 1973), and anti-discriminatory practices. In the process feminist ideas and values played an important role. Our own experience in consciousness-raising and study groups, tied to our distrust of patriarchal knowledge, institutionalised authority and leadership, led to the conviction that democratic and collaborative learning relationships were more likely to enhance the self-esteem and confidence of women than traditional, didactic and tutor-dominated methodologies. The influence of feminism usually guaranteed a commitment to equal opportunities and anti-discriminatory practices in general, encouraging levels of awareness and responsiveness which were not nearly so common in mainstream provision.

Some have chosen, in this respect, to pay tribute to the inspiration of Illich and Friere (1972), both of whom were sufficiently removed from the more immediate British context and experience to be considered theoretically and practically interesting. But in terms of women's studies and women's education, we were already building up our own ideas and ways of working, based on the importance attributed to personal knowledge by the women's liberation movement, the commitment to collectivism, the deconstruction of traditional forms of authority and wisdom, and the linking of our developing theories to transforming practice and social change.

In university provision the more enlightened adult education departments all established their 'popular liberation fronts' by the early 80s – some with more conviction than others. At Southampton, for example, the women's education programme grew out of the department's community education programme in the late 70s, in circumstances of initial tolerance but increasing alarm. The contemporary politics and traditional roots which those of us involved used as our inspiration were the notions of women's autonomy and working-class independence. In creating the Women's Education Centre in Southampton in 1981, used mostly by working-class women and run on the basis of decision-making, participation and control by its members, we weathered an increasingly hostile political decade, during which time the attention of the university became more punitive as we became less dutiful, and as the effects of Thatcherism and New Right thinking became increasingly destructive.

After countless attempts to 'supervise' the politics of the curriculum, 'inspect' the collaborative relationships between the students and the tutors, 'raise' the fees, 'cut' the childcare, 'change' the collective organisation to an externally recruited management structure, matters came to a head in 1986. Attempts by the university to withdraw all funding from the creche, sack part-time tutors and require women on benefits to pay course fees provoked a lively press campaign and vociferous demonstration in support of the Centre's work, which involved former members and sympathetic adult educators nationally, as well as current members of the Centre and their children. The effect of the demonstration and press campaign was to shame the university into making concessions. Of course the authorities blamed the government. But whilst the former freedoms of the universities, the WEA and the LEAs were being systematically reduced, and, like other public services, becoming customised and accustomed to the requirements of the market, we continued to sustain our autonomous position for a further five difficult and defiant years (Taking Liberties Collective, 1989).

Meanwhile, a more acceptable variety of women's education was gaining ground within the academy, which should not be underestimated. A continuing legacy of second wave feminism has been the development of academic women's studies programmes, which are now established in almost every British university, at both undergraduate and postgraduate levels. It is unlikely that this creation of a new academic specialism would have occurred so quickly and so strongly without the impetus of feminism or the experience provided by developments rooted in adult and community initiatives.

In many ways it has been Access courses which have become the beneficiaries of women's education programmes in the 70s and 80s. No one is any longer in any doubt that considerable numbers of women, presented with the chance of returning to education, will grasp the opportunity with considerable enthusiasm. The rhetoric of Access is still more persuasive than the reality, however, when the costs and consequences of education are measured against the need to earn a living, the regulations surrounding benefits, the dearth and cost of childcare support and the total lack of government commitment to providing realistic grants. Yet women have increasingly become the 'targets' in new and expanding education 'markets'. The attempts which many of us made, and the classes which we pioneered in the 80s, in order to make 'really useful knowledge' accessible to 'disadvantaged' groups, especially working-class and black women, have now become an industry. In the process, however, Access has become a fairly middle-class affair. No self-respecting FE college is without its Access provision, comprised not exclusively, but predominantly, of lower-middle-class women. No self-seeking university is without its franchise deals and credit transfer schemes, aimed at maximising its quota of 'non-traditional' students within the overall constraints imposed on student numbers. In the process, of course, something of the politics and the passion has been lost. What counts as the culture and the curriculum of Access, what informs the logic of accreditation, what gets assumed in the promotion of APEL (Fraser, 1995), for example, owes less to the arguments about cultural politics and critical intelligence, feminism and empowerment, than to the need to generate 'customers' in line with the ideological and political consequences of applying performance indicators and free market economics to the practices of education.

Viewed from the changing political circumstances of the middle 90s, at which point the party political tide is clearly turning, and the present Conservative government looks much less omnipotent – even to its own supporters – than at any other time in the last 15 years, it is salutary to consider what we have won and lost, and what we must now do to advance the political and learning interests of women in adult and continuing education.

1979 was the year in which Gloria Gaynor provided the still quite youthful, born again and politically unsophisticated women's movement with one of its contemporary anthems – 'I Will Survive'. It was also the year which saw the inauguration of Margaret Thatcher as Britain's first woman Prime Minister. Those who had their wits about them could see that this was no ordinary chop-and-change of government. I can remember being at a meeting about funding for a women's education project, in a room rented from the Labour Party, at which a woman stood up and spoke passionately and eloquently about the severity of the impending backlash. We listened, mesmerised by the conviction and implications of her warnings. But we thought that she exaggerated. Like almost every other 'innocent abroad' we were unprepared for the degree, the disdain, the daring and the destruction which was to accompany the relentless resurgence of the 'radical' right.

As the 80s progressed, the women who signed up for a Second Chance in education, a Fresh Start, or a New Opportunity, got both 'richer' and poorer. Women from those cultural and social groups which were already well-represented in adult education provision began to take advantage of Access and women-centred courses which were much more relevant and responsive to the concerns of women seeking education as distinct from transitory diversions and trivial pursuits. When fees were required, they paid them.

At the Women's Education Centre in Southampton we continued to give priority to working-class and unwaged women and to keep the costs of coming to an absolute minimum. Those who joined our classes did so with greater difficulty, in spite of mounting obstacles, in relation to growing desperation and with dwindling expectations, as the decade wore on. The numbers of women living in poverty, on their own with children, under the scrutiny of the state, and in a climate of reaction to the ideas and concerns of feminism increased in direct relation to monetarist economic policies, cuts in benefits and public services, the buoyancy of right wing ideology and increasing levels of unemployment.

As the political issues for working-class, unwaged and black women became increasingly determined by the feminisation and racialisation of poverty, the restructuring of the economy, and the restructuring of the welfare state, the response of adult education displayed a growing tension between its own struggle to survive government cuts and reorganisation, and feminist attempts to hang on to scarce resources for women's education.

Faced with education institutions reneging on their previous commitments to community education and to the poor, equal opportunities initiatives became as out of date as popular democracy in Quangoland. In this respect, some feminists, like many erstwhile social and cultural workers, became advocates and exponents of the 'new realism' and took the line of least resistance.

One of the problems with the liberal and middle-class domination of the early women's movement, as many black and lesbian and working-class women had already begun to point out, was the confusion in loyalties caused by professional status and some residual allegiance to the rules and regulations of the men in mainstream organisations. Such was the hostility displayed towards 'extremism', the ridicule attached to left wing 'lunacy', and the irrelevance attributed to feminism – provoked by the New Right, cultivated by the media, and largely undefended by the liberal left – that many wavered and collapsed against the strain.

But it would be unfair of me to blame feminism for failing to defend women's education from the material and ideological assault of 'radical' right thinking and policy requirements – policies which also made virtual mincemeat of local government democracy, trade union rights, the health and welfare services and the pursuit of critical intelligence as distinct from training. Feminism, it was said, was no longer necessary, now that the only deterrent to women's equal opportunities was our own inertia. Tokenism in high places, supported by competitive individualism and libertarian propaganda, welcomed in the 'post-feminist' age. Part of the logic of New Right strategies was to co-opt, neutralise and discredit potential sources of opposition, like feminism, and to wipe from the collective consciousness the memory of subversive movements which might give a voice to resistance and provide real evidence of alternative ideas and ways of operating.

Within universities the preoccupations of many academics became distracted by the passing intellectual fashion called postmodernism, which in turn became entrenched in some women's studies courses (Jackson, 1992). The reclassification of women's studies into gender studies began, and the debates became increasingly obscure, fragmented and particular. Courses were increasingly put together by those who had no roots in the resurgence of feminism, no experience of front-line feminist politics, no interest, as far as one could tell, in praxis. The intellectual sophistication of feminist-derived theories soon placed them above reproach in the male academy, however, measured by the proliferation of publications, the erudition of their scholarship, and the growing numbers of students choosing to study them. It was not long before men also joined the queue to teach about women and gender in relation, for example, to masculinity, identity and sexuality. It looked as though 'feminist knowledge' had at last arrived.

Increasingly, however, the arguments of postmodernism were used to make intellectual sense of the alleged fragmentation of the Western women's movement, just at the moment when issues to do with class, ethnicity, social difference and sexuality were being most fiercely contested. Except that the obscurity of the endeavour frequently appeared more alienating and immaterial to women's lives than the ill-formulated but well-intentioned essentialism it sought to displace.

The arrival of women's studies and gender studies in universities and colleges has been, of course, an achievement to be relished. It is no longer so possible for patriarchal institutions to retain their distinct privileges and powerful influence over the intellectual reproduction of malestream ideas once women have begun to occupy positions of leadership and initiative. But the battles are far from over.

Whilst Audre Lorde (1981) was warning of the dangers of incorporation (in the original, political sense of the term), insisting that 'the master's tools will never dismantle the master's house', others of a radical persuasion also disputed the effectiveness of strategies based on becoming 'dutiful daughters' (Rich, 1980) and seeking recognition by demonstrations of relentless reasonableness and moderation in the face of continuing sexism, or by lending credibility to tokenism (Taking Liberties Collective, 1989).

The promotion of selected women in systems sustained by men revealed that recognition often had its price. The price was gratitude, loyalty and obligation. Too often they provided the examples set to others, the role models, the evidence of opportunity that closed the doors on more serious or fundamental challenge. Too often those who 'made it' lent credibility to an otherwise continuing concentration of white male control. But in 1994, 10 years after 'power dressing' had become an art form practised by new style femocrats, and 'Women into Management' courses had become an outpost of the enterprise culture, the numbers of women in key management positions in industry had again begun to fall, and the women who had broken through the academic glass ceiling, in ways that have helped to transform the patriarchal nature, culture and control of education, remained few and far between.

And none of which has done very much to advance the interests of the majority of women in society, whose material circumstances and access to equal opportunities actually deteriorated as the Thatcher years ground on.

In these circumstances, the attachment to postmodernist approaches among some academic feminists has done little to assist in the struggles that have preoccupied the vast majority of women. A well-known convert to the new orthodoxy has been Michele Barrett, former Marxist feminist, now writing books with Anne Philips like *Destabilizing Theory: Contemporary feminist debates*, which turns out not to be about a range of feminisms, as one might expect, but which is exclusively about postmodernism. According to Stevi Jackson (1992) 'the points of reference for most postmodernist feminists are not other feminists, but theorists such as Lacan, Derrida and Foucault'. It is not simply that 'these are men', and therefore 'to be avoided', but that they are men who speak from a position which is not sympathetic to feminism. Their influence may have helped to provide some temporary kudos to women disciples in the male-dominated academy, but their influence has played into the hands of those who are pleased to see women's studies de-radicalised, who find the study of gender less challenging, and who have no particular interest in women's liberation. The concerns of postmodernism – to do with linguistics, culture and identity – are far from accessible to the general feminist reader. And in their most extreme expression come with a denial of any form of material reality.

The function of the feminist curriculum in education should not have been to obscure, to mystify and to restrict entry into its insights. Otherwise it becomes a self-indulgent, inward-looking, elite activity that acts to exclude others, rather than enable them to learn. The feminist curriculum, as it relates to the concerns of women in the workplace, in low-paid employment and the home, must be grounded in the experiences, the victories, the problems and the aspirations of women surviving in these situations. All of which are immensely serious material realities. Grounded in such a way as to make connections with the lives of other women, to make political sense of everyday experience, to develop understandings that enhance consciousness and which lead to political and social action for change. Given the discrepancies of wealth and power between North and South, the growth of fundamentalism, the re-emergence of nationalism and the fairly basic inequalities between men and women revealed daily in the reconstitution of Eastern Central Europe, it is imperative to do this in a context which transcends ethnocentric and particularist dimensions. Not in the postmodern sense of neo-pluralism but in recognition of complexity and difference as well as commonality.

In these circumstances women's education is most useful when it is concerned not with postmodernism but with 'really useful knowledge'. The kind of knowledge that supports women, in the company of others, in the business of transforming our lives. The kind of knowledge that shifts the emphasis from victims to survivors. From customers to activists. From impotence to creative anger. From those who desist to those who resist. The kind of knowledge that assists women in various and real sites of struggle, including those which are personal and private, to confront the everyday experiences of inequality and power relations which help sustain the logic and the authority of the *status quo*. In other words, to help women bring about change, in historical circumstances which may not be conducive, but in ways that are a matter of survival.

In declaring the death of 'big ideas' and of historical and structural explanations of social inequality and power, postmodernism has, in my view, gone too far. Certainly it was appropriate to recognise the politics of difference and diversity, and to underline the many ways in which global theories of social progress and social change are flawed by simplification, inconsistencies and contradictions. These are, after all, the same theories that second-wave feminists had already begun to challenge in terms of their silences and misrepresentations about women.

But in providing the philosophy to explain the end of totalitarian categories, in favour of more local narratives and multifarious identities, and helping to legitimise emerging ideologies associated with free choice, free market economics and free enterprise, writers like Lyotard (1984) and Vattimo (1988) in seeking to challenge much of what was previously 'taken for granted' have, in the process, acted as a mirror image of the wider political and economic movement to the right.

The intellectual enthusiasm for postmodernism among some academic feminists needs to be properly understood. At worst it has become a revitalised agenda in favour of relativism and pluralism. A collapse into individualistic reductionism that could destroy the possibility of collective action and suppress political will. In which the concept of power, influenced by the ideas of Foucault, has been displaced into the spaces between minimal encounters, and the disparate exchanges and negotiations of everyday life. At best it simply confirms what feminists have always said about the personal nature of the political, in which large issues both grow out of and get reproduced in small ways, in the day-to-day negotiation of relationships based on unequal amounts of power. But to invert the telescope, as postmodernism then chooses to do, to consider the particular in the foreground, without registering the collective, material, deep-seated impact of the structures in the background, is to ignore the strength and influences of forces that help to shape the conditions in which the particular happens. The refusal to consider 'big' questions on the grounds that 'global categories are inaccurate', and 'there is no such thing as certainty or truth' is, of course, politically convenient for those who benefit from power on a big scale. If discrepancies based on 'race', wealth, power and gender can no longer be addressed, how can there be any effective challenge to social, sexual and economic systems that distribute their rewards and penalties unequally? It is clearly premature to speak about the death of grand narratives in relation to the significance of capitalism and patriarchy, for example, when both sources of power so obviously continue to be reproduced and reconstituted.

When earlier feminists talked of patriarchy, it might have seemed like the kind of ahistorical, culturally specific, grandiose concept that distorted the significance of other oppressions, such as racism and imperialism, in ways that made resistance or change seem impossible. But these were grounds for refining and developing our theories, and using words more carefully. Not for defining out and distracting attention away from the nature and predominance of male power.

Put plainly, the issue is a question of political significance. Does the shift from structural, economic, patriarchal and political explanations of women's subordination, towards subjective, cultural and linguistic preoccupations with the character, style, and meaning of identity, for example, advance or paralyse the possibility of women's independence? I suspect the former seems too big to contemplate, the latter seems too small to matter. In practice we cannot afford to abandon either. Systems of oppression, like experience, require both deconstruction and reconstruction in the interests of our liberation.

The amelioration and transformation of women's material circumstances requires political consciousness, political resistance and political action. It also requires courage. The somewhat philosophical and linguistic preoccupation of postmodernism has helped to divert some varieties of academic feminism away from being a subversive social movement, aligned to the women's liberation movement, and engaged in direct action, in favour of a cerebral, inward-looking, elite activity that denies the possibility of widespread transformation brought about by committed social and political action for change. In such circumstances it is vital to hold onto the lessons that earlier feminist ideas have taught us, in order to continue to relate political consciousness and understanding to the lived experiences of the vast majority of women. Women who, in different cultures and different circumstances, still have to make sense of the world from positions of low pay, no pay, racism and poverty. Women whose capacity for survival, and whose potential for resistance, is not in question but who can be assisted by the ideas and information that rescue women's lives from oblivion, that make connections between women, in ways that 'name the enemy' and 'shift the blame' from themselves and each other, onto forces much more powerful than the pathology of individuals.

Teaching women's studies at Ruskin, as I now do, underlines all the problems associated with building and sustaining a vision of alternative practice in the current educational and political climate.

Ostensibly Ruskin has much to recommend it. It has a history closely associated, in the literature of adult education at least, with the radical tradition, reflecting across the years the tension between education as a tool of liberation and an instrument of social control. But its commitment to working-class constituencies, to socialism and the labour movement, and in turn to women, has always been contradictory. In 1909 the Plebs Strike drew attention to Ruskin's ambiguous position in relation to 'really useful knowledge' and to Oxford University. The Plebs League was a socialist fraternity, which although inspired by Marxist politics, was itself quite authoritarian (Brown, 1980) and sexist. In February 1970 the first National Women's Liberation Conference chose Ruskin as its venue but feminism didn't enter the college curriculum until over 20 years later.

In 1976 the college provided the speaking opportunity for James Callaghan, the then Labour Prime Minister, to lay the groundwork for subsequent Conservative education policies, concerned to narrow the curriculum, and direct the attention of education towards the needs of industry.

Like the best and worst of those in the organised labour movement, it has taken Ruskin as long as any on the left to come to terms with the contradictions of the old left and those who are the 'postmodernisers' and to acknowledge the different concerns of women and black people in narrow definitions of the class struggle.

In such circumstances, the prospect of students learning about feminism, a curriculum which recognises both structural oppression and cultural diversity, which prioritises women's experiences of the world, and insists upon confronting prejudice and developing anti-discriminatory practices, all provide real challenges to closed minds and vested academic interests – even in a college like Ruskin. It also challenges the workerist mentality and crude patriarchal priorities of some of its more traditional students. Issues to do with unreconstructed masculinity and sexual harassment are probably no more endemic at Ruskin than other organisations in which men and women work together, but the increasing presence of women's studies students and the declared intention to 'shift the culture' of the college as well as the curriculum, means that life in a residential community is far from being a simply academic affair.

At the same time, the ongoing pressure from the government, fronted by the Further Education Funding Council, remains determined to draw the residential adult colleges into the same market-driven, cost-cutting, commercialised system of provision, in which others in adult and continuing education have already been forced to operate. It is not, as has been argued elsewhere in this collection, a system which encourages critical thinking or cultural resistance. Quite the reverse.

Dogged by the Old Left and bullied by the New Right, it is still not an easy time to be speaking of feminist knowledge, or holding onto learning principles about asking questions as distinct from collecting credits. At a recent conference organised by NIACE on 'Quality Assurance in Education', Terry Melia of the FEFC boasted about his ability to 'grade everything that moves on a five-point scale'. And as Cilla Ross (1995) argues elsewhere in this collection, part of the consequence of modularisation, accreditation and quality control has been the simplification and the acceleration of the time set aside for critical thinking. With adult students who have missed out on previous educational success, this represents yet another deprivation. GNVQs in further education have already made a mission out of multiple choice answers that can be reduced to ticks on sheets, which can then be marked by a machine. In adult and continuing education, increasing variations on meaningless qualifications proliferate, like so much confetti, whilst no one has required Oxbridge to modularise, accelerate or standardise its courses.

In this kind of climate, it is as important as it ever was in women's education to make the subject matter of what is learned relate to the cultural, material and political condition of women's lives. And to the expectation of our liberation (Thompson, 1983). Otherwise we collude in re-ducing women's experiences to silence or absence in the guise of brevity. We collude in keeping women in their place, attuned to the logic of an unequal and oppressive society.

In the development of the women's studies programme at Ruskin we are using the history and intensity of the recent past, and what has hap-pened to women, as the starting point from which to rebuild the road to feminism. It means repeating and relearning many of the lessons we thought we'd learned already. It means making sure that women, many of whom don't remember much about life before Thatcher, know that they come from other, deeper roots, with traditions that are based on re-silience and courage; and from generations of women who have experi-enced victories and triumphs, as well as defeats. It means learning not simply academic knowledge, devoid of political significance and pur-pose, but seeing knowledge as a tool which can be used to raise aware-ness and provoke resistance. It means un-learning the rules of competitive individualism prescribed by the proponents of the New Right in favour of collective learning and collaboration. It means not al-ways looking for a leader but becoming oneself an activist, who knows that it takes trouble and it takes courage to be free. It means, as it always did, seeking the connections between the things we know from within ourselves; how these relate to the experiences of others; building theories to understand the world more clearly as a consequence; and finding the courage to make the difference.

In this way the feminist curriculum, when it is focused with preci-sion, understanding and illumination, can assist in the process of con-sciousness-raising and social transformation; which remains, and continues to be, the first line of defence against the persistence of inequal-ity and oppression.

References

Brown, G. (1980) 'Independence and incorporation: The Labour College Move-ment and the WEA before the Second World War', in Thompson, J. (ed.) *Adult Education for a Change*, Hutchinson.

Fraser, W. (1995) 'Making experience count ... towards what?', in this volume.

Freire, P. (1972) *Pedagogy of the Oppressed*, Penguin Books.

Illich, I. (1973) *Deschooling Society*, Penguin Books.

Jackson, S. (1992) 'The amazing deconstructing woman', *Trouble and Strife*, 25.

Johnson, R. (1979) '"Really useful knowledge": radical education and working class culture', in Clarke, J., Critcher, C. and Johnson, R. (eds) *Working Class Culture: Studies in history and theory*, Hutchinson.

Keddie, N. (1980) 'Adult education: an ideology of individualism', in Thompson, J. (ed.) *Adult Education for a Change*, Hutchinson.

Lorde, A (1981) 'The master's tools will never dismantle the master's house', in Moraga, Anzaldua (ed.) *This Bridge Called My Back*, Persephone Press.

Lyotard, J-F. (1984) *The Post-Modern Condition: A report on knowledge*, Minnesota University Press.

O'Rourke, R. (1995) 'All equal now?', in this volume.

Rich, A. (1980) 'Towards a woman-centred university', in *On Lies, Secrets and Si-lences. Selected prose 1966–78*, Virago.

Ross, C. (1995) 'Seizing the quality initiative: regeneration and the radical project', in this volume.
Rowbotham, S. (1973) *Hidden From History*, Pluto.
Spender, D. (1982) *Women of Ideas*, Routledge Kegan Paul.
Taking Liberties Collective (1989) *Learning the Hard Way: Women's oppression in men's education*, Macmillan.
Thompson, J.L. (1983) *Learning Liberation: Women's response to men's education*, Croom Helm.
Vattimo, G. (1988) *The End of Modernity: Nihilism and hermeneutics in post-modern culture*, Polity Press.

Eleven

Making Experience Count ... Towards What?

Wilma Fraser

> *Is it possible that we practitioners may also be unwitting agents of the very oppression or limitations we seek to transcend by our good practice? (Mulligan and Griffin, 1992)*

Most educationalists, whether in the fields of adult, further or higher education, have by now at least a nodding acquaintance with the work which has been undertaken in the area of accrediting or assessing prior learning (APL). APL's importance lies in having legitimised the inclusion of prior learning within assessment procedures across the spectrum of vocational and non-vocational certificating bodies.

In other words, the principle of including prior learning – whether towards the awarding of, for example, National Vocational Qualifications (NVQs), BTEC or RSA diplomas, or in granting access to, or advanced standing within, higher education (HE) – has now been generally accepted as a means of acknowledging greater individual potential by valuing the importance of diverse sources of learning and the competences to be derived from them.

Broader-based facilities also abound. A number of providers, including Goldsmiths' College (University of London), the Workers' Educational Association (WEA) and the Open University (OU), have developed programmes under the general heading of Making Experience Count (MEC). These concentrate less on specific and directed outcomes, whether vocational or educational, and instead provide a space in which participants reflect on the learning gained from their experiences and their current situations. They may then take stock of their needs and aspirations and decide upon possible next steps.

Some of these broader-based programmes have sought recognition from their local Open College Network (OCN). In these cases, participants may submit a portfolio of their learning 'outcomes' for external verification and accreditation. Because the learning outcomes within the MEC approach are not specifically tied to the competence requirements of a receiving institution or vocational assessor, there is theoretically greater scope for drawing upon learning gained from a broader range of experience.

This is why a number of practitioners within the field argue for a distinction between APL and APEL – the Assessment or Accreditation of

Prior *Experiential* Learning. They contend that APEL preceded APL as a
means of valuing the diversity of individual experience and included
both formal and informal sources of learning. Increasingly, APL has restricted the types of learning and experience which may be utilised because its formalisation within certification procedures has demanded a
greater systemic fit between the relevant competences of the individual
and the specific requirements of the awarding body, employer or institution. Thus, much of the potential for valuing the range of individual experience, and finding creative outlets for its expression, is being eroded
as market forces increasingly hold sway over issues of vocational and
educational relevance, and, by extension, of personal and social value.

In 1991, the WEA South Eastern District ran a pilot series of six experiential learning courses, entitled Making Your Experience Count, which
fell within the potentially broader APEL category.

The project comprised:

- A programme for the unwaged, both women and men, run in
  conjunction with a local education centre.
- A programme for women, the majority unwaged, run in
  conjunction with Brighton Women's Education Branch of the
  WEA.
- A course for women who were known to Social Services and run
  in conjunction with the latter.
- A course for women and men with acute learning difficulties, run
  in conjunction with local Mental Health organisations and
  voluntary contacts.
- A course for women and men in management positions within
  the Ford Motor Company, run in conjunction with the Ford
  Employee Development and Assistance Programme (EDAP).
- A pilot programme for women and men who wished to use
  APEL as a 'fast-route' access course to the part-time degree and
  diploma programmes at the University of Kent. (This was part of
  a larger pilot organised by The Learning From Experience Trust
  and financed by the Department of Employment.) [1]

Although I had facilitated MEC courses for a number of years, the diversity of provision within the one project afforded a unique opportunity
to examine MEC's potential across a range of differing 'target groups'. [2]
And what began as a typical WEA initiative, outwardly modest yet educationally ambitious and innovative, soon revealed the deeper complexities within the whole MEC/APEL endeavour; and the tutor team and I
were forced to question the very principles upon which MEC/APEL's
supposed potential for empowerment were predicated.

At one level, the learning gained from facilitating these courses justified our holding to the distinction between APL and APEL and I shall return to this issue later in the discussion. But as the work progressed it
became apparent that the very notion of 'counting experience' reveals a
complexity that reaches far beyond the easy polarisation that such a distinction suggests. Indeed, the rhetoric surrounding AP(E)L's potential as

an instrument for greater individual fulfilment all too often masks what is actually its incorporation within a restrictive societal conformity.

I shall argue that part of the problem lies in the theoretical underpinning to the whole endeavour. I shall then discuss some of the particular issues which arise for the women on our courses who comprise the majority of our MEC students.

'Adults Are What They Have Done'

The key to the heart of the MEC/APEL endeavour is the reflective process which will open the door to the learning derived from experience (Kolb and Fry, 1975). The underlying assumption is of the self as narrator – a unified 'I' – who can recollect experience and turn it into learning. To put it simply, we experience, we reflect, we generalise and then we act. 'Learning' is understood as a process which operates in any number of formal or informal situations. It is not restricted to scholastic or vocational environments but includes the learning gained from the myriad quotidian experiences we all encounter as we perform the various roles our social obligations demand of us. The intention of the MEC programme is to facilitate understanding and thence 'ownership' of the learning process which will lead, in turn, to enhanced self-esteem and increased self-confidence.

The process is in accord with the andragogical approach to learning which states basically that 'adults are what they have done' (Knowles, 1980). And this approach is reflected in the numerous publications offering lesson plans and programme notes to facilitate the reclamation process.

Many students regard that process as an end in itself, for the programme is seen as providing a diagnostic space in which adults may explore their prior experiences in a safe and non-judgemental environment, extricate the learning gained, and utilise that learning according to the nature of their own goals and aspirations. At this level we can applaud the liberatory potential that MEC offers:

> I thought I was just a housewife but this course has made me value just how much my caring and nurturing entails. I feel better about myself.

Yet, whereas we would never wish to decry the experience of individual empowerment that MEC courses can offer, deeper reflection brought home to us MEC/APEL's fundamental paradox.

As long as recognition of the individual's learning process remains within the heart and mind of the student concerned, we can encourage the journey of discovery and applaud the outcome of increased self-esteem. But when students seek others' acknowledgements of the relevance of their new-found learning, for example, to vocational or educational requirements, they must articulate that learning in a manner which will meet the approval of an external reader – and assessor. Private concerns have now become a matter for public adjudication.

So where is the problem with this? If 'adults are what they have done' then we should welcome the broadening of perspective which encourages recognition of hitherto unsung achievements and paves the way for access to greater opportunity. This was certainly our heartfelt belief when we began the MEC project. However, theory and practice rarely walk hand in hand. Our work with Making Experience Count has laid bare the muddle, inconsistency and contradiction at the heart of our endeavours.

On the one hand we argue for the space in which students may explore their potential and thence exercise greater control over their lives. On the other hand, we as a team became all too aware of the glibness of the term 'adults are what they have done' because it is predicated upon a model of individualistic achievement which fails to address either societal inequity or the sheer irrationality so often at the heart of our humanity. 'The thousand natural shocks' also include the lessons learned, sometimes much more painfully and tragically, from experiences that we are subject to as socially-constructed members of different cultural, economic and gendered milieus.

AP(E)L assumes that 'competences' learned in one sphere can be utilised and applied in a number of different contexts. But how realistic is this for students who fall within that broad classification – the 'disadvantaged'? For those at the margins of political, economic and social power, the notion that they 'are what they have done' sounds more like a slap in the face than a term of encouragement; and we are all reminded that there are far greater barriers to opportunity and fulfilment than simply the acknowledgement of individual potential.

All modes of social engagement are regulated by discourses which, in turn, reflect the relative powers and equities measured out by cultural, political and socio-economic interests. MEC/APEL courses are no exception. Whether we are talking about individuals at the first stage of private recollection and reflection or at the point where they seek public recognition for the value of their experiences, regulatory practices both inform and construct each step of the way. We organise our lives according to narrative structures of greater or lesser effectiveness, which, in turn, depend upon our relative distance from society's loci of control. And the extent to which we self-censor our experiences, 'select' the most 'relevant', and 'choose' the arenas where we can utilise the learning gained, reveals the nature of those regulatory practices, if not always their goal and purpose. To put it crudely, it tells us who, or what, is pulling the strings.

This is why Making Experience Count is a double-edged sword. It operates at the margins between our private and our public selves because it intervenes at the sites of self-disclosure, selection, relevance and control. In begging the question – 'count towards what?' – it can either 'cut the ties that bind' or sever our connection to perhaps the most creative parts of ourselves because they are not 'relevant'.

This brings me back to the distinction between APL and APEL. My concern is that current implementation of APL is increasingly reflective of a reductionist and outcome-oriented approach. This is not to denigrate the work of many colleagues in the field who are striving to retain the potential inherent in validating experiences which may have hitherto been denied or ignored, and counting them towards educational or vocational enhancement. But, once again, it is the way in which experiences 'count towards' that causes my disquiet.

Leaving aside for the moment the fundamental paradox in the MEC process which I have discussed above, it is nonetheless true to state that APEL includes experiential or informal learning whilst APL increasingly does not. It is largely restricted to prior certificated or vocational learning because its value is more often couched in its relevance to the currency of the market place. Much government funding has been spent in developing APL as a means towards acquiring NVQs – it is intended to increase vocational competence. Inevitably, APEL's broad-based claim that diverse forms of experience can constitute sources of learning is being muted by the clamour for particular and 'relevant' knowledge which will match the units of 'competence' delineated by the industry lead bodies who set the NVQ agenda. (Although some claim that such reductionism will be tempered by the broader requirements of the more recent General National Vocational Qualifications.) In other words, the translation of competences from one arena to another is restricted to prior experiences which have a direct bearing upon the nature of work being assessed. Indeed, the inclusion of prior learning from any source is under threat as NVQ assessors demand evidence of competence in the work currently undertaken. There are two reasons for this. The assessment of prior learning, if it is to be fair and comprehensive, is a time-consuming and therefore expensive process, particularly if it is conducted at individual as opposed to group level. The other problem concerns the nature of 'translation'. How much easier it is to assess an employee on the basis of her current work and practices than become involved in the much more complicated task of matching past practice to current relevance – particularly as past practices become obsolete within shorter and shorter spaces of time.[3]

Of course, APL is not used solely in pursuit of vocational enhancement. Many of the 'new' universities (erstwhile polytechnics) – and a growing number of 'old' – incorporate AP(E)L within their admissions procedures, whether to grant access or advanced standing. The theory, once again, is that learning can be acquired from a range of experiences. Once articulated in the form of 'general' or (even) 'generic competences' the parity between the skills involved in, for example, running a voluntary self-help group and the knowledge required to embark upon a social work qualification may be self-evident. The reality is that HE institutions differ in the degree to which such parities are accepted. Academia also delineates its own codes and prescriptions against which an individual's informal learning may all too often be deemed irrelevant and inappropriate. Thence it limits the range of 'acceptable' prior learning to that which falls within, and may be measured against, those codes and prescriptions.

Yet it would be simplistic and misleading of me to appear to be positing an easy dichotomy between MEC/APEL as good practice, liberating potential in an open-ended and self-enhancing way, and APL as bad practice, sacrificing process and empowerment at the altar of an out-come-oriented market religion. I would hold to a distinction between the two for the reasons I have outlined but I would hesitate to place relative values on either in terms of what they promise the student. APEL appears to offer the greater potential, but once we start to analyse the process we become aware of profound epistemological faultlines which necessarily reverberate, with equal depth, in terms of educational and political delivery.

The APEL process begs three basic questions:

- The concept of a unified subject enjoying equality of opportunity.
- The concept of 'experience' as coherent, consistent and a site for rational intellectual excavation.
- Parity between learning gained in one arena and the skills and competences demanded by another.

In other words, the act of articulating the MEC/APEL process goes to the root of what constitutes the private and public spheres. And any form of assessment, whether formal or informal, reveals the degrees to which those spheres are constructed.

Gendered Reflections

The crucial question for theorists and practitioners alike is how experience actually impacts upon the learner so that the knowledge gained can be retained and utilised in different contexts and in the future. The proliferation of materials aimed at facilitating this process, including those published by The Learning From Experience Trust and the Open University, urge that the student begins the reclamation process by depicting the events of her life in some epistolary or diagrammatic form. She is urged to include the painful events because they often represent particularly rich veins from which learning may be mined. This is not a surprising assumption. The belief that 'we understand through our suffering' is the bedrock upon which many religious and psychoanalytic discourses are based.

But in order to extricate the learning gained and be able to use it – in order to complete the learning cycle – we have to be sufficiently distanced from the suffering so that rational reflection may take place. At its most basic, therefore, this approach is founded on the belief that our lives present linear journeys, and that chronological distance from significant emotional experiences will allow for the rational appraisal that the reflective process represents. Some practitioners acknowledge that there are risks attached. In the pilot version of a *Profile Pack* from Macmillan, students are reminded that they are:

> *concerned with the learning and not the experience itself. If you are still trying to 'cope' with the emotion, you are not in a position with this experience to articulate what you have learnt from it. Do not embark on*

*reflection about emotionally charged experiences if you have not already
dealt with the emotions that are likely to surface.*

Of course, this advice accords with our common sense belief that
'time heals all ...' and in our own initial work with MEC we debated the
nature of our roles and responsibilities within the learning environment.
Were we 'educators' or facilitators of a therapeutic process? Most of us
agreed with the advice echoed by Macmillan, and some of us, myself included, eschewed the 'lifeline' approach altogether; preferring to encourage our students to glean their learning and transferable skills from 'safe'
experiences such as previous jobs, community work and domestic responsibilities.

In retrospect, I am astounded by my own naivety. Domestic responsibilities do indeed furnish an enormous range of transferable skills, as
Butler (1993) has persuasively argued, as long as we adhere to the andragogic model that 'adults are what they have done'. But few would
contest the fact that the domestic, or private, realm is often the source of
sustained pain and conflict in terms of who women are. In other words, if
we base the MEC/APEL process upon some form of andragogic journey,
then there is every likelihood of eliciting a wide range of transferable
skills. However, this is not the same as facilitating a learning process if
we are to regard learning as a dynamic intervention involving critical
analysis of who and why we are.

Thus is it is my contention that reflection is not simply a vehicle for
reclaiming learning from pain, neither is it just a vehicle of cool appraisal
for assessing the potential for skills transferability. Although it can function as medium for both, I believe it is very often, and much more profoundly, the cause of pain. This is not in the sense of unearthing old
traumas but in the realisation of, and the connection with, the implications which cohere around the initial painful event. Reflection can thus
call into being the deeper complexities in the formation of experience and
thence generate experience anew.

In a fascinating project, Crawford *et al.* (1992) have explored the implications of research undertaken into the nature of women's and men's
memories. They illustrate the discourses generated by social imperatives
and the power that these discourses hold in the formation of our gendered selves. They conclude that women are still largely socialised in
terms of their relations to others. They are 'burdened' with responsibility
for maintaining the 'existing web of social relations'. In uncovering the
'clichés' that have formed our internalisation of these cultural imperatives, women may be enabled to effect change through redefinitions of
their sense of self. But if we accept that our social imperatives are gendered, then I conclude that the reflective process is also a gendered process and will, of necessity, involve women and men in different struggles.

Our work with MEC has illustrated the truth of this statement. We
have seen that the reflective process for a woman so often involves un-
ravelling the conflict, or tension, between her-self defined in relation to
others and her strivings for autonomy – and the struggle can be extremely painful. This is why it is so important that the reflective process

for women is undergone in conjunction with others. As Crawford *et al.* point out, 'we can change our own constructions, but change can be threatening, and so we need to do it together'.

This has obvious implications for the value of APEL programmes which are undertaken as distance (or sole) learning packages. There are two issues which need to be considered. The first needs no repetition; women need the support of other women if they are to unravel the 'clichés' which have constructed so many of their 'choices'. The second also has profound resonance for the nature of the educative process. For the conclusion that we are socially constructed in relation to others – and this is true of both men and women, although via different processes – means that our social reconstruction is also effected in conjunction with others, which, if utilised, provides a means of challenging the polarity between dependence and autonomy.

Conclusions

So what are the implications for an educative process which seeks to 'make experience count'? As I have already suggested, the andragogic model upon which MEC/APEL is based can prove useful in eliciting the skills gained in one arena and highlighting their potential transferability. And it is understandable that students' recognition of the possible value of skills which they have hitherto taken for granted or denied can lead to enhanced self-confidence and greater self-esteem. However, I believe that most work undertaken in the field of MEC/APEL is conservative and reductionist, and serves to maintain the *status quo*. If we are to embark upon an educative process which offers genuine possibilities for creative change, then we have to engage with the factors which constrain our understanding of who, and why, we are.

The underlying principle remains the need to address the 'nature' of our socially constructed experiences. One of the fundamental premises underpinning women's education, and certain other forms of experiential learning and adult education practice, has been the assumption that we should 'start from where the students are'. We are familiar with the commonplace injunction to 'begin with what the students know from their own experience and then move on to the general and theoretical implications'. It is a cornerstone of good facilitative practice. But we have already noted that the realm of the experiential is not simply a bedrock for rational excavation. I therefore offer the following guidelines for those who, like myself, seek to 'make experience count' as a transformative learning process.

Facilitators must problematise the experiential from the outset. This requires a supportive environment. Learning operates at the interface between the individual and the social. It is therefore a given that MEC should operate as a group process to unravel the 'clichés' upon which our sense of our experiences is based.

Thus, the nature of our experiences should be examined for traces of the broader discourses which inform them. This means acknowledging the dynamic power of the reflective process.

New experiences will emerge as a result of the conflict between old assumptions and fresh understandings. This will generate a range of emotions, including anger and fear. Space must be given to incorporate these emotions into a broader analysis in the hope of effecting change.

If we attack APL for its narrow reductionism, we have to be wary of the MEC/APEL evangelism which, by fostering the 'uniqueness of the individual', is actually maintaining the ethic of difference upon which our social constructions are based. Our work with MEC has illustrated the contradictions inherent in our notions of empowerment. It has also reminded us of the dangers that lie in forgetting that the learning process is ultimately a social process which will have profound educational and political implications.

(I am indebted to the excellent team of MEC tutors in the WEA South Eastern District for their commitment to working through the complexities and contradictions that the MEC process entails. I am also extremely grateful to the untold numbers of students who have worked with courage and honesty in the struggle to 'make their experience count'.)

Notes

1. For a full account of this project, the reader is referred to: West, L. and Fraser, W. (1992) *The Assessment of Prior Experiential Learning in Universities' Admissions Procedures,* University of Kent.
2. A full account of this pilot scheme and the broader issues which have arisen from our work with MEC is discussed in Fraser, W. (1995) *Learning from Experience,* NIACE.
3. The English National Board for Nursing, Midwifery and Health Visiting is striving to retain an experiential component in the professionalisation of health carers: 'An essential feature of the Framework is that it is based on the accreditation of prior and experiential learning (APL/APEL). It recognises the contribution that all forms of learning make to the quality of professional care offered by nurses, midwives and health visitors' (*Adding Up the Past. APL/APEL guidelines for good practice,* ENB, 1992).

References

Butler, L. (1993) 'Unpaid work in the home and accreditation', in Thorpe, M., Edwards, R. and Hanson, A. (eds) *Culture and Processes of Adult Learning,* Routledge.

Crawford, J. *et al.* (1992) *Emotion and Gender: Constructing meaning from memory,* Sage.

Knowles, M. (1980) *The Modern Practice of Adult Education: From pedagogy to andragogy,* Follett.

Kolb, D. and Fry, R. (1975) 'Towards an applied theory of experiential learning', in Cooper, C.L. (ed.), *Theories of Group Processes,* John Wiley.

Mulligan, J. and Griffin, C. (1992) *Empowerment through Experiential Learning: Explorations of good practice,* Kogan Page.

Twelve

The Dying of the Light? A Radical Look at Trade Union Education

John McIlroy

> *If the workers knew enough, if as a class we'd been really trained and intelligent we'd have done it by now, done it a generation ago. Only we haven't done it and you'll find out why (Raymond Williams, Second Generation).*

The trade union education which developed slowly from the late 1920s stood in distinction to the democratic, emancipatory tradition of workers' education represented by the National Council of Labour Colleges and the WEA. Where workers' education focused on economy, society, the means of political change and the role workers would play in this as labour movement activists, trade union education emphasised the mechanics of day to day dealing with capital, the practical information and skills workers required as trade union representatives. The two streams intermingled and the post-war period saw attempts to fuse them, best represented in some of the long university day release courses. The pull of the practical, narrowly defined, proved strongest. The universities, the WEA and some unions persevered with social and political education. The dominant trend exemplified by the TUC in the day-release courses for shop stewards sponsored in the educational bodies from the mid-1960s prioritised workplace industrial relations. As union membership increased from 1968 and as the state increasingly sought to involve the unions in economic and industrial relations policies to which the activities of shop stewards were important these tendencies were strengthened. Under the Social Contract they were institutionalised, with direct state funding provided for specified categories of course and statutory rights to paid release for union representatives to attend courses.

It is relevant to what came later that this produced little reflection on fundamentals amongst adult educators. Intent on dealing with expansion and the space and potential that still existed for broader education even within TUC programmes they dwelt lightly on purpose and limits. There was, for example, little examination of the roots of trade union education in TUC General Secretary Walter Citrine's attempts to develop a new orientation to the state and marginalise ideas of workers' control, and TGWU leader Ernest Bevin's attempts to use it to create a professionalised, top-down trade unionism and sideline rank and file opposition (Clinton, 1977: 39; Topham, 1992: 53). The role of the state, central to past debates, received little address. Not until Roger Fieldhouse's work was published in the 1980s was stock again taken of the limits state and educational institutions placed on any radical trade union education (Fieldhouse, 1985).

Critiques from the political left were rarely acknowledged (see, for example, Dutt, 1963; Cliff, 1970: 218; Hyman, 1979: 57–8). Nor, critically, was the conception of trade unionism which informed union education and the alternative conceptions which should inform a radical approach. Perry Anderson's aphorism, unions do not challenge the existence of society based on class divisions they merely express it, is well known (Anderson, 1967: 264). However, in their role as agencies for the expression of working-class activity unions provide a key site for working-class education. Moreover the quality of this will be influenced by the form of trade unionism which develops, for Anderson's general estimation neglects the *varieties of trade unionism*, from business unionism to syndicalism, which express class conflict in different ways and which many produce different educational projects. During the 1960s and 1970s the TUC was attempting to construct a *corporatist trade unionism* capable of engaging in fruitful and enduring political exchange with the state. This required centralisation, at the level of the movement, with a greater role for the TUC and at the level of the affiliated unions, with greater integration of the workplace organisation, which constituted a problem for economic planning and incomes policy. This in turn required the construction of a more predictable and proceduralised industrial relations (McIlroy, 1995: Chapter 3).

The conception of trade unionism embodied in trade union education centred strongly on trade unionism as collective bargaining. The 'needs' of activists were diagnosed by union professionals in terms of the skills required for reformed workplace bargaining. Union representatives did not 'need' to bother themselves with the economic or political dimensions of corporatism, with unions' relations with the state, with economic planning and incomes policy. Explicit address of politics and ideology was excluded from much of union education (McIlroy, 1985a). In retrospect it appears clear that the role of adult educators should be to redress this extraordinary deficit, address trade unionism as well as education, re-assert trade unionism as part of a wider movement with industrial and political wings and a political and economic programme. And rehabilitate the activist as a democratic actor *beyond the workplace*, debating the political and economic framework that constrained workplace activity, discussing alternatives to existing policy, placing themselves in a position *to make choices* and struggle to implement them.

Yet the 1970s was a time of blithe optimism in which these concerns figured minimally, and developments in union education were heralded as 'the Great Leap Forward' in generally uncritical celebration (Caldwell, 1981). What was lacking amongst the enthusiasm was any precise critical analysis of what was happening. This affected even radical projects such as the collection *Adult Education for a Change*, which we may take as a reference point. The reach towards critical theory that informed other contributions was less evident in the two chapters dealing with the unions.

Geoff Brown predicated a fine exploration of the pedagogy of Independent Working Class Education and the WEA between the wars on its lessons for the content, objectives and 'nature of the new provision for working-class education' developed by the TUC. His conclusion – the WEA approach offered a better model – was brief and handicapped by the leap in his text from 1939 to 1979. Brown's search for inspiration in the past for renewal of workers' education in the 1980s possessed little purchase on the contemporary curriculum and pedagogy of TUC courses. For these had moved significantly in the direction of skills-based training, qualitatively different from the issue-based education of the inter-war years he had examined. Moreover no note was taken of what critical address there had been by the left of the attempts by the TUC from 1964 to create a centralised scheme of basic training with standardised curricula and teaching methods increasingly prescribed for classes at the expense of political education and student democracy (see, for example, Topham, 1964; Park, 1969; Fieldhouse, 1971). Brown observed that democratic control by students was 'a vital ingredient in working-class education absent in TUC provision' but considered that the effective conferment of Responsible Body status on the TUC by the direct grant had 'clearly been an advance for the Labour Movement'. Brown took a benign view of the impact of state funding on union education. Nor in his conclusions did he return to his earlier comments that the politics of the National Council of Labour Colleges were diluted by dependence on right-wing union leaders which placed the NCLC in some ways under greater constraint than the state funded WEA (Brown, 1980: 110, 114, 124–5).

Mel Doyle, like Brown, concentrated on the central role of the TUC regional scheme. He foregrounded the role of WEA industrial branches in involving workers from TUC courses in social purpose education of their own making, a development which would in turn impact on the TUC scheme. The rapid expansion of TUC courses and the WEA's role in the scheme had limited attempts to focus on wider perspectives. Consequent tensions within the WEA produced accusations that it was becoming a training agency for the TUC. The way to renew workers' education was to 'extend the definition of trade union education', within the TUC scheme and interactively outside it, by bringing workers into the mainstream of the WEA via industrial branches. History, Doyle averred, was working this way: 'expansion has fuelled expansion and will continue to do so. The only restraints will be limitations on resources'. The future would see a bigger and better trade union education with its historic social purpose stream revived (Doyle, 1980: 137–140).

The untheoretical and unproblematic progressivism of these accounts was only disturbed in the text by Jane Thompson's brief reference to internal disputes in union education and Sallie Westwood's terse comment that closer analysis would probably disclose a programme which offered incorporation of workers into capitalist relations rather than empowerment (Thompson, 1980: 242; Westwood, 1980: 38). The majority of these involved in union education in 1979 were probably even more sanguine than Brown and Doyle.

The Impact of the New Right

I feel that you have always given the concepts of 'utility' and 'practicality' a content which is much too mean and narrow (Gramsci, Edinburgh Letter LXXIII).

Until 1979 the development of union education was conditioned by state support for strengthening trade unionism as an agency of economic order. The role which quasi-corporatist policies culminating in the Social Contract accorded unions produced important procedural and organisational concessions. Membership of TUC unions increased from 8.8 million in 1968 to 12 million in 1979. Trade unions were viewed as a new 'fifth estate' of the realm and their future appeared secure. All this now changed. At the heart of New Right politics lay the view that the 1945 welfare compromise and the quasi-corporatist attempts to shore it up from the 1960s had failed to stem economic decline. Trade unions were incapable of controlling and delivering their members and the legitimacy and power consensus politics had conferred on them had exacerbated economic problems. The path to economic regeneration ran through the rehabilitation of the market; attenuation of state regulation; recantation on state responsibility for full employment and the welfare of its citizens; the renovation of individualism; and an entrepreneurial culture. Collective bargaining and trade unionism should be progressively weakened by legislation withdrawing union 'privileges'; political exclusion; set piece confrontations with public sector unions; an ideological onslaught on collectivism; and, crucially, by allowing employment to find its market level. These policies reduced membership to 7 million by 1993, weakening trade unionism and collective bargaining without, as the two neo-Conservative recessions bespeak, solving the problems of economy and society.

From 1979 union education was increasingly defined by the fact that the paymaster was no longer the supportive social democratic state of the post-war years. Disorientated by neo-Conservatism, the TUC developed no successful alternative to their redundant corporatist impulse. The defeat of the miners' strike in 1985 foreclosed on the strategy of resistance. The 'new realism' developed from 1983 by a TUC apparatus which had always attempted to curb resistance was based on seeking a subordinate accommodation with Thatcherism. Its failure was accompanied by continuing significant decline in union membership and power and in the specific weight of the TUC (McIlroy, 1995: Chapters 5, 10). This was the essential context to developments in union education. None of it was inevitable. It was the result of a combination of factors from luck, statecraft and political nerve to the response to the labour movement and in a small way trade union education.

Reading off New Right ideology, the existing structure of financial and statutory support for union education should have been quickly dismantled: quite apart from the now tenuous legitimacy of collectivism, unions as private organisations should resource their own training (Anderson, 1987). In contrast, the state's evolutionary and gradualist attack and continuing employer support demonstrated the complexities and limits of Thatcherism. It certainly never developed any distinctive antagonistic analysis of union education (McIlroy, 1995: Chapter 6). Norman Tebbit, Secretary of State for Employment 1981–1983, for example, supported the maintenance of state finance on largely pluralist grounds: better trained shop stewards were likely to make a better contribution to industry (Tebbit, 1989). His utilisation of union education was specifically political. In sustained dialogue with right-wing union leaders who opposed the TUC boycott of state funds for ballots as part of the oppositionary stance towards employment legislation, Tebbit underscored the inconsistency of taking money for union education whilst boycotting it for ballots. The TUC argued that state finance for ballots would compromise their independence – an argument they had used until 1974 to oppose direct state finance for education (TUC, 1970). Tebbit rejected termination of state aid for steward training and determined to demonstrate strings could be attached to this funding as easily as to funding for ballots (Patterson, 1982; Auerbach, 1990: 120–1; Tebbit, 1989). Ministers who advocated termination of an embarrassing relic of 1970s-style corporatism were restrained. Funding was sliced, with part of the grant now available only for courses whose content was approved by employers.

The TUC did not fight. In the 1970s it had asserted its sole right to control steward training: it now conceded an employers' veto over courses with minimal protest (Lloyd, 1983; *Tribune*, 1983). A TUC review appears to have convinced the education department that it was now dependent for resources on the state (Jobbins, 1982; TUC, 1983). Trade unionists pointed out that lack of resistance would stimulate further encroachment (Gravell, 1983). Ministers do not appear to have been overly concerned about the impact of steward training in strengthening the unions. But they felt that whilst most of it dealt with 'relatively neutral issues, the content of courses has over-emphasised a union view which could be seen as hostile to employers' (Lloyd, 1983). The employer-ratified courses were seen as readjusting the balance and providing a shot across the bows.

To reverse Kipling: once you have taken the state's geld you'll never get rid of the state. A further initiative prompted by Education Minister Sir Keith Joseph sought to exploit the TUC's dependence by the introduction of grant for courses dealing with 'the importance of economic realities in the functioning of industry'. 1986 saw another slice at the salami. The government declared its intent to limit rights of paid release to courses dealing with issues for which stewards were recognised by employers for the purposes of negotiation. The new restrictions were introduced in the Employment Act 1989. The rolling programme of change saw state funding falling 20% in real terms between 1984 and 87. The continuing pressures were evident in TUC statements that the government had 'sought to place unacceptable conditions upon grant aid for 1986–7' and that civil servants had 'queried the educational validity of TUC course material on the privatisation of public services' (TUC, 1986: 11; 1991b: 15). Right-wing MPs and journalists questioned the continuance of state support, reinforcing the climate of insecurity and compliance (House of Commons Debates, 1987: 10, 11; Anderson, 1987; Doyle, 1988).

TUC dependence and subservience and the reality of state surveillance of union education through the 1980s was demonstrated in 1991. DE officials complained about the political nature of a book used on TUC courses, *Working Women*, and criticisms of government policy in it. The matter was brought to the attention of the Secretary of State for Employment, who threatened withdrawal of grant unless the book was banned from courses. TUC education staff took a decision in liaison with the General Secretary but without any discussion with the education or women's sub-committees to ban the book. Critics were informed that they should live 'in the real world', that there should be no protest about the matter and that greater care than ever should be taken to down-play criticisms of government in union education materials (McIlroy, 1993: 43–9).

The TUC expressed support for the employer-led new vocationalism of the 1980s despite its relative exclusion from it (TUC, 1989; 1990b). With changes in the funding and organisation of the further education sector from 1990 it began to take steps to assimilate union education to the new vocational training system by introducing NVQs into courses (TUC, 1991a: 57). Despite this the government announced in 1992 that the state grant would be phased out by 1996.

Political hostility was accompanied by internal decline, which made the TUC's objective of 180,000 student places annually in the 1980s the purest moonshine. The number of 10-day shop steward courses fell from 1208 with 15,700 places in 1980, to 762 with 9546 places by 1987, and 512 with 6000 students by 1992. There was a large increase in shorter workshops but follow-on courses and courses for health and safety representatives also fell significantly. By 1994 TUC education was in serious disarray (TUC, 1994). Even within its own terms the TUC had failed to successfully defend its position and had compromised its independence. By the 1990s, as one TUC representative commented, 'the government appeared able to determine TUC policy making and educational provision through the political use of public money' (TUC, 1991c). The Department of Employment's remark commending TUC acquiescence in the banning of course materials, 'the TUC has co-operated fully' (McLeod, 1991), summed up the thrust of its bureaucratic manoeuvring under neo-Conservatism.

Far from being broadened and radicalised to deal with the radical challenge of Thatcherism the curriculum of courses remained geared to technical training for organising and bargaining as the very basis for organising and bargaining was being disrupted by an economic, political and ideological offensive. Yet any real explicit political and economic analysis to deal with this remained absent from courses. This was the real failure, one which cannot be underestimated. Political and campaigning issues were dealt with in short one- or two-day propaganda workshops outside the mainstream provision. Overall, as the TGWU commented:

> subject matter has tended to be limited to what can be called the *'non-political'* or *'non-controversial'* aspects of trade unionism. By far the greatest amount of TUC and individual trade union courses concern themselves with what is essentially training (Cosgrove, 1983: 63).

By the mid-1980s TUC education was set firmly in the world of the new vocational training, with packaged courses commissioned for bureaucratic delivery by facilitators operating pre-determined techniques. Far from the WEA stimulating a broader approach it was increasingly reactive, playing with the universities a marginal role. Doyle's comments on the nature of the WEA proved prescient. The equivocation of the districts resulted in the loss of 17 new posts in trade union studies in 1979, a milestone which along with continued internal dissension seems to have signalled to the TUC the Association's ultimate unreliability (Fieldhouse and Forrester, 1984: 8–14).

In the early 1980s some districts minimised trade union work, others maintained a strong position. But the initial justification for involvement, the defense and extension of a liberal address of issues and critical discussion, faded (Fieldhouse and Forrester, 1984: 11; *Trade Union Studies Journal*, 1980: 2). Involvement in TUC courses was increasingly on TUC terms. By 1989 the WEA was providing 235 10-day release courses compared with over 700 a decade earlier, and a large and growing majority of TUC work was concentrated in the FE sector (*TUSJ*, 1990: 18). The WEA's detailed policy statement in that year acknowledged: 'the WEA can no longer claim to be a national provider of trade union education'. Whilst it urged the WEA to sharpen the definition of its specific contribution to union education the report was informed by no assertion of philosophy distinguishing the WEA from any other deliverer of the TUC package. It could cite few examples of successful industrial branches; the document as a whole was limp and uninspiring (WEA, 1989: 14, 28–30).

Measured against the hopes of 1979, TUC education in the Conservative years provides a study in failure. State incursion first silenced the TUC and then, as in the *Working Women* episode, compromised its dependence, before administering the final *coup de grace*. The state's policies went uncontested: maintenance of existing structures was a function of the government's careful step by step approach, not the opposition of the TUC. The 1970s was a decade of trade union struggle against state initiatives and sharp resistance continued in the period until 1985. It was completely absent from education, despite the possibilities it may have yielded. This area was defined by the TUC in bureaucratic terms. No case for a broad, independent, state-supported education was ever developed and publicised in the movement and wider. The TUC's annual reports in the 1980s had a section headed *Campaigns*. There seemed to be a campaign for everything. Union education was a vehicle for campaigns on employment legislation, the political funds, the check off. There was never a campaign for union education.

This was seen as the subject of polite 'begging to differ' in smoke-filled rooms intended to refine state initiatives at the edges. The idea that the TUC is the hapless prisoner of its affiliates is without foundation: it initiates policy and has its own stance on a whole range of issues (see, for example, Dorfman, 1983; Trower, 1990; McIlroy, 1991). Similarly the TUC Education Department has some autonomy, and, as can be seen from the *Working Women* episode or the favourable stance on NVQs, power to take decisions and initiate policy. It too has viewed engagement with the state since 1979 as engagement without struggle, whilst the absence of any great interest or alternative conception on the part of left leaders meant there was little pressure in this area.

What was largely absent from the 1979 accounts of Brown and Doyle was the anti-educational ideology of mainstream trade union education and the extent to which its custodians perceived it as training functionaries in the pre-established norms of trade unionism and the efficient and loyal execution of hierarchically prescribed tasks. Its business was training the voluntary labour force of trade unionism to adapt to pre-set forms of industrial relations rather than critically interrogate and transform them. Steward training was conceived as the reproduction and reconstruction of established authority relations in industry and union. It sought legitimacy and compliance for established policy, crucially political exchange with the state, and was perceived as the subject of partnership with state and employers, albeit one which the TUC was *primus inter pares* (McIlroy, 1985a,b). This was organic to a wider bureaucratic conservative philosophy of trade unionism which provided strong ballast against radical initiatives and radical teachers.

But if the TUC was not prepared to explore the limits of the possible, what about the teachers? In 1979 there were TUC courses in most WEA Districts, many university extra-mural departments and 140 further education colleges. There were around 200 staff involved full-time on trade union courses and a further 90–100 spending 75% of their time on this work (TUC, 1979: 190). What role did they play in the developments sketched? An examination of its inner landscape may shed light on union education under Thatcherism, the difficulties educators had to confront and the limits of resistance.

Once Upon a Time in the North West

It was right to struggle against the old school but reforming it was not so simple as it seemed. The problem was not one of model curricula but of men ... (Gramsci, The Prison Notebooks).

In 1979–80 a small group of tutors involved in courses in the North West of England began to develop a rudimentary critique of TUC education. We were concerned, in retrospect in an unclear way, at the growing centralisation and standardisation exhibited in the move to programmed materials, greater control from Congress House and the deskilling of the educators. We could not credit the idea that the key deficit in trade unionism was the inability of union representatives to interview members, handle grievances, prepare a negotiating brief or possess command of legislation. In response to the conflicts over the Social Contract we felt a strong need to relate skills development to address of purpose and policy and viewed external prescription as an impediment to this.

Nonetheless the courses I worked on – a collaborative effort between Manchester University and the North West WEA – represented at around 35 10-day courses a year the second-largest provision in the TUC region and provided significant educational opportunities. As well as courses dealing with basic skills, courses for senior shop stewards of 30 days' duration discussed economic and political issues as well as neglected organisational matters such as industrial action (Campbell and McIlroy, 1981; McIlroy, 1984). Rights at Work courses provided the opportunity to address many of the issues then confronting the movement. There was a – largely unavailing – attempt to build a WEA industrial branch (McIlroy and Brown, 1980). A two-year Certificate in Trade Union Studies at the university was informally supported by the TUC, securing the basis for more intensive study, whilst I taught a number of courses for full-time officers notably on industrial tribunal procedure (McIlroy, 1983a). I enjoyed a close partnership with the TUC Education Officer, a former NCLC organiser and his successor, both of whom shared many of my preoccupations and until 1981 played a leading role in development in the region as did other later dissident tutors, particularly Bruce Spencer (Connell, 1990: 8).

I appreciated the threat Thatcherism represented. Following discussion with other tutors I wrote in *Tribune* arguing the inadequacies of the collective bargaining basis of much union education and the need to decisively reorientate it in a political direction to meet the challenge of the new Conservatism (McIlroy, 1980). An influential paper by Tony Topham also emphasised the need for change to prioritise the battle of ideas and foreground understanding of the current political situation and economic policies which constrained collective bargaining and alternatives to them (Topham, 1981).

The TUC moved in the opposite direction. With the advent of a new officer in 1981 the 30 day courses at Liverpool and Manchester were terminated without explanation and courses for full-time officers soon met a similar fate. Displeasure was expressed at the lack of enthusiasm WEA tutors exhibited for TUC materials and teaching approaches and stronger emphasis on their use began to emerge. I incurred reproof for the wide range of materials I used in teaching labour law. There was refusal to circulate to other tutors materials which raised criticisms of TUC policy. This problem was resolved with the removal of the 10-day Rights at Work course from the curriculum. Representing a group of worried tutors, Alan Campbell of the University of Liverpool, Bruce Spencer of the West Lancashire and Cheshire WEA and I met with the TUC officer. We were asked to put our concerns in writing with the promise that the paper would be placed before the Regional Education Advisory Committee for debate (see Spencer, 1984). On receipt of the document he refused to circulate it or table it for discussion. Although I acquiesced in this I quickly received a letter removing me from the committee on which I had served for some years.

In early 1982 it became clear that the TUC was attempting to undermine certificate courses at the Universities of Liverpool and Manchester.
Bruce Spencer was warned as co-ordinator of the WEA–TUC courses in
Liverpool not to distribute leaflets about this course. When Bernard
Foley, the university tutor responsible for the course, remonstrated he
was informed that only TUC literature would be 'authorised' for circulation, that the TUC had 'considerable reservations' about certificated
courses and that such courses undermined recruitment to TUC courses
and took resources away from them (Foley, 1982; TUC, 1982a). A well argued demolition – the students on the courses were past, present and future students on TUC courses whilst the termination of such courses
would simply lead to the loss of university resources for union education
– produced no response (Campbell, 1982). In Manchester the TUC undermined recruitment by writing to individual union education officers stating they did not support the course (TUC, 1982b).

It was clear that problems were stemming from the TUC's attempts
to dictate the content and method of courses. There was:

> insistence that all courses should follow an extreme and ill-founded
> form of student self direction. The TUC continually attempted to
> interfere in the organisation and conduct of courses brushing aside long
> established educational practice and belief (Campbell, 1988).

Matters deteriorated further when the TUC circulated a paper
marked 'Discussion Document' inviting comments. A group of tutors
wrote a detailed response refuting its simplistic notions of student centred learning. It was condemned out of hand by the TUC officer, the
REAC explicitly refused to discuss it and its signatories were informed
they had no right to circulate documents to fellow tutors without the per-
mission of the TUC! The WEA District Secretary attempted disciplinary
action against one of the signatories on the grounds that the WEA's good
relations with the TUC were being impaired and instructed her that she
must in future consult him about any controversial publications. She was
at the time the editor of *The Industrial Tutor*! At Wigan College the TUC
inquired whether Ted Mooney, another signatory, had been disciplined
(North West Tutors, 1983).

By now a group of around a dozen tutors were meeting regularly.
We understood what was occurring in the context of the TUC's attempt
to control and standardise all courses it sponsored within the constraints
of the categories for which grant aid was available to avoid critical attention and maintain state support. Filtered through a crude and energetic
local officer this was producing a momentum towards the exclusion of
those who would not accept the TUC's prescriptions on content and
method. In a situation where Open University materials were being challenged we saw the axing of issue-based courses and courses on legislation as attempts to placate the state and the pushing of student-centred
learning and the forced abdication of the tutor as a means of evading issue-based learning. The TUC was refusing to even begin to *test the limits*
of state aid. Yet it was committing considerable effort to stopping us

teaching about issues we were encouraged to teach about in our other classes with full-time and adult students.

For us this evasion of any critique and understanding of Thatcherism in the education of activists was strengthening its purchase and diminishing the union response. Some of the concerns I and other tutors sought to introduce into the curriculum can be seen from pamphlets and books written throughout this period (see, for example, McIlroy, 1979; McIlroy and Campbell, 1979; Campbell and McIlroy, 1981; McIlroy, 1981; McIlroy, 1983a; McIlroy, 1984; McIlroy, 1985c; McIlroy, 1988). And from contributions I made to left journals. We attempted to raise these issues in *The Industrial Tutor*, the WEA's *Trade Union Studies Journal* and more widely in response to TUC initiatives and though a number of articles were published (Whitston, 1982; McIlroy, 1982; Edwards *et al.*, 1983; Brown *et al.*, 1983) it was again difficult to secure the proper conditions for genuine educational debate.

In response to an article by a member of the TUC Education Department three tutors submitted an article to the *Trade Union Studies Journal*. The editors asked for around 60 changes mostly related to style and 'tone' and also requested elimination and softening of criticisms. The article was resubmitted with a statement that any further changes would require discussion and that a request for further substantial revision would lead to the withdrawal of the piece. At least four months passed between submission and publication with no attempt made to contact the authors. The article appeared with whole passages removed because they were critical of the TUC Education Department and with an invitation to debate the remnants. After months of correspondence involving the General Secretary and National President of the WEA an offer was made: the excised parts of the article would not be published but instead the authors were invited to respond to a subsequent piece which criticised their views. When they did so the article was refused publication (McIlroy and Spencer, 1984: 49–50).

Members of the TUC Education Department had been willing to write for both journals. Until their views were criticised, when they retreated to their tents. As *The Industrial Tutor* commented:

> *when invited to reply to a series of articles they refused to do so on the unsubstantiated grounds that the articles were inaccurate. This is a disturbingly uneducational approach. If the criticism of the articles could be backed up, why not set the record straight? The TUC Educational Department claim to be experts in the approaches and methods required by trade union education and to have developed several. They also claim the prerogative of training tutors. In any other area of education those who make such claims justify them through a developed literature ... for any serious educator a challenge to one's ideas requires a detailed, argued response. This is particularly obligatory in TUC education. If it is to be anything it has to be an equal partnership between educators employed by the TUC and educators employed by universities, the WEA and the colleges. It is a block to progress if one voice is not heard (The Industrial Tutor, 1984: 4).*

The TUC refused to lend their voice to debate, were not interested in partnership and were determined to silence critics. They possessed a number of other control mechanisms in addition to packaged content and methods. In Liverpool, where Bruce Spencer had built up the largest provision of TUC courses in the country, a core of full-time tutors was supported by part-time staff often economically dependent on this work. Bruce had performed the difficult task of organisation and allocation of work with patience and judgement. The TUC officer now began to sponsor particular part-time staff against full-time colleagues, exploiting economic dependence to ensure pedagogic compliance. This was often accomplished through 'the briefing system'. The TUC increasingly insisted that only tutors who had completed their briefings in London could teach on particular courses: recalcitrant staff were refused briefings, the TUC then insisting they could not teach courses. The TUC began to usurp WEA prerogatives, selecting tutors for courses and with growing ascendancy over the District Secretary, playing a key role in new appointments. After all the TUC was the monopoly client and the WEA dependent on it for a very large slice of its income as its grant was cut back in the early 1980s (Evans, 1987: 163).

When Spencer raised the issue of the WEA's autonomy and integrity, pointing out that an outside body was controlling content, methods and staff selection for courses, he was informed that the TUC officer – unelected and unaccountable to anybody outside Congress House – was acting as the students' representative. He was also criticised for endangering the relationship and found himself frozen out of briefings and courses (Spencer, 1983; North West Tutors, 1983).

The TUC adopted similar approaches with colleges. At Blackburn College long-serving tutors critical of TUC education were progressively undermined through meetings with the principal and local trade unionists which downgraded their role and boosted the stock of more co-operative junior staff. At colleges in Bury, Rochdale and St Helens part-time tutors and staff from other institutions were imported to teach courses in local union offices to freeze out established tutors. In Warrington staff were informed that students were being directed away from the college because of refusal to allow TUC officers to sit on appointment panels (NW Tutors, 1983).

The recruitment process was an important control mechanism. All recruitment passed through the TUC office and in Manchester, where there was more than one provider, those with (short-lived) access to the running totals reported courses recruited to the university-WEA were being transferred elsewhere. When union officers approached tutors for specific courses and were referred to the TUC they reported the TUC would only support the course if mounted at the polytechnic. The market in education was taking a grip, except that choices were made not by the students but by the TUC. There was no great fall-off in demand in Manchester: what was occurring was steerage of work away from the university-WEA to the polytechnic, where by now three part-time tutors worked with three full-time staff (Brown, 1982; Brown *et al.*, 1983).

This constituted a difficult context for discussion about the future of trade union education. In 1983 critical tutors organised two open conferences in Liverpool and Manchester to discuss this issue from a number of viewpoints. I wrote two more articles published in *Tribune* and *The New Statesman* and appeared on Channel 4 discussing union education (McIlroy, 1983b,c). At this stage a decision was taken to remove me from TUC courses. In October 1983 the TUC attempted to cancel the course I was due to teach the next day and informed the university that owing to a shortage of students no courses would be mounted at the university in the following term. Such was the shortage of students that in January 1984 the polytechnic was unable to staff the courses allocated to it. Rather than transfer them 500 yards down the road they were removed outside Manchester to Tameside.

A protracted saga ensued. The TUC REAC condemned a petition signed by 300 union officers, stewards and MPs, emphasising the situation had occurred through shortage of students and their objection to a higher education setting (Richards, 1985). When groups of stewards specifically requested courses at the university in writing they were informed in writing that the TUC decided where courses should be held and who tutored them and the ready made courses transferred elsewhere (Outten, 1985; TUC, 1985). A detailed complaint signed by 14 tutors from eight educational institutions produced no change. Requests from the university for proper arrangements with an agreement for a specific number of courses per annum were rejected by the TUC on the grounds it was impossible to give such guarantees. Already in 1983 such a guarantee of 360 hours teaching a year had been given to the polytechnic (NATFHE, 1983: 7). A detailed formal complaint by the extra-mural department to the head of the TUC education department produced only an acknowledgement.

The TUC approached the polytechnic, stating there was insufficient tutorial capacity to meet demand in Manchester and requesting five new full-time appointments. When the Director, kept in ignorance of the true position, was appraised of the fact that there were five tutors at the university and WEA – three of them specifically funded by the DES to teach trade unionists – without sufficient work, he gave the TUC short shrift. Their ingenuity was far from exhausted. They now sought the transfer of the work from the polytechnic to the FE sector under the auspices of Manchester Education Committee. Attempts to create a unified centre involving all parties were foiled by statements from the TUC such as 'TUC national policy would preclude a co-ordinated approach between the City, WEA and University' (Manchester Education Committee, 1985: 12).

The amount of time spent on this issue was becoming excessive. Extra-mural departments are far from dedicated to trade union education, still less forceful support for disputes about it. Availing myself of offers of courses from the TGWU I did not escape difficulties, for some of these courses were funded through the TUC. Attempts to exclude me from meeting with the TGWU education officer to discuss courses and insistence that TUC teaching materials were used continued. Concern was expressed at the 'suitability and balance' of my approach, foresight was demanded of all materials to be used on courses and assurances were sought that I would not 'promote anti-TUC views'. The TUC declared it would 'continue to monitor my teaching' (TUC, 1985b).

Meanwhile the situation in Liverpool continued to deteriorate, revolving around the TUC's 'extremely rigid attitude to courses and repeated attempts to decide who should teach which courses and generally interfere in the running of them' (Chapman, 1984: 2). Whilst the District Secretary continued to argue that the problem was simply too many tutors competing for too little work, others insisted that this had to be related to 'undue interference by the TUC in course provision and the WEA's acquiescence in this'. The TUC 'wished to safeguard its government grant by controlling course curricula' and was favouring those tutors willing to be controlled (Connor, 1985; Turnbull, 1985). Part-time staff claimed they were being victimised because of their association with critics. The only woman tutor claimed two-thirds of her work was given to a man who had never taught on these courses because of her criticisms of TUC policy (Chapman, 1984; Turnbull, 1985).

Bruce Spencer took out a grievance against the WEA, arguing that his job was being made impossible and that the Association must 'reaffirm that we will co-operate with the TUC but not be dictated to by them' (Spencer, 1983). As the dispute continued he resigned, citing pressures from the TUC. By now some tutors felt that 'the only conclusion one can draw is that this District of the WEA is not in fact an independent body in its trade union studies work but acts merely as an agent of the TUC' (Campbell, 1988). In 1985–6 the TUC negotiated with Liverpool City Council to establish a centre in a local college. Despite the advice of the university that they should oppose this the WEA went along with the creation of a competitor. In return for its opposition the university was now pushed out of TUC courses:

> *thus the Department of Continuing Education has been effectively excluded from the TUC Educational Scheme. This has taken place without notice, despite our planned commitment of 240 teaching sessions during 1987–8 or explanation despite the Department's participation in the TUC Scheme for almost twenty years (Campbell, 1988).*

By the end of the decade none of the 14 tutors who had addressed a collective complaint to the TUC in 1983 were involved in TUC education. To a person they were still involved in the Labour movement as union officers, MEPs and as tutors in the schemes of individual trade unions with a more imaginative approach.

Reflections for Radicals

Everything I have written underlines the importance to the intellectual of passionate engagement, risk, exposure, commitment to principles ...

and being involved in worldly causes (Said, Representations of the Intellectual).

I have recounted these episodes because we need awareness of the barriers to working with working-class students in a really educational way and the difficulty of opposing established power in attempting to do so. In these times where much of the education of adults is commissioned by organisations on the market with parameters set by institutional power-holders they possess a relevance beyond trade union education. Many texts ponder the problems of a radical pedagogy. Few dwell on the social constraints on its realisation and the lack of a proper basis for its development (see, for example, Youngman, 1986: 234–5; Collins, 1991: 94*ff*). Moreover brief references in the literature (Field, 1988: 228–31) are giving way to more detailed and erroneous accounts which justify erasure of democracy and suppression of critical, social purpose education on the altar of the 'success' of technical training – evidence of which, as the TUC and TUC education has staggered from one defeat to another, is conspicuous by its absence (Holford, 1994: 142).

Holford excuses the TUC's behaviour by appeal to the good record of the region – despite the leading involvement of those attacked in building that record (Connell, 1990: 8). He transmutes victimisation of experienced critical tutors and their replacement by the inexperienced and compliant into 'the management of resource allocation'. He then diminishes matters, asserting that only myself, 'Manchester University and to a lesser degree the WEA' were involved. At least 19 tutors from nine different institutions were removed in one way or another from teaching TUC courses in the North West in this period. Finally he notes that my own exclusion was – this from a man who urges wider discussion of trade union education – 'in the context of his very public criticism of the TUC's educational approach'. That is all right then: the bounder deserved everything he got. Such is the decline in educational integrity and the growth of time-serving masquerading as realism – 'decisions were sometimes arbitrary, hard choices had to be made' – with which we are presently confronted (Holford, 1994: 142, 248, 245).

We can enter all sorts of caveats. Perhaps we should have behaved more diplomatically, argued and publicised our case better, built more alliances. Many in trade union education were not very interested. The saga demonstrates not only the limits of radicalism but of educational principle in this area of work. The problem is not simply that the illiberal apologetics cited above – how can any education worth the name come out of the petty manipulation, bullying and silencing of voices I have described? – can emanate from somebody who worked for the WEA throughout this period. Unfortunately it represents a powerful current in adult education. Criticism and refusal is sometimes necessary, even against all the odds. Our case was influential in some areas and but for our efforts TUC orthodoxy would in all probability have continued unchallenged. We achieved no reorientation because of the powerful factors we confronted. Operating in a market situation dominated by one supplier, where institutions and tutors competed on TUC criteria, where there was pressure to maintain a flow of courses, where some educators were being pushed to be entrepreneurial and others to get jobs, little attention was paid to, and some irritation exhibited at, what was perceived as abstract and expensive educational discourse which could upset the apple cart.

We argued that any renewal of workers' education would necessitate:

> *the freedom of tutors and class to pursue the argument wherever it might lead and by whatever methods they chose. It would require tutors to rightly regard themselves as intellectuals, in no matter how small a way, not as technicians governed by external edicts. None of this is true of the 'core' of trade union studies in 1986 (Healey et al., 1986: 5).*

The majority of tutors, however, regarded themselves precisely as technicians with restricted autonomy, fully adjusted to delivering pre-packaged, standardised curricula and pedagogy on behalf of external authority. Some argued they were 'serving the labour movement' despite the lack of democratic accountability of TUC professionals and the necessity for a degree of autonomy for educators and students. Others conceived of themselves, as one university teacher put it, 'as guns for hire', available to execute pre-determined commissions and eschew criticism of the client. This lack of independence and mission cannot simply be ascribed to changes in the ideological context since 1979. Conformity and co-option always had its rewards. Long before Thatcher some university 'industrial studies' tutors conceived themselves as entrepreneurs offering their services on the market to employers and unions (Houlton, 1971). Such a tradition was always present in further education. Under the rhetoric, the disintegration of any *active* distinctive philosophy of workers' education in the WEA long preceded Thatcherism. These tendencies were strengthened after 1979 primarily by changes in the political and material context. In some cases Pavlov seems to have more to contribute to explanations of change in adult education than Stuart Hall. Change the funding rules and if you don't change educational beliefs you change actions. Make the TUC a responsible body and dispenser of funds, strengthen competition in a cold climate and you reform the stimulus-response pattern in the educational market and the behaviour of many of those who continue to spout old philosophies when fine words butter no parsnips but sit silent when the stakes are down.

Of course it is more complex than that. Many tutors in trade union education have a genuine wish 'to serve the movement', understood in static, hierarchical terms with conflicts of politics and interest inside it erased. Others are infected with workerism, one polytechnic lecturer going so far as to pronounce – in the 1980s – academic freedom a bourgeois illusion. Others are *entrists* who stubbornly and parochially refuse to examine the system in which their classroom operates because they feel they can implement their own political goals once the classroom door closes. Still others are driven more by material pressures: in a situation of high unemployment they need the work on the hirers' terms.

Many are socialists who unlike their counterparts in other areas of education refuse the collective elaboration of a critique of the organisation, goals and philosophy of the educational sub-system in which they work, confronting it only in 'common sense' terms. The position is not helped by the divided and marginal position of staff in three different trade unions. The Society of Industrial Tutors, an umbrella organisation dedicated to the liberal education of industrial workers as trade unionists and managers, provided an arena for debate but was criticised by TUC-loyal tutors as managerialist in the 1970s and leftist in the 1980s.

All of this is wrong: the principled teacher *must* pursue an always elusive relative autonomy, rejecting subordination and the sacrifice of critical independence to union leaders, civil servants, politicians or university functionaries. The pedagogic intellectual, as against the technician, will possess a restless spirit of distrust of established authority and refusal of conformity, questioning orthodoxy, seeking to raise the embarrassing questions that are conveniently overlooked. He or she will be a relentless opponent of institutional expediency, engaged but critically aligned, attempting to represent the unrepresented, 'speaking truth to power', rather than serving it (Said, 1994: 9, 63).

The intellectual will be committed, in no matter how small a way, to searching, to finding out what it is all about, to theory, to struggling to understand what he or she is doing as part of a systemic endeavour beyond the classroom. Intellectuals will possess a powerful conception of themselves as teachers and leaders. They will struggle to develop pedagogic craft and critical self-interrogation, asserting the need for the education in which they work to privilege independent thought and classroom democracy. Unlike technicians they will negotiate and debate with representatives of 'the labour movement'. Committed to that movement, but with full knowledge that it is a site of conflict and division and its objectives, policies and processes are developing and contested, their response to attempts to insist they follow a particular organisational line or approach (usually that of an established leadership) will be: *non serviam*. At this particular unfavourable conjuncture, the creation of organic intellectuals within the working class envisaged by Gramsci is related amongst numerous other factors in the economic and industrial struggle to the development of critical 'new' traditional intellectuals in this mould. Radical intellectuals will not confuse education with conversion. They will insist that trade union education addresses competing conceptions of trade unionism and the context in which it operates, its internal relations and the issues confronting it with the object of raising consciousness, developing strategic vision and encouraging educated action. In short they will take trade unionism, education and themselves seriously.

The education of trade unionists espoused by the radical intellectual will be very different from that resourced by the technician. Refusing theory the technician does not escape its consequences. TUC pedagogy, whether through the explicit package or 'other directed, self-directed' learning, has been created to ensure control lies with those who wish to reproduce trade unionism as essentially an industrial bargaining agency.

To reduce trade unionism to collective bargaining is to purvey one limited conception of trade unionism, minimising or ignoring its organic political role. To identify trade unionism with the workplace is to fragment and diminish trade unionism: for success it needs to have its roots in the workplace but reach far beyond it. To confuse trade unionism with technical skills is to reverse priorities and trivialise trade unionism.

The drift is towards formation of industrial subalterns rather than political cadres, as skills training displaces the critical engagement with purpose, policy and politics of which skills are sinews, not substitutes. The strengthening of the mechanistic and conservative competency approach can only reinforce a *status quo* in which the TUC has moved towards a variety of business unionism, sees collective bargaining as a means of increasing productivity and profits and denies 'any inherent conflict between capital and labour in the workplace' (McIlroy, 1995: Chapter 10). It is the inadequacies of trade unionism which TUC education reproduces: its weakness as a social movement; its lack of participation; its limited strategic vision and political purchase; its lack of a cadre of activists able to think, discriminate, decide and lead. And it is simply not good enough for a national union centre to shrug its shoulders and say 'yes all that is important but it should be done elsewhere' (Grant, 1990: 13). An education dedicated to technique wrenched from critical understanding can only produce ineffective organisers and bargainers.

This has as much to do with the conservatism of the TUC as state funding *per se*. The categories of courses for which grant was available agreed in the 1970s met the objectives of both the state and the TUC. Under Thatcherism state funding acted as a pressure against a radical widening of the curriculum but it is doubtful if the TUC itself wanted any such widening. Certainly there was little pressure amongst trade unionists, nor, as we have seen, amongst educators. The lesson is not that engagement with the state should be eschewed but that it requires understanding of its limits, struggle and the application of power if it is to prove fruitful for the working class (Poulantzas, 1978; Zeitlin, 1985). And that will not be forthcoming until a radical vision of trade union education is anchored in a renewed vision of trade unionism. We are still very far from that.

Futures

It eluded us then but that's no matter – tomorrow we will run faster ...
(Scott Fitzgerald, The Great Gatsby).

The challenges facing the unions today are clear. How can they make good membership loss in the face of hostile industrial and labour force trends, the move from manufacturing to services, large to small workplaces, public to private industry, full-time to part-time work, sustained large scale unemployment, a move to global economy? How can they develop a new collective oppositional culture which appeals to women workers in the service sector rather than dockers or carworkers? How can they restore a supportive legal, economic and political framework surely essential to any real recovery? It is this agenda which should be explicitly at the core of any relevant trade union education. Yet as the TUC's embrace of NVQs demonstrates, the march of technicism continues whilst other factors also strengthen the educational bifurcation in which politics, policy and strategy are the province of the leadership and the skills required for their execution the role of activists. The growth of managerial conceptions of trade unionism which downplay activism and democracy in favour of professionals servicing members as consumers is deeply antagonistic to any broader radical education and cuts with the moves to NVQ shop stewards.

Realistically we can hope for little from the TUC scheme, which is not to understate the continuing importance of the union centre in establishing the terms of legitimacy and ethos in union education. Its dependence on state funding has caused serious problems. Without temporary support from the TUC development fund its courses would have been in serious trouble in 1993. Cutbacks in courses and organisation are planned as it is clear that affiliates will not make up the loss of grant. The move to NVQs is, for all the fine words, driven by financial needs: to ensure continued funding from the Further Education Funding Council. It has been criticised on a wide front. Crucially its emphasis on competence, on *doing*, evicting knowledge and understanding, suppresses critical thinking and classifies the success or failure of shop stewards in terms of their ability to meet purposes ultimately set by state agencies, particularly the Department of Employment. The independence of union education is finally compromised and its content tied to state control. In the context of well publicised critiques of NVQs by academic researchers and the National Institute of Economic and Social Research the TUC's adoption of the system has been criticised by 'a majority of union education officers' (Howard, 1994; McIlroy, 1993).

There is an alternative which would link in these courses to Access routes and higher degrees. If, as it seems, certification is unavoidable this appears a more educational route but, of course, less consonant with the training tradition entrenched at the TUC. For those interested in real trade union education, this path – it is not without its compromises – seems the one to follow, perhaps working in conjunction, if possible, with the TUC but also affiliated unions. The residential colleges such as Ruskin and Northern College have developed a variety of courses in this mould and key unions such as the TGWU and Unison have been supportive of a wider social education. The TUC itself has joined the scramble for certification in supporting Diploma courses in a number of colleges. The TGWU has supported a range of one- and two-year courses in politics and economics with the universities of Surrey, Leeds, Liverpool, Manchester and Northumbria. Unison has developed similar work with the universities of Manchester, Nottingham and Sheffield (Fisher, 1989; McIlroy, 1989; Fryer, 1990). The likelihood is we shall have to look to specific projects like this rather than a national system. But above all there is a crying need for closer links and more debate as to the future of trade union education in the context of the more open situation created by the disappearance of state funding.

Radicalism in union education remains weak. Yet the game is far from up. The conditions that bred trade unionism rooted in class conflict and exploitation still exist. And the education of trade unionists remains of key importance to any development of radical adult education, for, despite important changes in structure and consciousness, class remains the dominant social antagonism and trade unionism its necessary basic reflex (McIlroy, 1995: Chapters 1, 10). Our hope lies in the *limits* of the ideological change wrought by the New Right and the real potential for change in the political situation.

References

Anderson, D. (1987) 'Academies of union unrest', *The Times*, 9 December.

Anderson, P. (1967) 'The limits and possibilities of trade union action', in Blackburn, R. and Cockburn, A. (eds) *op. cit.*

Auerbach, S. (1990) *Legislating for Conflict*, Clarendon Press.

Beynon, H. (ed.) (1985) *Digging Deeper – Issues in the miners' strike*, Verso.

Blackburn, R. and Cockburn, A. (eds) (1967) *The Incompatibles*, Penguin.

Brown, G. (1980) 'Independence and incorporation: the Labour College movement and the Workers' Educational Association before the Second World War', in Thompson, J. (ed.) *op. cit.*

Brown, J. (1982) *Relations Between WEA and the TUC*.

Brown, J. (1983) 'Trade Union Studies: Day Release Courses with the TUC', Memorandum to WEA.

Brown, J., McIlroy, J. and Spencer, B. (1983) 'Fundamental questions about student-centred learning', *Trade Union Studies Journal*, 7.

Caldwell, P. (1981) 'State funding of trade union education', *Trade Union Studies Journal*, 3.

Campbell, A. (1982) Correspondence with TUC re. Diploma courses.

Campbell, A. (1988) *TUC Provision in the North West*, University of Liverpool Department of Continuing Education.

Campbell, A. and McIlroy, J. (1981) *Getting Organised*, Pan Books.

Chapman, P. (1984) Statement on Constructive Dismissal.

Cliff, T. (1970) *The Employers' Offensive*, Pluto Press.

Clinton, A. (1977) *The Trade Union Rank and File: Trades Councils in Britain 1900–40*, Manchester University Press.

Coates, K. and Topham, T. (1969) *Trade Union Register*, Spokesman.

Collins, M. (1991) *Adult Education as Vocation*, Routledge.

Connell, J. (1990) 'In memoriam: Jim Millar', *The Industrial Tutor*, vol. 5, no. 1.

Connor, D. (1985) 'WEA courses', *Times Higher Education Supplement*, 28 June.

Cosgrove, F. (1983) 'Re-shaping trade union education', *The Industrial Tutor*, vol. 3, no. 8.

Dorfman, G. (1983) *British Trade Unionism Against the Trades Union Congress*, Macmillan.

Doyle, M. (1980) 'Reform and reaction – the Workers' Educational Association post-Russell', in Thompson, J. (ed.) *op. cit.*

Doyle, M. (1988) 'Editorial', *Trade Union Studies Journal*, 17.

Dutt, R. Palme (1963) 'Notes of the month', *Labour Monthly*, September.

Edwards, C., McIlroy, J., Mooney, J. and Spencer, B. (1983) 'Student-centred learning and trade union education – a preliminary examination', *The Industrial Tutor*, vol. 3, no. 8.

Evans, B. (1987) *Radical Adult Education: A political critique*, Croom Helm.
Field, J. (1988) 'Workers' education and the crisis of British trade unionism', in Lovett, T. (ed.) *op. cit.*
Fieldhouse, R. (1971) Correspondence, *WEA News*, September.
Fieldhouse, R. (1985) *Adult Education and the Cold War*, University of Leeds, Leeds Studies in Adult Continuing Education.
Fieldhouse, R. and Forrester, K. (1984) 'The WEA and trade union education', *The Industrial Tutor*, vol. 3, no. 9.
Fisher, J. (1989), 'Industrial studies: an example of university-union co-operation', *The Industrial Tutor*, vol. 4, no. 9.
Foley, B. (1982) Correspondence to TUC regarding Diploma courses.
Fryer, B. (1990) 'The challenge to working class education', in Simon, B. (ed.) *op. cit.*
Grant, A. (1990) 'Trade union education: a TUC perspective', *The Industrial Tutor*, vol. 5, no. 1.
Gravell, C. (1983) 'Trade union education: will state funding lead to state control?' *Trade Union Studies Journal*, 8.
Healey, E., Campbell, A., McIlroy, J. and Spencer, B. (1986) 'Beyond industrial relations training', *Trade Union Studies Journal*, 13.
Holford, J. (1994) *Union Education in Britain: A TUC activity*, Nottingham University Department of Adult Education.
Houlton, B. (1971) 'Supply and demand relationships in industrial adult education', *The Industrial Tutor*, September.
House of Commons Debates (1987–8) vol. 123.
Howard, S. (1994) 'No verifiable quality', *Morning Star*, 26 August.
Hyman, R. (1979) 'The politics of workplace trade unionism', *Capital and Class*, 8.
The Industrial Tutor (1984) Editorial, vol. 3, no. 9.
Jobbins, D. (1982) 'TUC plans to rescue shop steward courses', *Times Higher Education Supplement*, 3 December.
Lloyd, J. (1983) 'Unions accept employers right to ratify courses', *Financial Times*, 15 March.
Lovett, T. (1988) *Radical Approaches to Adult Education: A reader*, Routledge.
McIlroy, J. (1979) *Trade Union Recognition: The Limitations of Law*, Studies for Trade Unionists, WEA.
McIlroy, J. (1980) 'Politics and the trade unions: why the issue is one the Labour movement must take up', *Tribune*, 10 October.
McIlroy, J. (1981) *Trade Unions and the Closed Shop*, Studies for Trade Unionists, WEA.
McIlroy, J. (1982) 'TUC stage 2 – an opportunity to change course?', *The Industrial Tutor*, vol. 3, no. 6.
McIlroy, J. (1983a) *Industrial Tribunals: How to take a case, how to win it*, Pluto Press.
McIlroy, J. (1983b) 'Lessons in conformity', *New Statesman*, 23 September.
McIlroy, J. (1983c) 'Beyond the workplace', *Tribune*, 16 December.
McIlroy, J. (1984) *Strike! How to Fight – How to Win*, Pluto Press.
McIlroy, J. (1985a), 'Adult education and the role of the client – the TUC Education Scheme 1929–80', *Studies in the Education of Adults*, vol. 13, no. 2.
McIlroy, J. (1985b) 'Goodbye Mr Chips?', *The Industrial Tutor*, vol. 4, no. 2.
McIlroy, J. (1985c) 'Police and pickets' in Beynon, H. (ed.) *op. cit.*
McIlroy, J. (1988) *see* McIlroy (1995) below.
McIlroy, J. (1989) 'Back to the future', *Adults Learning*, vol. 1, no. 3.
McIlroy, J. (1991) *The Permanent Revolution? Conservative law and the trade unions*, Spokesman.
McIlroy, J. (1993) 'Tales from smoke-filled rooms', *Studies in the Education of Adults*, vol. 25, no. 1.

McIlroy, J. (1995) *Trade Unions in Britain Today*, 2nd edn, Manchester University Press; 1st edn, 1988.

McIlroy, J. and Brown, J., (1980) 'Giving the workers what they want', *Adult Education*, vol. 53, no. 2.

McIlroy, J. and Campbell, A. (1979) *Picketing Under Attack*, Studies for Trade Unionists, WEA.

McIlroy, J. and Spencer, B. (1984) 'Methods and politics in trade union education – a rejoinder', *The Industrial Tutor*, vol. 3, no. 10.

McLeod, D. (1991) 'TUC booklet on women withdrawn', *The Independent*, 15 June.

Manchester Education Committee (1985) *Report on Trade Union Education*.

NATFHE Trade Union Studies, Manchester Polytechnic (1983) *Who Cuts the Cake?*

North West Tutors (1983) *The TUC Education Scheme in the North West: A cause for concern*.

Outten, D. (1985) Correspondence with TUC re shop stewards courses at Long and Crawford.

Park, T. (1969) 'Trade union education', in Coates, K. *et al.*, *op. cit.*

Patterson (1982) 'Hint by Tebbit on union cash', *Daily Telegraph*, 23 August.

Poulantzas, N. (1978) *State, Power, Socialism*, Verso.

Richards, M. (1985) 'TUC and tutors clash', *Times Higher Education Supplement*, 9 June.

Said, E. (1994) *Representations of the Intellectual*, Vintage.

Simon, B. (ed.) (1990) *The Search for Enlightenment*, Lawrence and Wishart; 2nd edition, 1992, NIACE.

Spencer, B. (1983) Grievance – Bruce Spencer, Industrial Tutor, WEA.

Spencer, B. (1984) 'Collective bargaining and the rights at work courses', *The Industrial Tutor*, vol. 3, no. 9.

Tebbit, N. (1989) Correspondence with author.

Thompson, J. (ed.) (1980) *Adult Education for a Change*, Hutchinson.

Tolliday, S. and Zeitlin, J. (eds) (1985) *Shop Floor Bargaining and the State*, Cambridge University Press.

Topham, T. (1964) 'Shop stewards and workers' control', *New Left Review*, 25.

Topham, T. (1981) 'The need for political education', *The Industrial Tutor*, vol. 3, no. 5.

Topham, T. (1992) 'Education policy in the TGWU 1922–44. A tribute to John Price', *The Industrial Tutor*, vol. 5, no. 5.

Trade Union Studies Journal (1980) Editorial, 2.

Trade Union Studies Journal (1990) 'WEA/TUC provision', 20.

Tribune (1983) 'TUC to let employers vet training courses', 19 August.

Trower (1990) 'British Trade Unions and "1992" ', MA Thesis, University of Manchester .

TUC (1970) Evidence to the Russell Committee on Adult Education.

TUC (1982a) Correspondence with University of Liverpool regarding Diploma Courses.

TUC (1982b) Correspondence to TGWU regarding Certificate Courses.

TUC (1983) *Report*.

TUC (1985) Correspondence with University of Manchester EMD re shop steward courses at Long and Crawford.

TUC (1985b) Correspondence to University of Manchester Department of Extra-Mural Studies, November, December.

TUC (1986) *Report*.

TUC (1989) *Skills 2000*.

TUC (1990a) *Report*.

TUC (1990b) *Joint Action Over Training*.

TUC (1991a) *Report*.

TUC (1991b) *Report of Annual Meeting of Chairs and Secretaries of TUC Education Advisory Committees.*
TUC (1991c) Women's Committee, Minutes.
TUC (1994) Trade Union Education Review Group, Minutes, 16 March.
Turnbull, M. (1985) 'WEA tutors', *Times Higher Education Supplement*, 5 July.
WEA (1989) *Report of the Working Party on Trade Union Education.*
Westwood, S. (1980) 'Adult education and the sociology of education: an exploration', in Thompson, J. (ed.) *op. cit.*
Whitston, K. (1982) 'Breaking fresh ground. The new TUC introductory course', *The Industrial Tutor*, vol. 3, no. 6.
Youngman, F. (1986) *Adult Education and Socialist Pedagogy*, Croom Helm.
Zeitlin, J. (1985) 'Shop floor bargaining and the state', in Tolliday, S. and Zeitlin, J. (eds) *op. cit.*

Thirteen

Learning in Working Life: The Contribution of the Trade Unions

Keith Forrester

For many thousands of people, participation in the educational opportunities offered by their trade union has been an important and salutary experience. Entry into some form of trade union education has not only provided the member with a greater awareness of issues and strengthened activity in the workplace, it has also developed a number of valuable personal skills and overcome many unhappy earlier educational memories. Trade unions, more than any other organisation, have the possibility and therefore the responsibility for unlocking the learning potential amongst its membership to the benefit of both the individual member and the trade union. The record of the Trades Union Congress (TUC) and individual unions' educational programmes for involving large numbers of working-class students is impressive. The problems besetting the current provision, however, are considerable and threaten to qualitatively undermine future developments. This chapter outlines these difficulties. It suggests that present funding crises and increasing difficulties associated with paid educational leave compound other problems which have characterised this provision over the two previous decades. The main argument in the chapter, however, is the importance of strengthening and widening the learning opportunities available to the membership, now and in the future. Encouraging and meeting the learning aspirations of the membership requires, it will be argued, participation by the trade unions and the TUC in the rapidly changing context of post-compulsory education and recognition of the changed employment context of the 1990s. Instead of an educational provision centred around 'assisting representatives to carry out their functions as responsible officers of their union and to promote trade union competence in the conduct of industrial relations and in improving trade union organisation' (TUC, 1987: 3), there is the urgent need, it is argued, for a broader-based provision that engages with the membership's changing experiences of working life, of growing societal inequalities and apparent disintegration of inner city life.

Encouraging members to participate in an educational practice that addresses problems in the workplace as well as in the wider community at a local and global context is an argument for renewal within trade union life and, more urgently, in democratic understandings and practices. For want of a better description, we have labelled this broader role for trade union education as 'working life education'. Three examples are chosen to illustrate the direction that such a working life education might take. Reformulating trade union education to include these (and other) areas, it will be argued, offers the possibility of a wider membership engaging more systematically with the harsher and, often, bewildering circumstances of the 1990s. As the conclusions to the article suggest, the future direction and format of trade union education will be a significant determinant not only on the nature of trade unionism but also on the skills, understanding, confidence and activities of people to shape and influence their lives.

Trade Union Education in the 1990s

As Holford (1994: 241) has argued, 'the TUC education schemes weathered the eighties rather better than a number of other educational institutions – and arguably rather better than the trade union movement itself'. By the mid-1990s, however, the institutional framework characterising trade union education over the previous two decades looks increasingly unlikely to provide the basis and momentum necessary to survive the current problems. The immediate problems are two-fold. First, there are the serious problems arising from the governments vindictive decision to phase out, over a three-year period from April 1993, public funding for trade union education of its lay officials. In 1996, the TUC would need to raise around £2m in order to maintain its level of provision in 1992. Secondly, over the last decade, there has been the increasing difficulty of lay officers obtaining paid educational leave. The 10-day-release courses for workplace representatives, for example, declined from a peak of around 1200 courses in 1979–80 to 546 in 1991–92. Health and safety courses have similarly declined but not so dramatically. Short courses, usually of a single day duration, grew in importance throughout the 1980s. Finally, whether as a result of the above two problems or for reasons unconnected with them, the rapid move by the TUC towards an accredited, competency-based model of provision for its lay officer courses could add a further cluster of difficulties to be overcome in the immediate future.

Of course, the problems confronting trade union education are but a part of the wider problems facing trade unions in the 1990s. At one level, the impact of a Conservative government from 1979 onwards on British trade unions has been well recorded and much discussed (Coates, 1989; Hyman, 1989; Hall and Jacques, 1983). Reams of statistical data supplement commentaries illustrating how, on any of a dozen or so different indicators, trade unionists, their organisations and their activities have been crippled or qualitatively damaged under the impact of anti-union legislation, two economic recessions, a hostile ideological onslaught and mass unemployment. In line, however, with commentators such as MacInnes (1989) and Kelly (1988), it can be argued that:

with some notable exceptions, British trade unions have weathered the recession remarkably well. Membership and density have declined, but less than in previous recessions: workplace organisation has remained largely intact and is still expanding in the public sector; union finances are fairly sound; real wages for many of those in work have increased since 1981; and unions were completely successful in the political fund ballots despite the alleged unpopularity of the unions' political voice (Kelly, 1988: 289).

The continuing loss of jobs in the mid-1990s, especially from the larger workplaces, in a period of economic growth, together with fundamental changes in the labour market and upheavals resulting from the earlier waves of privatisation and deregulation, are and will continue to severely test the resilience of trade union organisations (Pendleton and Winterton, 1993).

At another level, however, the damage to trade unions has been more complex and possibly more profound. The economic and industrial relations environment of the 1990s is characterised by a number of important and significant changes to that of two decades ago. These changes, coupled with the increased uncertainty resulting from four consecutive political defeats in the general elections, has resulted in a certain loss of nerve and sense of purpose and an undermining of collective confidence and direction. The weakening of a collective identity and sense of solidarity, expressed and reinforced in the culture and communal relationship of many sections of the working class has instead been increasingly replaced by a receptiveness to individualism and to claims on behalf of 'the national interest'. The ending of 'organised capitalism' as Lash and Urry (1987) put it, suggests that a particular type of labour movement and its associated modes of action are disappearing. Collective confidence in a series of earlier relationships, with the state, the Labour Party and the membership, are, in the 1990s, seen as problematic and in need of renewal and reformulating. As a sympathetic observer of European trade unions reported in 1993, 'This year, the TUC celebrates its 125th birthday. The best present it can give itself is to put the past 125 years on hold and spend its 126th year learning from others how organisation, policy and ideas may be used to rekindle the fire that its many enemies in this country would like to see extinguished' (MacShane, 1993). Trade union education, it could be argued, has an enhanced importance and centrality within a context of 'the weakening of a collective identity and sense of solidarity', and in the early to mid-1980s there were signs that the TUC recognised this to be the case. There were, for example, the excellent materials produced on 'tackling racism', 'working women' and the 'beating apartheid' workshops. Towards the end of the 1980s, however, it was clear that trade union education was not going to be the principal or even a significant force of the TUC and the trade unions in confronting the accumulating problems resulting from the Thatcher governments. The end of the 1980s and early years of the 1990s witnessed no significant attempts to reverse the steady downward spiral of provision in the number of courses provided or, more importantly, in the nature and format of the provision. By the mid-1990s, as was outlined above, future provision was facing a number of severe problems.

More fundamentally though, weaknesses within the national provision of trade union education that have remained hidden since the mid-1970s have resurfaced 20 years later to further constrain and narrow the options available to the unions. Despite, for example, the mass explosion of provision and students attending courses in the late 1970s and early 1980s, education or, more accurately, learning, never became an integral defining characteristic of trade union activity. They might have, comparatively, done a lot of it, but it was never organisationally or intellectually central to the structures and work of trade unions. Education was the responsibility of the education departments and their officers and was divorced, often rigidly, from the remainder of the organisation. This isolation within trade unions was, secondly, mirrored within the wider educational world. Perhaps as a result of the quarrelsome relationships with some of the university extra-mural departments, the Workers' Educational Association and other sympathetic voluntary groups, there was never seriously attempted, never mind created, a broadly-based educational alliance of sympathetic tutors and institutions. The development of a network of trade union studies centres within the further education college system in the 1970s was an important part of any possible educational alliance. The overwhelming focus on class-contact hours within the college sector, however, ensured limited autonomy for the future to initiate learning programmes or projects that supplemented or developed the core day-release provision for lay representatives. From the early 1980s onwards, the energy and efforts of college tutors, outside their teaching commitments, has centred around the grind of ensuring sufficient recruits for the advertised lay representatives courses. Creating a 'critical mass' of tutors and researchers in the further and higher education sector, not directly tied to the core provision of the 10-day-release programme but involved in a developmental, experimental and supportive role would have provided a valuable national resource. Such an alliance was a possibility up until the mid-1980s. Unfortunately, the explosion of student enrolments towards the end of the 1970s provided the basis for the easier (and certainly less politically painful) option of using outside educational resources as passive servicing agents, rather than as collaborative partners.

A third weakness that has traditionally characterised trade union education over the last 20 or so years has been the absence of any serious focus on the 'missing audiences'. While priority for any union must be given to the education of its present and future lay officials, the absence of learning strategies designed to involve, for example, particular trade union communities or the general membership remained a strategic shortcoming. The inadequately funded and designed (and short-lived) Open School initiative in the late 1980s exposed the organisational and conceptual isolation of the TUC provision, despite the efforts of a small number of college tutors and the responsible TUC education officer. The success of the NUPE 'Return to Learn' scheme throughout the country provided evidence of the exciting possibilities of a membership education initiative characterised by a solid, old-fashioned labour-intensive adult education practice. As the funding problems around the turn of the decade in the 1990s grew more acute, short courses, including the valuable campaign workshops, assumed greater significance and helped stave off, for a short period, the accumulating problems confronting continuing provision.

The government-initiated problems facing trade union educationalists, then, are formidable. Within a broader scenario, however, working-class education opportunities have been carefully nourished and, in many instances, blossomed. As Fryer (1990) has illustrated in his survey of current working-class learning initiatives, there are grounds for optimism. The growth of women's' studies, of new opportunity courses and accompanying growing literature, as illustrated in the WEA's *Women's Studies Newsletter*, provide examples of growth areas throughout the 1980s. The exciting educational fall-out from women's involvement in the 1984/5 miners' strike continues to be felt in the pit areas. Interrelating to these women's studies have been the local groups of the University of the Third Age and, in parts of the country, the rapid development of worker-writer networks. Educational work with the myriad tenants' organisations has been discussed elsewhere in this volume, while black studies programmes, often resourced through community-based Afro-Caribbean centres, are not uncommon in large conurbations. Often fragile and sometime intermittent, such varied learning groups represent impressive and exciting initiatives committed to exploring changing, often competing, conceptions of culture and the community in difficult, hostile circumstances.

Similar initiatives and explorations were less evident in the labour market, employment-related fields, despite the substantial changes in the understandings and experiences of working life over the previous two decades or so.

Working Life Education

As the debates and voluminous literature around 'de-industrialisation', the 'second industrial divide' and 'post-Fordism' continue to demonstrate, the endemic structural weakness of the British economy and the restructuring of the economic base has resulted in dramatic upheavals in the labour market and a parallel growing trend of inequality. From the end of 1990 to mid-1993, for example, there was a shocking loss of some 1.67 million jobs (in full-time equivalents). The poorer 50% of the population had 32% of total incomes in 1979 and only 25% by 1990–91. The virtual abolition of the Wages Councils and the rise of, mainly female, part-time jobs, has once again placed concerns of 'social exclusion', 'underclass' and 'displaced persons' alongside the urgent need for economic recovery programmes, in this country and elsewhere. Youth and adult experiences of working life have been transformed over the last two decades and are increasingly characterised by falling standards of living, temporary or long-term absence from employment and increasing insecurity.

Making sense of these changed material circumstances and growing insecurity within a supportive, collective learning environment has been, and remains, an important part of the adult education agenda. The mushrooming of imaginative feminist learning projects in the 1970s onwards illustrated the vitality and enthusiasm possible within circumstances of limited resources and overwhelming patriarchal control. For most trade unionists, the educational opportunities available from their trade union and their employer have not provided the basis to engage with processes of profound economic and political change. Tackling issues of racism and gender is of course integral to the TUC day-release provision but as the list of topics suggested in the 'Review of the TUC's Education Service' indicates, the courses are heavily influenced by the increasing difficulties of immediate workplace concerns (TUC, 1987: 25). The descriptions and struggles of working life (or non-working life) that increasingly characterise the personal, domestic and collective experiences of adults is not reflected sharply enough within the learning opportunities currently available. As Fryer (1990: 277) puts it, 'the focus of vigorous adult study today should be not only on education for and by working class people, but also about the working class as a topic of study, a range of experiences and as an agency for social change. In character it should be both analytical and practical'. In addition to the increasingly threatened agenda of trade union education, with its necessary emphasis on workplace lay officer induction, skills and collective bargaining focus and in addition to the job-specific vocational education and training (VET) minimally available in many workplaces, there is an argument for a more varied and wider conceptual learning experience. For want of a better term, we have called this 'working life education' suggesting a learning agenda for trade unions that expands the understandings of the social, political and economic transformations of recent years through critical judgment and independent study encouraged and shaped by the trade unions. Linking theoretically and organisationally the increasingly fragmented experiences of those in and out of work has become more urgent. For many millions of citizens, it is only through their trade unions that there is a chance of educationally making sense of the bewildering and often painful dislocations and aspirations characterising the 'free-market' society of the 1990s.

What are these 'more varied and wider learning experiences' that require linking through the trade unions? The remaining sections in this chapter will illustrate a number of possibilities that have remained hidden, undeveloped and embryonic, it will be argued, within the ambit of the trade unions but that have emerged 'from below' in the 1980s.

The Unemployment Experience

Unknown to the vast majority of trade unionists, there has been since the early 1980s a network of Unemployed Workers' Centres (Forrester and Ward, 1986; 1990). In 1994 some hundred such centres existed in England and Wales, attracting at the last count around £5–6 million in funding per year from outside bodies (mainly local authorities). Organised through the TUC and responsible to the TUC Regional Secretaries, the Unemployed Workers' Centre (UWCs) range from small 'voluntary'-run centres through to the large urban centres employing between six and 15 workers. Childcare facilities, reprographic and printing services, employment rights and welfare benefits expertise and computing skills are but a small selection of the services available through many of the centres. Often sharing their premises with a variety of other voluntary organisations such as 'Gingerbread', the local 'Child Poverty Action Group' or with a neighbourhood community association, the UWC's represent a considerable organising resource of valuably acquired skills and expertises rooted in the community and usually centrally part of local networks. Publications such as the *Lambeth Women's Handbook: A guide to services and benefits* or research documents such as *A Price Worth Paying?* and *Employment Training: One year on* from the Wakefield Centre in Yorkshire illustrate the imagination, organisation and skills used in informational and agitational activities. Users of the Centres number many tens of thousands. Usually seeking employment-related information or solutions to social service and welfare problems, user demands on the Centres often present acute workload problems for Centre workers.

The primary focus of any Centre's activities is not the workplace or collective bargaining. Support for workplace struggles and campaigns is certainly an important feature of the larger urban UWCs as was witnessed during the 1984/5 miners' strike but the workplace is generally only a part of the focus in the Centres. More important are social security provision, Income Support, Employment Training, single parent support facilities, homelessness and housing issues, the council tax and, finally, health-related issues. Interestingly, but perhaps predictably, the majority of people using the Centres are not trade unionists and know very little, if anything of trade unions. Women users are well represented but not ethnic minority communities, preferring possibly their own self-help support organisations. Educational activities within the Centres are a continuous feature of most Centres and range from campaigning workshops – usually around social security and 'workfare' issues – to classes run by the Workers' Educational Association. Some Centres offer skills-type courses on computers while others concentrate on the informal topical discussion group. Making trade union banners or developing lay-out and poster-making skills are other examples of education activities. A Centre worker with responsibility for education is not unusual in the non-voluntary UWCs.

The significant missing part of the UWC picture is the trade unions and their members. Largely absent as a presence in the work and campaigns of the Centres are the millions of experienced trade unionists, with their valuable organising and political skills, who have lost their jobs in the 1980s. The local Trades Union Councils, formally linked to 'their' UWC, are by and large indifferent to the Centres. For most trade unions, as opposed to the TUC, there remains an ignorance of the existence and facilities available to them 'out there' in the community. More importantly, the trade unions are failing to influence a different and 'new' audience of Centre users. At a most minimal level, UWCs could be used as effective recruiters of new members. The 'Link-Up' campaigns of the Transport and General Workers Union and 'low-pay' campaigns of the shop workers' union and Unison, for example, explicitly targeted such audiences in their drive for new members, but failed to use the Centres. Not only do trade unionists fail to build relationships with their Centre but there is separate education provision for those in work and those out of work, each with its own network of providers and own different learning agendas.

There exists then, it is argued in this section, the organisational and conceptual basis for strengthening the understandings and activities of both those in and out of work. Integrating the activities of the local UWC with various trade union branches in the vicinity would strengthen the resources and facilities available to both audiences as well as widen the concept of learning and campaigning agendas. Leaving some hundred resource centres, with their 200–300 full-time workers, marginalised and peripheral to the activities of the trade unions is a luxury that can no longer be afforded.

If 'working life education' must reflect the experiences of being out of work or being only marginally in work, it must also reflect the learning possibilities available to trade unionists while in work.

Workplace Learning Experiences

Trade unions, and in particular the TUC, have in recent years greatly increased the importance attached to workplace education and training. As part of its programme and campaign for full employment, the TUC for example has prioritised 'life-long access to education and training' (TUC, 1993b: 5). Similarly, a key feature of its future priorities and agenda is the promotion of 'joint action on training in particular at workplace and employer level (whether public or private sector)' (TUC, 1991). The recent TUC document *Working in Partnership for Quality Training* reports on a number of initiatives involving trade unions, sometimes in partnership with their employers and/or the local Training and Enterprise Council. Much of the impetus behind the increased interest and activity by trade unions in workplace learning has resulted from government policy initiatives simplistically, and often mistakenly, linking skills shortage and reforms of the vocational education and training (VET) system with Britain's comparatively weak economic performance. The introduction, for instance, of National Vocational Qualifications (NVQs) has provided the political and collective bargaining space and opportunity for trade unions to discuss with employers a wide variety of learning opportunities for their members while at work.

The nature and direction of this workplace learning agenda is an agenda still to be contested and detailed. As NIACE has persuasively argued in a number of reports, there is no way that the National Education and Training Targets (endorsed by the TUC) are going to be met unless there are 'radical changes in the way in which education and training in the UK is organised and financed. The targets cannot be achieved without extending the "learning community" far beyond those who have traditionally participated in education and training' (NIACE, 1993: 4). Our own research into employee VET experience and aspirations in the retail sector clearly demonstrates the very minimal opportunities available (Forrester, James and Thorne, 1994). A successful eventual outcome to this 'contested agenda' of workplace learning by the trade unions could transform the learning experience and aspirations for millions of trade unionists at work. The stakes are high. Trade union education, we are suggesting, is more than the training of future lay officers: it must centrally involve learning at work. The opportunity is there but there are a number of inter-related policy issues that require further discussion and effort by trade unions, the TUC and sympathetic educationalists.

Most obvious of these 'inter-related policy issues' is, for example, the system of National Vocational Qualifications (NVQs). While strongly agreeing with the need for workplace accredited learning by employees and the development of transferable core skills, we have strong misgivings over the competency-based model of learning underpinning the NVQ system. We share the conclusions of the Smithers report for Channel Four television where they state, 'For the best of motives, and from a romantic and impractical idealism, NCVQ seems to be perpetrating a disaster of epic proportions' (Smithers, 1993: 41). Secondly, learning at work, while generally designed to improve task-and job-related performances, is much more than this. It is unlikely that any workplace or sector will achieve its task- or job-related goals without providing a much wider learning environment. As the Union of Shop, Distributive and Allied Workers (USDAW, 1991) has argued, 'we also need to dispel the myth that all training and skills, or aptitude development, is only important in relation to paid employment. Personal development training and the opportunity to enhance skills, pursue interests or develop aptitudes is an important quality of life issue'. VET in the workplace with the appropriate support services in terms, for example, of guidance, childcare and eldercare will allow employees (mostly women) with family responsibilities to pursue workplace learning opportunities. As USDAW puts it, 'We are also arguing for increased investment in ourselves as working people. We are arguing for social justice as much as economic growth' (USDAW, 1991). There are numerous examples of workplaces embarking on these (mis-named) 'employee development' schemes (Forrester, Payne and Ward, 1993).

A third inter-related issue that requires attention by trade unions on behalf of their members is the whole development of 'accreditation of experiential learning'. Awarding accreditation and legitimating the learning (and unrecognised skills of trade unionists) while at work is an area of increasing importance for both employers and those in further and higher education. As in most workplace learning initiatives, the involvement of trade unionists and especially part-time employees is likely to be ignored unless learning at work becomes a central concern of trade unions and a broader 'trade union educational' function.

This section has argued that workplace learning is too important to be left to the employers or to narrowly focus on job-specific learning. For many millions of employees and trade unionists, their opportunity to participate in 'life-long learning' will be determined by how forcefully and resolutely trade unions manage to transform the narrow concerns of vocational education and training.

Membership Learning Experiences

The third type of 'more varied and wider learning experiences' that, it is argued, require incorporating within the ambit of 'trade union education' centres on membership learning. As was suggested earlier, educational initiatives designed to involve the members have not been successful. The labour-intensive requirements of most membership-driven schemes have not suited the mass-based delivering system created by the TUC, around the day-release model, over the last two decades. Given the changes in working patterns and hours, together with the changes in composition of the labourforce, involving employees and trade unionists through education is of greater importance today than before. A possibility of overcoming problems may well be available through trade union-led workplace learning developments, as outlined in the section above. There are, though, other possibilities. The success of the NUPE (now Unison) 'Return to Learn' scheme has indicated that it is possible to involve members in their own time around a sustained programme of learning. In the Yorkshire and Humberside region, the vast majority of these members have never attended a union branch meeting, are mainly part-time women workers, know little or nothing about their union but were prepared to enrol on the 'Return to Learn' course in comparatively large numbers. As trade union educationalists have confirmed almost daily, trade unionists value highly the opportunity to learn in a safe and trusting environment. 'Their' trade union provides this non-threatening context in a way unmatched by any other agency. Evening classes, linked weekends or Sunday schools or, more ambitiously, open and distance learning programmes are delivery systems yet to be successfully exploited by trade unions. The exception to this general case is the example of the planned Unison Open College. This exciting development, centred around four stages or phases, is designed to introduce members to learning (phase 1) around basic skills, literacy and numeracy (with the help of Workbase) and eventually, to support members' learning activities, in association with tutors from further and higher education, at a more advanced level. 'Return to Learn' and 'Women, Work and Society' are developed 'modules' on this learning progression. Combining vocational and non-vocational learning opportunities, accredited through the Open College Network and part of a credit accumulation and transfer system, the Unison Open College developments represent the most systematic and coherent attempt to date of a trade union determined to place membership learning strategies at the centre of its activities. The agreement between the Manufacturing Science and Finance Union with the University of Leeds is, similarly, an attempt to progressively develop an accredited independent study programme eventually targeted at the entire union membership.

Interestingly, recent 'distance-learning' initiatives and membership education have purposively moved away from a conception of trade union education dominated by a collective bargaining agenda. While a labour market and unemployment related context provides the backdrop for the learning outcomes, the immediate objectives are driven by wider social, political and educational priorities. Issues of inequality, of democratisation and of learning progression, for example, are evident as strong themes in the provision. An explicitly political consideration (political with a small 'p') informs and shapes the agreed learning agendas, at a pace and at a level determined by the student.

Conclusions

Membership education that makes the connections between increasingly disparate and fragmented adult experiences remains an area to be further explored and developed through trade union education. Making sense of the council tax, of unemployment, of the Single European Market, together with occupational health and safety and related collective bargaining issues requires an enhanced and not a curtailed education service within trade unions. The selected examples used in this chapter for such a widened conception of education by the TUC and member trade unions are not 'new': they are longstanding issues within trade unions. They are, however, 'new' in the sense of the political openings and opportunities currently available in the 1990s. They are already the focus of a minority of trade union efforts and activities. They lack, however, a conceptual and organisationally integrated and strategic role within the provision of trade union education.

The possible return of a Labour government in the mid-1990s is seen by some trade unionists as the best and most likely solution to the serious financial and paid educational leave problems facing TUC provision. This could well be the case, although the lack of any detailed and concrete proposals within the Labour Party around the notion of lifelong learning remains worrying. The argument in the sections above, however, have suggested a direction in trade union education that moves beyond the day-release provision for shop steward education. Involving the wider membership in a variety of diverse learning pathways, in a way that extends the enthusiasms, insights and commitment of the members, is a major task that can no longer be postponed. The very nature of the future movement is largely dependent on this task. The previous 10 years have witnessed accumulating difficulties for trade unions and their members: unlocking the potential within the membership represents the single most important element in the necessary restructuring and renewal of trade union activity as a collective movement for democratic advance.

The scale and depth of the problems besetting the economy and large parts of the social fabric after some 15 years of Conservative rule are too severe for trade union education to remain locked within the important but limited ambit of the lay representative day-release model. As indicated earlier, no other organisation matches the ability of trade unions to potentially mobilise important working-class communities around learning programmes designed to confront these problems. The tasks facing the trade unions in the coming decade, irrespective of which party is in government, are too great to permit trade union education to continue within its present marginal and unassuming ambition. It is too important to be allowed to maintain a provision characterised by smaller numbers of participants and smaller numbers of courses.

The present problems confronting trade union education, as mentioned earlier, in the final instance revolve around issues of trade unions as 'learning organisations'. It was suggested that, irrespective of the numbers of shop stewards attending day-release provision, trade unions as organisations have failed to make the transition into such organisations. 'Education' remains as an activity for an increasingly small group of members, organisationally and analytically distinct and separate from the 'real' or 'main' activities of the organisation (and often on inferior terms and conditions of employment from other officers). As the last four or five years have demonstrated, education facilities and resources are often the first area to be curtailed in a period of contraction. A 'working life' education, by contrast, is an argument for the increased importance of learning to be organically part of all major policy initiatives by a trade union. Such a strategy of learning is beyond the resources and expertise of the trade unions alone and instead requires the collaboration and mobilisation of all possible resources from within the local authorities, the voluntary sector and from further and higher education. Involving those people and members out of work, as well as enhancing the learning opportunities of those at work will not only contribute towards improving performance within the workplace but equally important contribute towards the development of a more 'tolerant society, committed to active citizenship and a more fully developed democracy' (NIACE, 1993: 6).

References

Coates, D. (1989) *The Crisis of Labour. Industrial relations and the state in contemporary Britain*, Philip Allan.

Forrester, K., James, J. and Thorne, C. (1994) *Training Matters. Vocational education and training in the retail sector*, USDAW.

Forrester, K. and Ward, K. (1986) 'Organising the unemployed? The TUC and the Unemployed Workers' Centres', *Industrial Relations Journal*, vol. 17, no. 1, Spring.

Forrester, K. and Ward, K. (1990) 'Trade union services for the unemployed. The Unemployed Workers' Centres', *British Journal of Industrial Relations*, vol. 28, no. 3, pp 387–95.

Forrester, K., Payne, J. and Ward, K. (1993) *Adult Learners at Work. Final Research Report*, Department of Adult Continuing Education, University of Leeds.

Fryer, B. (1990) 'The challenge to working-class adult education', in Simon, B. (ed.) *op. cit.*

Hall, S. and Jacques, M. (1983) *The Politics of Thatcherism*, Lawrence and Wishart.

Holford, J. (1994) *Union Education in Britain. A TUC activity*, Department of Adult Education, University of Nottingham.

Hyman, R. (1989) *The Political Economy of Industrial Relations: Theory and practice in a cold climate*, Macmillan.

Kelly, J. (1988) *Trade Unions and Socialist Politics*, Verso.

Lash, S. and Urry, J. (1987) *The End of Organised Capitalism*, Polity Press.

MacInnes, J. (1989) *Thatcherism at Work*, Open University Press.

MacShane, D. (1993) 'State of the union', *New Statesman and Society*, 21 May.

NIACE (1993) *The Learning Imperative*, NIACE.

Pendleton, A. and Winterton, J. (eds) (1993) *Public Enterprise in Transition. Industrial relations in estate and privatised corporations*, Routledge.

Simon, B. (ed.) (1990) *The Search for Enlightenment: The working class and adult education in the twentieth century*, Lawrence and Wishart; 2nd edn, 1992, NIACE.

Smithers, A. (1993) *All Our Futures. Britain's education revolution*, Channel Four Television.

Trades Union Congress (1987) *Review of the TUC's Education Service*, TUC.

Trades Union Congress (1991) *Towards 2000. A consultative document*, TUC.

Trades Union Congress (1993a) *Employment Charter for a World Class Britain. Negotiators' handbook*, TUC.

Trades Union Congress (1993b) *Working in Partnership for Quality Training*, TUC.

Union of Shop, Distributive and Allied Workers (1991) *Training for the Future*, USDAW.

Fourteen

Popular Education and the State: A New Look at the Community Debate

Keith Jackson

> *Owen was telling the working man that he had a right to 'learn what he is in relation to past ages, to the period in which he lives, to the circumstances in which he is placed, to the individuals around him, and to future events'. Men were learning by collisions, but there were targets that made the clash meaningful and worthwhile. The range of attitudes to education ... had ... come to include the attitude which involved participation in social action.*

This is how Harold Silver (1965) concludes his seminal work on popular education. Twenty years ago echoes of his ideas bounced around debates in adult education, in the voluntary and statutory sectors, with sufficient resonance to re-invigorate ideas and practices. Could these ideas, it was asked, have significant meaning for adult education in a troubled 'welfare state' when they meant so much in the formative stages of the capitalist state itself? The outcome for adult education practice of the debates was small and took place mainly on the margins of the state education system, but, as is often the case, its marginality brought a kind of strength. New practices which eventually become part of the professional mainstream frequently emerge on the margins of economic and political organisations, where it is possible for radical spirits to explore and experiment.

Marginal Manoeuvres – The Community Debate

In the 1970s, this phenomenon was one of the sources of the concept of community adult education which eventually had some influence on professional practice. The development directly influenced aspects of the Russell Report in 1973, which argued that there was a strong case for expanding provision for 'the socially and culturally deprived, living in urban areas' which would often 'have to be of an experimental and informal character' (Russell, 1973: 22, 95).

The Russell Committee did not accurately represent some of the experiments it encouraged but there is merit in re-examining the Report and its context. It causes one to focus on issues of policy and practice which are important now, and to do so in a way which recognises both continuity and fundamentally changed circumstances. The issues I have in mind include the definition of adult education and its role within the wider education industry, relations between adult education, social classes and social movements, and certain aspects of the relations between civil society and the state which bear on educational practice.

As a starting point, therefore, it is useful to recall briefly some aspects of the debate which took place around community adult education in the 1970s. At that time, we[1] noted the implications of importing late colonial community development into Britain's working-class neighbourhoods. Romantic notions of recreating the old 'spirit of community' added a confusing gloss to this process. Such policies and practices were, to say the least, as much concerned with controlling and determining the direction of change in communities facing crisis as they were with enabling people to take greater control of their lives. Cynthia Cockburn succinctly summarised this view when she demonstrated convincingly how community development was built into the corporate management of change in cities (Cockburn, 1977).

There was also a strong element of 'blaming the victims' when community projects emphasised the local characteristics or origins of a 'problem' or 'crisis'. There were some awkward associations, deliberate or accidental, with the culture of poverty school, and with loose notions of a sub-proletariat, when people adopted, for example, restricted notions of 'working-class culture'. I remember my delight in a colleague's characterisation of some community education 'theory' as a form of collective lobotomy on working-class communities.

What remained, then, after the limitations of a community focus in adult education had been stripped away? By engaging with communities one was forced to recognise people's interests and concerns as part of their whole lives when political and economic processes were increasingly fragmenting them. We also confronted a greater degree of collective awareness of this among the groups we met in this context than conventional academic wisdom at the time might have indicated.

This engagement had important consequences for the practice of many people involved in adult education. It led some of them to re-examine the form and content of existing practice when it seemed inappropriate for constructing the proper relationship between educational resources and people who were organising around their interests. I found R.H. Tawney's crucial reflection on the relations between education and social movements particularly useful in reflecting on these practices.

If I were asked what is the creative force which has carried forward educational movements, I should reply: the rise of new classes, of new forms of social structure, of new cultural and economic relationships. All these movements have regarded eduction not simply as an interest or an ornament. They have regarded it as a dynamic, and there is nothing at all surprising or regrettable in that. Knowledge has been sought in fact to meet a need. That need has been sometimes intellectual, it has been sometimes religious, it has been social, it has

> been technical, but the process by which it is satisfied is as much
> educational in the latter case as it is the first ...
> If you want flowers you must have flowers, roots and all, unless you are
> satisfied, as many people are satisfied, with flowers made of paper and
> tinsel. And if you want education you must not cut it off from the social
> interests in which it has its living and perennial sources (Tawney,
> 1926: 20, 22).

From this perspective the close engagement directly with the interests of community organisations in local community actions raised questions about the results of policies which, over the previous 50 years, had
incorporated into a state service some aspects of adult education which
had originally been associated with the working-class movement. [2] Were
we now failing to recognise the full experience of the adult education tradition which Silver describes, which had informed Tawney's understanding and had provided the energy which created the Workers'
Educational Association?

During the 1950s and 1960s significant developments in industrial
and trade union education by university adult education departments
and by the Workers' Educational Association and universities had re-in-
troduced a more direct engagement with the organised working class,
but the focus and content did not take into account some important aspects of working-class experience, particularly in communities where
material and cultural inequalities were most evident.

A definition of 'working-class' adult education was one of many in
the debate about the meaning of community adult education, which involved contesting views about the contemporary political economy. It
helped to identify some characteristics associated with working-class
adult education in Britain whose early forms Harold Silver had explored
so sensitively. Among these characteristics I would emphasise at this
stage: the view that adults bring something which derives both from
their experience of adult life and from their status as citizens to the educational process; that adult education is based on a dialogue rather than a
mere transition of knowledge and skill; that education is not only for personal development and advancement but also for social advancement;
that adult education constructs knowledge and does not merely pass it
on; that adult education has a dialectical and organic relationship with
social movements.

It was precisely by engaging directly with the interests of people in
working-class communities facing major problems, that adult education
seemed to have a real if marginal contribution to make in meeting the
challenge which they faced. This small contribution brought together resources in a variety of organisations large and small, both within civil society and the state. There is an extensive literature on the projects,
programmes and new forms of 'service delivery' and I shall refer to some
examples later.

Can we learn anything from this which is useful for practice today?
Do the conditions exist for similar forms of engagement with groups in
the community? Here I shall consider the possibilities and contradictions

of relations between adult education and public policy rather than seek to assemble evidence for community activity. I shall do this by comparing the Russell Report of 1973 with the policy statements surrounding the creation of a new Further Education Funding Council. The contrasting philosophies and language have clear implications for the contribution adult education might make 'in the community'.

The Russell Report and Its Concept of Adult Education

Margaret Thatcher, then Minister of Education, endorsed the Russell Report heartily and it could be said to reflect official thinking about adult education at the time.

At the end of its summary conclusions the Report declared:

The value of Adult Education is not solely to be measured by direct increases in earning power or productive capacity or by any other materialistic yardstick, but by the quality of life it inspires in the individual and generates for the community at large.
It is an agent of changing and improving our society: but for each individual the means of change may differ and each must develop in his own way, at his own level and through his own talents (Russell, 1973: xi).

What did Russell mean by 'adult education'? The term adult education was first used officially in the United Kingdom in 1919, when what became known as the Smith Committee, appointed by the then Ministry of Reconstruction, considered 'the provision for, and the possibilities of, adult education (other than technical or vocational) in Great Britain'. [3]

The 1919 Report found that the adult education movement was:

inextricably interwoven with the whole of the organised life of the community ... It aims at satisfying the needs of the individual and the attainment of new standards of citizenship and a better social order. In some cases, the personal motive predominates. In perhaps the greater majority of cases, the dynamic character of adult education is due to its social motive.

The report also noted that such adult education included studies which 'enable the student to relate his own occupation to the industry of which it is part, to appreciate the place of that industry in the economic life of the nation and of the world and to interpret the economic life of the community in terms of social values ...' Adult education was thus seen as a crucial part of the reconstruction of British society after the First World War.

The recommendations of the 1919 Report included a stress on the importance of adult education being organised to ensure the fullest self-determination on the part of students, including the courses to be provided and choice of teachers. This was a direct reflection of the way in which the Workers' Educational Association had been founded with the tutorial class at its heart; working-class groups organised as students to engage with the universities on an equal footing.

By today's standards, quite small numbers were involved in formal programmes in the years following the Report. Universities expanded extra-mural provision and there were some local authority programmes. Voluntary organisations played a major part. The WEA was the most substantial, but women's organisations and community associations, which created their own national organisation during this period, were very significant.

After the 1944 Education Act and for the period up to Russell's review local education authorities became the leaders. The scale of the demand for non-vocational adult education increased rapidly. Numerically, classes for personal interest, recreation and vocational purposes, greatly outweighed those which could be said to have the 'social motive', and the liberal adult education associated with the WEA and the universities was eclipsed as the dominant influence. In the early 1970s, therefore, Russell could not argue that in the majority of cases this was what provided its dynamic character. The role of the local authority was consequently reaffirmed as general provider of a comprehensive service which could meet the explicit and latent demand for courses of all kinds, but it was also proposed that the partnership with voluntary bodies should continue.

The strength of Russell was that it recognised the complex ways in which adult education, attended by millions for many different reasons, contributed to the general quality of life, providing opportunities for personal development and more effective citizenship. The report saw needs for what is called 'permanent education', which included remedial education where schools had failed, second chance education, and also updating to keep abreast of developments for everyone, regardless of qualifications on leaving full-time education. To these it added those needs which related to personal development – artistic and personal creativity, physical and sporting activity, and intellectual activity for enjoyment.

Finally, Russell considered adult education related to the place of the individual in society, giving examples of role education, concerning roles in industry or in the family and community; social and political education; community education for effective collective action; and education for social leadership. It could be argued that, as the 1919 Report had reflected the WEA in its stress on the importance of student self-determination, the Russell Report not only continued an endorsement of the WEA but also extended it to less permanent collectives in civil society, in the field of community action. There were, however, also a number of weaknesses in the Russell Report. Perhaps the most important one resulted from the brief which the committee was given. This meant that the needs of the economy, and the relations between education and training were barely addressed. Another was that it tended to blur the distinction between education and social service. And, partly as a result of this, the Report did not challenge much sloppy thinking in adult education, particularly concerning evaluation – how to test whether grand aims such as developing independent judgement or increasing powers of decision-making were actually being achieved.

Underlying the Report's weakness was the nature of the committee's brief and the framework of political and economic analysis which was assumed in its deliberations. Russell was asked 'to make recommendations with view to obtaining the most effective and economical deployment of resources to enable adult education to make its proper contribution to the national system of education conceived of as a process continuing through life'. The Committee was to be concerned only with the delivery of non-vocational adult education, making it more accessible and valuable as a public service. Indeed the Russell Report can best be understood as a latecomer at the end of a decade of reports in many fields which were responding to what were perceived as failures in the structure and processes of the welfare state. These included the Plowden Report on primary education, the Skeffington Report on town planning and the Seebohm Report on the personal social services.

These reports were all responses to a perceived failure, in the services which they examined, to engage with the interests of the poor, particularly those living in 'deprived areas'. Research evidence for this failure was reinforced by the demands of community action, which was widespread. The reports all prescribed a similar combination of remedies: new approaches to professional practice and management along with devices to encourage people to participate in the services they received. They represented stages in the development of a 'corporate management of cities' which we have noted earlier. Community adult education in its different manifestations included both elements of corporate management and of support for community organisations who challenged the outcomes of corporate management, and the premises on which it was based.

Russell shared with these reports a basic assumption that the political economy of the welfare state was itself not problematic. There was no break with the consensus which had dominated public policy since the 1940s, namely that the fundamental problems of a capitalist political economy had been resolved by a balance of class forces, with the state acting as a means of regulating the economy in order to ensure full employment and social justice. In seeking to tidy up the edges of the welfare state none of the reports considered that the problems they were addressing might be manifestations of a more fundamental crisis in the political economy.

There were of course people on the radical left of politics who recognised the crisis, emphasising different aspects such as declining profitability due to the demands of a highly organised working class and an associated explosion of public spending which could not be sustained. Also the radical right, with less political exposure in the UK but with a developing international collaboration,[4] was building up the critique which was to prove very effective before long in challenging the consensus.

Its brief, and the framework of political and economic analysis which it assumed, were the sources of both strength and weaknesses in the Russell Report. We can return to the lessons of this after we have considered adult education policy determined by a quite different brief and analysis. But we can immediately note that unlike recent policy documents on post-16 education, with their implications for adult education, Russell never became the basis for such public policy and the associated allocation of resources. Such an outcome no doubt indicated the low priority given to adult education and was in any case pre-empted by a more rapid reconstruction of international capital than welfare state reforms had contemplated, triggered off by the oil crises. The gathering pace of this reconstruction brought reductions in public spending and soon fuelled the ideological attack from the radical right which eventually dominated the 1980s.

The New FE Sector: Education and Training for the Economy

No such thing as adult education

Official descriptions of educational policy increasingly omit the concept of adult education at all. As a senior civil servant said a few years ago, 'There is no such thing as adult education today, only adults attending classes'.[5] He was giving an accurate reflection of government policy as it emerged.

The White Paper which was presented in 1991 as a radical policy for all post-16 education and training, concerned itself almost entirely with the 16–19-year age group (DES, 1991). Only two pages out of almost a hundred specifically refer to the learning needs of adults. Its overall aims are stated clearly as intending 'to meet the needs and aspirations of young people going into work' by ensuring that high quality further education or training becomes the norm for all 16- and 17-year-olds who can benefit from it, by increasing the levels of attainment and the proportion of young people acquiring higher levels of skills and expertise for employment (DES, 1991: 2). Its short chapter on education for adults merely tells us that this should be funded through the new Council where suitable and that other provision by local authorities should be supported as much as possible only through fees.

The FEFC is about vocational education, whereas Russell was about non-vocational provision. But our thinking about adult education today can gain by comparing their approaches. Clearly there is a wholehearted commitment to an economic dynamic, rather than Russell's social dynamic, the reservoir of human and material resources to which Russell referred is to be released by the FEFC for the good of the economy, not the good of society, assuming implicitly that there is no distinction of significance. While Russell was part of a process of reforming the welfare state and a response to its inability to deliver its promises, the new further education is part of the complete reconstruction of the welfare state in the interests of a market-driven society. This economic orientation is a significant contributor to the chief strengths of the current policies as they have been laid out in the White Paper, the legislation, and key documents of the FEFC.

Firstly, the White Paper declares in simple and radical terms that academic and vocational qualifications deserve equal recognition. This is by far the most serious attempt to break down the divide between education and training, between the academic and theoretical on the one hand and the vocational and practical on the other. When the Robbins Report recommended in 1963 the first post-war expansion of higher education, it seemed to assume that large numbers obtaining academic-style education would make the nation more productive. That questionable assumption is now completely rejected.

Secondly, there is a clear definition of objectives and of the means by which they are to be achieved. There is a strong drive, through the White Paper, the legislation and Treasury decisions, to increase the numbers of people in post-school education and to increase the proportion of the population with qualifications. Also, by noting that 'Young people and adults need a clear framework of qualifications to measure their success in education and training. We need to build up a modern system of academic and vocational qualifications which are equally valued' (DES, 1991: 16), the White Paper sets the scene for imagination in creating effective ways of evaluating learning outcomes for individual adults themselves.

Thirdly, there is a very welcome emphasis on learning rather than teaching. This is referred to at a number of points in the White Paper, noting its significance for the motivation of participants, particularly if they left school disillusioned with education, and for ensuring that individuals can find their own personal programme of development. The concept of dialogue in adult education might relate closely to this within the appropriate policy framework, and I shall return to the possibilities this creates for us now to address the challenge offered by some of the contradictions in Russell.

Funding Learning (FEFC, 1992) is a more hopeful document than many expected. It tried, in an interesting way, to articulate a standard unit of resource which funds learning programmes, rather than crude outcomes such as student numbers. There was a real attempt to seek sensitive ways of measuring outcome and quality, even to the extent of not ruling out complex qualitative factors such as value added.

These approaches to learning and to accountability for public funds in providing learning programmes are summed up in the language of quality management. The FEFC intends to deliver a 'quality service' to its 'customers'. And here's the rub. There is no doubt in my mind that something can be gained from a more rigorous approach to outcomes in adult education than was considered by Russell, but, if a great deal is not also to be lost, we must pick up some continuities and not allow market-driven policies to determine entirely the purpose and outcomes of adult eduction.

UK plc – The Frantic Thrust of Capital

Addressing economic needs, focusing on definite outcomes and evaluation of programmes, reinforcing the notion of quality management and value for money, integrating education and training, these are the strengths in the new further education sector, which result from responding to the economic challenge we face. But compared with Russell the scales have been tipped too far in favour of the economy, defined in market terms, rather than society. The concept of 'value for money' displaces the concept of social value to which Russell gave central place. This is the subtext to the replacement of 'adult education' with the notion of adults attending classes.

Russell's vision of a wide-ranging, comprehensive system of education as a process continuing through life is replaced by an allocation of resources in the Gradgrind tradition with four significant consequences:

- Russell's role education is narrowed to the role of active participant in the labour market
- a comprehensive service with local development plans is replaced by market delivery by competing suppliers
- whilst giving equal status to vocational and academic education a sharp division between vocational and 'leisure' education is introduced, with the latter precariously holding onto public funds
- social and political education is not even acknowledged.

A further education sector with wide responsibility for post-16 education, and therefore for adult education, appears to disregard the role of education in society at large, beyond the world of work in the economy. Consequently, whilst the division between academic and vocational was removed, an unnecessary demarcation between vocational and non-vocational education was introduced with serious consequences for achieving the sector's own objectives.

This apparently exclusive focus on the economy in the policy documents which led to the new further education sector is given greater significance for the present argument by the fact that the market-driven approach of the sector has eventually led to the adults being recognised as a key target group (WEA, 1994: 19), despite the disregard for adult education in the policy documents leading up to the new sector. 'Predatory FE colleges', as they were characterised in the *Times Educational Supplement* (2 December 1994), find themselves 'fatally squeezed between budget constraints and poaching'. In other words, 16 to 19-year- olds turned out to be too difficult a market for colleges if they were to achieve the target student numbers required to maintain funding in the new regime. Adult education is needed to make up the numbers, not because of its intrinsic value to individuals and society.

The new market language is widely used and penetrates into the heart of further education. In *The Guardian* on 26 January 1994, a mature student described some of her experiences of difficulties in a further education college, noting that the colleges have a great deal to offer and that mature students are 'hungry to buy their wares'. The following sales ploy to colleges, which arrived on my desk soon after *The Guardian* article, is also typical:

> Re: A vital contribution to the success of your college
> *I am writing to introduce you to a revolutionary new service which will help you college to succeed. There is no doubt that college managers are currently facing an unprecedented challenge in both senses of the word, that is a major opportunity and a major threat. You must respond to great changes in society and what it wants from education and you are at the focus of multiple thrusts of government policy to address the problems of 'UK PLC' (letter from DIALnet, PMS Communications Ltd, Birmingham, March 1994).*

So what's in a name? Why should we be concerned to preserve the concept of adult education. Why not provide a quality service of education and training for adults?

Harry Braverman (1974) has provided some of the most useful insights into this process when he discusses how the rapid advance of the market has taken an inward direction into the territory of our daily lives and human relations as well as an outward direction to new parts of the globe: 'In this process, capital which "thrusts itself frantically" into every possible new area of investment has totally reorganised society'. All activities and relationships, he argued, are transformed into commodities which can be bought and sold: caring for each other, young, old, or sick, playing together, having fun, relaxing and learning together. So what is the consequence of this for education?

Commodities are produced, marketed and sold to whomsoever can buy them, at a particular price. It doesn't matter what the consumer is like, or the use to which commodity will be put. It is, for example, irrelevant whether the consumers of education are adults or not, as long as they want the product and can afford it. It could be argued that this might have beneficial results. Education can be delivered effectively to mixed age groups, for example, to the benefit of all, and I believe this argument has some validity. But only if the negative consequences of purveying adult education as a commodity are also recognised.

Braverman describes some of these consequences clearly. 'The social structure, built upon the market, is such that relations between individuals and social groups do not take place directly as cooperative human encounters, but through the market as relations of purchase and sale' (Braverman, 1974: 277). 'In time not only the material and service needs but even the emotional patterns of life are channelled through the market' (*ibid.*: 276).[6] In a market exchange commodities are created for, not by, the customer. But education is a form of human exchange, which if it is to be effective requires participants to be creative partners.

There is evidence for the practical consequences of allowing the labour market commodity model to determine the availability of learning opportunities adult education. A survey in Central Birmingham found that tiny proportions of the population possessed qualifications and that these proportions decreased sharply in successive age ranges after 26 years of age (Birmingham City Council/Heartlands Development Corporation, 1989). The evidence suggested that people did not take formal vocational courses because they did not have the confidence or motivation to do so. Vocational qualifications are important, of course, and they are the most likely form of education to be presented effectively as a commodity since they have direct currency in the labour market. Conversely, however, people do not study for such qualifications when they perceive, accurately or otherwise, that their place in the labour market will not be improved thereby – either due to high unemployment or the low quality of much work available (Faure, 1972: xxviii). People will not choose education if they are not motivated and committed and are convinced that their interests, as they define them, will not be served by the process (Harrison, 1993; Uden, 1994; Council of Europe, 1992; Daines *et al.*, 1993).

On the other hand there is evidence that when people do not take up formal vocational courses because they lack confidence or motivation, they can begin learning through other kinds of activities. These are activities they undertake as people, as citizens, as members of society, not commodities in the labour market. Recent substantial studies on adult learning in voluntary organisations covering Health Education, Advocacy and Campaigning, Arts, Physical Activity and interests or hobbies showed that membership and activity brought a liberating sense of increased confidence (Elsdon, 1994). Even when formal learning and training programmes are involved in these organisations, informal learning remains significant. For many people who do become involved in formal learning, the major objectives which carry them forward are personal and social rather than the learning content which is explicitly offered to them.

Unfortunately, in recognition of this motivation to learn among adults, the competitive market model has led to colleges competing for community group activities to be 'anointed' for FEFC funding in order to expand their numbers, but there is not the same allocation of resources which Russell identified to ensure that genuinely appropriate educational practices are created. Community adult education in the 1970s, which improved the quality of the adult education service, as Russell acknowledged, did not operate in terms of a 'marketed quality service'. Additionally, the concern was not only with the motivation of individuals in terms of narrow self-interest. Improvements were the specific results of direct engagement with groups who defined their interests collectively in relation to their lives as they perceived them, not in order to meet target numbers of customers.

Also, whilst the current market model emphasises competition among providers, collaboration in response to demand was the hallmark of the engagement with community groups. The competitive marketplace is said to offer 'freedom' to the consumer, and to lead to better product quality. But this concept of freedom is very limited, as has been very apparent in many areas of public policy which directly affect the quality of personal life, and not just in education. Transport is a good example, illustrating the issues well. The market offers people the freedom to choose a car of this colour or that colour; it can also increase the opportunity for more people to buy cars. These are important outcomes but they do not offer the opportunity to people to determine the kind of transport they would like in the life they want to lead. Freedom to improve one's quality of life can better be achieved by collective and collaborative approaches to public transport rather than freedom in the marketplace, as many European cities have shown.

Post-Fordism Is Not Enough

One response by some critics to inadequacies of the market model in public services, is that we should recognise the opportunities of post-Fordist management (Murray, 1991). What we face now, they argue, is the result of applying the ideas and methods of industrial Fordism to public domains and they have not worked because they are inappropriate. Instead we should turn to the ideas and methods of post-Fordist management, giving priority to innovation, customised products and the flexible systems which such customisation requires. These require workers who are skilled and creative, and forms of organisation which are based in a complex inter-relationship of points of autonomy. Decisions are decentralised and take into account their own independent relationships outside the system. Indeed, it is a central feature of this approach that social relations rather than market exchange determines its character and it is held together by a shared culture emphasising the quality of such social relations.

However, present employment patterns in the labour market are based on a core of skilled permanent workers and a periphery of part-time or short-term workers, along with overlapping groups of short-term and long-term unemployed. This pattern will not be changed by post-Fordist management policies. If post-Fordism were to be the basis for adult education and training only core workers would obviously benefit (Ball, 1991; Metcalf, 1990; Morgan, 1994).

Moreover, whilst post-Fordist theories do offer real possibilities for a new integration of education and training they do not address a central issue. UK plc remains the concern. Russell treated adult education as if the economy did not exist, the FEFC treats training for the economy as if society does not exist. Post-Fordism incorporates society for business objectives just as much as did Fordism, but in more complex and sophisticated ways. Indeed this development is precisely in line with Braverman's argument, enabling capital and the market to transform social life in its own image.

A real alternative is to shift public policy emphatically away from education and training for UK plc towards education and training for a democratic society, in which political, social and cultural activity is given the same status as activity in the labour market.

Popular Education, Civil Society and Development

It is in this regard that we turn again to the particularity of 'community adult education' practice within adult education generally which was the starting point for this argument. By referring to 'communities' in that earlier debate we meant specified groups of actual people, not society as a whole and certainly not a market. In short, we used the term to indicate the 'place' and 'moment' of engagement with specific groups of people around their interests.

There were a variety of programmes within the 'community move-ment' which shaped adult education to serve the interests of groups in their relations with the state. People articulated their concerns not as ob-jects influenced by state policies to deal with 'problems', or clients of the state but as agents of change – as part of a movement which shared that consciousness. When we placed the key concepts of 'engagement' and 'dialogue' within the traditions of the British working-class movement, perhaps we failed to draw in the full range of international experience in which the concepts have been significant. Harold Silver's title *The Concept of Popular Education* should have pointed us more directly to a broader, less insular, tradition.

The adult education of engagement is associated internationally with the concept of popular education, popular not in the sense that it is well supported but that it is of the people. The term has never gained cur-rency in the British tradition. The dynamic of adult education referred to in the 1919 Report, quoted above, would in many other countries be as-sociated with popular education, which can be described as education for, and in response to, people as citizens (see, for example, UNESCO, 1978). Adult, in this sense, is defined, not as a person of a given age, say post-16, but a person with a particular status in society, with responsibili-ties and rights. These are not customers, but contributors to, and partici-pators in, learning for the ends which they consider to be important – both personal and social. Motivation to learn comes from being treated with dignity, as someone who can contribute to society as well as receive benefits from it. Thus, the most successful literacy programmes have been part of popular education in many parts of the world.[7]

The Importance of Dialogue

Popular education is also not about providing education but about dia-logue.[8] Both participants and professional educators bring significant contributions to the dialogue, with the result that there is learning on both sides. Within such learning programmes there is a development of knowledge and understanding which reflects people's lives and experi-ence, not merely a process of experts purveying their knowledge. Com-munity adult education was in part a British manifestation of popular education, responding to a considerable growth in community activity in the years before the Russell Report, and bringing together what Russell called, the 'critical study of society' in the liberal tradition, with a new understanding of the role of popular education on the part of adult educators.

Evidence of the outcome of this dialogue took many forms. In Liverpool David Evans has described the development of Writers' Workshops (1980). There was, for example, a contribution by participants in a community action project to academic research very similar to that which R.H. Tawney is reputed to have reported from his tutorial classes in the earlier part of the century.[9] There was a structured dialogue in which working-class adults drew on their own experience but also were part of a wider intellectual debate. The major adult literacy programme which began in the voluntary sector during the Russell period, particularly through a revived Settlement movement, included many examples where people learned to read and write through exploring their own lives and experiences, and what they wanted from life – in prose, poetry and song. Some of these groups came together in a national organisation to produce the impressive newspaper, *Write First Time*, which was a stimulus for significant developments in literacy teaching in Britain.

I mention these examples to give the flavour, not to pick any of them out as particularly significant among many examples. The notion of a dialogue between equals and citizens provides substance to the claim, in both the 1919 Report and the Russell Report, that adult education can make a particular contribution to the quality of democratic and cultural life. The minority of citizens who would join this dialogue in any one community might be regarded as an 'elite' (in Gramsci's terms they might almost be called 'organic intellectuals'), Russell envisaged state support for these activities as a contribution to a process of widening and deepening participation by many kinds of 'elites' in many communities as part of a comprehensive adult education service.

Adult Education, the State and Social Movements

The question we can now ask is whether conditions exist for an adult education practice which engages in this dialogue, when the national policy framework is determined by the Further and Higher Education Act rather than Russell's precepts. Seeking an answer to that question requires us to consider the present nature of relations between social movements, popular education and the state which can usefully start by an elaboration, based on more detailed recent research, of Tawney's valuable broad historical insight quoted earlier.

Eyerman and Jamieson, for example, examine 'social movements as cognitive praxis' (1991). In similar language to Tawney they argue that this 'cognitive praxis' is the social action where new knowledge originates. They follow Berger and Luckman's formulation of the social construction of reality – 'Society is constructed by "re-cognition", by recurrent acts of knowledge which go on all the time' – and propose that a social movement is not to be recognised primarily in terms of particular organisations but as 'cognitive territory', a new conceptual space in which groups, formal and informal, interact. That, they argue, is how social movements can be distinguished from action groups and single-issue protests. Social movements are not to be conceptualised merely as learning processes. However, what gives a movement its particular character, and distinguishes it from other movements, is its 'cognitive practice'.

> *No social movement emerges until there is a political opportunity available, a context of social problem as well as a context of communication, opening up the potential for problem articulation and knowledge dissemination. Not every social problem, however, generates a social movement; only those that strike a chord, that touch basic tensions in a society have potential for generating a social movement. As such, our approach tends to limit the number of social movements to those especially 'significant' movements which redefine history, which carry the historical 'projects' that have normally been attributed to social classes (Eyerman and Jamieson, 1991).*

This elaboration of Tawney's axiom is interesting. It suggests that popular education might be both a process by which a debate is constructed between existing knowledge and social movements, and also part of the means by which 'movement intellectuals' formulate and disseminate new knowledge. This can readily be observed over recent decades in, for example, the US civil rights movement, the women's movement and in popular liberation struggles against colonialism or neo-colonialism. What then of the 'community movement'? Was this a phase in the historical project of the working-class movement in which the welfare state consensus was challenged by alliances between left-wing intellectuals and the working-class organisations in urban communities? Or was it part of a particular movement with its own 'cognitive territory' and its own 'project' emerging in response to significant changes in the relations between civil society and the state?

Popular education seen as a dialogue within social movements can be in complete opposition to the state, as is clearly the case in liberation struggles, or it can receive state support and legitimation under certain circumstances. Such conditions prevailed in Scandinavia at the end of the nineteenth century and up to the present time, enabling the folk high schools to operate within but separate from the state (see note 8). They include an interpretation of democracy which is pluralist and which accepts a role for collective action in civil society, along with ballot box and the rule of law – action which may not only be opposed to the government of the day, but even seek to change by democratic means fundamental aspects of the power structure and of the state itself. In a less substantial fashion than the Danish folk high school movement, but nevertheless significantly for a pluralist democracy, the Workers' Educational Association took its place as part of a British adult education system. From this perspective it may be argued that Russell represented an acceptance of popular education within the community movement on the margins of the education system. If so the acceptance was precarious and short-lived.

By the early 1990s conditions had became distinctly unfavourable in the UK for the state to support popular education in this way. The nature of activity in civil society had been severely diminished; Margaret Thatcher had famously declared that there is no such thing as society and John Major's Citizen's Charter had set the official seal on a transformation from citizen to consumer. The British state became steadily more centralised and the political process less open to influence by independent sources of power such as trade unions and local government (see note 6). The new further education system reflects this relationship between the state and civil society.

Possibilities in the 1990s

There are many residues of the early 'engagements' we have identified in adult education within the new further education sector today. Some practices of community adult education, mainly in terms of curriculum, have been incorporated in the Access movement which has emerged since the 1970s. A network of Second Chance courses has maintained a tradition of community-based courses which have become associated with access. Other more formal courses in further education colleges retain some features of community education, but the pressures of the FEFC both for numbers and immediate Schedule 2 outcomes have severely reduced the possibility of a curriculum based on real dialogue.

If there are serious attempts to engage with the interests of social groups rather than provide them with a service there is no national focus. Perhaps the social problem to which the 'community movement' responded did not touch a basic tension in society, or maybe the ideology of the free market is itself the product of a powerful social movement. If so we shall, in Tawney's terms, have to recognise a customer-driven adult education as the educational expression of that movement 'roots and all'.

Another possibility is that the dialogue will re-emerge in the contradictions which are beginning to appear in market-oriented policies when they seek to determine the shape and pattern of civil society at all levels. A recent report evaluates the outcome of the whole range of programmes outlined in the government's 1988 Action for Cities package (Robson *et al.*, 1994). It identifies failures to utilise the skills and talents of people by concentrating on purely economic goals and proposes that autonomous community groups, as well as formal agencies, should participate in local coalitions to achieve more success. Considered from the perspective of the past 20 years the report seems to call for the wheel to be invented again. It recognises that the institutions of the state and the market are not sufficient means for social development; organisation in civil society is required, and not merely to provide volunteer care in the community which has been the role prescribed by government for the voluntary sector in the 1980s (Cook, 1988).

The European Union's recent Green Paper on social policy also recognises contradictions:

> *There is a high risk that the continued pursuit of present policies will lead ultimately to a dual society in which wealth creation is primarily*

in the hands of a highly qualified labour force, while income is
transferred to a growing number of non-active people as a basis for a
reasonable level of social justice. Such a society would not only become
increasingly less cohesive, it would also run counter to the need for the
maximum mobilisation of Europe's human resource wealth in order to
remain competitive (Commission of the European Union, 1993).

Market-driven policies are here seen to have serious consequences
for social cohesion and to be ineffective in realising the full potential of
people in society. The key phrase for educational policy here is 'human
resource wealth'. Human resource development will increasingly be the
context for adult education and training as governments seek both to
deal with the consequences of unplanned labour markets and provide
the basis for economic success as world competition increases. For example the press release of 15 September 1994 for the 'First Global Conference on Lifelong Learning' in Rome declared, 'Government Leaders, at
the recent G7 Summit, called for increasing investment in people through
better education systems, training and the development of a culture of
lifelong learning'. The conference programme is heavily dominated by
the post-Fordist industrial training world, with Sir Christopher Ball from
the UK as a Chief Conference Rapporteur.

We can see in human resource development, in contemporary form,
the same process which was community development and the corporate
management of cities in the 1970s. There is the same concern both to in-
duce change and to manage the consequences of change. For adult education, therefore, it might be appropriate to consider a similar debate
about the possibilities of a dialogue with those who face the impact of the
policies. Twenty years ago it was the meaning of 'community' and 'development' which helped to determine practice, now it is 'human resource' and 'development'. As they were before the issues are contested.

Recent Swedish research into popular education has drawn on the
critical sociology of Jürgen Habermas to interpret the role of popular
education in its social and political context, with particular reference to
his two key concepts of the system-world and the life-world (Gustavsson, 1994). In broad terms the first is demonstrated in the market and the
state, where the rationality is instrumental, focusing on goal-oriented efficiency. 'The system is driven by strategic action, rather than search for
right and truth, which carry risks for distorted communication in society.
The life-world is the sphere in society where individuals create their
identities, values and meaning and search for truth, rightness and
beauty'. Language is central in the life-world and the rationality is one of
free individuals communicating with each other, which Habermas calls
'communicative action'. Habermas proposes that the goal for a free society should be 'undistorted communication' and this points, it is suggested, to the dialogue of popular education as an appropriate
educational form.

Habermas' two worlds are not, of course, mutually exclusive. They
interact. But the continuing development of democracy and a sustainable
economic development requires that the system-world does not entirely

colonise the life-world. A strong case has been presented by some historians that the conditions for take-off into the industrial revolution in the West included a relatively open, free, and enquiring civil society, creating social institutions which were supportive of new developments in the economy and the state (Perkin, 1969; Hagen, 1964). In looking for solutions to the problem of current market-driven polices the European Green paper seems to suggest that this may also be true for further development:

> *The alternative would be to seek to create an 'active' society where there is a wider distribution of income, achieved by means other than simple social security transfers, and in which each individual feels able to contribute to production (as part of the search for full employment) but also via a more active participation in the development of society as a whole. An active society is also one which has the ability to provide an adequate supply of the 'collective goods' – such as education, health and social protective systems – which are required to ensure its innovative capacities and its ability to adjust quickly (Commission of the European Union, 1993).*

What Is To Be Done?

This exploration has indicated far more questions than answers. Can we identify anything approaching collective responses to the contradictions in the results of market-driven policies, comparable to those in the community which responded to the contradictions in welfare state reform 20 years ago? Is the current focus on a narrow approach to human beings as capital leading to resistance by anything which seems like a social movement? This is only the beginning of a list of questions which must be addressed. But there are some things which can be done. The praxis of marginal manoeuvres remains valid and there are indications in both the continuity and changes since the 1970s of a direction to be taken.

First, it is necessary to maintain vigorously a critique of the full implications of market-driven policies for adult education. What appear to be gains, for example the possibility of new resources, a welcome integration of education and training, or attention to outcomes, can continually be reviewed in relation to the social and human values we recognised in the Russell Report. If there are opportunities for adult education to enable a dialogue to take place around that critique, which can be useful for people to take action around their interests, practitioners have to be ready to respond in ways which current policy does not encourage, whilst recognising the possibilities of both continuity and change in this practice.

We can see some continuity from the period of the community movement, with similar contradictions becoming apparent. We saw that both the problem which led to the corporate management of cities, and the process of that management itself, provided occasions for 'learning by collision' in community action and citizen participation. Clearly there are many for whom public policy driven by a market philosophy has not worked. Communities face material and social problems which the market either creates or cannot resolve; human resource management is corporate management in a new guise, and people need to win specific victories for the quality of their lives within its contradictions.

However, there are important differences now. Collective responses in the community are not so apparent as they were in the 1960s and 1970s. A consciousness of being citizens within a welfare state has shifted to that of expendable commodities in the labour market, disempowering people and reducing expectations that our parliamentary democracy is capable of responding to, or even acknowledging, collective action in civil society as appropriate. People, therefore need a hard and realistic assessment of what is possible, and are able to identify specific changes which can be achieved in their communities and in their life chances.

So if adult education practice is to develop appropriately, there may need to be changes which take into account some approaches associated in the past with training rather than education, with more precise attention to outcomes. There might be a concept (and associated practice) of an integrated education and training for civil society rather than the market, the outcomes of which would be seen in social development and democratic processes, not merely economic development as required by currently dominant policies on education and training. This suggests finding new and effective means for identifying that outcomes have been achieved. Some of the weaknesses we identified in adult education might be addressed in this way.

The greater concern today with recognisable outcomes and with learning rather than teaching, which we have noted, is consistent with engagement in a dialogue about feasible change. The dialogue, however, must enable people to define the outcomes which are important to them as citizens and the learning and evaluation must be collective and not on a purely individual basis. This contrasts with the main forms of education and training currently available, which are narrowly geared to changes they can make to their opportunities in the labour market.

Interest in the work of Freire and other notable contributors to popular education played a significant part in the developing practice of the 1970s. An international perspective about the territory on which the contest of ideas and practice might appropriately take place is even more important today.

Starting from a different standpoint from the one adopted here Alan Rogers has usefully addressed some international issues of adult education and development (1992). He argues for adult learning programmes which combine formal and informal education in order contribute to the development of communities in ways which can be demonstrated as concrete outcomes. He contrasts adult education 'for individualism' in the West with adult education 'for social responsibility' in the Third World'. He trenchantly criticises adult educators in the West for having a poor record in evaluating the outcomes of their activities and suggests that to rectify this would be one of the advantages, among others, for adult education becoming more associated with development, as it is in the Third World.

Rogers' discussion of ways in which collective development goals and objectives can be set and their achievement identified is extremely useful. However, it is important to place this argument in the context of the tradition of popular education and 'learning by collision' in order that the dialogue may remain as open and democratic as possible. When Rogers analyses the role of the state in defining development objectives he gives too little attention to the present 'frantic rush of capital' which drives state policies.

Human resource development is a world-wide phenomenon. The collapse of the approach to socialism which was represented by the command economies has taken away a supporting framework for more democratic forms of socialism which included popular movements in the Third World. Their struggle to survive against the opposition of international capital, and particularly the foreign policy of the United States, has become hopelessly one-sided, and market-driven policies are evident everywhere. Community development as the corporate management of cities was an attempt by the modern state to create conditions for the development of the market, within a democratic, participative framework. That is also the full significance of the international attention to human resource management.

This leads to the final lesson of this comparison over a 20-year period. The degree to which an engagement with autonomous, independent groups within human resource development programmes can be given some kind of state support will depend on the framework of public policy and the importance it attaches to the quality of life in civil society. To identify possibilities we have critically to understand the political and economic context and to place an educational response within an international perspective. The contradiction to be addressed is not, as it was at the time of the Russell Report, in the British welfare state, but in the world-wide programme of structural readjustment, in industrialised nations and developing countries alike.

The biggest questions therefore remain. Will nation states adopt policy frameworks for development which are pluralist, which seek to extend democracy in terms of the power people have directly to determine their life chances, not merely indirectly through parliamentary-style electoral systems, and which define human beings as more than merely a resource, above all as more than human capital?

Only if this is the case can there be a role for popular education in education and training programmes in human resource development. There might then be some forms of engagement and not merely the delivery of a quality service to customers, generalising dialogue within communities as part of a debate on the possibilities of sustainable development for all. This is the way in which modern adult educational practice might seek to address the interests of people, as Robert Owen argued in our opening quotation. Or maybe the tradition of 'education by collision' cannot be supported by the state in the modern world political economy, and the tradition of popular education will continue in quite new ways outside state-supported systems.

Notes

1. I think the use of this collective term at certain points in this chapter, when referring to the earlier debate, is justified in that it refers to common themes recognisable in the literature of the debate with which I was associated along with other colleagues and referred to in later references.

2. See for example Ashcroft, B. and Jackson, K. (1974) 'Adult education and social action', in Jones, D. and Mayo, M. (eds) *Community Work One*, Routledge and Kegan Paul. The article focuses on the issue of engagement directly with the interests of working-class groups.

3. The main sections of the report were reprinted, with an introduction by R.D. Waller (1956) as *A Design for Democracy*, Max Parrish.

4. See reference to the role of the Mont Pelerin Society in Blunkett, D. and Jackson, K. (1984) *Democracy in Crisis*, Chatto and Windus.

5. This remark was made at one of the discussions about the role of residential colleges of adult education in the new system at the Department of Education and Science. It struck me as a vivid contrast with similar discussions around the Russell Report in which I took part 20 years earlier.

6. See Blunkett, D. and Jackson, K. (1984) *op. cit.* for an account of how the success, in some local authorities, of policies to improve the quality of services on the basis of collective provision and community involvement, rather than market choice, led to a systematic campaign against them by the Conservative government because their success and popularity offered an attractive alternative agenda to the local electorate.

7. The popular liberation movement in Nicaragua reduced illiteracy from 50% to 12% in the late 1970s and early 1980s (*Nicaragua Must Survive*, 1986, published by the Nicaraguan Solidarity Group and War on Want).

8. The work of Paulo Freire is most commonly referred to for illustration, although some commentators remove the analysis of political economy in his work and reduce it to 'non-formal education', but the tradition can be found in many political and cultural contexts. See, for example, Borish, S.M. (1991) *The Land of the Living*, Blue Dolphin, California, for a magnificently researched demonstration of the contribution which the folk high school movement made to Danish society. 'These enthusiastic hojskole people ... transformed the whole district. The battle for freedom and Folkelig self-control brought new forms of social gathering ...' The Danish 'folk' conveys the meaning better than 'popular' but the English word has more general currency between different international political traditions.

9. Parker, H.J. *View from the Boys*, David & Charles. Howard Parker was tutor to a Crime in the City education and research project involving a group of unemployed workers.

References

Ball, C. (1991) *Learning Pays: Interim report*, Royal Society of Arts.

Birmingham City Council/Heartlands Development Corporation (1989) *East Birmingham Survey*.

Braverman, H. (1974) *Labour and Monopoly Capital*, Monthly Review Press, New York.

Cockburn, C. (1977) *The Local State*, Pluto Press.

Commission of the European Union (1993) *European Social Policy: Options for the Union*, Directorate-General for Employment, Industrial Relations and Social Affairs.

Cook, Stephen (1988) 'To alms, citizens', *The Guardian*, 9 November.

Council of Europe (1992) *The Unemployment Trap*.

Daines, J., Daines, C. and Graham, B. (1993) *Adult Learning and Adult Teaching*, Department of Adult Education, University of Nottingham.

Department of Education and Science (1991) *Education and Training for the 21st Century*, HMSO.

Elsdon, K. (1994) 'Values and learning in voluntary organisations', Paper to the Voluntary Adult Education Forum's Annual Conference 22 February 1994 which summarises findings at the University of Nottingham Department of Adult Education.

Evans, D. (1980) 'Writers' workshops and working-class cultures', in Thompson, J. (ed.) *Adult Education for a Change*, Hutchinson.

Eyerman R. and Jamieson, A. (1991) *Social Movements: A cognitive approach*, Policy Press.

Faure, E. (1972) *Learning To Be*, UNESCO.

Further Education Funding Council (1992) *Funding Learning*, FEFC.

Gustavsson, B. (1994) 'Lifelong learning reconsidered', Unpublished paper to colloquium on Popular Education and Lifelong Learning Centre for Adult and Continuing Education, University of Western Cape.

Hagen, E.E. (1964) *On the Theory of Social Society Change*, Routledge and Kegan Paul.

Harrison, R. (1993) 'Disaffection and access', in Calder, J. (ed.) *Diversity and Disaffection*, Falmer Press.

Metcalf, H. (1990) *Releasing Potential*, NTTF/PSI.

Morgan, P. (1994) *Financial Times*, 30 April.

Murray, R.(1991) 'The state after Henry', *Marxism Today*, May 1991.

Perkin, H. (1969) *The Origins of Modern British Society*.

Robson, B. *et al.* (1994) *Assessing the Impact of Urban Policy*, Inner cities research programme, Department of the Environment, HMSO.

Rogers, A. (1992) *Adults Learning for Development*, Cassell.

Russell, L. (1973) *Adult Education: A plan for development. Report by a Committee of Inquiry appointed by the Secretary of State for Education and Science under the Chairmanship of Sir Lionel Russell CBE*, HMSO.

Silver, H. (1965) *The Concept of Popular Education*, McGibbon and Kee.

Tawney R.H. (1926) 'Adult Education in the history of the nation', paper read at the Fifth Annual Conference of the British Institute of Adult Education.

Uden, T. (1994) *The Will to Learn*, NIACE.

UNESCO (1978) *Experiments in Popular Education in Portugal 1974–76*.

WEA (1994) *Reportback. The magazine of the Workers' Educational Association*, vol. 1, Spring.

Fifteen

Beyond Subversion

Mae Shaw and Jim Crowther

With the onslaught of Thatcherism during the 1980s the strategy advocated for radical educational practice was essentially a subversive one. In the context of vocational preparation for community education practitioners, radical ideas were sown, if at all, in 'the nooks and crannies' of institutions and services. Though critical of the orthodox professional wisdom, radical ideas never managed to challenge the dominant ideology of practice. We argue that broad dissatisfaction with the current orthodoxy provides an opportunity for a radical agenda to be reasserted. Our analysis and argument are based on a critical reflection on our educational engagement, and in undertaking to write this we acknowledge that we too are attempting to put into practice a key theme that we advocate in our own educational work – the need to theorise practice.

To locate and make explicit the nature of our argument we need also to place ourselves as producers of the text. It is hard to discuss education 'in abstraction from material circumstances and ... [the] political project' (Harvey, 1993). Materially, we are located in an institution of higher education and are employed as lecturers in community education. In the growing contract culture of education, when many of our colleagues are on fixed-term contracts, we are privileged by a relatively secure form of employment. Influences which have shaped our own understanding of the purposes of education are intertwined with our experiences of class, geography and gender. We both work in Scotland but grew up elsewhere. Our experience of initial education was coloured by secondary modern schooling. We, at different times, returned to education as adults and, unexpectedly, find ourselves in the role of 'the educator'. How great an impact these experiences have had is difficult to say, and their meaning for us is less than clear and certainly not self-evident or privileging in any way. We have each been teaching in higher education for less than five years and prior to that had over 20 years' combined practice in the areas of community work and adult education. A theme running through our past work was one of seeking opportunities to develop a radical agenda and we see our current work as a continuation of that purpose. We also see our current practice as an attempt to prefigure ways of working in the field.

It would be difficult to unravel cause and effect in a biography, because of the complexity; nevertheless, it has shaped in us a scepticism about an education which fails to recognise a central distinction, as Dewey (cited in Giroux, 1992: 80) would have it, between education as a function of society and society as a function of education. For us, the purpose of education has to be linked with the aim of 'acting on' society to challenge the many forms in which power, privilege and discrimination are manifested and the inequalities that creates.

It is important to recognise the limitations which arise from our context of work. We are employed in a formal educational system which has much more in common with the reproduction of existing inequalities than it does purveying critical knowledge for social transformation. What is more, this system is entrenched in a period of educational reaction which has further added to these constraints; a reaction which has, amongst other things, taken the form of the application of a highly prescriptive competency-based framework to the vocational preparation of community education workers. During the past five years pre- and post-qualifying courses were re-organised to meet the competency requirements laid down by CeVe – the acronym for Community Education Validation and Endorsement – which is sponsored by the national quango for community education in Scotland, the Scottish Community Education Council (SCEC). Despite the prescriptive framework, however, we believe it would be a mistake to indulge in an effective self-censorship rather than explore the possibilities for a more radical practice to emerge. We take heart from the Gramscian perspective which emphasises the role of ideas as a material force and the necessity of making theory and practice explicit (Forgacs, 1988; Femia, 1987). Whilst acknowledging that the formal education system is not a traditional site of knowledge for transformation, we agree with Johnson's point that, although academic knowledge forms are the most appropriate focus for 'reproducing social elites and adding an educational justification for inequalities' they nevertheless 'have harboured ... opportunities for critical thinking' (1988: 27). It is those opportunities we wish to explore.

In recognising, along with Meekosha (1993: 190) and others, that there are 'many sites of power, many sites of resistance, and that struggles are temporary and changing', we would argue that in the current context, where the very contestability of education as a concept is under threat, the struggle to challenge this homogenising project has become a prime focus for those who believe in education for liberation rather than domestication. What characterises an essentially contested concept (Gallie, cited in Hartnet and Naish, 1976) is the legitimation of oppositional stances, in their own terms. This is seen as offering 'permanent potential critical value' (*ibid.*: 84) in the discourse which emerges from diverse views. It would seem to us that the reassertion of education as an essentially contestable concept in these terms is crucial in keeping the discourse open at a time when it is being systematically narrowed in an attempt to 'cut the cackle, to damn the heretics and to exterminate the unwanted ...' (*ibid.*: 85) – carrying it out ideologically. This movement can be seen in the institutional community education field in Scotland (in common with developments elsewhere), which has seen the emergence of a paradigm which uncritically passes off its own view of community education as 'truth', by simply assuming the function of community education as self-evident and beyond dispute.

Community Education in Scotland

In Scotland the formation of local authority Community Education Services followed the publication of the Alexander Report (1975) and regionalisation of local authorities. The main problem the report attempted to address was the lack of any widespread participation in non-vocational adult education and the main strategy advocated to overcome this was the creation of an integrated adult education and youth and community service – the Community Education Service.

The report was a typical product of its time, in the same mould as the Gulbenkian and Russell Reports in England and Wales. It was riddled with pluralistic assumptions about society and its implicit values of consensus (see Kirkwood, 1990; Galloway, 1994). The focus was on the 'disadvantaged' (women, the unemployed, ethnic minorities, etc.), who were seen as being the main target group for the Community Education Service; based on a 'pathological' (Bennington, 1975) analysis of inequality in society. The corporatist strategy advocated involved the premise that structural re-organisation of service provision would offer a context whereby adult education workers would benefit from the informal approach common in youth and community work, together with their network of contacts within communities, whereas the latter group would benefit from the more rigorous and overtly educational approach seen as characterising adult education practice. As Kirkwood (1990) has pointed out the strategy was flawed, firstly, because it failed to take account of the 'human relations' element of this re-organisation (at this time, the numerical balance of full-time staff between adult education and youth work was 7:500) and also the contradictions and conflicts which followed in its wake. In particular, this manifested itself in relation to the hegemony of genericism in the Community Education Service – the notion that there is a single identifiable process transferable to the areas of community education practice (community work, adult education and youth work). Moreover, a key aspect to the success of the report was seen to hinge on the injection of extra financial resources (to appoint 200 adult education workers) which were never forthcoming; more importantly, for the argument developed here, the report was flawed by the absence of any theoretical discussion of the purposes of community education.

The absence of a theoretical discourse on community education also characterised subsequent national policy documents on the training of community education workers – the Carnegie Report (1977), Scottish Community Education Council (1984) and CeVe (1990). This failure to address theoretical issues has been highlighted as a fundamental weakness by Nisbet (cited in SCEC, 1984) and others, whose criticisms were accepted by policy-makers and then simply ignored as if they had never been made. In this theoretical vacuum some of the key ideas that have shaped policy and practice have, therefore, been drawn from a pragmatic, anti-theoretical tradition in community education. Thus the development of the Community Education Service has been largely divorced from some of the radical theoretical traditions which have characterised independent working-class education in Scotland (see Alexander and

Martin in this volume). We now turn to locate, and critically examine, the emergence of the competency-based approach which, we would argue, was nurtured by this anti-theoretical tradition which has dominated the Community Education Service. Furthermore, we go on to argue that the competency-based approach constitutes a paradigm shift which is fundamentally re-structuring the nature of community education practice.

Paradigms

A paradigm is a set of working assumptions which influences understanding of the purpose, process and nature of an activity (Marris, 1987). It serves to define what are appropriate problems and how they should be dealt with. Paradigms are never eternal. Their latent contradictions, 'blind-spots', inconsistencies and anomalies provide grounds for the emergence of new and competing paradigms. It would be an oversimplification to suggest such breaks between paradigms occur in an articulated way; the transition from one to another involves some fluidity, an ebb and flow as ideas and practices within the emerging paradigm and the discourse it generates become dominant. Nevertheless, what is a crucial feature of paradigm shifts is that old understandings are not simply adapted or added to; instead, they are reinterpreted and redefined in line with altogether different purposes. New paradigms may appear to contain some of the same language of the old but they only do so by giving it new meanings. As Giroux (1992) points out, paradigms involve creating a new language which lends meaning to the concepts, values and beliefs intrinsic to it; a process which, we would argue, has been evident in the development of competency-based training and which supports our view that we have witnessed a major paradigm shift.

It would seem to us that two dominant philosophies underpinned the training of community educators in the United Kingdom up until the mid-1980s. The first involved a 'folklore-philosophy' which embraced knowledge rooted in practice and common sense, and on-the-job training rather than formal theory and college work, which some argue has left a legacy of anti-intellectualism in community education (Pountain, 1994). The second had its roots in humanistic psychology in the form of human awareness training and group dynamics (Smith, 1988: 82). An influential source of this philosophy was the National College for Youth Leaders which was established following the recommendations of the Albermarle Report (1960). The professional ethos which emerged assumed a canon which embraced non-judgementalism, non-directiveness, and implied the neutrality of the professional role. It was also characterised by an uncritical attitude to theory. Major influences on training were the works of Rogers, Maslow and writers in the nativist tradition, the basis of which is the notion that there is an original 'me' waiting to blossom given only a 'nurturing and accepting but otherwise neutral environment' (Neher, 1991: 95). Therefore, the experience students brought with them to their training was seen as a primary resource for their learning – as long as they could 'get in touch' with it – and this experience was privileged over other modes of understanding. Translated into the curriculum of training this led to a heavy emphasis on knowledge and understanding of groups and groupwork techniques, person-centred counselling, discovery learning, T-Groups and active learning applied primarily to the area of youth and community work.

Arguably these influences on training involved a double paradox for the practice of community education. First, for a service aspiring to some notion of collectivity, the emphasis in training surprisingly centred on individual growth and development with little consideration of the wider context within which it occurred. Structural barriers to change and the unequal distribution of power which they implied were obscured by this emphasis on individual change. Because power relationships were not explicitly addressed through this approach, the assumed value base of the profession operated within a conceptual power vacuum. This failure to theorise power and make power relationships explicit meant that professional values were susceptible to colonisation in a changing context. Second, the non-directive role of the worker eschewed systematic consideration of teaching methodologies and curriculum development (Kirkwood, 1991). It was also suspicious of and hostile to theory. Leigh and Smart (cited in Smith, 1988), in asserting that by the late 1970s many youth service trainers had gone overboard on psycho-therapeutic approaches, comment:

> *in the excitement with which the Service embraced some apparently powerful methods, it once again lost sight of purposes ... any thinking or analysis is stigmatised as task-centred, and construed as evading the all true realm of feeling (53).*

As Edwards and Usher point out, 'it is precisely through its articulation with liberal humanist ideas that discourses of competence are powerful ... not simply within the formal structures of education and training but, more important, over and through learners' (1994: 9). Ironically, therefore, the competency-based approach can be seen as a development of a seemingly more liberal paradigm on the grounds that an assumed (rather than articulated) value base was easily reinterpreted towards different purposes. The theoretical vacuum created by the absence of debate over the purposes of community education has allowed it to be filled by a methodology which substitutes function for purpose. The seductiveness of the liberatory language which surreptitiously connected with the humanist tradition helped to conceal the true nature of the competency-based approach. By abstracting the process from the broader context some argued that it was a useful framework for assisting workers to clarify their job, in the context of inherent and troublesome ambiguity (Blacke, 1992). We would argue, however, that despite the benign language of 'empowerment' associated with the humanist paradigm the growth of a competency-based approach in the training of community educators constitutes a paradigm shift. It has involved the redefinition of purpose and processes clearly linked with ideological and market considerations rather than educational ones, giving old language new meanings in a way that obscures its true nature. It is the implications of this paradigm that we now turn to examine.

The Competency-Based Approach

We would argue that pressure to redefine and change the nature of the training of community education workers, through the 1980s, has involved four interlinking developments: the trend towards genericism, the convergence of political and professional agendas, the increasing centralisation of power and changes in the labour process. Firstly, in the corporatist context of the 1960s and 1970s where participation was seen as necessary to policy implementation, the role of 'process worker' served to create a distinctive niche for community education. The advent of genericism, with its emphasis on process over purpose, effectively served to depoliticise the community education worker's role. Not surprisingly, therefore, in the changing context of the 1980s and 1990s, this role, with its implicit 'neutrality', has been colonised and reinterpreted in the service of a deeply political project. Secondly, there has been a convergence of professional interest in up-grading the pre-service qualification (Hamilton, 1991), with wider changes in the political context of vocational higher education. The exposure of higher educational institutions to the market has resulted in institutional mergers, a proliferation of new universities and a more competitive approach to student recruitment, amongst other things (Rustin, 1994). One result of this has been the elevation of community education diplomas into university-validated degrees. Thirdly, in the current context of entrenched hostility to public expenditure the Scottish Community Education Council (SCEC) has been increasingly dominated by the government's agenda. One expression of this relationship is the way in which CeVe (a sub-committee of SCEC) has been able to claim the monopoly on the definition of community education and assert its purpose as a functional one. Fourthly, the post-Fordist notion of 'flexible specialisation' is reflected in the increasing polarisation between 'core workers' (the process specialist; qualified community education workers in full-time employment) and the casualisation of 'peripheral' (unqualified) face-to-face workers. A key function of this flexibility is that it enhances managerial control (Williams, 1994).

The managerial culture which has been pervasive within this new paradigm relies on the privileging of certain kinds of knowledge. That is, knowledge which supports notions of quality assurance and value for money. Managerial control over the agenda of community education supports and reinforces a functional approach rather than engaging with issues of power. As Jeffs and Smith point out (1993), the rise of competences is associated with the development of Taylorist principles of scientific management, involving the separation of mental and manual labour and the creation of a labour process involving the sub-division of labour and its overseeing through time-and-motion studies and linked cost-accounting procedures. Translated into the context of community education training, this has resulted in the detailed specifications of a series of tasks which, it is assumed, can be behaviourally and unproblematically measured by explicit performance criteria. These tasks are arrived at by a functionalist methodology which puts the emphasis on measuring how functions are performed rather than on why they are seen to be important. A further implication of this methodology is that it oversimplifies reality. Performance criteria have to be clearly specified as if the tasks engaged in by the worker are all of an unproblematical kind. Complex issues of values, power and ideology and their embeddedness in social interactions are ignored.

It is no coincidence either that the functional analysis of community education is claimed to have emerged from 'the field' as a reflection of what constituted best practice, whereas in reality it (in the form of CeVe) consisted disproportionately of senior managers and representatives of voluntary organisations and local authority employers (Jeffs and Smith, 1993). In addition to this, as we argue elsewhere in this chapter, the seductiveness of the competency-based approach (with its implied commitment to liberal humanist values) has found some willing adherents amongst community education workers. The competency-based paradigm necessarily involves a narrowing of educational experiences both for 'would-be' workers and those people they engage with through their work. The emphasis on 'competences' – which specify a discrete series of technical accomplishments – rather than 'competence' understood as a virtue, 'a general sense of excellence and goodness', undermines the qualities necessary for a liberatory education in that the intellectual, social and moral debates informing practice are stripped away and replaced with education seen as a technical exercise (*ibid.*). Crucially, the engagement of workers in exploring and critically engaging with the experience and meanings people subscribe to is devalued through a process based on checklists of mechanical performances.

What has deepened the influence of the competency-based approach has been its ability not only to routinise issues of power but to render individuals responsible for their own surveillance through a checklist system of appraisal and evaluation – 'atomising and itemising' (Edwards and Usher, 1994: 5). It is this recognition of the exercise of power through 'autonomous authority' (Fromm, cited in Rees, 1991), however, that begins to offer opportunities for the emergence of a more critical educational culture and praxis.

To ignore issues of power means that questions about context, purpose and pedagogy are removed from the discourse and replaced by narrow concerns about skills and output; 'politics are reduced to administration' (Dale, 1989: 24). The irony of this is that its advocates claim precisely the opposite: that is, the neutrality and objectivity of their approach.

In the technicist approach, the purpose of community education is immediately locked into an adaptive one where 'useful knowledge' is disseminated in order to enable people to adapt to the 'reality' of their experience. A radical approach to education which deals with 'really useful knowledge' begins with the practical and collective possibilities for 'acting on' the world. The representation of competency-based training as an organic development, which provides a framework for the evaluation of practice hitherto lacking, has not only fulfilled a significant function in the professionalising of community education, but it has also renders power invisible behind the 'rationality of administrative or organisational procedures' and 'power which is not recognised is not negotiable' (Melucci, 1988).

This trend can also be understood in terms of changes in the social control of expertise in society, involving more direct state regulation of the knowledge and skills of experts than previously existed, in the form of anonymous authority exercised by the professional community (Jones and Moore, 1993). Dale (1989), in recognising the limited nature of autonomy in education, distinguishes between 'licensed autonomy', that which prescribes structure but allows some lassitude in content and delivery, and 'regulated autonomy', which prescribes structure as well as the nature of content, leaving flexibility only in the delivery. In the competency approach 'regulated autonomy' occurs by the specification of outputs – the performance tasks which have to be achieved – rather than by crudely delineating content. Because of the form of this control, however, there is space where the 'closure of competence' (Edwards and Usher, 1994) can be resisted. So, for example, the setting of criteria for evaluation can at least be used to keep open issues of power. By framing performance criteria in terms which expect 'a critical examination of the values informing community education', instead of 'articulation of the values underpinning community education', the contestability of the terms can be made explicit whilst also locating them in context.

We would not wish to present an over-optimistic scenario in that the 'regulated autonomy' of providers has to be seen in a context of increasing centralisation of power over the definition of community education. The emergence of CeVe in Scotland is the result of a political context which has begun to monopolise, and submerge, the professional agenda. Courses, therefore, which do not meet the requirements of CeVe run the risk of being put out of business by not being professionally endorsed, the recent fate of Edinburgh University's Diploma/MSc qualification in Community and Adult Education.

What is also becoming increasingly clear is that the pervasiveness of the competency-based approach requires a strategy which goes beyond the 'nooks and crannies' of ideas about practice, beyond subversion, and into the heartlands of education for practice, requiring us to address fundamental issues of both purpose and process, and to work towards developing a new paradigm.

Critical Intelligence

Making power visible requires critical reflection on both the professional and political agendas shaping practice. At a political level, the assertion of the sovereignty of the individual as customer within the rhetoric of choice has been a key feature of the New Right's strategy, aimed at presenting and having accepted as valid and appropriate, a view of the world which neutralises power relationships, recasting them as a purchasing function within a market relation: a vision, as Martin (1992) points out, based on the ideology of possessive individualism, which is aimed at transforming the way we think about, and evaluate, institutions and society in accordance with market criteria. Education as a relationship between people is turned on its head in this process, and instead becomes a market relationship between customers and businesses. Inverting this relationship, putting it back on its feet, requires a re-engagement with questions of purpose which are explicit about the way in which invisible power constructs the 'problems' that often constitute the field of practice.

In examining the way problems are constructed Schon argues that: 'It is not by technical problem-solving that we convert problematic situations to well-formed problems; rather it is through naming and framing' (1987: 5). In this problem-setting model, power is rendered visible in the understanding of the need to question the source of the problem (naming), and a recognition of the exercise of power in defining it, leading to a reframing in Schon's terms. Manning (1991) identifies social problems as 'what powerful and influential people think they are'. By identifying power relationships in the defining of problems, we can begin to locate the notions of problem-solving within a politics of education, which names and frames, and not merely as an outcome of skills-based training.

In addition, the connections and contradictions between theory and practice need to be made explicit, providing both a context for testing the coherence and consistency of practice and the relevance of theoretical positions when tested against 'lived experience'. A way of conceptualising this notion, which aims to build a bridge between 'actionless thought and thoughtless action' (Johnston, 1992), finds expression in the idea of theorising practice.

Theorising Practice

We would claim that our role in vocational educational programmes in community education begins to emerge dialectically from this notion of rendering power visible: engaging with purpose and context. We have to offer alternatives to the technicist approach, harnessing competence-based approaches to a clear educational purpose which aims to develop critical practice. At a practical level we should acknowledge the ambiguity (Martin, 1987) of community education and consider the values, assumptions, knowledge and understandings informing professional practice and arising from it as resources for theorising practice and judging the adequacy of existing theory. Our aim is to promote a reflective and critical culture rather than parading 'community education principles' as ikons to be worshipped. This analysis has implications for curriculum, content and pedagogy.

We see a radical agenda for education developing from a view that places the individual within a collective context and enables an active and critical engagement with issues of power. 'Acting on' the world requires an understanding of the relationship between theory and practice in terms very different from those expressed in the competency paradigm. Instead of 'opening up' issues of purpose and practice, theory is conceived in terms of a set of tools to do the job. The atheoretical functionalism of the competency approach assumes a problem-solving, technical role for the worker – much as, say, a craftworker might solve the technical problems involved in producing an artefact. What this neglects of course is the role of theory in creating problems for practice, in terms of raising questions about the purpose and nature of a worker's intervention. Rather than simply aiding problem-solving, theory is a way of problematising reality.

In working with students to reconnect theory and practice we see the necessity of examining issues which arise from the processes of demystifying and acting-on the way social problems are constructed. To contrast, for example, the 'Women in Fear of Crime' police initiative offered in many community settings with the Zero Tolerance Campaign, opens up questions of power, purpose and context in a way which has direct influence on the nature of the professional intervention. In this example, to broaden the discourse to male violence, rather than fear of crime, begins to build a way of critically analysing initiatives such as 'Women in Fear of Crime', an initiative which ultimately individualises women's responsibility for their safety and technicises the problem (techniques for survival), disguising a highly ideological purpose which focuses on the victim and not the perpetrators.

Similarly, the current ubiquity (locally at any rate) of parenting initiatives can be seen in the same way. In a context where ideological dogma on the role of the family is represented as a social problem requiring technical solutions (e.g. parenting skills) the focus of intervention can be shifted by locating these initiatives in their wider context. By opening up the issue of power and purpose from the outset a critical culture develops in which the field of practice becomes the focus of inquiry. Within this paradigm, parenting skills and survival techniques become merely useful knowledge, abstracted from their social context. In practical terms, the curriculum is influenced by how these issues are addressed.

Working Towards a Critical Culture

Whilst recognising that the current context of higher education, with its emphasis on marketisation, would not seem an ideal setting to nurture a critical culture, we would argue that in order to resist 'self-surveillance' we need to develop counter-hegemonic strategies, linking them to broader public concerns in a way which opens up and challenges the prevailing wisdom. In seeking to provide ways in which students and practitioners can gain access to a broad range of ideas and perspectives and develop and share their own, we can begin to broaden the boundaries of the discourse by re-connecting with radical traditions and reclaiming what has been corralled as marginal, so that a diversity of arguments are represented. In our own context, the development of a cheaply priced journal (in collaboration with practitioners), for example, which encourages workers to theorise their practice and argue their positions, aims to provide both a forum for the active development of ideas and a stimulating resource. We also see active collaboration between 'the field' and 'the college' to produce and disseminate texts and organise inspirational seminars as a way of cutting through the compartmentalisation which can result from entrepreneurial pressure. It is also incumbent upon us to seek opportunities to act in solidarity with those groups who are resisting the market logic of their own positions; disabled people, young and older people, black and ethnic minority people, gay and lesbian people, working-class people. By offering students the opportunity to hear and engage with authentic voices of resistance, alliances can be made which go beyond the confines of the institutional context.

In a context where process is often substituted for purpose, there has been a predictably contradictory response from practitioners. On the one hand, our own impression from feedback received from practitioners is that there has been a loss of confidence about the purpose of community education; even if the confidence of the 1970s and 1980s was based on a questionable paradigm. It would seem to us that there is now an acute fear that the functions of community education will be gradually reformulated to legitimise the activities of the 'enabling state', at worst 'helping people to tolerate the intolerable' (McShane, 1993: 160).

This growing recognition has caused many workers to realise that what is missing from their professional lives is a clear idea about why they are engaged in community education and towards what purpose. This is reflected in our own Institute in the number of practitioners enrolling for award-bearing and in-service courses which are framed around theorising as compared with those offering purely skills development. It seems to us that this indicates a growing demand for knowledge which goes beyond the technical and this offers significant opportunities for those of us engaged in higher education.

On the other hand, some practitioners are very comfortable with defining themselves as technicians and clerks; it is easier to explain your role in functional terms. For them to be exposed to a line of critical thinking that calls their own experience into question and, at the same time, raises fundamental questions about what education might be and what social purpose it might fulfil, is both threatening and difficult. Referring to the same dilemma in relation to his own students, Giroux claims: 'they don't have a frame of reference or a vocabulary with which to articulate the centrality of what they do. They are caught up in a market logic and bureaucratic jargon' (1992: 16).

In recognising and engaging with the politics of education rather than training we can also be seen to be politicising the process of education in the minds of the 'students'. This brings to the fore the question of the agency and the role of the 'educator'. To embrace the purpose of acting on the world rather than simply adapting to it, the role is shifted from mere functionary to critical educator, engaging in dialogue with students about what kinds of social relationships underpin the learning process and what kinds of experience can be brought to bear on larger questions of principle. This conceptualisation of experience represents a critique of the paradigm in which students' experience is reified above other learning resources. In arguing that 'a sense of voice' is crucial to the politics of education, Giroux also points out that 'experience never simply speaks for itself' (1992: 175) and that it needs to be critically engaged with.

Power can also be rendered invisible by limiting people's perceptions of what constitutes their experience and what possibilities there are for new experiences. To focus purely on functional analysis and performance indicators reduces the agenda for discussion to caricature. If we are to engage with students on issues arising from purpose and experience, we need to provide opportunities for them to develop arguments, defend positions and come to a view which can be articulated and reviewed or renewed in light of new experience. This, we agree, will provide them with a confidence of purpose and grounds for practice, which the identification of performance indicators never will – separating, as it does, practice from context.

Conclusion

Hegemonic projects, as Williams (1976) has noted, are never complete. They have continually to be made and re-made in the light of shifting circumstances and resistance. Similarly, the competency movement has also to be seen as part of an historical moment rather than as its endpoint. By reasserting the essentially contested nature of education the limitations of the competency paradigm are made clearer. Acknowledging the ambiguity of community education; giving a central focus to issues of power in engaging with notions of value, purpose and process; and recognising that the contested nature of education has implications for our own educational and institutional practices, opens-up an alternative agenda for vocational preparation. The imperative is to develop a paradigm which sees the job of education as developing critical intelligence, and not just producing 'those who merely have some of the knacks and tools of the trade', as Dewey so aptly puts it (quoted in Hartnet and Naish, 1976: 118); a paradigm which engages with questions of purpose and context.

The competency-based approach has meant an excessive narrowing of focus and impoverishment of what is seen to constitute the purpose of community education. In attempting to render power visible, in identifying a strategy of exposing the substitution of function for purpose and the passing off of the former as unproblematic, the strength of the competency-based approach is undermined. Making theory explicit and reflecting on practice provide the resources for theorising which cut through the narrowness of the competency approach and enables us to work towards clearer educational purposes.

Power invariably produces resistance in one form or another. In the space between intent and outcome we can begin to develop counter-hegemonic strategies. Recognising organisational constraint is not the same as submission to their ideological underpinning. In the prescriptive educational environment of the 1990s it is essential to examine the reality of relative autonomy in our own context. It seems to us that there is a further conceptualisation of relative autonomy in education, which seeks to address the relationship between education and the 'reconstruction of alternative public spheres' (Giroux, 1992: 159). Opening up the issues for debate within our setting, and within the field, provides a public sphere for contesting the very idea of what education is about.

This is the imperative: to articulate and promote a view of education which recognises a responsibility to challenge the hegemonic understandings which currently dominate education in debate, policy and practice.

Acknowledgements

We are grateful to Ian Martin, Lyn Tett and Alan Ducklin, who commented on an earlier draft of this paper.

References

Albermarle Report (1960) HMSO.

Alexander, K. (1975) *The Challenge of Change*, HMSO.

Blacke, F. (1992) 'But what is it you actually do? Competence-based training in community education', *Journal of Contemporary Community Education Practice and Theory*, vol. 2, no. 2, Moray House Institute.

Bennington, J. (1975) 'The flaw in the pluralist heaven: changing strategies in the Coventry CDP', in Lees, R. and Smith, G. (eds) *Action Research in Community Development*, Routledge Kegan Paul.

Carnegie, E. (1977) *Professional Training and Education for Community Education*, HMSO.

Calouste Gulbenkian Foundation (1968) *Community Work and Social Change*, Longman.

CeVe Scotland (1990) *Pre-service Training for Community Education Work*, Scottish Community Education Council.

Dale, R. (1989) *The State and Education Policy*, Open University Press.

Edwards, R. and Usher, R. (1994) 'Disciplining the subject: the power of competence', *Studies in the Education of Adults*, vol. 26, no. 1.

Femia, J. (1987) *Gramsci's Political Thought*, Clarendon Press.

Forgacs, D. (1988) *A Gramsci Reader*, Lawrence and Wishart.

Galloway, V. (1994) 'Community Education: A liberatory cultural action approach', Unpublished MEd dissertation, Moray House Institute.

Giroux, H. (1992) *Border Crossings: Cultural workers and the politics of education*, Routledge.

Hamilton, R. (1991) 'Professionalisation: meeting the needs of community educators?', *Scottish Journal of Adult Education*, vol. 10, no. 1.

Hartnet, R. and Naish, M. (1976) *Theory and Practice of Education, Vol. 1*, Heinemann.

Harvey, D. (1993) 'Class relations: social justice and the politics of difference', in Squires, J. (ed.) *Principled Positions: Postmodernism and the rediscivery of value*, Lawrence and Wishart.

Jeffs, T. and Smith, M.K. (1993) 'A question of competence', *Journal of Contemporary Community Education Practice and Theory*, vol. 3, no. 1, Moray House Institute.

Johnson, R. (1988) '"Really useful knowledge" 1790–1850: memories for education in the 1980s', in Lovett, T. (ed.) *Radical Approaches to Adult Education*, Routledge.

Johnston, R. (1992) 'Education and unwaged adults: relevance, social control and empowerment', in Allen, G. and Martin, I. (eds) *Education and Community: The politics of practice*, Cassell.

Jones, L. and Moore, R. (1993) 'Education, competence and the control of expertise', *British Journal of the Sociology of Education*, vol. 14, no. 4.

Kirkwood, C. (1990) *Vulgar Eloquence*, Polygon Press.

Kirkwood, G. (1991) 'Fallacy: the community education worker should be a nondirective facilitator', in O'Hagan, B. (ed.) *The Charnwood Papers*, Education Now.

McShane, L. (1993) 'Community care', in Butcher, H. *et al.* (eds) *Community and Public Policy*, Pluto Press.

Manning, N. (1991) 'What is a social problem?', in Loney, M. *et al.* (eds) *The State or the Market?*, Sage.

Martin, I. (1987) 'Community education: towards a theoretical analysis', in Allen, G. *et al.* (eds) *Community Education: An agenda for educational reform*, Open University Press.

Martin, I. (1992) 'Community education: LEAs and the dilemma of possessive individualism', in Allen, G. and Martin, I. (eds) *op. cit.*

Marris, P. (1987) *Meaning and Action: Community planning and conceptions of change*, Routledge.

Meekosha, H. (1993) 'The bodies politic: equality, difference and community practice', in Butcher, H. *et al.* (eds) *op. cit.*

Melucci, A. (1988) 'Social movements and democratisation of everyday life', in Keane, J. (ed.) *Civil Society and the State*, Verso.

Neher, J. (1991) 'Maslow's theory of motivation: a critique', *Journal of Humanistic Psychology*, vol. 31, no. 3.

Pountain, D. (1994) 'Anti-intellectualism, post modernism and community education', *Journal of Contemporary Community Education Practice and Theory*, vol. 4, no. 2, Moray House Institute.

Rees, S. (1991) *Achieving Power: Practice and power in social welfare*, Allen and Unwin.

Rustin, M. (1994) 'Flexibility in higher education', in Burrows, R. and Loader, B. (eds) *Towards a Post-Fordist Welfare State?*, Routledge.

Scottish Community Education Council (1984) *Training for Change*, SCEC.

Smith, M. (1988) *Developing Youth Work*, Open University Press.

Schon, D.A. (1987) *Educating the Relective Practitioner*, Jossey-Bass.

Williams, F. (1994) 'Social relations, welfare and the post-Fordism debate', in Burrows, R. and Loader, B. (eds) *op. cit.*

Williams, R. (1976) 'Base and superstructure in Marxist cultural theory', in Dale, R., Esland, G. and MacDonald, M. (eds) *Schooling and Capitalism*.

Sixteen

Training the Community: The Case of Tenant Training

John Grayson

Over the past few years, definitions of 'training' have subtly changed. This has certainly been the case in the world of community work and community skills training. This short survey of some of the recent debates will focus on the field of tenant training. Housing has been a key battleground in the struggles around redefining the welfare state. The role of tenants and their organisations has also changed dramatically in response to government initiatives and the restructuring of the housing market. The case of tenant training sheds light on wider political pressures on the world of community training, and also suggests some possibilities for radical action in a very bleak landscape.

Many of us in adult education in the 1970s attempted to confront the elitist dualism of 'education' on the one hand and 'training' on the other. We believed that to fuse the notions – by using them interchangeably – was to signal our contempt for the 'secondary modern' track for working-class people. To misquote Raymond Williams, 'Education is ordinary'; in fact we argued that it is really 'training' for the middle classes. I now firmly believe that we were wrong to uncritically continue the support for the term 'training' into the changed political and economic climate of the 1980s.

The Political Transformation of Training

In the years of the Thatcher governments training was starting to take on much more clearly charged political meanings. As Ann Wickham points out: 'In a period of increasing unemployment and deep recession training has become what it never was before, a central political issue' (Wickham, 1986). Training for the labour market is now obviously problematic. The labour market itself has fundamentally changed. What was a male industrial workforce has now become a majority female and part-time labour force, dissolving old certainties. And despite the evidence that at best the economy will produce 'jobless growth', state programmes targeted solely at training for jobs now dominate the funding regimes of much of higher and further education and community development and adult education. It is becoming more apparent that this labour market philosophy for adult education and training actually has much wider and deeper implications. Other values and ideologies have become attached and practice has been fundamentally distorted.

It is not perhaps widely recognised that these structural changes in the labour market have produced a nervousness and anxiety in government circles. It is often forgotten that it was only really in 1983 that Conservatives finally realised that they could have unemployment, with its powerful disciplinary effects on organised labour, *and* win elections. Prior to this the 1981 urban uprisings had forced the government into headlong retreat, literally throwing money at the MSC and job programmes. 'Riot Money' appeared each summer to keep young, volatile groups off the streets. These same groups are now being forced, or enticed, into further education, simultaneously to further launder unemployment figures and to occupy and incorporate a still potentially dissident generation. Training becomes an incorporation strategy as well as labour market strategy, a theme to which we will return.

Two Crises: the 1890s and the 1990s

In the late nineteenth and early twentieth centuries there were also public state anxieties on training, then expressed in terms of 'technical' education. Competition with Germany and other industrialising economies had increased middle-class anxieties about the capacity of the working class both to work and to fight. The Victorians had already developed a state bureaucracy whose practices reflected political discourses dominated by the classification and demonisation of working-class groups. It is certainly no accident that in the current crisis we also have social policy debates dominated by half-formulated theories of a threatening 'underclass' made up of 'idle thieving bastards' (Bagguley and Mann, 1992). For an historical comparison consider the 'social explorers' of the late nineteenth century venturing into working-class areas like Jack London's 'Great Abyss'. The state in the two periods even polices 'ghettoes' in similar ways – 'rookeries' in Victorian Britain, Broadwater Farm in Thatcher's Britain (Davis, 1989).

In Britain today alongside these moral panic theories goes a national obsession with classification and labelling, again not unlike the Darwinian obsessions of the early twentieth century. An industrial and political crisis is seen as partly a result of 'skill shortages' or lack of a qualified and certificated workforce. But certification or 'accreditation' has to be placed within a general political climate linking classification and labelling with the imposition of 'social control'.

Cultural Change and Education

This process of labelling and categorising is probably inefficient in its own terms and is unlikely to have the effects that people claim for it, but its cultural and ideological effects are profound. 'Changing the culture' of education and training has been an overt aim of Conservative governments in the 1980s. Contract cultures, bureaucratised 'document' and 'output' monitoring of education achievement and process, have almost driven out liberal pluralist assumptions of professional and academic control or influence. Testing, examinations and central control of curricula are thought necessary to control the socialisation of a new generation. As John Clark has recently pointed out, the left is now driven to defend 'standards' against the finance-led philistinism of the right wrapped up in arguments about 'quality' (Clark, 1992).

This changing culture has meant almost a wholesale acceptance of 'competency-based' NVQs, despite the fact that crucial sections of industry (e.g. Ford) reject this minimalist approach. Those of us still influenced by strategies based on developing a 'counter-hegemonic' culture are confronted perhaps not by a homogeneous 'Thatcherite' culture but certainly by a one-dimensional approach. The 'accreditation' and NVQ model *is* ideological and exclusive. There is little space left in funding and auditing regimes for other models. Even a pluralist argument would demand *other* routes, *other* approaches. Moreover, a highly centralised system of accreditation standards and curricula, on past records, will simply act as a barrier to working-class participation in educational programmes. We may be involved in one of the periodic upskillings of the middle classes which have regularly appeared since World War 2, but these have usually entailed the *exclusion* of working-class students from real opportunities (Rustin and Finch, 1988). We perhaps should remember the promise of the Open University launched by Jennie Lee, an ILP stalwart of the 1930s. The Open University is now the single largest providers of MBAs and business degrees, and refuses to publish the occupational and class composition of its students.

The NVQ revolution is also set to 'colonise' other educational and social territory. The vogue for 'access' programmes from the late 1980s created innovative notions of accreditation around the Open College Network. With this came, however, an assumption that most areas of civil society could in theory be accredited – childrearing, advice giving, self-help activities, voluntary work and organising, etc.

Training and Community Development

To some extent these linked developments in accreditation, NVQs and certification in general have invaded the practice of community development and community work. Accreditation and the struggle for professional qualifications has always been an important strand in community work. The origins of recent community work 'in and against the state' has meant that there has been a continuous debate on 'unqualified' workers and the job market in community development (Scott, 1990). This debate now entails a link between the Federation of Community Work Training Groups, a key actor in the community work campaigns in the 1980s, and the development of NVQs in the field of professional training.

There is an obvious attempt to simply absorb the larger voluntary organisations into the territory and culture of private capitalism. The 'contract culture' and business sponsorship and partnerships assume (via the

liberal theories of Charles Handy *et al.*) that organisation theory and wa-
tered-down management theories can deal with the problems of any organisation in civil society. Thus the Open University Business School has
launched a Certificate in the Management of Voluntary Organisations,
and the RSA has offered its Advanced Diploma in Community Skills.
'Management' and managerial values are now firmly at the centre of a
whole series of Higher Education Certificate and Diploma courses for
workers in the voluntary and community sectors.

It is also the case that practically all community development work
with 'community organisations' has a core element of 'training'. Clearly
this is to some extent simply a response to funding regimes. But what is
often overlooked is the fact that this emphasis on training carries with it a
threat of the restructuring of core values in community work and adult
education. Most models of 'training' after all clearly assume inequalities
of information and power between trainees and trained.

At the level of community groups and activists, 'training' can often
distort values of community work. Professional middle-class workers in
community development settings promote 'training' almost as a metaphor for their role and function in working-class communities. Even 'participative' training places the community worker in a powerful role and
one that gives meaning to an otherwise vague presence in the community. [1]

With the collapse of a challenging politics at community level, 'training' gives a role for community workers, for community activists, even
for the local state as funders and facilitators. But what is it *for*? There always has been in much community work a model of an active *participative* democracy confronting *representative* models of democracy. The local
council becomes part of the problem for local 'community' democracy.
'Training' becomes a way of equipping the participants in this shadowy
community politics to function as actors in a democratic play at local
level.

The central problem of course is that active models are impressive
when actually connected with an overall active, even perhaps anarchist
project for revolutionary change. When disconnected and locked into
'neighbourhood' or 'community' projects they actually become disempowering processes. As C. Wright Mills pointed out many years ago,
power allocation is a 'zero sum game'. If some groups gain power it is at
the expense of other groups – they lose power and political conflicts are
inevitable. It is also the case that power can never be given, it can only be
taken. Importing notions of 'competences' and 'accreditation' into activists' training hives off their activities in a neatly sanitised, hermetically
sealed area of social life – an area outside political life. Perhaps at the
crudest level, community activists used to connect with or join trade unions or political campaigns and groups. They now achieve level 4 on
their Open College accredited training programme and gain 'self-confidence' and 'assertiveness' instead. 'Therapy' models have always been
offered to working-class groups; they now come with ready-made 'outputs'.

Threats to Radical Pedagogy: The Response of Northern College

The new 'vocationalism' and 'accreditation mania' is also a major departure from adult education and political education practices. Opening up educational possibilities for working-class community and political activists has always been part of these practices, but the educational processes have been seen as consistent with, and supportive of, political practice, at least in theory. Student-centred methods in TUC day-release courses, the critique of medical and other 'science' in health and safety courses, and the universal rejection of individualised competition and examination-based curricula, all these elements were not accidental but functional in educational programmes. The methods reflected the theory and political principles. They followed an historical tradition which linked political education to social 'movements', an historical tradition dating back to the Owenite Halls of Science and Chartist schemes of education. The relationship of these movements to the state's education programme was always problematic, often subversive, and at times (for instance in the NCLC) separatist. It has proved in the end totally impossible to incorporate 'training' into this tradition. The TUC may argue that NVQs have a huge liberating potential in industrial training but this already sits uneasily with its implications for the practice of trade union education. [2]

The adult residential colleges (Coleg Harlech, Northern, Fircroft, Co-operative College, Ruskin, Plater and Hillcroft) sit within this historical tradition. In fact a few years ago they were perhaps about to be strangled by it. But the colleges have in very different ways attempted to meet the challenges of the new definitions and new state funding arrangements.

At Northern College since its foundation in 1978 there has been a declared commitment to offer educational programmes to resource community organisations through short, part-time, residential courses. Local authorities in Yorkshire, Humberside and Derbyshire have enabled the college uniquely to provide a wide range of free residential courses for community activists. This experience has suggested that alternative radical models can survive the onslaught of the new cultures. Key elements in Northern College practice are:

- partnership arrangements with community organisations to provide 'tailor-made'courses to respond to their perceived needs
- 'negotiating the curriculum' of courses by use of outreach tutor organisers from the College to work in meetings and community-based sessions to write draft course outlines with community activists
- developing networks with the WEA, federations of tenants' groups, women's aid organisations, Gingerbread, Homestart, Credit Unions, etc. The networks then develop their own agenda of training with the college. They often select participants for programmes at the college. This allows a more equal process of negotiation than is normal in purely neighbourhood-based work with individual groups

- an institutional bias towards unqualified working-class students, with positive action policies in favour of women, black groups and people with disabilities. Courses at the college are free to groups and individuals. The college works with professionals as students only so far as that work opens up educational programmes with community activists.

The college has based its practice on familiar models. Some of the staff have over the years carried traditions from the 1970s based on the ideas of Freire and Highlander. Trade union education of the 1970s and the 'Russell' and CDP community-based work of the period were also clearly influential. But the college has certainly not been immune from external state pressures. It has always offered half its 130 or so places to students on a Diploma course (now reduced from two years to one year) a qualification established independently, with an elaborate system of external assessment of 'long essays' by a large panel of senior academics from a range of universities. It has also grappled with the more recent establishment of the FEFC and pressures towards accreditation. Northern College has had courses accredited with the South Yorkshire Open College for the past few years. Recently in partnership with Sheffield Hallam University and the South Yorkshire Open College it has established a joint accreditation system as part of the development of the new Northern Institute for Continuing Education (NICE). The key element in this new system is framework or 'generic' accreditation, which sets down the principles of accreditation but allows a great deal of flexibility within it. The accreditation programme will not include all part-time courses. Around 3000 students attend mainly three- or five-day courses and a negotiated programme of courses with trade unions and community groups will be retained.

The radical practice of the college will also be retained by agreements with partner organisations. Links to UNISON's distance learning programmes and the TUC day-release programme in the region have already been forged. With voluntary and community organisations an experiment in 'participative accreditation' is being developed. With the national Credit Unions network, with Gingerbread, with a Community Centres course (involving Community Matters, the Community Development Foundation and ACTAC, a network of community architects and planners) and with Barnsley Tenants' Federation, the college is working with development workers and activists to write courses which the organisations' members are demanding. The development work includes residential consultation courses to establish priorities in terms of content and advice on how and where the courses should be delivered. It also includes 'Do It Yourself' training courses (perhaps the equivalent of conventional Training the Trainers courses) to build in control of programmes with activists. There are obvious dangers in this approach but the fact that the college is offered as a resource sharing experience with peers rather than 'providing' accreditation is already proving popular with community organisations.

The model of 'participative accreditation' emerged from work the college undertook with tenants' organisations and Sheffield Hallam's School of Urban and Regional Studies to establish the Institute of Housing accredited National Certificate in Tenant Participation and Control. In fact the Northern College's work with the tenant movement since the establishment of the college in 1978 provides some useful lessons for radical practice in the whole field of community training.

Housing, Welfare and Tenant Training: A Case Study

The Conservatives have actively intervened in the housing market since 1979 and their attitude to community organisation on council estates sheds light on their wider aims for training in the community development field. Tenant training offers a case study demonstrating the changing definitions and processes in recent years.

Up to the early 1980s organisation amongst local authority tenants and squatting campaigns were seen as classical 'movements' comparable to trade unions or other working-class movements (Lowe, 1986). Some doubts had already surfaced on the left but the 'discovery' of the 1915 Glasgow Rent Strike anchored the tenants into traditional categories. But the early 1980s shook these assumptions: housing became *the* issue through the Conservative 'Right to Buy' campaigns, which arguably won the 1979 General Election for Thatcher. The ideological offensive completely wrong-footed the left. One could argue for altruism on the working-class tenant's doorstep, but it was impossible to argue a policy which seemed not to be in the financial interests of working-class tenants at all. It is often forgotten just how successful this 'cultural' offensive was. It created a smokescreen behind which the Conservatives managed to cut spending on housing far more successfully than other sectors of the welfare state. Spending was reduced by 55% between 1979 and 1985; in contrast social security spending was actually increased by 36%, health by 24% and education by 6% (Cole and Furbey, 1994: 195).

In fact it seems credible that the Conservatives were encouraged by this early success to gamble on a series of initiatives to undermine local authorities as landlords. First through the 'Right to Buy' and Estate Sales, then through 'Stock Disposals' and 'Voluntary Transfer' later in the 1980s. The government came unstuck when mobilising their fantasies about the return of the private landlord. The 1988 Housing Act with its peculiar formulation of 'Tenants' Choice' also infamously included the procedure of counting abstentions in ballots as indicating support for transfer to private landlords. Housing Action Trusts (HATs) emerged and were quickly exposed as a way of transferring housing stock to private housing corporations after modernisation. After amendments in the Lords the HATs became subject to ballots. In a process akin to the 'own goal' they scored in the political levy battle with the unions, the Government managed to mobilise a massive reaction from Labour councils and tenants' organisations. All proposed HATs were overwhelmingly rejected after highly effective campaigns by tenants. Moreover many councils began to actively 'sponsor' tenants' associations for the first time.

A New Strategy: Incorporation of the Tenants' Movement

This failure proved an interesting learning experience for the Thatcher government. It seems likely that they received advice from their consultants on HATs that continued confrontation with tenants would be counterproductive. Co-operation and the promotion of tenants' role in management would be much more effective. Thus a dual track approach emerged. On one track the Government continued a programme of massive cuts in housing spending and attempts to transfer tenants from local authorities. On a separate track attempts were launched to detach active tenants from a directly political confrontation role by aggressive selling of a Tenant Participation message. [3]

Tenant Management Organisations (TMOs) had meant up to the late 1980s co-ops. The Conservatives were never really interested in ownership co-ops. Their history had suggested that very few groups were likely to use this route to leave local authority ownership (Birchall, 1988). Glasgow and some London boroughs had experimented with Tenant Management Co-ops as a stage on from decentralisation of housing management. The TMCs gave tenants management powers over repairs and rent collection, though not over rents or allocations in most cases. Anne Powers at LSE and some colleagues set up the Priority Estates Project (PEP), which rapidly became adopted by the DoE as a favoured consultancy. PEP developed the EMB (Estate Management Board), a variant of the TMC with a closer link to the Council through a management agreement. The DoE also sponsored a range of other consultancies and secondary co-ops. They became arms-length agents to develop 'tenant management' of local authority housing. This process was exactly comparable to LMS (Local Management of Schools) and the development of school governors in education, and trusts and fundholders in the NHS. Managing the crisis of government funding in this way has become standard throughout the welfare state. The blame for service cuts is neatly deflected onto local, apparently democratic or responsive management rather than their political fundholders.

The DoE also encouraged the development of TPAS (Tenants Participation and Advisory Service), which had started as an experiment in Scotland and gradually came to dominate the field of 'participation' through consultancy work, conferences and publications. TPAS has been forced into becoming a virtual quango of the DoE, although supported by affiliations from tenants' organisations and landlords. Its reluctance to encourage political confrontation with government can be seen in its campaign on Compulsory Competitive Tendering for Housing Management – 'Compulsory No, Competitive Yes': some of us are still trying to work this one out!

The net effect of all these developments was to gradually suck in a huge percentage of tenant activists into a network of collaborationist organisations and institutions. As in other sections of the welfare state, apparently libertarian notions of 'participation' and 'community involvement' were used to create a culture within which expenditure cuts and staffing cuts could be managed. If 'knowing who to blame' is the essence of representative democracy the Conservatives have managed to successfully obscure the channels of accountability.

The Political Importance of Tenant Training

The cement which held this initiative together was training. Councils appointed tenant liaison officers who 'trained' tenants to enable them to organise associations which could be 'recognised' by the Council. PEP and TPAS developed 'conferences' with workshops, usually at luxurious venues which began to socialise tenant leaders into a round of events and courses based on 'management' rather than their traditional roles of campaigning or political organising. In April 1994, with the government's 'Right to Manage' regulations, training in the community reached a new level of sophistication. In various parts of the country the Institute of Housing, a traditionally very conservative body, has sponsored a Certificate in Tenant Participation and Control. The Joseph Rowntree Foundation commissioned Sheffield Hallam and TPAS to produce a study of training which linked developments to traditions in community work and adult education (TPAS/Sheffield Hallam University, 1993). The DoE turned to Glasgow University for a study which rigorously identified competences and training outputs for TMOs. A set of comprehensive manuals has been produced which identify and cost each development phase and the appropriate training needed. [4]

This ideological and training offensive is linked to the introduction of CCT (Compulsory Competitive Tendering) for housing management. Tenants have been allotted a role in drawing up and monitoring management contracts. Again priorities for tenant training are dominated by DoE agendas. There are few tenant activists at present who have not been on a CCT 'course' in the past few months.

Radical Initiatives in Tenant Organisation and Training

Since 1988 there have been attempts to revive more traditional forms of organisation. Tenants' Federations have continued to develop and a National Tenants' and Residents' Federation has emerged. But within these newer organisations 'political' elements have tended to be marginalised. Practically all Federations and Associations have written constitutions specifically disclaiming any 'political' role. The one remaining independent Tenant Resource and Information Service (TRIS) based in Newcastle closed in 1993, starved of funds by the DoE and local authorities. The survivors (e.g. TPAS) are all sponsored either by local authorities or the DoE direct. The NTRF is a relatively weak organisation compared with some tenants' organisations of the past and probably owes its continued survival to links with state-funded bodies like TPAS through shared memberships.

But there is still a massive membership of tenants' organisations in Britain. Inevitably the restructuring of the housing market will lead to conflict and reactions from tenants. It is significant that no 'management' agreements include the right to fix rents. Indeed the banks have recently managed to limit tenant representation on Housing Association boards with the argument that representatives would inhibit development by restricting rent increases. Yet inexorably council and housing association rents continue to rise well above levels of inflation.

The government has signally failed to dent the power of Labour housing authorities, particularly in the North of England. Leeds and Sheffield each have over 70,000 council houses, Barnsley between 1981 and 1991 lost only 13% of its housing stock. Training and sponsorship approaches have meant that CCT rather than rents or homelessness still dominates tenants' agendas, but for how long? Already there is evidence of a revival of tenant 'levies' to finance organisations to avoid reliance on council or government grants.

Indeed, it can be argued that although training for tenants has become part of a managed process of ideological mystification and incorporation, as with state initiatives in the past, space has been created also for more radical initiatives. At Northern College tenants' courses have been organised since 1978. A programme of courses has been developed directly with federations and associations. The National Certificate course at the college and Sheffield Hallam University was developed with tenant activists. A conference of representatives from Federations (over 50 delegates) gathered at the college to discuss training in the tenant movement. They welcomed an initiative originally aimed at 'co-operative' models to develop a national course in Tenant Participation and Control. In the Yorkshire region an exhaustive (and exhausting) process of consultations and joint steering committees was established between the college and university, TPAS the NTRF and local Federations. Two of the modules were written at Northern College and at Fircroft. Tenant delegates suggested interviews to establish the principle that tenants should see themselves as responsible to their organisations and that housing workers (the course was developed as joint training) should demonstrate commitment to tenant participation and control. Tenant representatives continue to be involved in interviews and the Certificate awards meeting.

This model of active involvement by tenant organisations is now being developed within the college's accreditation framework. Barnsley Tenants' Federation are acting as a pilot area to establish with the college a training programme developed by them and college staff and taught by tenants as well as college tutors. The impact of this process of co-operation and partnership is already apparent in existing college courses for tenants.

The 'wider' (i.e. political) context of housing appears on curricula as an integral element. Interestingly, students have welcomed the inclusion of sessions on the history of tenants' movements: examining their 'roots' is as important to them as uncovering the 'hidden' history of other working-class groups and movements. Tailor-made workshops and courses are designed and organised by staff and Federation or Association activists. A standard five-day course is offered each term called 'Housing in the Community', and workshop weekends are targeted at the large network of tenants' groups in Yorkshire and Humberside. Workshops deliberately aim to address current political and organising challenges. Housing courses combine history and political analysis of the development of Council Housing and Housing Associations, with skills sessions (lobbying councillors, running committees) and action plan preparation.

Some joint courses have been developed with housing workers and councillors, a few at Northern College but more extensively in Birmingham, through Fircroft College. The links with the unions which seemed to be emerging in the mid-80s (Homes and Jobs campaigns, etc.) are now only apparent in a few areas (Newcastle is one). Joint union/tenant organisation training is still extremely difficult to organise. UNISON publishes *Public Housing*, a regular newsletter monitoring government initiatives. The Centre for Public Services (CPS) and the Local Government Information Unit (LGIU) also continue to provide critical consultancy and advice services. There are also still examples of radical initiatives surviving on estates, within projects, and even on City Challenge programmes. It seems that community 'capacity building' initiatives in regeneration (*sic*) programmes can also offer opportunities to adult educators – if they can stomach the jargon and language! Little of this practice is chronicled. Since the demise of *Community Action* magazine there is no national network connecting this work.

Thus spaces do still exist but radical practice can only occupy them effectively if training for incorporation and mystification is challenged. As Tom Lovett has recently pointed out, the choices are clear: 'We can either settle for a limited view of community development, one which is much more instrumental, more concerned with necessity such as learning through doing, opening up resources, encouraging dialogue, providing training, but not concerned with encouraging dreams of a new society. Or we can seek to become more actively involved in a process of critical thinking, a process of action and reflection' (Lovett, 1991: 27). The principles of such practice are well covered in other contributions in this collection. Recent experience suggests that there is little time to lose.

Notes

1. The Federation of Community Work Training Groups has a number of useful publications. See also CETU, FCWTG and Northern College, *Training and How to Enjoy It*, 1989 and CETU's *Training and How Not to Panic*, 1992.
2. See the debate in *Industrial Tutor*, vol. 5, no, 7, Spring 1993, particularly the article by John Field.
3. The Conservatives should have followed the remarkable lead of their Scottish Housing Minister, the Earl of Ancram, who, two years ear-

lier, stated that 'Consultation alone is not sufficient; what is required is the direct involvement of tenants wherever possible in the actual management and delivery of the housing service ... It means devolving real control over policy and resources at the local level ... resulting in a strengthening of local responsibility and democracy', *Scotsman*, 11 November 1986.
4. See *Training for Tenant Management*, HMSO, 1994; *Learning to Manage*, HMSO, 1994; *Preparing to Manage*, HMSO, 1994; and *The Guide to the Right to Manage*, HMSO, 1994.

References

Bagguley, P. and Mann, K. (1992) 'Idle thieving bastards? Scholarly representations of the "Underclass"', *Work, Employment and Society*, vol. 6, no. 1, March.
Birchall, J. (1988) *Building Communities the Co-operative Way*, Routledge.
Clark, John (1992) in *Open Socialist: The newsletter of the OU Students' Association Socialist Society*, Summer.
Cole, Ian and Furbey, Rob (1994) *The Eclipse of Council Housing*, Routledge.
Davis, Jennifer (1989) 'From "rookeries" to "communities". Race, poverty and policing in London 1850 to 1985', *History Workshop*, 27, Spring.
Lovett, Tom (1991) in O'Hagan, B. (ed.) *The Charnwood Papers*, Education Now.
Lowe, Stuart (1986) *Urban Social Movements*, Macmillan.
Rustin, M. and Finch, J. (1988) *A Degree of Choice?*, Penguin Books.
Scott, D. (1990) *Positive Perspectives*, Longman.
TPAS/Sheffield Hallam University (1993) *First Stage Training for Tenant Participation*, Joseph Rowntree Trust.
Wickham, Ann (1986) *Women and Training*, Open University Press.

Seventeen

Seizing the Quality Initiative: Regeneration and the Radical Project

Cilla Ross

Adult education responses to the current turbulence in the world of work [can be] ... criticised as assuming a one-dimensional view from above, pre-empting an understanding of the producers' concrete experience. Rather, this experience is frozen into the pin-head size reality of skills or skill deficits, and encapsulated in a curriculum which mirrors social divisions and hierarchies. ... The ideology of unlimited economic growth ... fixates the learners to choices which do not provide real alternatives, individually or socially. The adult education enterprise must therefore also be criticised for its profound lack of a critical and Utopian perspective, particularly with respect to the issue of work and production (Hart, 1992: 200).

Institutionalised educational provision, the 'increasingly individualised nature of participation' and government emphasis on markets, voca-tional education and training have all helped to blur the meaning and orientation of adult education in recent years (Field, 1991: 128). In Britain, where educational policy appears to be crisis-led and shaped by the need to re-order the contradictions of late capitalism, there has, in addition, been a serious failure by educationalists to contest the dominant views expressed by government in the public domain or to provide an imagina-tive alternative analysis of the future of work and its relation to educa-tion. This failure to 'seize the initiative' has forced many of us to believe that never before has education been so obviously in need of a rejuve-nated, relevant, indeed utopian philosophy.

The difficulties encountered by the radical and liberal adult educa-tion projects in particular have been profound. The radical tradition asso-ciated with working-class education (however this is defined) is of immense historical and political significance and remains a motivating force for many practitioners, but its inability to provide a contemporary framework for a coherent and confident alternative to orthodox adult educational practice is manifest. It is true that social and political changes have served to undermine the radical project, but the problem runs much deeper and relates to the intellectual contradictions exposed in the tradi-tion as it engages with late twentieth century society. The liberal tradi-tion, on the other hand, as Field points out, 'while far from dead ... has neither a popular nor an institutional base strong enough to bear its more all-encompassing aspirations' (Field, 1991: 128).

Educational aspirations which were to 'help the working class achieve its own emancipation from ignorance and bondage' have failed, in Field's view, because they were rooted in 'a labour movement paradigm' which was thrown up at a particular phase of capitalist development (Field, 1991: 136). The 'working class humanism of labour' has 'lost its force; it is able to inspire neither a sustained critique of capitalism and its political economy; nor, and perhaps more significantly, is it any longer able to inspire an alternative conception of social being – that is a utopia and a means of achieving it' (Field, 1991: 137). Field's conclusion finds resonance with all but the most optimistic educational practitioner.

The problem is compounded by the contemporary experience of adult education workers, who, in common with deskilled/restructured workers everywhere, find their confidence diminishing. Notions of flexibility and multi-skilling – those changes most closely associated with capitalist restructuring – have filtered down unevenly to reshape both the theory and practice of education (Westwood, 1990). Language, ethics and behaviour have all been transformed to accommodate market-driven change and to host many of the processes integral to neo-Fordism. Exhausted, bemused, defensive, no longer sure of our ground, many of us work in an inhospitable ideological terrain and grapple interminably with practical, intellectual and ethical questions. Is the disintegration and apparent disappearance of a praxis which sought to reflect the relationship between education, democracy and class consciousness and which was occasionally brilliant, often muddled and usually flawed, an outcome of a changing constituency, a new labour and social paradigm? Are we, have we been, hopelessly out of step with people's feelings, intellectually bankrupted and displaced in a world which has passed us by? Most disturbing are those questions which raise the perennial issue of exploitation. In 'taking' education to the people, are we caught up as active agents of crisis management living at best symbiotically, at worst parasitically off ravaged lives?

This chapter inevitably touches on some of the philosophical and organisational problems facing the radical educational practitioner in the light of contemporary restructuring, but this is by no means its main focus. My chief concern here is to identify ways in which radical adult education practice can be not simply revitalised but redefined and remade – strategies not only for survival but also for renewal. Some strategies – working in community bases, responding to group demands – are familiar and they are implemented wherever there is 'space' for them. But in this chapter I want to consider an initiative which the radical practitioner is not only in a position to seize but should seize: that of determining and defining the form and quality of adult educational provision. I shall argue that this strategy is increasingly viable because there is some indication that students, as individuals and in groups, are reviewing their attitudes towards education and paid work and that despite the difficulties associated with modularisation and accreditation these initiatives (coupled with increased access) can be reworked to the advantage of both radical project and student – a view formulated by my experiences as a freelance in the old industrial regions. Here, technical change, jobless 'growth' and labour market re-structuring has not gone unnoticed(!) and many in these regions are facing the future with a new realism shaped by frustration and disappointment. With education no longer seen automatically as a passport into work but increasingly as an 'end in itself', some students are expressing hostility towards government emphasis on vocational courses and modularisation and are demanding instead continuity, coherence, relevance and quality in provision.

That these demands are not simply self-interested is a further theme of this paper. Although there is some truth in the view that 'the vast majority of our fellow citizens do not wish for the transformative pedagogy we want to foist upon them' (Barry, 1993), largely because dominant ideologies have done their job so well, this is too crude a generalisation and fails to acknowledge the tough thinking of those who do indeed want to change the communities in which they live. This feeling for community change is not invalidated by a desire for life improvement through increased access to commodity culture. Whilst few would see themselves 'at the barricades', many have a sense of social responsibility, wish for a different sort of society, are dissatisfied with this one and are willing to try and 'convert' others in their communities to an educational paradigm which fosters a discussion and understanding of mutual experiences. In other words, as I shall suggest, it may well be the case that there are enough people who are once again seizing the initiative and deciding what constitutes, for them, 'really useful knowledge'. In this context, the primary responsibility of the education worker is to respond by rethinking the relationship between education and work (Hart, 1992: 12), democratising and deepening the educational experience and adopting a new (or revisited) honesty in all approaches to working with adults (Barry, 1993: 34; Barry and I share the term but we use it for different ends). In 'disadvantaged' regions like South Yorkshire – where adult education is as much about social regeneration as a preparation for a diminishing labour market – this honesty must reflect a realistic appraisal of what is and what might be possible. I shall offer examples of my own practice and the ways in which I believe a reworked radical adult education agenda can find sustenance in striving with students for a different kind of quality in educational provision.

Before the issues of content and quality are examined there is a need to clarify, briefly, the ideological framework within which some of us in South Yorkshire – particularly in the Workers' Educational Association – are attempting to work. Although many of us have been shaped by the 'radical tradition' we are trying to revitalise our work by seeking models which on the one hand reject the current market ethos, but which on the other are only partly concerned with recapturing lost ground. Tradition is important, but to anticipate the future we need to use the term in its less familiar sense as an active, making process (Williams, 1990), a matrix of ideas and strategies which can be re-worked and newly determined collectively, before it is 'handed down'. We would not deny that we carry with us assumptions to do with the need for social change through mutual empowerment or the powerful impulse to 'politically educate'. But we do not approach students with an inflexible, pre-determined agenda based simply on our own definitions of reality. Instead we engage with students and groups confident that we have left behind the sort of 'deficit theory' which was embedded in some earlier discussions about community-based and working-class education. (I am indebted to John Grayson of Northern College for the term and the debate around it. See the criticisms of the deficit approach in Thompson, 1980.) Our aim is to value subjectivity and to place this on an equal footing with the 'objective' facts of a particular experience or relationship. By building on work previously done in the region we are able to work with students to construct learning frameworks which both acknowledge these subjectivities and help to generalise and socialise them. As a consequence, the idea of education as a collective enterprise which reflects new traditions based on self-determined notions of 'really useful knowledge' is taking root. And by working with those other than the traditional male working class – women, the unemployed, the insecurely employed – we are no longer hampered by some of the unrealistic and often exclusive aspirations of earlier radical educational theory. As key actors in the restructured workplace and as primary servicers of family debt, women are under immense pressure to train vocationally. Yet there are signs that the problems inherent in service sector jobs in the region and the destruction they have seen wrought on their own families and communities have encouraged some women to demand courses which make political sense of their experiences or which will place them more centrally in relation to decision-making processes. The difficulties associated with encouraging men to participate in educational initiatives (Carr and Williamson, 1994) are as incisive here as elsewhere and we do not underestimate the fact that the priority for most people in the region is to obtain remunerative paid work. But we have become conscious that in the old steelmaking and coalfield communities – where 'the end of the working class' thesis has an abstract and unreal quality, a philosophical and semantic obscuration of a culturally and economically confused reality – a new realism is emerging.

This realism is in part based on a growing awareness by students that a clutch of credits, or even a degree, do not necessarily guarantee a job. Whilst many do return to education in the hope and expectation that this route will enhance their success in the labour market, an expanding minority, whilst still choosing to take the 'education' option, are seeking courses related to their own interests or the collective interests of their region. One indication that attitudes might be shifting is shown by the response of some students towards vocational education:

> *Everyone in the coalfields will be able to use a word processor ... or have a degree in business studies ... but that doesn't mean there are any more jobs. If everyone can do it, it'll drive wages down anyway. Bugger it, I'm doing history (student in Barnsley).*

And:

I think you've got to study what you think is important. With technology there's no point in training for something that will be out of date straight away ... there's no jobs anyway. You might as well do something you think will help people, that you're interested in (student in Stocksbridge).

This view of reality might well be construed as a natural reaction in a region which has seen very little in the way of job creation, but there is an underlying and unconscious relationship with the ideas embedded in an earlier radical education tradition. Knowledge is sought for its own sake but it is also sought as a way of understanding and resolving contemporary problems – it needs to be 'really useful'. The sentiment expressed a century and a half ago in the *Poor Law Guardian* 'What we want to be informed about is – how to get out of our present troubles' (Johnson, 1979) finds an echo in the words of one ex-miner currently studying on a WEA community history course:

I just want to have a go at trying to sort things out. And I don't want to be told what courses I've got to do. We know what needs doing here (student in Sheffield).

In line with earlier radical thinking it would seem that 'really useful knowledge' must be relevant to the problems experienced in life, non-specialised, wide-ranging but comprehensive. One woman studying the experience of her pit village since 1860 sums up the problem of specialisation well:

I get them mixed up. How can you talk about politics without talking about economics or women or history. You need to know about them all at once. That's the only way you get to understand what's happened (student in Barnsley).

And:

It's difficult to know whose fault it is, the government, new technology. But you just know that something's gone wrong. I don't know if you can do anything about it but I don't think the government can, either. At least we are here and can make a go of getting things moving. The sort of jobs round here are no answer. I've done new technology courses but that's got me nowhere so I want to do other education. about the history of women and the coal industry (student in Barnsley).

Although it would be unwise to assume that discontent, or indeed any of the trends identified and discussed here, can be automatically transformed by a radical agenda, it is also the case that adult education workers can respond imaginatively and with integrity to the expression of such views. One of the ways in which the radical tradition can be reworked (recaptured?) is for the adult education worker to begin from where the student is, *wherever that may be.* Subjective experience, expressed in 'feelings', impulses, hunches and views, motivates people and promotes a particular agenda – in this case a rejection by some of orthodox vocational education. This rejection can be immediately 'picked up' by adult education workers who can then work with students to build appropriate models (accredited or not) which put students in charge of shaping, administering and sometimes tutoring their own course. It is essential that students are given the opportunity – where possible – to determine what it is they want or feel they need to learn. The WEA for example (fortunate in this region because of its existing structures and its support from 'no-strings' European funders) runs tutor training programmes in which community group participants are 'trained up' to work through self-determined issues with others in their communities. Once groups have decided what it is they want to study we are able to respond to their demand for 'really useful knowledge' by working with them to determine the content of courses, provide resources and speakers, offer research methodology workshops, etc. For example social history is now taught in community centres and the syllabus reflects the needs of local women to interpret their own and their families' experiences with both the content and the focus of the course controlled by themselves. The Somali community in Sheffield is researching its own community experience by using oral testimony to examine the cultural impact of the ending of a traditionally nomadic way of life. The project has been supported by practical community history workshops which have generated central intellectual issues. South of Rotherham, where one of the last pits in production closed in 1994, a group is working on the recent history of the community and the ways in which the pit's closure might reshape the local landscape. The group decided that they need to uncover the recent economic, technological, social and political history of the making and unmaking of the community and that this can only be achieved by picking their way through competing interpretations and assessing them critically as a group. A reading group concerned to examine key academic texts is now developing. In addition, a new WEA/HE initiative, 'The Making of Contemporary Communities', has been established to explore the art, music and cultural life of the region and juxtaposes this with a rigorous examination of economic, social and political structures. The emphasis is on students acquiring discerning practical and intellectual skills, producing their own community research and developing the critical awareness to do this. Whilst it might be expected that an examination of the changing geography of coal and steel production is seminal in South Yorkshire, equal emphasis is given to discussion about the kind of strategies which may be appropriate for the regeneration of the region and its communities.

Art, opera, music, writing, history, politics, tenants' and women's groups are at work all over the region and many are intent on setting their own social and political agenda. Such initiatives do not of course generate formal employment nor do they, in any immediate sense, make people more employable, but they do enable those involved in them to make sense of fragmentation and to work together to overcome it. They have been constructed not by the external, expert, adult education worker but by the groups themselves. All of these courses are aimed at the reconstruction of confidence and are about enabling people to make connections between experiences – a thing that an increasing number of students express the wish to do. The job of the adult education worker is to resource the groups, encourage a critically informed inter-disciplinary approach, provide support structures and information and, crucially, enable people and groups to work through their own ideas and take charge of them. If the initiatives do not seem immediately radical in scope, it is important to remember that there are as many 'transformations' possible as there are 'socialisms' (Williams, 1988).

A second indication that attitudes towards contemporary educational practice are changing can be found in the way in which some students now question the related issue of modularisation. Any distortions that modularisation might be causing in further or higher education is immensely worrying, but its impact on adult and community education – inevitable as franchising and partnership arrangements are built to safeguard funding requirements – is what concerns us here. Whilst many students welcomed the 'broad brush' approach implied by modularisation (an echo of a growing support for multi-disciplinary interpretations and thematic approaches) some suggest that modularisation is failing to meet their needs:

You just start doing something, getting used to something, then your 10 weeks are up and you're shifted to something else. You don't get to know things properly (student in Leeds).

We have 10-week modules and that's just long enough to get talking in your group. Then it's on to another thing and you feel its always rushing to get you on (student in Barnsley).

If you really want to discuss things you have to get to know each other and come together as a group. That's the only way you'll sort things because you can share the problems and try and work things out. But with these modules you don't get time to think, then it's credit this and credits for that ... there's no chance of doing anything in depth (student in Leeds).

Modularisation is clearly inadequate as a means of generating the type of discussion essential to either social regeneration and empowerment or the regeneration of a radical education project generally. Whilst modularisation might be an appropriate framework for learning if a critical and informed foundation has already been laid, as a mechanism for stimulating a coherent, trenchant and connected analysis of say, local capitalist social relations, or the changing geography of production it is clearly too insubstantial, too tokenist, *too rushed* for the needs of many with whom we work. The attitudes of some students in the region towards modularisation suggest that anyone challenging this structure would meet with a surprising measure of support and enthusiasm. In some adult and community education settings students are being offered froth rather than food and in the rush to accumulate credits in a modular framework – a framework which can be likened to one of those 10-day coach trips which fleetingly visits 20 countries and endorses a 'been there, done that' mentality – they are not being encouraged in any meaningful way to deepen the context of their learning. Crucially there are growing signs that some students feel intellectually 'short-changed' and frustrated by the modular system.

Modularisation is in place but it remains possible to work democratically and trenchantly with students to build a more flexible and relevant framework. For example in this region a broadly interdisciplinary Combined Studies Programme has been devised *by students* and validated externally. Literature, History, Art, Music, Health and Community Action are studied over six terms and each term includes not only 10 taught sessions but two group support sessions, study skills sessions, dayschools and a weekend residential. The Combined Studies team has worked closely together to produce detailed study packs which pull out and deepen links between disciplines and which direct students to complementary themes. Tutors are also responsible for supporting a small number of students over the two-year period to ensure continuity and the mutual evaluation of both the course itself and the students' progress within it. It is therefore possible to rework current educational models with reference to both earlier traditions, when two- or three-year unaccredited programmes were common, and the contemporary demands of students.

To summarise, then, there is now a serious constituency acclimatised to the idea of 'doing' education with others in groups, who share the view that gaining formal qualifications will not necessarily guarantee (in the foreseeable or indeed any future?) much of an improvement in their labour market position. Some students, conditioned to unemployment, are choosing to take courses which are unrelated to the demands of the labour market. Partly as a result of this, they seem eager to devise and engage with imaginative courses which reflect neither individualism nor an instrumentalist attitude toward education, but the concern to work with others to understand the collective experience of change. A second development is that some students – newly aware of their currency as learners in a climate of relative expansion – are questioning the type of increased access provision on offer, particularly modularisation. It would seem that students feel more confident about making such criticisms because of their own assessment of the relationship between education and paid work and because education has been demystified and rumbustiously pulled down to earth. This has resulted in a third development, whereby socially and critically conscious students are convinced that they have the ability (indeed the right) to plan, organise and shape initiatives, and also that they can do so according to their perception of 'really useful knowledge'. So in this region at least there is still (just) 'sufficient space around the edges' (Thompson, 1993) for initiatives which, if not 'subversive', are relevant and overflowing with potential, in ways which contest the meaning and significance of education and which arrive at rather different definitions from that currently being promoted.

Taken together it can be argued that these developments signal a 're-source of hope' for those who continue to see education as a tool for indi-vidual and social change, though it would be unwise to ignore the possibility that the spatial fix of this region might well have generated a particular and unrepresentative response to social and economic cleav-ages. But if these shifts in attitude are underway – and it seems likely that challenging educational trajectories will continue to emerge as polarisa-tion deepens – then it is here that the question of quality and the relation-ship between the adult education worker and the quality initiative arises. If students are beginning to demand quality provision within a frame-work of 'really useful knowledge' *as perceived by them* then we must strive as workers to create and sustain that provision.

This in itself would not be difficult. I have offered some examples of good practice and many of us already work to exacting intellectual standards, but for the enforced introduction of funding-related accredita-tion systems. Accreditation has largely been welcomed by students, in-cluding those cynical about outcomes, and by some workers who view accreditation at pre-Access level as a means for wider access into more formalised education. Yet many would agree that education workers are hindered from a full engagement with the quality agenda by the enforced introduction of funding-determined accreditation systems. Although committed voluntarists continue to dispute the philosophical basis of ac-creditation many of us are working with it as creatively as we can. What is more difficult to come to terms with are the unexacting standards ap-parently required by some accreditation models. This is not the place to raise associated philosophical and semantic difficulties – what are stand-ards? who measures them? what are they for? – but most people working in education would agree that some accreditation models appear to have surprisingly low expectations of students. In terms of the quality agenda this has potentially devastating implications for students. Just as impor-tant is the way in which we, as adult education workers, deal with these models. Disturbingly there are signs that some of our thinking on this is-sue is both defensive and muddled and that some of us, unintentionally, are compounding the already poor educational qualities inherent in the new accreditation systems with a further dilution in quality of our own making. For this, the radical tradition is in some sense to blame. Integral to the belief system of the radical practitioner is the knowledge that the 'ordinary' working-class adult student has the same potential and ability as the more 'advantaged' student and that the reason why this potential has not been fully realised is that such students have been denied access and opportunities. It has usually been argued that 'disadvantaged stu-dents' need more time to express their abilities and few would disagree with this. However, accreditation systems tend to work on the principle of the lowest common denominator and, partly as a result of our tradi-tion of collectivity and loyalty to the potential of our students, we are now, for different reasons, as intent as those from other educational tra-ditions on pushing people through the system as quickly as possible and *all at the same time*. Students are no longer able to take their time to work with any profundity through issues and there is a very real danger that they will be denied an opportunity to make connections and understand key issues in a meaningful way. Crucially, if we are (often inevitably) caught up in 'progress' routes which insist on the notion of students achieving by moving 'upwards' we are failing those who need or want to move 'sideways', that is, to carefully and meaningfully deepen their knowledge. Poor practice can also be located in some adult education practitioners' engagement with APEL (Accrediting Prior Experiential Learning). No one would wish to undermine the notion of increased access (and it is right that prior experience should be suitably assessed), but in addition to the philosophical dangers inherent in APEL – particularly those to do with agency and substance ((Usher, 1992) – it is difficult to identify in much of our current practice the long-term benefits for students other than the valid one of increasing confidence and the more intellectually dubious one of a quicker access route to qualifications.

If we address the needs and demands of adult students, particularly but by no means solely in the old industrial regions, honestly, and if I am right and there are signs that a cultural sea-change taking place in the educational expectations of students, then we need to be very careful how we interpret and implement accelerated learning practices. If more students are concluding that paid work of any kind is elusive and that the courses they take need no longer be solely related to the labour market and their place in it, then accelerated learning tracks have little meaning. Education really is for life. The process of seizing the quality initiative lies in our contesting, in partnership with students, dominant values about learning agendas and contemporary delineations of standards.

It is vital that the radical education practitioner does not underestimate the nature or potential of these changes. Because of the role we have, indeed because of our own traditions, we should be well placed to work to deepen the resources that everyone takes into their life experiences. If we have kept faith with one reasonably uncontroversial tenet of the radical tradition, it is that education is a tool for social and individual transformation and for generating constructive thought and action. Not only does it have to be sharp enough to uncover and cut through existing social and economic arrangements, it also has to have the strength and flexibility to forge new social trajectories. If what we have to offer as radical practitioners is found wanting, we need to rethink and reconstitute what we do.

Crucially, if change is being signalled by students and groups and we misjudge, misunderstand or fail to respond to this with integrity then we are not only denying ourselves the possibility of working collectively towards a more utopian project shaped by new (as yet unknown, unimaginable!) radical agendas, we will have ignored the social, political and economic realities some students are choosing to confront. Those who are committed to alternative priorities to those determined by the market and the interests of government and industry, need to network and work together towards different goals.

We can begin by being clear about what the causes and consequences of recent government interventions in education have been and start talking honestly about what is to be done and how we can build a praxis that is unhampered yet informed by tradition. We need to reclaim our own definition of what counts as 'quality' in education. Some students have suggested to me that fragmented educational systems are intellectually frustrating, patronising and underestimate the student's potential. What they want, they claim, is continuity and purpose. If this is so, those concerned with contemporary developments need to be unafraid of introducing 'long', intellectually rigorous courses which are amply backed up with study skills and research methodology. Modularisation can be elongated and deepened by intimately connecting and relating themes so that a team of tutors work together with students to create coherent courses with a social purpose. Students working on accredited courses could be vigorously supported when they wish to redefine 'academic progress' and assert their perception of 'really useful knowledge' by moving 'sideways'.

Finally, in terms of content and form, everything we do must consistently be in solidarity with those with whom we work, which means working together for connectedness, relevance and a rigorous and informed knowledge – indeed a revisited quality in analysis and understanding. My own experience suggests that it is possible both to reflect contemporary experience but also to challenge the pessimism so apparently endemic to the experience of living and working in Britain. It is from this conviction that we must start.

References

Barry, M. (1993) 'Learning, humility and honesty', *Adults Learning*, October.

Carr, M. and Williamson, B. (1994) 'Coal was our life', *Adults Learning*, January.

Field, J. (1991) 'Out of the adult hut: institutionalisation, individuality and new values in the education of adults', in Raggatt, P. and Unwin, L. (eds) *Change and Intervention: Vocational education and training*, Falmer Press.

Hart, M.U. (1992) *Working and Educating for Life: Feminist and international perspectives on adult education*, Routledge.

Johnson, R. (1979) '"Really useful knowledge": radical education and working class culture, 1790–1848', in Clarke, J., Critcher, C. and Johnson, R. (eds) *Working Class Culture: Studies in history and theory*, Hutchinson.

Thompson, J. (1980) 'Adult education and the disadvantaged', in Thompson, J. (ed.) *Adult Education for a Change*, Hutchinson.

Thompson, J. (1993) 'Learning, liberation and maturity', *Adults Learning*, May.

Usher, R. (1992) 'Experience in adult education: a postmodern critique', *Journal of Philosophy of Education*, vol. 26, no. 2.

Westwood, S. (1990) 'Adult education and "new times"', *Adults Learning*, October.

Williams, R. (1990) *Keywords*, Fontana.

Williams, R. (1988) *Resources of Hope*, Verso.

Eighteen

Amman Valley Enterprise: Adult Education and Community Revival in the Welsh Valleys

Sonia Reynolds

Community Ownership

> *I wanted to leave the village. There was nothing to do, my children were growing up and were either at school or bored, with nowhere to go (Original AVE group member).*

We were a small group of women, drawn together by a series of exhibitions organised by the council for voluntary service, at local primary schools. We continued to meet whilst the children were at school, in the local community hall. Over a number of weeks the ambition developed to use a set of offices, owned by British Coal Open Cast Executive (BC), which lay derelict and rotting on the edge of one of the villages, for educational activities. [1]

Between us we had skills and knowledge, although mostly uncertificated (ranging through domestic and childcare, to office and clerical skills, computing and management), which we wanted to share and develop to our own and if possible the community's benefit.

In October 1987 BC handed over the building. All of the windows were broken and boarded, the building's fittings had been reclaimed by some of the more enterprising members of the community and water was coming through the roof in several places. A few thousand pounds and some 'in kind' assistance, to aid renovations, were received after applications to charitable trusts. Progress, however, still depended squarely on voluntary labour. For some of those involved, the level of the responsibility they were taking on was clearly intimidating and the working group reduced to five during the next few months of DIY activity. Some of the group had been born and bred in the valley; their local knowledge and connections proved key to gaining local support, and a number of local craftsmen, some directly related to those involved, others simply inveigled through appeals to their community spirit, assisted in piecing enough of the 15-room building back together to enable the first classes to take place from Easter 1988.

Although hard at the time, this initial period of physical work and coffee-break planning sessions cemented relationships in the group. The initial courses, put on by various local statutory education providers, included Welsh conversation, spinning and weaving and assertiveness for women. These bought in new activists, so further strengthening the group. To the present day this has been the method of growth. Local people participate in courses and enjoy the feeling of ownership and progress that the enterprise emanates. They become members and volunteers; the next step is nomination onto the board and/or employment. Education, therefore does not stop with courses. It exists at AVE in its broadest definition. Progression is through involvement and activism and it is the ability to involve and enthuse individuals which has enabled AVE's growth from what was initially a totally voluntary self-help group, to the valley's principle community education and development agency. AVE is now a company limited by guarantee with charitable status. It utilises five sites for educational provision and has established five community businesses: commercial trading companies run by volunteer boards, promoting the local economy through recycling profits to community benefit. There are a total of 38 staff, all but four of whose jobs are financed through earned income.

Developing Education

Unemployment runs at 21% in the valley. The communities were built around the coal industry and 1988 saw the beginning of the end with the closure of Abernant colliery. This resulted in 600 redundancies and in 1993 after two reductions in staff, the last mine in the valley, Betws New Pit, closed. The area is dominated by vast open-cast developments which provide limited employment opportunities with short-term contracts. Other large employers have tended to move to rate-relieved sites along the M4 corridor. Hence 95% of all local firms employ fewer than five people, making Amman Valley Enterprise a large-scale employer locally (West Wales TEC, 1990).

There is a very high level of people on benefits of all kinds, with a disproportionate number on invalidity. Wage levels for the few jobs available are amongst the lowest in the country and a lot of employment is part-time, temporary or casual (West Glamorgan County Council and Lliw Valley Borough Council, 1993). People are therefore loath to give up definite levels of long-term benefit for similar income through an uncertain job. They are, however, bored, isolated, disempowered and additionally disadvantaged due to lack of transport and affordable social and leisure facilities.

> *I take it as it comes but nothing's happening around here. I do get depressed but my children take my attention away from the depression. My wife working part-time helps keep our income and sanity (Labourer, age range 31–40, quoted in Gibbon, 1993).*

Coal mining, as the primary industry over many years, did not simply provide employment but a whole social and cultural structure. Workers were trained by the employer, to a high standard for the industry's requirements, ensuring employment. Contributions from mine workers built and maintained Workingmen's Institutes and Welfare Halls. These were managed by local committees and their provision included cinema, theatre, library, education and social centres, whilst often housing doctors' surgeries as well and informal advice services open to all. The death of the mining industry and the decline of the National Union of Mineworkers, means no money to maintain halls. The largest Welfare Hall in the Amman Valley has been semi-derelict for years and is now scheduled for demolition. [2]

The advance of microprocessor-based technology, knowledge of which was not required for underground work in the mines, has overtaken the workers' skills (Reynolds, 1992). Technological developments also affect entertainment, once obtained through the rich social and cultural life of the valley, now largely replaced by the home video recorder. Possession of videos is not a mark of increased quality of life here, but an essential and often the only means of affordable home entertainment. The effect on community life is negative, however, increasing family and individual isolation.

With its strong union, linked to the once permanent provision of employment and social and cultural activity, the deep mine coal industry was paternal in the extreme. Its loss has endangered the community, leaving it unprepared for any alternatives. The majority of the population are used to being employees and lack the skills, or desire for the much-heralded salvation of self-employment or small business development (Trotman and Lewis, 1990; Welsh Office, 1988). There is a tradition of community self-help and liberal adult education, however, and the initial, very ordinary classes run by AVE attracted many, particularly women who previously had no outlet as they did not want, or felt unable to go to, local pubs or participate in the very male-dominated culture of the Rugby or CIU clubs.

> *I don't know what I expected at the start, but spinning and weaving was fun. Classes gave me somewhere to go so I thought it must also be helpful for others. I didn't think so much would come out of it or so many people would depend on it! (early course participant and later group member).*

Educational provision at AVE is demand-led. Traditional surveys of community needs, undertaken by questionnaires, had resulted in the provision of poorly-attended courses. We realised that in a small community people responded to such enquiries (especially when presented by or linked to people they knew), as they felt that you wanted them, too. AVE now develops provision by constantly responding to needs vocalised more actively by people involved in local developments.

In addition to the 38 staff, there are now over 45 individuals who are associated, voluntarily, with the overall management and day-to-day running of the various community enterprises. For the majority of these, their first step over the threshold was to participate in a course. Community business development and community education provision are now mutually dependent, with course participants progressing to management and/or paid work, whilst more people come to AVE because the word is out that jobs are available. The high level of dependence on voluntary commitment brings both difficulties and great benefits. Through their involvement, volunteers and staff alike have identified new education and training needs for themselves, and for staff, local community leaders and the community in general. Course provision, thus initiated, has in its turn, brought in new participants from the wider community. Needs analysis is therefore ethnographic and continual, directly facilitated by the close involvement of local people.

Community Access

Prior to provision being developed at AVE, the nearest accredited education or training available was at further education colleges six miles to the west or 12 miles east. A limited number of classic adult education evening classes were available, within the valley, but there was no daytime provision. Redundant mine workers would be offered perfunctory counselling by British Coal Enterprises, aimed at 'resettling' them in any employment, as quickly as possible (Trotman and Lewis, 1990).

Amman Valley Enterprise aimed to bring provision out into the community, and was one of the founder members of the Valleys Initiative for Adult Education (VIAE) network, which was created to promote the role of adult education in the survival and development of valley communities. The strategy was based on a belief that removing people from their communities, for the purpose of education, all too often succeeds in isolating them, not just physically but emotionally, culturally and socially. The brain-drain from the valleys, initiated by the need for employment, can only be accelerated if people grow away from their community through the educational process (VIAE, 1990).

At each colliery closure, starting with that at Abernant, VIAE organised all the local education providers to come together for the provision of 'pit head' educational guidance. In the Amman Valley, as a response to mine workers who took advantage of the guidance sessions, the Department of Adult Continuing Education, University College Swansea (DACE) in partnership with AVE (DACE funding, AVE facilities and joint expertise!) put on initial short courses, including one in basic computing.[3]

These courses were broad in their remit. The intention was not simply to upgrade existing skills or implant new ones, but to provide a useful and informative breathing space, build on experiences and allow access to information and quality counselling to enable participants to make informed choices. It was hoped that participants would gain a broader sense of the possibilities open to them and have access to information, to inform those choices. The outcome should be one of knowing and understanding, rather than just of doing, personal development not simply skills acquisitions. The provision was therefore to be truly 'education', not simply 'training'. Often such provision depended on high levels of voluntary effort on the part of all involved (funding was often partially through the European Social Fund, which is for vocational training alone and normally recognises only quantitative not qualitative outcomes).

A total of 44 courses per year now run, whilst the same educative activity permeates all undertakings and learning is therefore not simply course-based. Most provision is at the original AVE offices site, but also at four 'outreach' centres, with the new resources centre, located more centrally, undertaking a fast expanding role. Increasingly, courses and activities are certificated, ranging from Open College Network accredited community management or Oriental Cookery, through BTec Business and Finance or City and Guilds Information Technology to Access to Higher Education. Plans are advanced for registration of the principle catering business as an NVQ centre, whilst the rapidly developing credit framework in Wales may enable the provision of a mixed access route to locally provided part-time degrees. [4]

The move towards certification was prompted through both student demand for qualifications (which all employers seemed to require), and new funding methodologies, put in place by the FEFCW, which require certifiable outcomes (FEFCW, 1994). It is fortuitous that AVE had an active involvement with the development of the South West Wales Open College and Access Consortium (SWWOCAC), which offers the only way to certificated and therefore funded and affordable provision, developed directly to meet the needs of the local community.

Courses are put on through partnerships with all of the statutory providers in the area, [5] although some of the more developmental provision has been funded through development agencies or European sources. [6] Parents with young children are supported by creche provision for all day-time courses and classes are mostly finished in time for children to be collected from school. Whole groups of people, once disenfranchised by distance, domestic commitments or cost can participate in education within their local community; and this builds confidence, knowledge and skills to inform decisions about their own future and that of their community.

Community and Individual Progression

Education in its broadest sense is the primary tool of community development, empowering local people to take control of their own destiny. One of the first problems encountered, however, was that of raised expectations. People involved, especially women, could not progress to higher levels of education or employment if it was not locally available, blended with their domestic commitments nor supported by affordable childcare. AVE, itself, at the end of 1989 had reached the limit of what could be provided through totally voluntary effort. Urban Aid funding was applied for, but refused, because both Local Authority and Welsh Office policy, at the time, was that such funding should be pump-priming (and mainly revenue projects would need to be self-sustaining after the initial funding period). The management group started to discuss the urgent need to move towards income generation, whilst still subsidising education and creche provision and facilitating all forms of progression.

The value of AVE activities was, however, recognised by some of the education providers. Neath Tertiary College and the South Wales Workers' Educational Association applied for some additional funding which provided for the employment of two of the volunteers for seven hours per week each, over and above their voluntary involvement, for 12 months. This extended the range of courses offered, at that time, to include a greater number which were certificated. The addition of paid workers also allowed AVE to concentrate on improving the organisation's long-term financial base.

Through the VIAE network AVE activists learnt about assistance for the development of community business from the Welsh Development Agency (WDA). Several of the original AVE members were interested in creating employment opportunities for themselves as well as others.

Community Business development had several advantages: grant-aided start-up, voluntary boards of directors, with all profits going into community benefit (which in AVE's case meant improving facilities for education locally), and the provision of employment for local people. Initial business ideas proved far too complex. On the basis of a feasibility study it was concluded that the best way to progress was to turn currently small, essential activities which were undertaken by AVE into viable business activities. Those activities which were initially selected were childcare and catering, the classic 'female' activities, in which the majority felt relatively confident.

There was a sense that this move into business activity was a logical progression within a developing, holistic view of communty revival. The new businesses and the education and development activities rapidly became mutually dependent.

'Lots of Tots'

Childcare had been provided as support for course participants since the beginning. With the growth in the number of courses, it became harder to provide this adequately with volunteer workers. Whilst this had enabled a free service to be provided, it is a general principle, within AVE, to pay workers wherever possible. AVE was approached by several local mothers asking if a Cylch Meithrin (Welsh language pre-school play group) could be started. The Welsh Office provides support grants to Welsh language play groups, to promote Welsh language development. So it was decided to run a Meithrin for two-hour sessions, three mornings per week, and grants allowed places to be offered at the rate of 60p per session, whilst staff were paid the full rate for the job. Courses were then organised, to coincide with the Meithrin sessions.

Meithrin sessions were soon full, with long waiting lists, so there was a proven demand. The decision to set up a day nursery as a community business, however, brought a change of attitude and culture. No more was this a partially voluntary, grant-supported operation, but a day nursery business, under contract from the Welsh Office to provide the

Cylch Meithrin service in the locality. 'Lots of Tots' offers full day care from 7.00 am to 6.30 pm, for children from birth to eight years of age. Alongside this there are 10 two-hour sessions per week of the Welsh language play group, in which all of the children of the relevant age group are regarded as participating, even if they are there for the whole day. This arrangement subsidises two or more hours of their care, thus keeping charges down, whilst improving their skills in Welsh. Discussions were also initiated with social services, and there is now provision for children with special needs in the valley too, when previously they had to travel to the nearest towns.

The availability of full day care enabled the organisation of full day courses, such as 'Women into Technology', which is provided by the DACE with ESF funding. The relationship between this type of provision and the nursery business is symbiotic, however, for the nursery, desperate to keep its charges as low as possible, is now dependent on the relatively high fees available through the ESF provision. Constant work is required, to ensure continued European funding for these and other programmes, to secure the educational provision and ensure 'bread and butter' income for the nursery.

The Children Act (1989) made it a requirement for all childcare workers to have a minimal level of qualification. This caused some concern for 'Lots of Tots' as, although the manager was NNEB trained, the majority of the staff were totally unqualified. Many had children of their own and could not travel or afford the courses on offer. After some discussion with social services, AVE, in consultation with its own childcare workers and other local groups, developed a 150-hour course, meeting the demands of the Act, to be delivered during school hours, on one day per week, over one year. The course is unusual in that it concentrates on aspects of community-based provision, and incorporates further educational and careers guidance. It is accredited by the OCN. With the help of West Glamorgan LEA, it was offered at very low cost (free to 'Lots of Tots' workers) for those involved in local childcare provision and play groups. Some participants on the first year of this course have now enrolled on other provision at AVE and the course will continue to run. AVE also plans to make the now fully piloted and accredited programme available to organisations in other communities.

Although 'Lots of Tots' provides an invaluable service to the community through employing local people, enabling parents take up available employment and providing for youngsters who have special needs, it will never do much more than cover its own costs. As a community business, the profit motive is subordinate to the community benefit.

The Women into Technology (WIT) and later people into technology (PIT) courses enthused many people and AVE soon found itself with a number of willing ex-course participants volunteering, in the hope of eventual work. A much greater level of competence and experience in information technology is required by employers than was evident in the newly qualified students. Women, in particular, found it nearly impossible to get paid work or a chance to develop their skills, because of childcare pressures. So the idea of setting up an Information Technology community business was developed. This would be a fully commercial operation, whilst employing ex-course participants as a 'bridge' between study and full employment.

ABACAS

A small group of PIT course 'graduates' were assembled and with some long-term AVE activists they formed the board of Amman Business and Computer Associated Services (ABACAS). The idea was to use the equipment now owned by AVE to enable ex-students to undertake, on a commercial basis, computer-based clerical work which was required by AVE itself, and by local organisations and residents. Since its inception, ABACAS has constantly identified new possibilities for technological enterprise and AVE has responded to learning needs through negotiation with its FE college partners. Places on courses in desktop publishing and computerised accounts can be assisted with TEC career development grants as ABACAS can ensure employment, if the course is completed. These courses raise the skill levels of those who work for the business on a casual basis. Whilst gaining work and IT experience, those involved often participate in management of the business. The increased confidence in their new skills often results in people taking up more complex jobs, within the AVE group of companies, or relativity well-paid jobs within the locality. And it is not unusual for those who no longer work for ABACAS to continue as board members, where their experience and new contacts can be of great use.

ABACAS, although a separate legal business, is now the administrative arm of AVE and it is hoped to develop it further by local and telephone/computer networking, into a fully operational Telecottage. [7]

The most recent business innovation breaks the mould as it will be a community co-operative. Cymorth o'r Cwm (Help from the Valley) is a consultancy co-op, which will draw on the considerable expertise of staff and volunteers, including management committees and board members, to undertake highly-paid consultancy work throughout the area. This is seen as yet another progression route for all involved, building on the reputation of the organisation as a whole.

Problems for Long-term Planning

AVE has recently opened a new resources centre in the valley, two miles from its original base. In April 1994, it received further support from the Welsh Office, through the Strategic Development Funds, for the provision of counselling, educational guidance, support for further community business developments and general community development provision. It must be noted, however, that this funding was almost certainly forthcoming because of AVE's ability to generate a proportion of its own income. The majority of funding opportunities are provided only for new, innovative activity, thus stretching organisations/resources to the limit (as underlying core management still has to be undertaken with no additional income).

A tender to Dinefwr Borough Council to run its civic function rooms as a community business was successful in 1993 and the enterprise is employing participants from its own courses, alongside other local people. This has enabled a relationship to be developed with the tourism industry training board and a training restaurant is envisioned, along with a series of day schools on topics ranging from the 'environment' to 'community development'. Drama workshops for young people are also possible. All of this could be organised immediately; the needs exist, but resources are not available to employ someone to organise this non-commercial activity, and it must be slowly developed with voluntary effort, whilst trade builds up to a sufficient level to partially support such activities. All involved in the enterprise, however, can see that such activities would bring in more business and that in the long-term, community development and the commercial operation would both benefit from initial development funding.

Three of the five AVE-initiated current business activities are breaking even or providing a small profit. Cymorth o'r Cwm is negotiating a contract for community business support work with the Welsh Development Agency. A total of 38 people are employed under contract, with many more working casually, and a number have proceeded to employment elsewhere. Several adults from the valley have gone on to higher education as a result of courses and involvement at AVE.

Services to the community include education, childcare, advice and community development services whose results include youth provision, collective tenders for community care contracts, credit union developments, leisure facilities and employment development. All this means that the enterprises' reputations are highly respected, although they are still not secure. Concerns for the future centre around the many changes affecting developmental activity; legislation on Unitary authorities set to be activated earlier in Wales than the rest of the UK, [8] possible mergers or even closures in the further education sector which could destroy long-valued partnerships, new funding methodologies for education which do not currently allow for the extra costs of provision in communities, away from the college base, and the removal of accredited access provision from the remit of higher education institutions, constant changes in criteria for TEC funding and many other legislative or market-oriented changes.

Reinventing the Welfare State

At the height of the coal industry, the Welfare Halls and chapels provided for all the needs of valley communities. They did it by the same sort of collectivist action that is now characteristic of the community enterprise movement (Francis, 1989). In the late 1980s and early 90s, communities such as those in the Amman Valley suffering from the gradual breakdown of publicly provided services have had to turn back to self-help traditions, with both their strengths and their dilemmas for community development.

Acknowledgment

Some of the material contained within this chapter was collected whilst undertaking UFC-funded research for the Department of Adult Continuing Education, University College Swansea.

Notes

1. The author was a founder member of Amman Valley Enterprise, and remains fully involved.
2. Decision of the Gwaun Cae Gurwen Rugby Club (owners of the hall) reported at a Welsh Development Agency, Rural Initiative meeting 1993. A Strategic Development Grant Application to turn the derelict site at the centre of the village into off-road parking was granted through West Glamorgan County Council, December 1993.
3. University College Swansea Department of Adult Continuing Education is currently running the first year of its Community University of the Valleys Programme of part-time degree provision at the DOVE Centre in Banwen. It is hoped that this will act as a pilot for provision at other centres.
4. The Wales Modularisation and Credit Based project is currently entering its second year of activity. Its brief is to implement a credit framework in the further education sector. The project is working with the Welsh Open College Networks, which have already approved some 2000 units of assessment and are undertaking accreditation of unitised mainstream college programmes during 1994/95. (See *Adults Learning*, vol. 6, no. 7.)
5. The majority of courses offered at AVE are negotiated between the education sub-group of the AVE management board and one of the local FE or HE providers or the LEA. AVE establishes the need and provides course administration, the provider presents the course and may supply the tutor or use a tutor identified by AVE. Providers include Neath Tertiary College, Carmarthenshire College of Technology and Art, West Glamorgan Community Education Service and University College Swansea Department of Adult Continuing Education. Other learning programmes are developed by AVE, often in partnership with other bodies, and funding is sought through the TEC, Europe or some other source for their presentation. Organisations worked with in this respect include Community Enterprise Wales, co-operative development agencies and SWWOCAC.
6. AVE was an active participant in the Valleys Initiative for Adult Education PETRA programme, 1990 to 1993. PETRA is a Task Force initiative which concentrates on vocational training for young people in preparation for adult life. Funding has also been accessed through ERDF and ESF funds.

7.   The idea of the Telecottage was born in Denmark and developed in Sweden. Other terms in use include electronic village halls and community teleservice centres. They refer to a combined workplace and training centre which provides the local community with low-cost access to information technology. For further information contact The Planning Exchange, 3 Worsely Road, Manchester, M28 4NN.

8.   Twenty-two unitary authorities have been created in Wales from 1 April 1995. Already committees across council boundaries are being pulled together to prepare the way for shadow authorities and in the next year the role that the new authorities decide to take in vital areas such as social services and education will be decided. The implications for community organisations, especially those which will continue to be located on authority boundaries, are enormous, yet their ability to affect decisions is minimal.

References

Further Education Funding Council Wales (1994) *Recurrent Funding Methodology*, FEFCW.

Francis, D.H. (1989) 'Socio-economic and cultural problems of declining industrial regions: the case of the south Wales valleys', in Alheit, P. and Francis, H. (eds) *Adult Education in Changing Industrial Regions*, Verlag Arbeiter-Bewegung und Gesellschaftswissenschaft.

Gibbon, Russell (1993) *Some choices for Amman Valley Enterprise Ltd in assisting Amman Valley people respond resourcefully to loss of work*, study supported by West Wales TEC, available from Amman Valley Enterprise.

Higher Education Funding Council Wales (1994) *Continuing Education: Future funding arrangements (W93/10HE)*, HEFCW.

Reynolds, Sonia (1992) *Access to Education and Training: A survey of the needs of mineworkers redundant from Betws Colliery*, project commissioned by the Department of Adult Continuing Education, University College Swansea, through the Valleys Initiative for Adult Education.

Trotman, C. and Lewis, A. (1990) *Education and Training: The experiences and needs of miners redundant from Cynheidre and Betws Collieries in South Wales*, Valleys Initiative for Adult Education.

Valleys Initiative for Adult Education (1990) *Next Step for the Valleys: Regenerating communities through adult education*, VIAE.

Welsh Office (1988) *The Valleys Initiative: A Programme for the People*, Welsh Office.

West Glamorgan County Council and Lliw Valley Borough Council (1993) *Amman Valley Regeneration: Sub-strategy for the Upper Amman Valley*.

West Wales Training and Enterprise Council (1990) *Corporate Plan, 1990–93*, West Wales TEC.

Nineteen

Formal Systems: Working from Within

Chris Duke

This chapter starts from the abiding fact that large formal organisations control extensive resources and influence many life opportunities. There is little evidence that power and influence are becoming more widely dispersed away from large organisations, Schumacher and government favour for small enterprises notwithstanding.

Many who work in adult education and other social sectors face a personal, moral dilemma about working within the constraints of a school, college or other organisation where they may be able to influence and modify only modestly and marginally what it does and how it does it. This can be a private dilemma, barely recognised and almost taboo. For the individual a decision to move may be a function of job boredom, frustration, perceived new opportunity for enhanced influence and satisfaction, or chance. The rationale may follow later. There can be tension between those who get out and those who stay within. Means and ends, virtues, vision and results, can get confused. In writing about those who adhere to a radical vision while working within the formal organisation, and of the opportunities for influence which they may enjoy, I touch also on the situation of those who work as radical activists 'on the outside'. The focus is particularly though not exclusively on the university.

Size, Beauty and Comfort

At least since Schumacher first published *Small is Beautiful* in 1973 critics of the size, power, anonymity and bureaucracy of the modern large organisation have sought or predicted its displacement by smaller, closer, more intimate and perhaps more flexible bodies. In Britain we are frequently reminded how large a proportion of the workforce is employed in SMEs (small and medium enterprises). Support for such enterprises is a familiar reprise of government economic rhetoric.

There is however no evidence that decomposition to smaller units is a common trend. To the lay person, aggregation of corporations through merger and takeover appears the dominant pattern in the industrial, business and financial sectors as well as in the media. Few of us know any longer who owns and is responsible for brand-name products familiar in the high street and the supermarket.

In the education sector, while aggregation and amalgamation as such have not been significant in the university core of higher education, the development of associational and validating arrangements may point in that direction rather than just towards collaboration. Nurse and midwife education is following the route of amalgamation and merger which affected teacher education earlier, with the rapid disappearance of small local colleges following the loss of small local hospitals. Newly independent further education is already experiencing college mergers, with large aggregated institutions in Sheffield and the Potteries leading the way, and others following suit. Adult education centres and institutes appear increasingly to be struggling to survive and to sustain an identity; for small institutions the choice may be between closure and being absorbed into a larger organisation. We may extol the beauties of smallness, but we have to acknowledge the continuing hegemony of the big.

Meanwhile an administration which rhetorically favours minimal government in an economic free market continues to tighten the strings of central control in almost every sector of its considerable influence. This includes, for all the talk of institutional autonomy and academic freedoms, the education sector, as those working in school, FE, and HE administration well know.

An eminent retired professor, sending a reference about promotion to another senior colleague himself in his mid-sixties, added that this was a good time to retire. To a jollying remark to a junior colleague to 'cheer up, it may never happen' I got the less frivolous riposte, 'it already has, I've been here three years'. There are morale problems in many parts of the education system about constrained resources and government-inspired interference, especially at present over the National Curriculum in schools, new contracts as well as new curricula in FE, and quality assessments in HE.

Adult education permeates all of these, especially the whole post-compulsory, or tertiary, system in the sense that the majority of students are adult and post-experience. Here it dominates numerically; yet adult educators may feel marginalised and morally threatened in terms of their particular professional identity, purpose and ethic. It is not just the size, nor necessarily the formal bureaucracy; more perhaps the sense of compromised integrity as outcomes-driven criteria and non-negotiable curricula appear to take over their work – witness controversy about the accreditation of non-award-bearing adult education in HE and about vocational and similar utilitarian purposes in FE, to which much 'formal' community adult education has migrated.

Getting Out and Staying Within

I have not studied systematically the reasons why adult educators choose to leave formal organisations. It might be an exercise worth attempting. I am however aware of the significance of this question, reflecting on the careers and locations of those (see for example the contributors in Thompson, 1980) who provide intellectual leadership to adult education in this country. They include the co-editor of this book, Jane Thompson, who left a traditional extra-mural department and the formal sector for many years before returning to a specialised college within the formal system, Ruskin, where she joined Stephen Yeo. Keith Jackson also left a leading extra-mural department, and prominent community development team, for the same long-term adult college fringe of the formal sector, first Northern and then Fircroft College. Fellow-Liverpool department activist Tom Lovett joined the Ulster department, a place where community and development have a special meaning, using it as a base to create and lead the People's College in Belfast – again on the very fringe of the formal university system. Colin Fletcher has moved from an unusual 'old university', Cranfield, to an adult and community oriented 'new university', Wolverhampton. Others, like Sallie Westwood, J.E. (Teddy) Thomas and Paula Allman, have stayed within the extra-mural sector or even joined the academic mainstream. Thomas has worked for six years as a senior central university manager, while retaining his (radical) adult education identity. On the other hand one of our great gurus, E.P. Thompson, after moving from Leeds for Warwick, left it to freelance for the peace movement and related causes, for the rest of his life. Finally, Alan Tuckett moved from a local authority education service to the country's central adult education position, as Director of NIACE, where he sups with a wide range of continuing education and training people while retaining what may accurately be called radical vision and purpose, and facilitating the publication of this volume from that position of influence.

Anecdotally I am aware of reasons why people leave: the push of bureaucracy, distaste for patriarchy, resentment over new demands and new rigidities, personal conflicts and individual idiosyncrasies, through to the pull of a purpose and cause working outside the formal structures of the education system – as a feminist, environmentalist, peace worker or animal liberationist, for example. Others have left education system positions to go to formal non-for-profit organisations working for North-South relations, development, or a similar cause.

There is at least a third category, and possibly a significant one numerically and apropos the theme of this chapter: those who stay in and work minimally within a formal system, but decline to identify with it or commit significant effort thereto, working rather, from this base, for causes beyond. This has been an important hidden aid to voluntary or community movements in the past, channelling time and other resources out from the institution. Tightening accountability and the pressure to 'do more with less', in the Vice-Chancellors' recent phrase, may have narrowed down (though not completely closed off) that option, and personal moral solution, for a number of people.

The Case for Working from Within

What I wish to argue for in this chapter is the desirability for at least some in the adult education movement (as I believe we can still call it) to work from within: not just to draw salary and poach some photocopying or wordprocessing time, but to engage deliberately, purposefully and to some effect with the institution itself, so influencing its culture, activity and even perhaps its mission.

The first reason for doing this is simply the persistence and influence of large formal systems. As long as they control so much of society's resources, and determine so much of the life experience and opportunity of most of its members, directly and indirectly, turning one's back on them is myopic. They are generally more likely to change through influence from within than by assault from without. The most potent external forces for changing formal organisations are economic and political, but these are not easily placed at the disposal of adult educators. Universities and their academics in particular have claimed a special responsibility for representing not just freedom of thought but the values and long-term purposes of society, of equity for example, rather than just economic gain or efficiency (Halsey, 1992; McIlroy, 1993; NCE, 1994; Taylor; 1993).

Not all, not the most radical, and perhaps not the best, adult education can develop within such structures. The cutting edge of radical adult education will almost inevitably be in the non-formal community sector. Resources may be lean but vision and commitment can mobilise huge energies and great courage – to protect the environment, to protest for peace, to struggle for women's liberation or to confront a particular form of injustice and corruption at a particular time and place. Change, especially change to vision, social direction and community values in such an area as racism, can be assisted by legislation and good employment practices, but relies more on non-formal adult education and informal learning in the community and the media, usually not identified separately as adult education at all. If cultural change is a bottom-up affair it may be pressure from outside that works best. And sometimes, certainly, social movement adult education can generate political effort and will sufficient to change formal organisations.

A second ground, or rather another variant of the argument, is that formal organisations dispose of the educational resources placed in the public domain which belong to 'the community' collectively. We are prone, for sound democratic and pedagogic reasons (I have come to dislike the separatist professionalising connotations of 'andragogy'), to speak of learning rather than education. NIACE, while retaining its title and the term Education, neatly circumvents this by referring also to adult learning. Learning is, or can be, universal, often relying not at all on deliberate educational effort, but abandoning the latter for the former may also mean abandoning the claim to educational budgets and resources which in equity should be shared by all in need, and in terms of need might more logically be distributed in a pattern inverse to the present one. Radical adult educators who turn their back on the formal education system, its resources and its influences over life chances, are thus leaving the field to the opposition. I argue therefore for sustaining engagement with the education system as an institution and a key sector of the social structure, and with the particular formal institutions of which it is comprised.

Note also that educational institutions are an increasingly significant part of the social landscape of the learning society. They represent a form of cultural as well as economic continuity. It is not just the great universities like Bologna, which with colleagues from all over the world recently celebrated its nine-hundredth anniversary and, one assumes, some abiding educational values. The Chairman of the Further Education Funding Council, in a May 1994 seminar at the University of Warwick, pointed out how transient were the large employers in the Coventry and Warwickshire region over the past 20 years, and how significant a feature of the cultural as well as economic landscape colleges actually were. Influencing the character, future contribution, or mission and 'soul' of the college of further education could be a worthy adult community education enterprise. If this seems too highflown, contributing to how its access objectives are practically carried out may sound more attainable yet end up being not very different.

The third argument for working from within is rather different. It is that our comprehension of formal organisations, their dynamics and potential for transformation has greatly increased of late. Skills of manipulation have been known, practised and celebrated since Machiavelli wrote *The Prince*, and for longer, but the study of organisations, their internal and external environments, organisational learning and organisation change, is quite new, stimulating and important. The concept of the learning organisation, and the new awareness of organisation culture, following on Schon's and others' characterisation of the reflective practitioner, opens up new possibilities for working in organisations, and for working on them from within. These insights and understandings do perhaps show us a new way to break open the alienating, monolithic sense of the large organisation, to which Schumacher did not lead us. It is not just the practical skills of staff development, and the understanding of new organisational forms and new ways of building learning into work organisation and work practices, which should excite adult educators. The very idea of organisation culture, of evolution and impermanence for survival – consciousness raised by Toffler and others in the States through to Handy in Britain today – can be liberating (see for instance Morgan, 1986). It may suggest the possibility of changing the workplace from within.

An Autobiographical Note

I found myself a *de facto* adult educator working in a formal institution (a big London polytechnic) by accident: almost all my students were adults, and suffered some obvious educational disadvantage, most commonly anchored firstly in social class and secondly in ethnicity. I became a modestly radical innovator from a humble junior position because I was concerned about giving value to the students I met, and because I found there were real opportunities to contribute to curriculum development, in the broadest sense, in a time of change. When I 'came out' as an adult educator and moved to one of the great extra-mural departments as a young lecturer, I was accepted as an institutionally acceptable Young Turk (a) to the credit of the powerful professor chairman because he was able to tolerate dissent, (b) because I was seen to hold dear the equity (as well as the academic) values of the Great Tradition and (c) because I was hard-working and productive enough not to be easily discounted or dismissed.

Eight formative years in two large higher education institutions gave me a sense of elbow room, common purpose, integration, and integrity, in and with my work, bureaucratic irritations and a few disappointingly venal colleagues notwithstanding. From this came the confidence that one can achieve some results without sacrificing all purpose in such settings, but admittedly two dangers: (a) optimistic naivety about capacity for change; and (b) the temptation to rationalise shortcomings and ignore what does not appear achievable. I cannot argue, therefore, (a) that all educational institutions offer a benevolent and malleable environment for purposeful adult education, or (b) that all the purposes of radical adult education can be attained by working from within. The claim, rather, is that enough can be achieved to make it worth trying to change from within, and that changes in the wider environment to do with life-long learning, learning organisations and the learning society make the argument more rather than less tenable.

My two subsequent positions carried much more senior formal responsibility, but the authority I have been able to exercise in them differed. The causes of difference are instructive. Going to the new Directorship of Continuing Education at the quite new, yet very wealthy, well-established and, one has to admit, conservative Australian National University, I took rather naively at face value a commission to help it become more community-oriented through continuing education. It took me some years to realise that in reality it was my lot to add some further decoration to a successful university, but more as additional medal than as any kind of institutional transformation. This was never explained, possibly never truly recognised by those who planned and oversaw the creation of the new Centre.

My own organisational learning, both theoretical and applied, was concurrent, but too late to influence the fate of the Centre (the path of which was probably almost predestined, irrespective of the leadership). The result was the creation of a largely free-standing unit, high in energy, purpose and productivity and very well-recognised beyond the walls of the institution and indeed beyond the shores of the country. It was however no more than a marginal component tacked on to the core university: welcomed for its decorative and public value, appreciated for its visibility in the local community and through high-profile, highly-publicised national events involving national figures, convenient for passing over some of the public community tasks that fell to the university. It was also a source of friction when it raised questions about the nature, purpose and identity of the university and its contribution to the wider society. Rather than influencing the university itself and working from within, my role became one of sustaining an extra-mural empire within the university, protecting it from academic conservatism and ring-fencing its resources so that it worked as almost a free agent in the wider world. This was not exactly a failure, for much good work was done over most of the Centre's time. But nor was it an example of working for larger institutional change, as distinct from segmenting off resources to work for adult education largely outwith and out from the university base.

I narrate this in order to illuminate more clearly what I now try to do, and why I feel committed to 'working from within', at the University of Warwick. We are what our past has made us, as well as what new experience makes us into. The influence of my Australian experience on my self-administered 'job description' at Warwick is now obvious, even to me.

Warwick when I joined it was barely 20 years old, with a challenging reputation: excoriated by E.P. Thompson for its partnership with business, ambivalent about its reputation as Mrs Thatcher's favourite university, a place which I was warned off by a close friend and colleague in the British university extra-mural community. It has however lately won a place as very highly successful by the more conventional criteria of teaching and research reputation, as well as for good financial management and, incidentally, a large and diverse continuing education portfolio. It ranks about fifth in the Funding Council's Research Selectivity exercise, giving it elite standing, and an aspiration, tucked in, in the restless prestige race, behind Oxford and Cambridge, with the big civics and other prestigious young universities trying to close the gap behind.

The relatively high morale and sense of confidence make this a good university in which to work. But what is the point from the perspective of a committed adult educator? Part of the answer is that the society needs foci of intellectual and academic effort dedicated to the study and transmission of adult education itself. So research centres for continuing education and international education and development such as now exist at Warwick are an important part of the profile and contribution of at least some universities. The regional resource centre afforded for advanced study and training in adult education is part of what the university offers its more local community. Adult education is acknowledged and treated as part of Warwick's social structure and tapestry along with the other professional and occupational areas to which the university contributes. That achieved, the art then is not just to sustain a strong department but to ensure that it retains the sense of direction and social purpose which connects it with a wider adult education movement.

The larger part of the answer however is that British (higher) education, like its supporting society, is prone to segregate hierarchically into a class or quasi-caste system. It would be easy for Warwick to gravitate almost entirely to the private school and middle-class end of the spectrum of universities, reinforcing a dichotomy between closed, elite universities for the more wealthy and successful, and poorly provided, lower status open access universities for the commoner masses, including those adults who are entering higher education for the first time. This is socially undesirable, both for the university itself as a socialiser of its students and for the shape and character of our society at large. Warwick is unique among leading research universities in balancing research excellence with access and community service in its mission and strategic plan, but the challenge is to hold this balance in the university's mission, so that research excellence and A-level selectivity do not entirely displace community service and local partnership.

Warwick's access numbers are modest by new university standards, and are at risk as the growth of higher education is curtailed by the Treasury, but they remain significant. Its part-time degrees stand out among the 'old universities', and its partnership with local colleges of further education for non-traditional students are more outstanding still. Arguing for these, and seeking to protect them despite diminishing resources and fiercer competition for research reputation is an important if modest contribution to the larger purpose and process of securing adults' right to education, including access (wider as well as more) to the best.

In still less obvious ways there are opportunities while working from within to promote the values as well as the cause of radical adult education. In my own case and present experience this includes attempting to promote good equal opportunity practice within the university (whether with formal overall responsibility or simply as one member of the university community) in areas of gender, ethnicity and disability; putting around the idea that lifelong learning and development, through staff development and in other ways, is for us as well as for other people; supporting access for local people to facilities such as the library. Much of this is a matter of small gains, losing a little ground here and winning some back there. Cumulatively, this is what makes the identity and culture of the institution, perhaps with occasional high points when the mission statement or strategic plan comes up for review. What is true centrally holds also departmentally and at lower levels.

This may sound like an apologia for not fighting harder, though the conservative control of peer group pressure can be daunting enough. Fortunately not everyone chooses to work for adult education, access, opportunity and change from within; alliances across the (now well-permeated) boundaries of institutions are also essential. What matters is a measure of mutual tolerance and understanding between overt and closet radicals to nurture such alliances. I recall ideological posturings – often from the security of a tenured job within an elite institution – by some who refuse to make the effort to work with the grain of the organisation and achieve tangible change, preferring the purity of pulpit posturing. The feel-good factor may be high, but the objective results are commonly nugatory, or actually negative. As our understanding of organisation development and the 'learning organisation' matures, there is every reason to hope that, with purpose, persistence and mutuality of effort, we can win back lost ground in our educational institutions and make some new gains too. The idea of university, as well as universities' contribution to adult education, is there to be played for.

References and Other Sources

Becher, T. (1989) *Academic Tribes and Territories: Intellectual inquiry and the culture of disciplines*, SRHE and Open University Press.

Brookman, J. (1994) 'Divisions between "town and gown"', *AUT Bulletin*, January 1994.

Duke, C. (1992) *The Learning University. Towards a new paradigm*, SRHE and Open University Press.

Duke, C. and Merrill, B. (1993) *The Winding Road – Widening opportunities for higher education*, Employment Department and University of Warwick.

The Economist (1994) 'Universities. Towers of babble', 7 January.

Fulton, O. (ed.) (1989) *Access and Institutional Change*, SRHE and Open University Press.

Halsey, A.H. (1992) *Decline of Donnish Dominion*, Clarendon Press.

Morgan, G. (1986) *Images of Organization*, Sage.

McIlroy, J. (1993) *Access and Elitism in UK Higher Education*, Edmonton, Athabasca University.

National Commission on Education (1994) *Universities in the Twenty-First Century*, London, NCE.

NIACE (1993) *An Adult Higher Education*, NIACE.

Schumacher, E.F. (1974) *Small is Beautiful*, Abacus, Sphere.

Taylor, R. (1993) 'Continuing education and the accessible university', *University of Leeds Review*, 36, pp 313–330.

Thompson, J.L. (ed.) (1980) *Adult Education for a Change*, Hutchinson.

Tierney, W.G. and Rhoads, R.A. (1994) *Enhancing Promotion, Tenure and Beyond. Faculty socialization as a cultural process*, Washington, ERIC and George Washington University.

The Times (1994) article on the status order of universities by Peter Scott, 7 February.

Yeo, S. (1991) *Access: What and whither, when and how?*, Department of Adult Continuing Education, University of Leeds.

Twenty

Adult Learning in the Context of Global, Neo-Liberal Economic Policies

John Payne

> *There are places, but for me, inevitably, this is the place to begin. What I shall try to do, here, is a new kind of enquiry, with ourselves involved in it (Williams, 1964: 298).*

In *Second Generation*, Peter, an Oxford undergraduate whose father is a shop steward at the city's car-works, turns away from the university model of 'pure', objective research. At best it changes nothing; at worst it simply stands aside from popular struggles and confirms the position of the powerful. This latter position is illustrated through the voice of Michael Swinburne, an industrial relations 'expert' who says on a TV programme about the strike at the car factory: 'The truth probably lies somewhere in a shifting series of greys' (*ibid.*). It was Williams's intellectual strength that he was able to think in strong, clear colours at a time when the left had already begun its long march towards fudge and compromise.

What I am trying to do in this piece of writing, then, is to see how my own personal experience and working life (especially in the decade 1983–93) fits into three broad areas of interest:

- a view of the purposes of, and appropriate methodology for, adult education research. In this essay, I have chosen to develop a theory of the location of adult learning in the context of global neo-liberal economic policy, in two areas of practice with social actors: my own practice in the London Borough of Wandsworth (1983–90) and the experience of popular educators in Nicaragua during the Sandinista period (1979–90) and the period since the election of the Chamorro government (1990–present). I shall show how the retreat of the state has been matched by a growth of private sector adult education, with oppositional practice increasingly located in the non-governmental sector
- the global economy and the hegemony of neo-liberal economic theory. I shall show how the activities of the World Bank (WB) and the International Monetary Fund (IMF) have attempted to impose neo-liberal economic policies in the countries of the South. Despite the discourse of 'aid' and 'development', the actual result has been increasing poverty in the South and a

widening gap between incomes in South and North, on the one hand, and within individual countries in both North and South, on the other hand

- the tendency to view education as a private consumption good rather than a public service. To take the UK as an example, Esland has argued persuasively that discussion of education and training in the UK has been characterised by a 'discourse of blame', through which all social and economic ills are ascribed to a single cause – the failure of the education and training system to produce workers with the skills required by the economy (Esland, 1991: v). This ideological position is usually traced back to prime Minister James Callaghan's Ruskin College speech in 1976, which coincided with the imposition of an IMF-negotiated deflationary package, including large cuts in public expenditure, on the British government. Esland argues that a crucial feature of the 'discourse of blame' is that: 'It has also provided legitimation for the imposition of a market forces model on the education provided by schools and colleges' (*ibid.*). What is at stake for conservative thought, then, is the neo-liberal economic model, with its emphasis on cutting public expenditure and subordinating all aspects of social life to its purpose – the maximisation of profit at a global level. At the same time, I shall explore the contradictory tendency for oppositional practice to relocate itself within this privatised sphere through the work of Non-Government Organisations (NGOs).

Informal Adult Education in the Inner London Education Authority (ILEA)

The penetration of the ideological shift outlined above was uneven, given the relative autonomy of local and national state in the late 70s to early 80s, and the determination of a number of Labour-controlled local education authorities (LEAs) to maintain high levels of public expenditure well into the 80s. Among them was the Inner London Education Authority (ILEA), the largest LEA in the country. The story of how ILEA was first strangled and then abolished by an authoritarian national government is too well known to be repeated in detail. Three stages are identifiable, each of which had an impact on my own work as an adult educator for ILEA.

1. The Greater London Council (GLC) phase (from 1983)

The GLC held responsibility for a range of public services and infrastructural matters across an area much wider than that of ILEA. From 1982 it was controlled by a left Labour majority under the leadership of Ken Livingstone. During this period, I worked closely with a GLC-funded community resource centre in Putney (London Borough of Wandsworth) to set up a series of workshop courses in support of voluntary organisations in the borough (Payne, 1987). Although a total of 130 organisations used the centre during its short life (1983–86), it was controlled through its management committee by working-class members of tenants' associations (TAs). In retrospect it was not, however, working-class militancy that gave the centre its focus, but the ferocious onslaught launched against the working-class by the Wandsworth Borough Council, which held local responsibility for important public services such as housing, social services, parks, recreation, street lighting and cleaning.

At the time, I made extensive use of Manuel Castells' work on urban social movements to try and understand what was happening. I emphasised that the tenants' movement formed a 'collective consumption trade union' (Castells, 1983: 316) which defended the city as use value rather than exchange value, a place to live in rather than a source of capitalist accumulation and profit. It was a social movement developing 'its own meaning over a given space in contradiction to the structurally dominant meaning' (Castells, 1983: 305). It was precisely the desire of Wandsworth Borough Council to transform the city to its own design (through privatisation of services, sale of public property to private firms and public housing to private individuals, massive cuts in public expenditure and services) that created a focused, coherent social opposition that fitted Castells' model of different parts of the social formation clashing for control of urban space. What is of interest is not whether the Conservative Party was consciously attempting to derive electoral advantage from its policies, but that its policies can be understood as central to the international neo-liberal project. 'Castells lives' in Wandsworth: our current struggle is over a popular open-air swimming pool which the council has closed and wants to redevelop the site for indoors bowls and tennis, with an international hotel next door to it!

What happened in Putney between 1983 and 1986 was a process full of ironies and contradictions:

- working with TAs meant confronting directly, and not always successfully, the conservatism of the white working-class. They were certainly not the 'Marxist co-operatives' (Patrick Jenkin), 'Marxists set on revolution' (Norman Tebbitt) or 'tinpot socialist republics' engaged in 'actions alien to our British character' (Margaret Thatcher) of the discourse of Tory derision!
- the use of two parts of the local state (GLC and ILEA) to oppose a third part of the local state (Wandsworth Borough Council)
- where TAs were strong, privatisation made little progress. Conversely, where they were weak, 'social cleansing' proceeded apace, with the decanting of whole blocks of flats for sale to middle-class incomers.

The educational work in support of this political agitation was very indirect, consisting mostly of courses in subjects such as banner-making, leaflet and newsletter production, committee procedure, media relations and so on. However, the inter-class solidarity established in the process led to two unintended educational outcomes, both after the closing of the

Putney Resource Centre and the abolition of the GLC. The first of these was a pair of oral history projects:

- *We survived*, an account of political and social history as lived by the members of the Putney and Roehampton Organisation of Pensioners (PROP). To emphasise the point about solidarity, I spent the Saturday morning before the 'course' started collecting signatures in the rain in Roehampton as part of the 'Save the Putney Resource Centre' campaign – a vain attempt to persuade Wandsworth to take over the funding from the GLC.
- Several years later I helped a small TA to write the history of their tower block (*Rising Above It*) in terms of their own early lives in depressed parts of Inner London (and elsewhere), the move to new model homes in Roehampton in the 50s but with no community facilities, the social problems that had arisen, and the response of the tenants movement to those problems.[1]

The second outcome was my involvement in the 1988 Housing Act workshops. During the winter of 1987/88, a small number of ILEA adult education workers met with Sue Gardener at the ILEA Adult Education Curriculum Development Unit (AECDU) to discuss responses to the Housing Bill going through parliament. This was the period of the radical conservatism of Thatcher's third term, following her General Election victory of 1987. Legislation included the 1988 Education Reform Act which, *inter alia*, abolished the Inner London Education Authority. The Housing Bill was the subject of nation-wide agitation in opposition to such proposals as Housing Action Trusts (HATs) and ballots to transfer the ownership of public housing into private hands. It was clear that at the end of the day, particularly when as in Wandsworth local government was of the same political colour as national government, small TAs might be left fighting ballots to privatise their estates. Sue Gardener saw this work as marking a new stage in the political agenda of adult education in London: 'I think the good practice embodied in the Housing Bill work was trying to attend to political agendas outside and not drive them from the relatively weak and detached position of Adult Education – trying to work out how to be genuinely instrumental and informative' (letter to the author, 10 July 1994).

In Roehampton, assisted only by one part-time tutor (a TA activist) and with the approval of the Adult Education Principal and Administrative Officer, I was able to put on a series of two-hour workshops which eventually reached over 500 people in a community centre, adult education centres and tenants' halls and rooms. The format challenged some preconceived notions about 'informal community education'. Numbers at most workshops were quite large; in the first half of the meeting I would explain in didactic fashion the government proposals and their implications for housing in London (including homelessness and equal opportunities) and the tutor-activist would talk about campaigning issues; after a tea-break a local TA leader would chair a question and answer and discussion session. It was an interesting example of the way that formal educational methods could be inserted into an informal context in which paramount importance was placed on the dissemination of knowledge and the building of collective strategy.

2. The Cuts Period (from 1986)

Disaster struck the ILEA Adult Education (AE) service a little at a time. From the mid-80s, rate capping [2] affected the ability of ILEA to respond to what it identified as educational need. Since schooling was a statutory service and AE was not, AE budgets suffered particularly badly (Payne, 1991). However, the impact of rate-capping was uneven: in some parts of the service it led to growing demoralisation, but in others it hastened the process of cultural change in adult education centres, with vocational and access courses (both of particular interest to women and black people) becoming a significant part of the work. Given that it was necessary to impose strict priorities in order to stay within budget, there was a decline in the number of 'leisure' courses, which were often dominated by middle-class people. As reflected above in my own practice, some informal adult education work continued, despite an increasing emphasis on accredited courses. Clearly both were important to people living in deprived communities, and indeed a number of the Roehampton tenant activists were studying GCSE English at the time the Housing workshops were held (1987/88).

3. 1990: Abolition

The abolition of ILEA in 1990 coincided with the arrival of the Poll Tax [3] and continuing pressure to cut local government expenditure. In the survey of adult education in Inner London reported in Payne (1991), half the new borough services reported a fall in budget from 89/90 to 90/91 and most a fall from 90/91 to 91/92. As one principal commented: 'if you're cutting adult education, you're bound to have a drop in student figures and if you then cut the budget further in respect of that, we're into a downward spiral from which we can't recover' (quoted in Payne, 1991: 7). There has been some recovery since 1991, but much of the force and direction of ILEA work has disappeared. Particular tendencies are:

- the increasing role of colleges and universities in making provision for adult students
- the loss of many of the London educational guidance services
- the loss of the generous fee concessions ILEA gave to the unemployed, older people, those on benefits and low wages, and their dependants
- rising fees and an emphasis on 'marketing' and competition between institutions.

It is clear that the most extensive AE services are now in the Conservative boroughs of Kensington and Chelsea, Westminster and Wandsworth. This is not just because of the way government grants favour these boroughs (e.g. in 1994/95 Wandsworth will claim more than

10% of the total council tax transitional relief for the whole of England, thereby keeping its position as the lowest-charging borough in the land). It is precisely because an emphasis on markets advantages those with power in the market: these three boroughs are among the richest in London. However, it would be over-reductionist to say that AE is simply back where it started – a consumerist service for the educationally advantaged. Towards the end of this chapter I want to celebrate the achievements of those adult educators across the country who have not lost faith and who still find spaces to colonise with oppositional practice.

It may seem a strange way to start a chapter which claims to deal with the global economy, to spend so much space on London in general, and one small corner of it, Putney/Roehampton, in particular. I want now to extend the argument and demonstrate more clearly how our 'little local difficulties' in London reflect not only a move from public service to market economy in the UK, but a wider international economic process which has engulfed most countries in the world. At the same time, as Sue Gardener points out: 'what strikes me now is how ill-equipped we were to use the global economic forces analysis at that time, and how hampered in our understanding by relying on a politics-of-adult-education rather than a politics-in-general' (letter to author, 10 July 1994). One of these is Nicaragua, a small, insignificant Central American republic which in the 1980s attempted to show that there was an alternative to neo-liberal economics, and that adult education had a role to play in that alternative.

Popular Education in Nicaragua

... and also, teach them how to read (Carlos Fonseca, founder of the Nicaraguan Sandinista front, the FSLN, in 1961).

For a number of UK adult educators, including myself, the decision of the International League for Social Commitment in Adult Education (ILSCAE) to hold its 1989 conference in Nicaragua gave us our first experience of life in the countries of the South. The achievements of the Mass Literacy Campaign of 1980, with the reduction of the illiteracy rate from 53 to 13%, are well known. But it also represented a certain view of literacy: as Luli Harvey, one of the UK delegates, wrote in a report on the visit:

The revolution was begun with a strong commitment to universal education and development.
In this context, education is seen as part of a comprehensive programme to empower the majority of the population so that they may participate in organisations that represent their interests, and through them, in the equitable development of their society. Public expenditure on labour and community organisations representing the poor increased dramatically, as did the membership, and those organisations were considered the foundations of public policies and programmes designed

to address the country's problems of poverty and inequity.
In order to participate fully, people must be able to read, to write, to
make calculations, to analyse, to criticise, to evaluate and reflect. The
creative forces of education are also needed to enable people to survive
during the reconstruction of their society – to raise standards of health
and nutrition, rates of production, levels of food self-sufficiency, and the
efficient use and conservation of resources (Harvey, 1990).

This broad view of literacy, founded in the social and economic reality of people's lives, is emphatically political. At the same time it recognises that all educational practice has a political basis. In the words of Raymond Williams, 'an education' is 'a particular selection, a set of emphases and omissions' (Williams, 1965: 145). And just as literacy (which dominates the North) is political, so is illiteracy (which dominates the South): 'The social production of structured illiteracy is a very important political process: a key factor in reproducing hierarchies of domination and subordination' (Lankshear, 1987: 142). It is also deeply ironical that the failure of the Sandinistas in the first years of the regime to think through the relationship between literacy in the dominant language, Spanish, and literacy for the peoples of the Atlantic Coast where English and a number of Indian languages are spoken, contributed to the destabilisation of the regime by the USA-backed Contra forces (Ortega, 1989).

By the time we visited Nicaragua in 1989, the educational work of the Sandinistas was already in reverse. The increasing illiteracy rate was a direct result of the economic crisis provoked by the USA trade embargo, the Contra war and the dislocation of daily life (Arrien and Matus, 1989). By 1989 only 76% of 7–12-year-olds were in school, with obvious implications for future patterns of adult illiteracy. At the same time, the strength of the educational work we saw lay in the interpenetration of adult education and civil society, in church and women's groups, in trade unions and community groups. This has enabled at least some of the work to survive the election defeat of the Sandinistas in 1990, and the imposition on the country of the type of neo-liberal economic policies approved of by the World Bank and IMF. Private education has flourished at all levels, while publicly-funded education for both children and adults has declined. The rump of the adult education work of the Ministry of Education has now formed as a non-governmental organisation (INIEP) dependent on outside support and assistance.

Why, then, did Nicaragua matter? Why was the might of US power put 'on the line' against a tiny, poverty-stricken country of only three million people? Why did leading US politicians risk their careers in the 'Iran-Contra' scandal, in which money from secret arms deals with Iran was re-cycled to the anti-Sandinista forces in Nicaragua? In a world dominated by the power of the multi-nationals and neo-liberal economic policies, Sandinista Nicaragua offered an alternative, an attempt to control a national economy in the interests of the people of that country. The failure of that project raises crucial questions about both the ability of national governments to challenge neo-liberalism and the continuing struggles of people within civil society, not least through adult education, to achieve a minimum of self-respect in their lives.

Neo-Liberalism North and South

It is the global impact of neo-liberal economic policies which provides the linking theme of this chapter. Public spending, whether in Nicaragua or London, is seen as a negative feature of an economy, always a cost, never an investment. The aim is to create markets for previously public services (health, housing, education) so that they can be enjoyed as private consumption goods by those with power (i.e. money) in the market.

To summarise:

1. The context: Structural adjustment policies (SAPs)

> Structural adjustment policies have been imposed on poorer countries as a response to the debt crisis, where it has become clear that loans to Northern financial institutions will never be repaid unless the economies of these countries are more fully integrated into the global market. Adjustment means more funds for export-oriented processes and international management, cut-backs to civil servants and often dramatic cut-backs to health, schooling and social services. Structural adjustment has also become a part of Northern day-to-day life as global economic shifts produce losses of jobs in one sector and the creation of new jobs in other sectors. In all countries of both the North and South the weight and daily responsibility for 'adjusting' to the changes has been on the backs of the poorest and most vulnerable persons in our respective societies (Hall, 1994).

2. The results: educational cuts

> The impact of SAPs on education has been especially severe. SAPs have sometimes directly cut back the education and adult education budgets or at other times have combined with the general weakness in world commodity prices to compound an already difficult economic situation. If we look at the UNESCO World Education report of 1991, we note a number of alarming situations. The gross enrolment ratio for first-level education in Sub-Saharan Africa actually declined from 77.1% to 66.7%. In Latin America and the Caribbean, nearly half of the children who start Grade 1 never finish Grade 4. ... It is not my intention to place the entire responsibility for these discouraging trends on SAPs, but I am in agreement with those who have said that the combination of SAPs, world commodity prices, internal policy weaknesses and centralisation of international social policy initiatives have combined to put the hope of an education for better lives for everyone in the world further away than ever (ibid.).

3. The response: non-governmental action

> *The African Association for Literacy and Adult Education (AALAE)*
> *catalysed the formation of adult learners associations in several*
> *countries. These associations are conceived, organised and managed by*
> *the learners themselves in order to cater to their need in each country.*
> *The associations have revealed and released creative energies at various*
> *levels – organisational, conceptual, time management. It is an*
> *experience which has to be seen to be believed. In this way it has been*
> *possible to help empower adult learners from organisations guided by*
> *their own world outlook and based on their value systems. Critical to*
> *this   approach   is   AALAE's   recognition,   acknowledgement,*
> *encouragement of, and respect for pluralism; for other people's ways of*
> *knowing and perceiving reality; as well as a celebration of diversity,*
> *symbiosis and social synergy (Wangoola, 1993).*

Resources of Hope

While the main debate in the North has centred on the future of the welfare state – continuing public support for the poor and marginalised – in
the South it has centred on the ability of local communities to pool their
own resources for survival on a day-to-day basis. In both contexts, there
are a number of points to be made which challenge the pessimism which
inevitably flows from the notion of an omnipotent economic determinism, and the remainder of this chapter will outline in brief these 'resources of hope'.

In the countries of the North there is a political limit to the extent to
which basic entitlements to health, housing and education can be denied
by the state to those people without market power because of their exclusion from the labour market (e.g. older people dependent on state pensions, the unemployed). *Theoretically* these limits are set by the tension
between, on the one hand, the economic demands of capitalist exploitation, and, on the other, capital's requirement of social cohesion which in
turn provides legitimacy for the 'democratic' state (Offe, 1984). The
growing political reversals of the Conservative government in the UK are
an indication that these limits may already have been passed. While there
is pressure on adult educators to prepare students for the labour market,
the non-availability of jobs means that in many cases adults are able to
use public funds to access long-term educational courses of real benefit to
them rather than short-term training courses. A major concern is, however, that the removal of many educational opportunities at a local, informal level may prevent precisely those who could benefit most from these
opportunities (the least skilled, women with young children, people living in deprived conditions on peripheral housing estates or in rural areas) are unable to get that crucial first step on the road to learning. The
gain in formal educational opportunities needs to be built on informal
education, rather than replace it, if the most deprived are to share the
benefits.

In the countries of the South there is an economy, culture and indeed education in poverty which enables people to survive without reference to the formal economy. The work of popular educators alongside these marginalised communities is a form of social commitment by adult educators which runs against the grain of the overall movement of resources from the public to private sectors, from the needs of local communities to the needs of international capital. In 1991–92, for example, of the loans to Nicaragua from the USA, IMF, WB and Inter-American Development Bank, 42% were used to finance external debt, and 27% to finance the inflow of consumer goods for the local elite (CIIR, 1993). The popular educators from the Sandinista Ministry of Education have set up an NGO called the Instituto Nicaragüense de Investigación y Educación Popular (INIEP) which continues the grassroots literacy work. [4] The work of this new wave of popular educators in Latin American is seen as eminently political, as the following extract from the final document of a recent international conference in Managua reveals:

Challenges for popular education
To define ways of strengthening the processes through which social movements can build democracy through their practices – educating people for participation.
To contribute to the democratisation process at a local level in ways that have an impact on public and global spaces.
To design a new utopian vision of democracy based on participation, in contexts where political education can take place and capacity for public activities can be increased. (Final document of the 2nd workshop/seminar on educational processes, 'Popular Education, Civil Society, Democracy and Building New Legal Rights', Managua, Nicaragua 15–19 March 1994. Translation by the author.)

In both South and North, civil society has become an increasingly important forum for a range of alternative ways of providing collective consumption services, including adult education, financed by voluntary contributions from government, individuals and charities. Non-government organisations are seen as an effective way of engaging the work and commitment of social actors such as shanty-town dwellers, peasant farmers and farm labourers. Aid from both international agencies (the IMF and WB), worldwide charities (e.g. Oxfam) and governments is increasingly channelled through these NGOs. In the case of the World Bank, this creates the somewhat curious spectacle of international capital proclaiming the primacy of women, environment and poverty as major issues in development (Martin, 1994). It remains to be seen how long this particular fig-leaf will remain in place! This has implications for education. It was noticeable that at the eighth international conference of ILSCAE (Bled, Slovenia, June/July 1994) a majority of both North and South delegates worked for NGOs of varying forms and sizes. Adult education has always depended on part-time, hourly-paid staff, but there has always been the prospect of secure, full-time employment as a goal to be worked towards. Increasingly, adult educators who want to work with poor, deprived communities must share at least some of the uncertainties of a world fractured between wealth and poverty, health and disease, peace and war. In Beck's terms, they must enter fully into 'the risk society' (Beck, 1992).

While empiricism does not allow people the luxury of transforming their world, it enables people to survive in it. The shift of educational resources from the pubic service to the private market sphere carries with it possibilities as well as losses. For example, an increasing number of employers are realising that one of the keys to a successful training policy to deal with changing production methods and market conditions is to support the ongoing personal development of their employees, including general education and basic education (Payne, 1993; Frank, 1993; Frank and Hamilton, 1993).

At the same time, the developments sketched out in this chapter have implications for the education and training of adult educators. The chief danger is exactly that technocratic rationality which Raymond Williams identified as 'Plan X' in his essay 'Resources for a journey of hope' (Williams, 1983). The insistent questions that adult educators need to be asked, and to ask themselves, are 'Who benefits?' and 'In whose interests?'[5] rather than beginning with the assumption that all adult learning is equally valid, equally important, and that the only issues for adult educators are how programes can be 'delivered' in the most efficient way. Down that road lies the hegemony of neo-liberal economic rationality and the political and ideological forces that support it. An understanding of 'Plan X' is an essential prerequisite for the committed adult educator. As Michael Collins has stated:

> *The obsession with technique, or technical rationality, has induced modern adult education to evade serious engagement with critical, ethical, and political issues. It has effectively sidelined adult education as a social movement and supports initiatives that tend to de-skill the practitioner's pedagogical role. Thus, the distinctiveness of adult education as a field of practice has been seriously eroded. Therein lies the deepening crisis. A renewed sense of vocation in adult education is invoked as a prelude to the orchestration of technique on a more humane scale and for the shaping of a genuinely reflective, emancipatory practice (Collins, 1991: 39).*

Adult education workers are, at the end of the day, no different from the rest of society. Many of us would wish that the world was otherwise. Many of us are committed theoretically to very different social and educational structures from those we work in at present. Yet within existing structures, I observe colleagues locating and filling spaces within which their curricular and pedagogical practices can 'make a difference' to the lives of students who for nearly 20 years have been at the sharp end of neo-liberal economic policies. Most people are not dupes of their circumstances. They understand only too well what is going on around them. That understanding and that resistance are indeed resources for the future.

In this context, the researcher has a role to play, too, alongside and in equal partnership with the practitioners of adult education:

- by identifying and celebrating the spaces within which alternative and oppositional work flourishes, and the social actors and social movements who occupy those spaces
- by exposing the contradictions inherent in the policy and rhetoric of those who hold power in education and beyond
- by working alongside practitioners to enable them to become more 'reflective', more conscious of the actual and potential meanings of their work
- by developing theory which resonates with adult educators' sense of their own work, its limitations and potential.

There is, still, a lot to be said for Voltaire's dictum in the face of global disasters: 'we must work in the garden'.

'Traveller, there is no ready pathway. We make your own pathways as we walk' (Antonio Machado).

A very modest Utopianism would appear to be the order of the day!

Notes

The ideas in this chapter have been discussed with, among others, Isolina Centeno, Sue Gardener and Carlos Tamez. I would like to thank them for their comradeship and help, and also the editors of this book for their encouragement.

For information about ILSCAE, please write to John Payne, 460 Merton Road, London SW18 5AE.

1. Both *We Survived* and *Rising Above It* are significant titles in view of subsequent events recounted in this chapter. Copies can be obtained from Fritz Luthi at Wandsworth Adult College, Hotham School, Charlwood Road, London SW15 1PN.
2. Rate capping involved national government setting a limit on local government expenditure and the level of local housing tax (rates) which could be levied to support that expenditure. It was an important step in increasing central government control and reducing the power of local government.
3. The Poll Tax was a method of financing local government based on a per capita taxation unrelated to housing or income. Popular opposition to the Poll Tax contributed directly to the downfall of the Thatcher regime in 1992.
4. Significantly, education and training work with Tenants' Associations in south London has been taken forward by Tenants' Corner, a voluntary group which inherited the resources gathered by Sue Gardener at AECDU.

5.   My thanks to Nell Keddie for keeping these ideas at the front of my mind.

References

Arrien García, J.B. and Matus Lazo, R. (1989) 'Nicaragua: diez años de educación en la revolución', *Cuadernos de Sociología* (Universidad Centroamericana), 9–10, pp 33–53.

Beck, U. (1992) *Risk Society. Towards a new modernity*, Sage. (First published in German as *Risikogesellschaft: auf dem Weg in eine andere Moderne*, 1986.)

Castells, M. (1983) *The City and the Grassroots*, Edward Arnold.

Catholic Institute for International Relations (1993) *Nicaragua. The price of peace*, CIIR.

Collins, M. (1991) *Adult Education as Vocation: A critical role for the adult educator*, Routledge.

Esland, G. (ed.) (1991) *Education, Training and Employment. Vol. 1: Educated labour – the changing basis of industrial demand*, Adison Wesley.

Frank, F. (ed.) (1993) *Not Just a Number: Writings about workplace learning*, Lancaster University Centre for the Study of Education and Training.

Frank, F. and Hamilton, M. (1993) *Not Just a Number: The role of basic skills programmes in the changing workplace*, Lancaster University Centre for the Study of Education and Training.

Hall, B. (1994) 'Adult education and the political economy of global economic change', in Wangoola, P. and Youngman, F. (eds) *Political Economy of Adult Education*, AALAE, Nairobi.

Harvey, L. (1990) 'Political education and revolution', *Community Education*, vol. 8, no. 3.

Lankshear, C., with Lawler, M. (1987) *Literacy, Schooling and Revolution*, Falmer Press.

Martin, K. (1994) 'The World Bank's work with NGOs', in White, H. (ed.) *The World Bank and the IMF: Some issues*, Development Education Association, Reading.

Offe, C. (1984) *Contradictions of the Welfare State*, Hutchinson.

Ortega Heg, M. (1989) 'Nicaragua: una nación multiétnica', *Cuadernos de Sociología* (Universidad Centroamericana), 9–10, pp 148–52.

Payne, J. (1987) *Adult Education and Social Movements: the Putney Resource Centre 1983–86*, Working Papers in Urban Education, no.1, Centre for Educational Studies, King's College, London.

Payne, J. (1991) 'Adult education in Inner London: a research report', *Adults Learning*, September, pp 8–10.

Payne, J. (1993) 'Too little of a good thing? Adult education in the workplace', *Adults Learning*, June, pp 274–5.

Wangoola, P. (1993) 'Adult education, the African crisis, and the role of AALAE', paper presented at the conference on 'Rethinking adult education for development', Slovene Adult Education Centre, Ljubljana, Slovenia, October 1993.

Williams, R. (1964) *Second Generation*, Chatto and Windus.

Williams, R. (1965) *The Long Revolution*, Penguin Books.

Williams, R. (1983) *Towards 2000*, Chatto and Windus.

Twenty-one

Popular Education in Northern Ireland: The Ulster People's College

Tom Lovett

The history of adult education is littered with examples of radical, independent initiatives designed to express their founders' commitment to the disadvantaged and the fight for justice and equality (Paulston, 1980). That radical tradition has suffered severe setbacks in the past 10 years as, under pressure from Conservative governments, the emphasis in adult education has shifted to vocational training to meet the needs of the economy (Westwood and Thomas, 1991).

Here in Northern Ireland adult educators have faced the same pressures. However, our social and economic problems are compounded by violence and sectarianism (McNamee and Lovett, 1987). In this situation some community educators have striven to find ways and means of contributing to the fight against sectarianism and the search for peace and justice for both communities.

One particular initiative, the Ulster People's College, was greatly influenced by this radical, independent, adult education tradition and has sought, since its establishment in 1982, to provide an accessible secular, neutral, venue where people from both communities could come together to explore common problems and perceived differences.

The College is an independent, cross-community education centre with residential facilities and a number of outreach workers concerned with education *about* the community, *across* the community. It is committed to the latter within the context of the need to explore and work for radical social changes, particularly amongst the disadvantaged. The founding members included people involved in trade unions, women's groups, community activism of various kinds and community education.

Background

The establishment of the People's College was obviously influenced by events and circumstances in Northern Ireland. However, it was also influenced by my own personal history and by my knowledge and experience of that radical popular educational tradition. All of these influences came together to generate the idea of an Ulster People's College.

Let's start with my personal autobiography. I was born in Ardoyne, a predominately Catholic, working-class housing estate in north Belfast in

1935. I left school at 16 to work in the local aircraft factory and quickly became an active trade union member. I started my adult education 'career' by attending classes in economics and social history organised by the Workers' Educational Association and the National Council of Labour Colleges. As I was later to discover, they were originally popular educational movements, with their origins in the labour and trade union movement of the early part of this century (Jennings, 1979; Atkins, 1981). I finished off my 'adult' education by winning a two-year scholarship to Ruskin College, Oxford (see Pollins, 1984 and also the chapter by K. Hughes in this volume).

The Liverpool Experience

So, at the age of 28 I became a graduate of that early popular adult education movement, fully aware of the role it had played in movements for social change. After graduating from Oxford University I decided to re-enter that movement and, in 1969, I was appointed WEA tutor organiser for central Liverpool.

My appointment was seen, at the time, as innovatory. The WEA felt that it had lost touch with its working-class roots and moved away from its earlier commitment to social change. I was appointed specifically to re-establish contact with working-class adults and communities in Liverpool; to explore how the WEA could respond to their educational needs and wants; to indicate what the latter might mean for the WEA nationally if it was to learn from the Liverpool experience. My account of that experience was eventually published in a book, *Adult Education, Community Development and the Working Class* (Lovett, 1982), which has influenced the theory and practice, not only of the WEA, but other providers of adult/community education.

The major influences on my work and approach were Illich and Friere. The former for his emphasis on alternative educational networks, the latter for his concentration on starting where people are, using their lives and the problems they face, as the basis and starting point for their own education; on education which would assist adults in challenging the cultural hegemony and creating their own vision of a new society.

Adopting this community development approach I had no problem in involving local people in a variety of educational and learning projects. I also learned a great deal from them and their struggles. However, I was anxious to return to my roots in Northern Ireland, where the 'troubles' had just begun, to see whether the lessons I had learned in Liverpool could be of some value in that divided community.

Community Education in Northern Ireland

Thus, in 1972, I took up an appointment in the Community Studies Division of the Institute of Continuing Education at the University of Ulster at Magee College, Derry, N. Ireland. The university had decided to commit itself to an unusually ambitious and large-scale development of community-oriented education. It was prepared to assist in seeking solutions to the social, economic and political problems of the province by putting its educational resources at the disposal of the community. I, somewhat naively and idealistically, decided to take these public mission statements at their face value and embarked on a programme of community education based largely on my Liverpool experience. Surprisingly, I found that, despite the violence and communal conflict, the same community movement I had found in that city was providing a bridge across the sectarian divide in N. Ireland. Working-class Protestants and Catholics were engaged in fighting the same problems of poverty, unemployment, redevelopment and the resulting alienation from those in authority. The situation was well summed up by a community worker in the Creggan area of Derry, a city profoundly affected by these changes:

> *When I think of all the social problems there are, I mean Creggan has everything. It's got poor housing. It's got people on low incomes. Those that are employed are on low wages; the majority are unemployed. When you're talking in terms of Creggan – widows, pensioners, single parent families – you name it, we've got it. We've got poor facilities medically; we've got poor facilities as far as shopping is concerned; no telephone, no place to post your letters. I sometimes think that if we were back in biblical days and John the Baptist was running around looking for a wilderness he wouldn't go to the desert, he would come to Creggan! (McNamee and Lovett, 1987: 135).*

It is obvious from the above comments that many of the problems facing the working-class in Northern Ireland are similar to those found elsewhere. However, in Northern Ireland they are compounded by violence and sectarianism. Some commentators see it as a society suffering from a vast nervous breakdown at community level, with the social fabric slowly disintegrating. This is far from the truth. The people are brave, resilient, humorous, friendly in the face of great change and adversity. They have responded to their troubles and problems with imagination and initiative. They have been involved in various forms of community action designed to protect and regenerate community life and to tackle the social, economic and cultural problems common to both communities – Catholic and Protestant.

This process of community action involved people from both communities, people with no politics, people with radical views, people with connections with paramilitary groups. It resulted in the formation of numerous community associations, tenants' groups, community resource centres, welfare rights centres, women's groups, co-operatives, etc.

These developments provided, for a short period, a bridge between the two divided communities emphasising their common problems, their common culture. It even had some influence on paramilitary groups like the Protestant Ulster Defence Association. One of their spokesmen commented:

We are aware that socially and economically we have more in common with our opposite numbers in the Republican (Catholic) side than we have with loyalist (Protestant) big-wigs. But, how are we going to put this over? What formula are we going to find to get the ordinary people of Ulster to vote on real issues which concern them and not on the entrenched sectarian issues into which we are brainwashed? (Lovett, 1985).

A Catholic community leader echoing the above sentiment said:

No matter what happens to the National question, in the final analysis the community struggle goes on, the struggle against the hopelessness and helplessness of ordinary people to manage to cope in a very complex society. We cannot separate politics from community action, no matter what we try to do about it, no matter how idealistic we may be (Lovett, Clarke and Kilmurray, 1983: 56).

This popular response in the 1970s presented community educators with a real challenge. It indicated that community education for peace and reconstruction offered a possible alternative to violence and conflict by building a united working-class movement based on local community action. Working with other colleagues, and in co-operation with a variety of community organisations, we responded to that challenge by establishing the Community Action Research and Education Project in the university. CARE become involved in the organisation and provision of a variety of workshops, seminars, conferences, classes and courses specifically concerned with cross-community issues and problems and designed to support and strengthen the community movement in N. Ireland. However, our response was limited by our institutional base and the fact that it was only one of a number of initiatives with very different agendas (Lovett, Clarke and Kilmurray, 1983: 56).

Like similar developments in Europe, North America and Australia, these initiatives reflected a wide range of activities and corresponding educational, social and political philosophies, sometimes openly stated, often not. The result was a certain pragmatic consensus which glossed over their ideological differences in favour of meeting local 'needs' and an emphasis on process, at the expense of content and direction.

However, by the late 1970s these ideological divisions surfaced in the debates between, and amongst, community activists and community educators. The pragmatic consensus weakened as people became more aware of the tensions and contradictions between these different approaches to community education and working-class community action. It was obvious that the latter had brought no great changes in the problems of poverty and inequality facing the working class in Northern Ireland. In fact their position had worsened considerably. There was little evidence that people had any more influence on the policies of major institutions. Local community action had, in fact, failed to make a major impact on the larger social and economic political structures in Northern Ireland. This is not to decry the small, but important, changes and victories at local level. However, community education did not present an alternative, radical, analysis and vision for those involved in this process. Instead, in the main, it had concentrated on access, second chance and a limited concept of training for community activists.

The Ulster People's College

At the beginning of the 1980s I and a group of community activists, trade unionists, community educators, peace workers and feminists met and agreed that what was needed was a reappraisal of previous efforts in the field, a conscious effort to determine our own social and political position and to choose an educational model or approach which reflected the latter.

The group felt that the community movement of the 1970s had been too romantic, too naive, too easily influenced by the popular educational theories and conventional wisdoms of the decade. They applauded the attempt to cross the sectarian divide to stress the problems common to members of the working class in both communities. However, they felt that this did not grasp the nettle of community division and conflict between the two sections of the working class. They agreed that it was necessary to combine the best in local community action and larger social concerns; to bring the fragments of social and community action together – community groups, trade unions, women's groups, etc. – to work towards a vision of a new society based on a radical analysis of existing structures and the lessons and aspirations of the men and women attempting to create new structures at local level; to stress objectives and content in education as well as methods and process.

From previous experience it was obvious that not all alternatives in adult education were necessarily radical. There were grave limitations in using formal adult education institutions for radical education and action, although this is not to decry the useful, and often innovative, work done by such institutions.

In attempting to support the development of a radical social movement, the group decided to go back to 'other dreams, other schools'. I was particularly struck by the work of the Highlander Centre in the USA, which I visited in 1979 and met its founder, Myles Horton (Adams, 1975). Highlander's maxim is 'Learn from the people and start education where they are.' Highlander has worked closely with various social movements in the USA: trade unions, farmers, civil rights. It has sought to educate people away from the trap of individualism and to reinforce those instincts which lead to co-operation and collective solutions to problems. It has survived from the early 1930s because of its craggy independence, its non-institutional base, its ability to adapt to new social movements thrown up by the working class and oppressed groups and, most important, its radical philosophy and perspective.

With this as a model and financial support from various trusts and charities, the Ulster People's College was established in 1982. It is situated in Belfast and has short-term accommodation for 30 people. This central resource is used to complement and strengthen the work in the field; to extend the process of action and learning in local communities; to bring together people from both sides of the religious divide, to reflect on their common problem; to learn from their different experiences and to discuss their cultural and political differences.

The College's Educational Approach

The College is primarily issue- and problem-oriented. It is not specifically concerned with access, second chance or certification. It is openly committed to radical social change and the concept of individual and collective growth and development. As well as providing space for workshops and conferences on social, economic and political issues of the day, the College is developing an alternative curriculum based on the issues and problems facing men, women and youth in working-class communities throughout Northern Ireland. It is also seeking to explore ways and means whereby men and women can play a larger part in the reconstruction of local working-class communities through the establishment of new forms of social and economic structures designed to meet local needs in a collective fashion.

Educational Objectives

The College has two major educational concerns:

1. Social and Economic Problems

To assist people in both communities who are concerned with, or involved in, the search for solutions to the many common problems facing Catholics and Protestants in the province, e.g. housing, unemployment, low wages, poverty, vandalism, changes in family and community life, lack of social and recreational facilities.

2. Cultural and Political Divisions

To help the two communities in Northern Ireland to communicate with each other, to appreciate and understand their respective traditions, to clarify the values and attitudes (social, political religious) inherent in those traditions, to search for their common history, to provide, in fact, a basis for a study of themselves. Labour history is an important instrument for this but the whole area of exploration requires the use of many instruments, language and literature, mythology and folklore, history and theology, economics and politics.

At a practical level its educational aims are:

- promoting a debate on the political situation in Northern Ireland
- looking at the political and constitutional options facing people in the province
- looking at the nature of the 'two traditions'

- assessing the role of the labour movement and its potential for the future
- analysing and assessing the political role of the major churches – Presbyterian, Roman Catholic and Church of Ireland
- investigating the area of civil and religious liberty and church and state in general. In particular the social role of the major churches in relation to the development or otherwise of the secular state and pluralism
- looking at the question of culture and identity
- looking at the social and economic differences between the two communities and between north and south
- identifying areas for further study and debate.

Educational Programme and Methods: An Anti-Sectarian Approach

The primary educational programme at the College takes the form of short informal courses of up to 10 weekly sessions. These are aimed at four groups:

- young people
- women
- community activists/trade unionists
- peace and reconciliation groups.

The structure of these courses follows a specific educational method. We begin by asking people to look closely at their own community, exploring the economic, social and cultural factors which influence their lives. This approach is based on the idea that a strong sense of where we're coming from is of fundamental importance in confronting the things which divide us from others.

The next stage of the courses seeks to identify in what areas and at what depth there are common concerns across the 'sectarian divide'. This analysis provides the basis for an exploration of whether there is, or can be, a 'common culture' or a common project which, though 'fragile' and uncertain, can evoke a commitment from members of the two communities. Common themes and problems which generally arise are in the areas of unemployment, health, housing, education and the relationship between the institutions of church and 'the common people'. An exceedingly important area, which the College had tried to emphasise by employing a Community Education Organiser with specific responsibility, is the situation of women. Among women's groups, an awareness of common struggles is particularly strong.

Only when time has been taken to establish community identity and areas of common cultural and social concern, do the participants on the course turn directly to community divisions in Ireland. This is done by looking at history, religion, identity, politics, once again using materials produced by the College.

An important point as regards this process and method is that members of both communities are together throughout the course. Another approach which we are using at the moment is to work with the groups separately and then bring them together for a residential weekend at the College to complete the discussions. These two different methods give a flexibility to the depth of the discussions. Certain issues can be aired more completely when only members of one's own community are present. On-going contact can allow stronger relationships between the groups to develop organically.

A final emphasis to be made at this point is that our whole educational approach seeks to be solidly *anti-sectarian* and not simply non-sectarian. In other words, we seek to explore the causes of sectarianism and not simply the feelings evoked. By looking at causes, we are better able to discuss the 'lines of action' along which these causes can be removed. Thus, we would not see it as adequate to 'respect the two traditions' but would look for assessments of what elements in the two traditions are progressive and what elements are in need of redefinition.

Longer Courses

Arising out of much of the pioneering work done in this field, the College now offers two part-time, year-long courses. These courses, which have been certificated by the University of Ulster, are offered by the two bodies. The first course, in Community Relations, is aimed particularly at providing the skills and knowledge necessary for effective cross-community work, particularly for those involved in work in the community with youth, community organisations and women's groups. The second course, in Community Development (which is assisted by a grant from the European Social Fund), seeks to give participants the knowledge and skills required for local community development, with a special emphasis on community economic and social regeneration.

A primary aim in both courses is to try and involve the participants' supporting organisation or community. The courses will thus be trying to integrate the work in local communities rather than simply giving a certificate to one person for their own career prospects.

Occasional Seminars and Conferences

Along with the regular educational work of the College, there has also arisen a tradition of holding occasional seminars and other courses addressing areas and issues of current and continuing interest. Following the basic ethos of the College, these events would all seek to analyse events and issues which affect ordinary people from the perspective of ordinary people. Thus a seminar was held on the situation of life sentence and SOSP prisoners (in Northern Ireland a person under the age of 18 who commits an offence which should entail a 'life sentence' is instead detained for the Secretary of State's Pleasure), focusing on the life sentence review procedure within the prisons. This seminar was attended by prisoners' families and support groups from the loyalist through to the republican side. A seminar was held on the Ulster Defence Association's Common Sense document, as an important contribution to the political debate by an organisation formed and led by working-class people. In June 1989 a seminar was held on the Irish language which sought to explore reasons for the difficulties facing the language revival in Northern Ireland. A very interesting feature of this day was the presence of people from the Protestant community, which led to an important debate on the nature of identity and the political options upon which much of the revival hinges.

A seminar was held in the College on Socialism and Sectarianism. Jointly organised by the College and the Belfast Trades Council, it began an important debate on the responses of the labour movement to the problem of sectarianism in Northern Ireland. Another seminar was held on the third anniversary of the signing of the Anglo-Irish Agreement in November 1988. This Alternative Review was held to examine whether and to what extent the Agreement had affected or improved or made worse the lives of people in working-class communities. Finally, a number of courses have been held looking at the issue of church involvement in the Northern Ireland problem. The most recent course has specifically taken a radical perspective, trying to analyse the way in which the churches have approached the question of power and powerlessness in Ireland. Many of these events have begun processes which continue in the form of future plans for follow-up meetings, report publications and formal groups which continue to reflect on these themes.

A Neutral Venue

Finally the College provides a neutral venue, with supporting services and resources, for a wide range of organisations and groups concerned to explore community divisions and/or identify common projects in their own particular field of endeavour. It also acts as host for groups from the Republic of Ireland, UK, Europe and America concerned with the Northern Ireland problem and anxious to know more about it. The College, in this instance, acts as an educational 'guide'.

Effectiveness of the College's Work

In trying to assess the work of the College in 'Bridging the Sectarian Divide' it is important to reiterate that the College seeks to be anti-sectarian in its approach. Thus simply bringing people from both communities together is, in itself, not the main purpose of our work. The College has to identify at least two main strands involved in this kind of work in Northern Ireland.

The first is developing the 'middle ground', trying to identify the elements of a common agenda which is not acknowledged by the prevailing 'stereotypes'. Another way of putting this is to say that there is a 'third way' between the nationalists and unionist positions. We would see a plurality of opinions on this among those who work in the People's College, some hoping for a unity among the people, others holding that a resolution of the constitutional question is necessary. We would hope that this plurality is defended.

The second aim, around which we would see more unanimity within the College membership, is to promote social change. If sectarianism is a result of specific social and class conditions, then working to create an anti-sectarianism society involves trying to change those elements of our present situation which promote sectarianism. In this process, education about social structures, government policy, people's responses and, perhaps most importantly, clarification of issues around identity, gives people the information upon which decisions can be made and options clarified.

Having these aims firmly in mind, how do we assess the College's educational work? Firstly, we recognise that we need to do more work on this, by following up those who are using our resources, and looking more deeply at methods of assessment. Empirical tests looking at attitude change are notoriously difficult to evaluate and are difficult to pitch, in the light of comments above about the 'middle ground'. Some of the comments we have had from people who have completed the courses indicate positive results from any perspective:

I realise now that many of my ideas were silly.

The history sessions helped me to understand why we are where we are.

I'm much clearer who I am.

These elements testify to the usefulness of having sessions on contentious areas such as history, identity and politics. They also testify to large and important areas which simply do not receive adequate attention within the educational provision currently available.

Another aspect which it is important to restate is that, by targeting certain groups, we hope to widen the impact of the courses. Instead of simply giving chances for individual personal development, we do emphasise the importance of collective educational effort. Thus the presence a group from a youth club, a group from a women's group, an activist from a community group or trade union means that there is more chance for the further dissemination of ideas.

Education Across the Community, About the Community

Paulo Freire's phrase 'Cultural Action for Freedom' perhaps sums up what the College is trying to do in all its educational work: an examination and exploration of people's communities in all their complexity in order to encourage the embracing of options which improve people's sense of identity, integrity, security and dignity. An emphasis on these manifestations of popular culture and politics from the base of society gives the People's College a specifically important function. One cannot think of many places where representatives of organisations from both extremes of the political spectrum feel able to come for open exchange and discussion. This brings a complex, and hard-to-handle edge, to many of the debates. Another important contribution to cross-community work is for activists and practitioners at the 'coal-face' of community relations to have a neutral and accessible platform to debate the complex issues involved in community work.

It is important to note that the Ulster People's College arose from a specific context. The explosion of community activity during the early part of the 'troubles' led to the belief that there was an alternative to community politics which would transcend the sectarian divide. It was partly a growing awareness that this transcendence was an illusion which led the College's founders to set up a cross-community education centre. Without an opportunity to explore precisely the issues that divide local communities, it was felt that continuing antagonisms would prevent coherent and effective campaigns on all kinds of pressing issues affecting working-class communities. Thus the dual aims of the College's presence arise from long experience.

The Ulster People's College has survived, over the last 10 years, because of its rugged individualism and the commitment of its founders and supporters to a specific educational agenda within the context of the search for peace and justice in Northern Ireland. It has had to struggle, like Highlander, to maintain its independence. It has been accused of being a 'Marxist' or 'communist' college. A great deal of energy has gone into seeking financial assistance from trusts and charities to keep the College open. It had, until recently, no full-time director or permanent staff and was run entirely by a group of dedicated volunteers. Their vision and determination has meant that, despite the retreat of progressive adult education forces over the last 10 years, at least one initiative has managed to survive as a testimony to the strength of the radical tradition.

References

Adams, F. (1975) *Unearthing Seeds of Fire: The story of Highlander*, J.F. Blair, N. Carolina.

Atkins, J. (1981) *Neither Crumbs nor Condescension. The Central Labour College 1909–1915*, Aberdeen People's Press.

Jennings, B. (1979) *Knowledge is Power: A short history of the WEA, 1903–78*, University of Hull, Department of Adult Education.

Lovett, T. (1982) *Adult Education, Community Development and the Working Class*, 2nd edition, Department of Adult Education, University of Nottingham.

Lovett, T. (1985) 'Contact and Reconciliation of Conflict: Community Education for Peace', Unpublished paper, University of Ulster, N. Ireland.

Lovett, T., Clarke, C. and Kilmurray, A. (1983) *Adult Education and Community Action*, Croom Helm.

McNamee, P. and Lovett, T. (1987) *Working Class Community in N. Ireland*, Ulster People's College.

Paulston, G.R. (1980) *Other Dreams, Other Schools: Folk colleges in social and ethnic movements*, University Centre for International Studies, University of Pittsburg.

Pollins, H. (1984) *The History of Ruskin College*, Ruskin College Library, Occasional Publications, no. 3, Ruskin College.

Westwood, S. and Thomas, J.E. (eds) (1991) *Radical Agendas? The politics of adult education*, NIACE.

Notes on Contributors

David Alexander is Senior Lecturer in Adult Education at the University of Edinburgh. He has carried out extensive research into community and adult education in Scotland. He has worked with community educators in Thailand, trade unionists in Swaziland, community health educators in India and is actively involved in worker's education in Zambia, where he worked for 10 years.

Paula Allman is a tutor on the Diploma in Adult Education and MEd in Continuing Education at the University of Nottingham. Her work is actively based on the work of Paulo Friere and is openly committed to the development of critical intelligence.

Jim Crowther is Course Leader, MAEd: Community Education at Moray House Institute of Education, Edinburgh. He was previously Adult Basic Education Organiser for Lothian Regional Council's Community Education Service.

Chris Duke is Professor, Chair of the Department of Continuing Education and Pro-Vice Chancellor of the University of Warwick. He was Secretary of the Universities Association for Continuing Education (formerly UCACE) from 1989 to 1994.

Keith Forrester is Senior Lecturer in the Department of Adult Continuing Education at the University of Leeds and is responsible for co-ordinating the extensive community and industrial work in the department. He works closely with a range of voluntary organisations, trade unions and community groups.

Wilma Fraser is a Tutor Organiser in the WEA South Eastern District with special responsibility for women's education and 'broad based access'. Recently, her research – both theoretical and practical – has concentrated on issues to do with 'learner managed learning'. Her book *Learning from Experience* is an account of the personal and pedagogic struggles undergone in seeking to retain the potential for social change within a particularly individualistic form of adult education provision.

John Grayson teaches Social and Labour History and Community Development courses at Northern College. He has worked for the WEA and in Trade Union Education, and has spent 10 years as a Labour councillor.

Katherine Hughes is the Co-ordinator of the Ruskin Learning Project. She also tutors on several courses at Ruskin College, Oxford and is particularly interested in developing programmes and materials for educationally marginalised working-class groups – the unemployed, older people, women and workers with little training.

Keith Jackson is the Principal of Fircroft College, Birmingham and has 30 years' experience in adult education. His publications include *Democracy in Crisis* with David Blunkett and a wide range of articles on adult education and popular education.

Hilda Kean teaches history and women's studies at Ruskin College, Oxford. Previous publications include *Challenging the State? The Socialist and Feminist Experience 1900 - 1930,* and *Deeds Not Words: The lives of suffragette teachers.*

Tom Lovett is the founder and chairperson of the Ulster People's College. He is Professor of Community Education at the University of Ulster and is active in community development initiatives in Northern Ireland.

John McIlroy is Reader in Sociology and Fellow of the International Centre for Labour Studies, University of Manchester.

Ian Martin is Lecturer in Community Education in the Department of Education, University of Edinburgh. He has a particular interest in the relationship between popular education and progressive social movements.

Marjorie Mayo is a tutor in Community Studies and Social Policy at Ruskin College. She has worked in a variety of settings in education, social policy and community development and published widely in these areas.

Rebecca O'Rourke is a Lecturer in Adult Continuing Education based at the University of Leeds' Middlesbrough Centre. She is the author with Jean Milloy of *The Woman Reader: Learning and teaching women's writing.*

John Payne has worked in further, adult and higher education, and is currently a researcher and writer on adult education. He is a committee member of the International League for Social Commitment in Adult Education (ILSCAE).

Sonia Reynolds is the Director of the Wales Access Unit and is also a voluntary community activist.

Cilla Ross works as a freelance tutor, writer and researcher in adult and higher education throughout Yorkshire. She is particularly interested in nineteenth and twentieth century politics, community and oral social history and the historical sociology of work, skills and technology.

Mae Shaw has been a community worker in the voluntary sector for 15 years. She is now lecturer in Community Work at Moray House Institute of Education, Edinburgh.

Tom Steele is a Lecturer in Adult Continuing Education at the University of Leeds and was previously Organising Tutor for the WEA in Leeds. He is author of *Alfred Orage and the Leeds Arts Club, 1893–1923*, and his *Marginal Occupations: Cultural politics and adult education 1945–65* will be published in 1996.

Julia Swindells currently teaches in the English department at Homerton College, Cambridge and has worked in most areas of education, including adult and community education. She is an activist in the Cambridge Labour Party. Her published work includes *Victorian Writing and Working Women: The other side of silence*, and, with Lisa Jardine, *What's Left? Women in culture and the labour movement*. She has also contributed to the radical feminist journal *Trouble and Strife*.

Jane Thompson is Tutor in Women's Studies at Ruskin College, Oxford and Research Associate at the University of Warwick. Previous publications include *Adult Education for a Change; Learning Liberation: Women's response to men's education*, and, with the Taking Liberties Collective, *Learning the Hard Way: Women's oppression in men's education*.

John Wallis is a tutor on the Diploma in Adult Education and MEd in Continuing Education at the University of Nottingham. His work is actively based on the work of Paulo Friere and is openly committed to the development of critical intelligence.

Martin Yarnit's career in education spans the range from extra-mural work, through the WEA to, currently, working as an LEA Officer in Sheffield. The connecting thread has always been a conviction that educational equality is a feasible goal.

Also Published by NIACE

Learning from Experience: Empowerment or Incorporation?

Wilma Fraser (WEA Tutor Organiser, South Eastern District)

APL/APEL is now a well-established practice in all forms of adult, further and higher education, offering a bridge between past experiences and future learning goals. But who gets to say which experiences, and whose, will count towards accredited qualifications? What is gained, and what is lost, in the translation of private experiences into the public sphere? This challenging and critical examination of current trends in learning from experience is based on a wide-ranging 'Making Experience Count' project and looks at experiential learning in relation to courses:

- at Ford Motor Company
- within outreach provision for marginalised groups
- with women
- with long-term unemployed
- in higher education
- with ethnic minority groups.

Offering both theoretical insights and unique practical wisdom, this book will be essential reading for all practitioners and managers in post-compulsory and professional education who really want to make experience count.

Wilma Fraser is tutor-organiser, WEA South Eastern District and honorary research fellow, School of Continuing Education, University of Kent.

ISBN 1 872941 60 5
paperback; 224 pages, incl. bibliography
£12.00

Engaging with Difference: The Other in Adult Education

edited by Mary Stuart and Alistair Thomson (University of Sussex)

> *It is our intention to open out a debate between adult learners and professionals which will help to reshape the changing map of adult and continuing education*

Who is the 'other' in adult education? The term is used here to refer to all those traditionally excluded from the full range of educational opportunities: women; adults with learning difficulties; members of ethnic minorities; older adults; people without conventional educational qualifications.

Engaging with Difference is a fresh and stimulating attempt to overcome the worn-out polarities of recent educational thinking, and urges instead a much closer engagement with learners in all their diversity. Among the topics explored are accreditation; open and distance learning; computer assisted learning; learning contracts; community care provision; refugee education; and education for an ageing population. A central theme of the book is autonomy and power in the learning process, and this is reflected in the range of student and tutor voices included in the book, voices which are not often heard in educational debate.

Engaging with Difference will be of interest to all involved in delivering and planning adult education in further and community education and in university continuing education. It will also appeal to those working in community and social care.

Mary Stuart and Alistair Thomson work in the Centre for Continuing Education at the University of Sussex.

ISBN 1 872941 59 1
paperback; 250 pages, incl. bibliographies
£12.00

Can They Do That? Learning About Active Citizenship

Derek Hooper, Annie Farrell, Jane Hedge and Tony Thorpe

An activity-based resource for return to learn and access courses, designed to develop students' understanding of the factors affecting rights, freedoms and access to services and the context of legal and democratic processes. The materials are intended for use in the development of practical skills and for students to use their experience as the basis for learning. The seven self-standing units cover:

- what is citizenship?
- law-making
- democracy and disability
- health
- education
- justice and the legal system
- belonging.

There is a guide to the aims and use of the materials, with examples of how the units may serve different courses. Each unit contains teachers' notes, student material and resources for further study. *Can They Do That?* will be of immediate practical relevance to all those providing college- or community-based courses for voluntary groups, women's groups, tenants' associations, self-advocacy groups, unwaged adults, school governors, etc. The material is also suitable for use in C & G Wordpower courses and for supplementary reading in various GCSE courses and for GNVQ Core Skills, particularly as it is written for adults.

Published in association with the Citizenship Foundation.

ISBN 1 872941 58 3
paperback; 104 pages
£12.00

About NIACE

NIACE: The National Organisation for Adult Learning is an independent advisory and development body promoting the interests of adult learners. NIACE works with national and local government, education providers, employers and the voluntary sector, and is active in research and development, publishing and conference organisation.

For further information, including a full list of current publications, please contact NIACE at:

21 De Montfort Street, Leicester LE1 7GE; tel 0116 255 1451.